THE LAW SOCIETY OF IRELAND, 1852–2002

The Law Society of Ireland, 1852–2002

Portrait of a Profession

Eamonn G. Hall & Daire Hogan

EDITORS

FOUR COURTS PRESS

Set in 11.5 pt on 15 pt Garamond by
Carrigboy Typesetting Services, County Cork for
FOUR COURTS PRESS LTD
Fumbally Court, Fumbally Lane, Dublin 8, Ireland
e-mail: info@four-courts-press.ie
http://www.four-courts-press.ie
and in North America for
FOUR COURTS PRESS
c/o ISBS, 5824 N.E. Hassalo Street, Portland, OR 97213.

ISBN 1–85182–695–5

Printed in England
by MPG Books, Bodmin, Cornwall

Foreword

It gives me very great pleasure, as President of the Law Society of Ireland, to introduce this portrait of the solicitors' profession. It is being published to commemorate the 150th anniversary of the granting of the charter of the Society, as an incorporated body.

Generations of lawyers have contributed to the development of the profession, and more broadly to the development of law and proper legal relationships as the core of an ordered society in Ireland. Outside their professional lives many solicitors have also achieved prominence in other fields of activity, including international sport, business, literature and politics. This history is a tribute, at the start of a new century, to the achievements of the profession and a portrait of the contribution which the Society has made to the representation and regulation of the profession.

Fifty years ago a memorandum for the government prepared by the Department of the Taoiseach noted that 'the Society have shown themselves to be a most business like body with a high sense of responsibility. Indeed it may be said that they have the most efficient vocational organisation of any of the professions.' That was a heartening if then undisclosed acknowledgement of the standing and efficiency of the Society at the time of the centenary of its charter. The Society and its members and all who work for it are committed to the upholding of the highest standards of professional life and to the most forward-looking, accountable and efficient form of professional organisation.

I am aware of the depth of knowledge which the contributors have brought to the subject of their chapters and of the hard work in the midst of many other calls on their time which has resulted in this handsome and most informative volume. On behalf of the Society I thank each of them and everybody else who has assisted in its preparation, not least in the selection of the photographs and other illustrations from the Society's records and elsewhere. I have no doubt that all who read this book will derive great enjoyment from it.

ELMA LYNCH
President
Law Society of Ireland
August 2002

Contents

Illustrations

Between pages 224 and 225

Contributors

JOHN F. BUCKLEY took the degrees of BA and LLB from UCD. He qualified as a solicitor in 1956. He was the Law Society's lecturer in conveyancing and land law from 1962 to 1972. He was chairman of the Society of Young Solicitors from 1966 to 1968, and president of the Dublin Solicitors' Bar Association for 1978/79. He was a member of the council of the Law Society from 1973 to 1987, serving two terms as chairman of its education committee and also as chairman of its publications committee and continuing legal education committee. He was junior vice president of the Society in 1983/84. He was the first non-North American to be awarded the Francis Rawle Award for services to continuing education by the American Law Institute-American Bar Association for Continuing Professional Education in 1991. He was a member of the Law Reform Commission from 1987 to 1996 and served as a judge of the Circuit Court from 1996 to 2001.

MARGARET BYRNE graduated from UCD with a BA degree in History and French and a Diploma in Librarianship. She joined the staff of the Law Society library in 1974 and has been librarian at the Law Society since 1978.

EAMONN G. HALL is chief legal officer of Eircom, chief examiner in constitutional law and consultant in judicial review to the law school of the Law Society. A graduate of UCD, UCG and TCD with degrees of BA, LLB and PhD, he qualified as a solicitor in 1974. A former president of the Medico-Legal Society of Ireland, past chairman of the Irish Society for European Law and the Incorporated Council of Law Reporting for Ireland, he served for three years as a member of the first Information Society Commission. He is a fellow of the Society for Advanced Legal Studies (London) and a visiting fellow and member of the adjunct faculty of law at UCD. Author of *The Electronic Age: Telecommunication in Ireland* (1993), Dr Hall was consultant editor of the *Irish Digest 1994–1999*, has served as the chairman of the editorial board of the Law Society's *Gazette* and has contributed chapters and articles to various publications, nationally and internationally.

DAIRE HOGAN qualified as a solicitor in 1973 and is a partner in McCann FitzGerald. He is a former president of the Irish Legal History Society. He is the author of *The legal profession in Ireland 1789–1922* (1986), and has contributed articles on the history of the profession and biographical studies of lawyers and judges in the nineteenth and twentieth centuries to a number of other books on legal history. These include studies of judicial appointments in Ireland 1866–67, the relations between Lord O'Hagan (lord chancellor of Ireland, 1868–74) and Lord Justice Christian, and most recently of R.R. Cherry (lord chief justice of Ireland, 1914–16).

KEN MURPHY has been the director general of the Law Society since 1995. A graduate of UCD, he qualified as a solicitor in 1981. From 1983 to 1995 he practised with the firm A & L Goodbody where he became a partner in 1990. He practised briefly as a conveyancer and then for a number of years in civil litigation. In 1988 he moved to Brussels and spent four years in charge of A & L Goodbody's office there, both then and subsequently practising in the field of EU law, in particular EU and Irish competition law. A former chairman of the Society of Young Solicitors, he was first elected to the council of the Law Society in 1983 and was re-elected eleven times, chairing many Law Society committees until his appointment as director general in 1995. As director general he has been the Society's main spokesman in the media and at Dáil committees. He has served on a number of Government and Courts Service-appointed working groups.

MARY REDMOND is a consultant solicitor at Arthur Cox which she joined in 2000. She is also deputy governor of Bank of Ireland Group, director of Jefferson Smurfit Group plc and of Campbell Bewley Group Limited. Author of *Dismissal Law* (1999) and of several legal articles, Dr Redmond, former Winter Williams Commonwealth Scholar and British Council Scholar, lectured in the Law Faculty of UCD and was a fellow of Churchill College Cambridge and later of Christ's College Cambridge before returning to Ireland to start her own employment law practice in 1985. She is a former member of the Employment Equality Agency, the Higher Education Authority, the Labour Relations Commission and the RTE Authority. In 1985 she founded the Irish Hospice Foundation and more recently The Wheel which networks community and voluntary groups.

Introduction

The Irish solicitor of today is a successor of the *fili* (poet) of pre-Norman Ireland. The *fili* was no mere versifier with a command of words, but was knowledgeable in several fields; one particular qualification of the *fili* was knowledge of the jurisprudence of Irish law. The profession of attorney and solicitor (one who is appointed to act for another), initially regulated by the courts and subsequently by statute, gradually developed following the establishment of Anglo-Norman rule in Ireland. Pursuant to the Supreme Court of Judicature Act (Ireland), 1877, all persons admitted as solicitors or attorneys were henceforth to be called solicitors of the Court of Judicature, but the title of attorney lives on in the designation of the chief law officer of the State as the attorney general. Today, the profession of solicitor remains one of the two principal classes of professional lawyer in Ireland.

The solicitor of today plays a significant role in the economic and social affairs of the nation. In the early days, it was said the medicine men held sway; in the middle ages and up to recent times, there were the clergy. Today, law and lawyers have a significant sway in the affairs of men, women and state. It is not an exaggeration to argue that solicitors have played and still play a role in the development of Irish society. This is partly due to economic advances, which in turn influence social change. For most of human history, economic advance within a lifetime would hardly be noticed; economic life, for all but an elite minority, amounted to a level of basic subsistence. Within the span of little more than a lifetime, industrialisation and technological progress, particularly the harnessing of electricity in all its forms, have changed the economic, social and cultural landscape of Ireland and the economic lives of its people. That transformation could not happen without a framework of law and lawyers who assisted in securing property and other personal rights.

The noted writer, jurist and judge, Oliver Wendell Holmes, in 1890 noted the contribution of lawyers in a corporate sense in the following words: 'The glory of lawyers, like that of men of science, is more corporate than individual. Our labour is an endless organic process. The organism whose being is recorded and protected by law is the undying body of society.' This book marks the 150th anniversary of the first grant of the charter in 1852 to the Society of Attorneys and Solicitors in Ireland, now the Law Society of Ireland, the professional body which educates, regulates and represents solicitors in Ireland. Patrick O'Connor, as president of the Society in 1999, established a working group with Elma Lynch in the chair and comprising John Buckley, Margaret Byrne, Dr Eamonn Hall, Daire Hogan and Ken Murphy with a view to publishing a historical record of the Society in 2002 on the 150th anniversary of the charter. This book, the fruit of the working group, considers facets of the 'corporate' history of solicitors and the institution known as the Law Society of Ireland.

Although this book is primarily a history of the structure and organisation of the solicitors' profession in Ireland, focusing on the Society, we would remark that there are many other aspects of the profession which might merit a wider study. As a contribution to local and professional history the Society would encourage members of the profession to make the back-ground of individual members and firms more widely known. A number of firms in different parts of the country can trace their roots over many generations, perhaps even a couple of centuries, often through direct descent from the family of the founding partners whose names they might still bear, and take pride in this heritage. Many other firms have been built up by persons who came to the law with no family background but with an instinct that the practice of law would be a useful and satisfying and hopefully remunerative career.

The structure of the profession in recent decades has been influenced to a large degree by the increasingly regulated and litigious nature of society, a greater awareness and concern for protection of human rights, and the complexity of laws and practices governing property, the environment, taxation, finance, information technology and intellectual property – everything in fact connected with economic growth. These developments both in forms of what might be regarded as personal law as much as in business law have necessitated the development of specialised knowledge and services by solicitors. They have been a force for the creation of specialist firms of varying sizes – in such fields as personal injury work, family law, criminal law – and of larger firms offering a wide range of specialised services, primarily in business law, to corporate clients and official bodies of one kind or another. From the perspective of 2002 it is strange to recall that as late as 1982 solicitors were subject to the traditional restriction of twenty members for the size of any partnership.

The significant growth in numbers in the profession in recent decades has been apparent not only within the traditional sphere of solicitors' firms but also within governmental and official bodies and in private sector businesses and financial institutions. These have not only seen the cost effectiveness of conducting much legal work in-house, and of having internal lawyers participate in and manage the relationship with external legal advisers, but have also appreciated the value which a legally trained mind can bring to any organisation and to business decisions. It is likely that, just as there has never been as many solicitors working in Ireland as at the start of this century, so there have never been more solicitors engaged, from within, in advising the official and corporate sector. The recognition of the value of an Irish legal qualification extends not only to that sector but also to law firms and businesses in other countries. In London, Brussels, New York and many other cities a significant number of Irish lawyers have played a full part in and been well accepted as members of the legal community. Many of them, after working abroad for some time, have brought their legal skills back to Ireland and enhanced the profession with the experience thus gained. We hope that this record of the profession will be of interest to lawyers and others, at home and abroad.

The initial three chapters, by Daire Hogan, deal with the history of the Law Society of Ireland up to the middle of the twentieth century. The first chapter sets out the story of the status of the profession in the eighteenth century, then divided between attorneys who practised in the common law courts of king's bench, common pleas and the exchequer and solicitors who practised in the court of chancery; it describes also the laws and practices which regulated the profession, and the developments and modernisation which slowly took place in the practice of the courts in the admission of attorneys and solicitors. This part of the book deals with the foundation of the Society as the body which was set up initially as a voice and representative for the interests of its members, and the grant of the Society's initial charter in 1852.

Chapter two describes the struggle of the Society over more than three decades, involving resort to Parliament, to end the supervision which the King's Inns had historically exercised over the profession, primarily through the requirement for solicitors to be members of the Inn. In 1866 the link was broken and the Society was given for the first time a number of educational and regulatory functions. These were enhanced in the following decades of the Victorian era, as a concept of greater profession-alism developed. The chapter describes the effects on the profession of the First World War and the War of Independence.

The third chapter deals with the challenges which independence and the Civil War brought after 1922. One development then was that the profession in Northern Ireland took steps to set up a separate body, the Incorporated Law Society of Northern Ireland, which assumed by law all the Society's functions in that jurisdiction. A new regulatory regime was introduced under the Solicitors Acts, 1954 and 1960, the latter of which resulted from some of the earliest litigation on constitutional rights. The story of those acts and the resulting litigation, and of the earlier introduction in 1929 of the requirement that solicitors should have a knowledge of the Irish language, gives a detailed insight not only into the profession in that era but also into the process of making law.

Dr Mary Redmond in her chapter on the emergence of women in the profession tells the story of how women have worked to overcome prejudice and to be admitted to, and gain equality within, the solicitors' profession. At common law, it was widely accepted that women were under a general disability by reason of their sex to become lawyers, and that a lawyer's work was not fit for a woman. She notes that it is difficult to believe that less than ninety years ago (a span of a lifetime) women in Ireland were prohibited from practising as solicitors or barristers or from serving as judges. The professional bodies and the courts in the early part of the twentieth century declined to admit women to the profession, and the background to this discriminatory attitude and the energetic campaign to change the law, culminating in the enactment of the Sex Disqualification (Removal) Act, 1919, is thoroughly examined. The number of women practising in the profession was small to begin with, and remained so for a generation, but the composition of the profession has been changing quite dramatically in recent years.

Dr Redmond, in her chapter, celebrates some of the many women who have achieved prominence in the profession and outside it. She does not refer, in this context, to herself but as editors we observe that Dr Redmond is one of the most distinguished lawyers of our time. She ends her chapter with the words of Moya Quinlan, first woman president of the Society, who said at a conference in Dublin in December 2000: '[M]uch remains to be done to ensure that in the future all will come to accept as a fact that women are lawyers who just happen to be women.'

Eamonn Hall, in his two chapters, chronicles some legal issues facing solicitors as individual members of a learned profession, and the Society, as the institution representing and regulating solicitors, over the last three decades of the twentieth century. The acquisition of the Society's headquarters at Blackhall Place, Dublin, in the late 1960s and 1970s is described. The move of the Society's headquarters from the Four Courts in Dublin to the former King's Hospital premises at Blackhall Place, 'one of the most beautiful' of Dublin's major buildings, is regarded as one of the great undertakings in the history of the Society. Another, albeit minor, milestone around that time, was the granting in 1971 of a right of audience to solicitors in the superior courts; some of the tension between the Bar and solicitors on the issue is of interest from today's perspective.

Delay and inefficiencies in the legal system, constant themes in the history of law, are discussed. A snapshot of time in the early 1970s of such delays and inefficiencies in the legal system in Ireland is presented. Some delays have been remedied; others are still with us. An effective operation of Ireland's courts is a critical element in the well-being of society; the establishment of the Courts Service in 1999 is welcomed.

In chapter six, Eamonn Hall examines issues associated with just and fair remuneration for solicitors, and the various related tensions that surfaced acutely in the 1970s. In this context, it is noted the Society argued that the stresses and strains on the modern solicitor and the frequent disruption of home and family life in the interests of clients should not be ignored by the State when regulating solicitors' remuneration. The contrast between the opportunities for solicitors who qualified in the 1950s (some of whom were forced to emigrate) and the era of the 'Celtic tiger', an unparalleled period of growth and demand for services of solicitors in the 1990s, is highlighted.

The manner in which solicitors obtain professional business, particularly by public advertising, has been a contentious issue over recent decades. Public advertising of legal services in the media is, in the history of lawyers, a recent phenomenon. Any advertising of that nature was regarded by many lawyers as unprofessional and strict rules were, until recent times, enforced by the council of the Society (under threat of disciplinary sanction), governing, for example, solicitors delivering lectures, writing articles and appearing on radio and television. These issues and how advertising by solicitors is regulated today are highlighted. Over the last three decades, several inquiries have been conducted by state bodies into aspects of the role and work of solicitors, including any privileges in the form of exclusive rights to perform any legal services and corresponding obligations, and these are examined.

The issue of the appointment of solicitors as judges of the Circuit, High and Supreme Courts is also considered. Other issues, including the protection of clients' finances, the maintenance of a compensation fund to compensate clients for financial losses arising from dishonesty on the part of solicitors and their employees and the unprecedented claims on that fund, are discussed. Finally, Eamonn Hall concludes by referring to the Solicitors (Amendment) Act, 1994 which, inter alia, gave the Society stronger powers to investigate and deal with complaints from the public against solicitors, and considers internal governance issues within the Society.

In his two chapters John Buckley deals with the significant changes in the Society's education and training programmes which have taken place in the last fifty years, and also reviews the Society's activities in the field of legal publishing during that period. In his chapter on legal education, he identifies the significant influences which led to the remarkable changes which have taken place over the last fifty years, not only in the nature of the education programme for solicitors but also in the physical surroundings in which the Society's courses have been conducted. So far from being required to trail around church halls, a sports clubhouse or dance hall and a university lecture room, students now have the use of a state-of-the-art modern building with a sophisticated information centre.

In his chapter on legal publishing, John Buckley traces the significant trail-blazing part played by the Society in the re-launch of legal textbook publishing in the State. In 1969, when the Society established its publications committee, the area was a desert. Within a period of ten years it had demon-strated that there was a market, as well as a need, for legal textbooks, showing the way for the commercial publishers who have transformed the desert into a flourishing garden.

Margaret Byrne's account of the library of the Society indicates how the desire for a proper library was a key element in the foundation of the Society in the middle of the nineteenth century, and how it has been a core element in the services provided to members since that time. The present library, opened in 2000, is a handsome successor to earlier library halls. The Society's librarians have had to respond to constant challenges, including the almost total destruction of the library in the Four Courts in 1922, and the extraordinary development of wider legal information sources in recent decades.

In the last chapter the director general of the Society, Ken Murphy, looks at how the profession, the Society and Ireland have changed since the centenary of the Society's charter was celebrated fifty years ago. He examines a number of the issues facing the Society today and the way in which the core values of the profession are coming under pressure from Government and other sources, and he reviews the constant challenge of change to meet the requirements of the profession and the public now and for the future.

We would like to thank all the contributors for their goodwill and courtesy and helpfulness in the preparation of this volume; their assistance in many cases has extended far beyond the preparation of their individual chapters. Although we have served as editors it has been a collective enterprise, and the advice and guidance and support of many people, among the contributors and elsewhere within the Society and the profession, have greatly eased our work. We thank all other members of the working group on the publication, and also Jim Ivers and Michael O'Mahony, and Margaret Byrne in particular for her co-ordination of the Society's input.

We thank also for their assistance in a variety of ways, which in a number of cases included the provision of photographs and other personal records, Michael Adams, Owen Binchy, Brian Bohan, Michael Byrne, Michael Carrigan, Tony Ensor, Patrick Farrell, Dermot Flanagan, Tony Hanahoe, Rosemary Kearon, Eddie Mackey, Eugene McCague, Frank McCormack, who compiled the index, Noel McDonald, Jim Milton, Eamonn Mongey, Michael Moran, Jo Noonan, Jacqueline O'Brien, Aoife O'Connor, Pat O'Connor, Elaine O'Doherty, Eugenea O'Neill, Brian O'Reilly, Peter Pearson, David Pigot, Eric Plunkett and Elizabeth Senior. We also are pleased to acknowledge the permission of the Director of the National Archives to cite an extract from the records of the Department of the Taoiseach (file DT S 13858, memorandum to government dated 28 July 1953), which appears in the President's foreword.

EAMONN G. HALL & DAIRE HOGAN
Dublin, August 2002

The profession before the charter of 1852

DAIRE HOGAN

Admission to the legal profession has historically been regulated by the courts, and lawyers are persons authorised to provide legal services to the community. Over the centuries the courts recognised the right of a litigant to appoint another person – originally an 'attorney' – as a representative in legal proceedings, and two principal classes of lawyers – barristers, and attorneys or solicitors – came into existence. Barristers were entitled to plead in court and attorneys and solicitors gave instructions to barristers and acted in legal proceedings preparatory to court hearings or in legal matters not involving litigation. Attorneys were attached to one or more (and from early in the nineteenth century, to all) of the three courts of common law – king's (or queen's) bench, common pleas and the exchequer, and solicitors were attached to the court of chancery. The distinction was finally abolished in 1877, when the separate courts were joined into a single Supreme Court of Judicature with a number of divisions, and 'solicitor' was thought to be the more polite term for the members of the profession. The word 'attorney' thus lost its precise meaning, although of course it continued to be used in ordinary speech. (The word 'solicitor' will generally be used in this chapter to designate both 'solicitors' and 'attorneys'.)

In the course of the eighteenth century what was previously a relatively informal manner of admission to the legal profession in Ireland was modified by a number of statutes and by rules adopted by the Benchers of the Honorable Society of the King's Inns. This was an unincorporated association of lawyers, governed by senior lawyers – including all judges – known as the Benchers, which was founded in 1539. Three years later it received a grant of the land of a dissolved monastery on the north bank of the river Liffey, a few hundred yards west of Dublin Castle and, after a period of dormancy, it was revived in 1607. A further reorganisation of the society in 1792 and in 1793 confirmed and set out the basis on which it exercised its very considerable influence over both branches of the legal profession, barristers and solicitors.

In the absence of hard data the arrangements that governed the admission of attorneys in Ireland prior to 1607 can only be a matter for speculation, but it would be reasonable to suppose that some system of apprenticeship operated and that some test, however cursory, would have preceded formal admission or permission to practise in the courts.

Attorneys were among the categories of legal practitioner admitted to the Inns on its revival in 1607. In 1629 there occurs the first recital of a crucial new rule to the effect that no one was to be admitted an attorney in any of the courts of Dublin unless he had first been admitted to membership of the society and that existing attorneys who were not already members of the society were to present themselves for admission early in the next ensuing Hilary term; otherwise they were to be struck off. Every attorney was required to keep one week's commons at the society in each law term.

The prominent position occupied by the King's Inns in the scheme of regulation is indicated by other evidence.[1] An Irish statute of 1715 which conferred rights of practice in the assize courts on attorneys who had been admitted to the superior courts in Dublin stipulated that such attorneys should first have paid their 'commons and other duties to the stewards of the Inns'. A second revival of King's Inns towards the end of the eighteenth century brought a spate of new rules of court that reaffirmed yet again the obligation of prior membership of the society. In 1789, the court of common pleas insisted, as a preliminary to entry, on proof of payment of the admission fee to the society, and in 1795 king's bench followed suit.

STATUTORY REGULATION

A number of statutes were passed at the end of the seventeenth century and the start of the eighteenth century which sought to compel lawyers to subscribe to oaths and prescribed tests and fines with the object of

---

[1] See generally Colum Kenny, *King's Inns & the kingdom of Ireland; the Irish 'inn of court', 1541–1800* (Dublin, 1992).

restricting the profession of law to members of the established church. The first of these statutes, which were repealed in 1792 and in 1829 (see below), was passed in 1698 and, having recited that 'papist solicitors have been and still are the common disturbers of the peace and tranquillity of his Majesty's subjects in general', it provided that solicitors (unless they came within the terms of the Treaty of Limerick, which ended the Williamite war in Ireland) should take oaths which were incompatible with certain articles of the catholic faith. This was replaced by a fresh statute and heavier fines nine years later (the existing fines on catholic lawyers 'being too small in respect of the great gains they make by their practice').[2]

The extent to which these statutes could be evaded by catholics and dissenters is uncertain and raises the same questions as the degree to which the other penal laws were enforced in practice. The fact that they were not completely successful in securing their object is shown by the amendments and extensions which were made from time to time in the early part of the eighteenth century, and the first statute regulating the solicitors' profession in any more general way was also intended to make these penal laws more effective. This act, passed in 1733, was entitled 'an act for the amendment of the law in relation to papist solicitors; and for remedying other mischiefs in relation to the practitioners in the several courts of law and equity' and was based in part upon a statute of the parliament of the United Kingdom ('an act for the better regulation of attorneys and solicitors') passed at Westminster in 1729.

Before 1733 'the right to exercise the profession of attorney-at-law in Ireland was attained by persons binding themselves to, or placing themselves in the office of, some admitted attorney for a certain period, and afterwards applying to one of the courts of law in Ireland for liberty to practise as an attorney in such court', in the words of a petition presented to parliament by the Law Society in 1858. Baron Pennefather of the court of exchequer commented in 1838 that prior to the seminal 1733 statute 'this court and the other superior courts in Dublin exercised, under certain regulations, the power of admitting attorneys as their own officers, to discharge the duties of the respective courts. It was thought right, however,

2 10 Will III (1698), c. 13 (Ir.).

by the legislature, that certain rules should be laid down by legislative enactments, reserving to the superior courts the power of exercising their original jurisdiction in such cases as, in their discretion, it might seem fit to do so.'[3]

The scheme of admission to the solicitors' profession laid down by the 1733 act, following the scheme applicable in England since 1729, was drafted with a view to 'preventing obscure and ignorant persons practising as attorneys or solicitors'. No person was to be admitted who had not been apprenticed for five years to a six-clerk (an official of the court of chancery) or to an admitted and licensed solicitor in England or in Ireland; indentures of apprenticeship were to be enrolled in the appropriate court(s) and an affidavit of due service as an apprentice was to be made out and sworn when the period had been completed.

The act also contained a short statement of the work of solicitors in relation to litigation; a person (other than a barrister) would be deemed to be acting as a solicitor and thus within the scope of the act if he

> draws dictates or abbreviates pleadings or transcribes or abbreviates any depositions or other evidence in order to be made use of in any suit either at law or in equity or takes upon himself the direction or management in any cause or suit or the defence thereof in the said Four Courts, or any of them, wherein he is not a party, nor concerned in interest.[4]

In 1773 a statute regulated apprenticeship in a more detailed way. The preamble to the act recited that it had become a frequent practice among the inferior classes of attorneys to take apprentices of low education, whose circumstances or conditions of fortune frequently induced them to be guilty of mean and improper practices to the dishonour of the profession. In each of the common law courts examiners – one officer of the court 'and four of the most reputable practising attorneys of the said court' – were appointed to inquire into the moral and educational qualifications of

---

3 Law Society, *Annual Report, 1858*; *In re Lyons* (1839) Ir Eq R 267 at 272.   **4** 7 Geo II (1733) c. 5 (Ir.), preamble, and sections 2, 3 and 6.

apprentices seeking admission as attorneys to practise in that court. These men became known as the 'moral examiners'. The act also provided that no apprentice should be admitted until he had attended the courts in Dublin for two terms for each of three years during his apprenticeship.[5]

This act resulted from the efforts of a group of solicitors who were anxious to improve the quality of the members of the profession, perhaps indicating also that over the years some members of the profession would have made efforts to maintain or consolidate rough and ready standards of professional respectability. They were led by Gorges Edmund Howard, a Dublin attorney who wrote plays and a number of books on court and revenue practice, and is best known perhaps for his collection of *Cases on popery*, published in 1775. He was instrumental in forming a society of attorneys in 1774, which was the first known association of solicitors in the country. In 1763 he had published some proposals for a reform of the laws, including heads of a bill for regulating the admission and practice of attorneys. These failed 'but with the most indefatigable pains and perseverance I was afterwards the means of obtaining a most effectual law for the purpose'.

Shortly after the 1773 statute was passed, according to Howard 'at several meetings of most of the principal attorneys in this kingdom who, some years before, had done me the honour to appoint me the president of the profession [which suggests that some informal committee had come into existence], all the delays, defects, and grievances in the practice and proceedings of the several courts which had occurred to them during the course of their experience were collected and digested and a memorial to have them corrected and redeemed was presented to several of the judges, who seemed to approve of it highly, yet little has been done therein'.[6]

That last statement was written in 1782 and is perhaps a better indication of what happened after the passing of the 1773 statute than is his description of it as 'a most effectual law'. The society of attorneys resolved to set up a committee (among whose members would be the attorneys appointed by the judges as the examiners under the act) to supervise the

---

5 13 and 14 Geo III (1773) c. 23 (Ir.), sections 1 and 6.   6 Gorges Edmund Howard, *Miscellaneous works* (Dublin, 1782), pp x and xxvi.

application of the new law and 'the regulation of the profession at large' and, as mentioned above, a memorial setting out proposals on 21 specific matters of law, procedure and practice was forwarded to the judges. The appointment of the 'moral examiners' was made by the judges in the various courts and must have led the judges from time to time to consult the attorneys practising in their courts, but the society of attorneys with its committee does not appear to have continued in existence for any length of time after it had been formed.

Howard's activities can be seen as an expression in Ireland of what a historian of English attorneys has described as 'a phenomenon that was common enough in the eighteenth century – groups of men with common interests meeting together for reasons that were primarily social and con-vivial, and finding that collectively they were able to do things for their common benefit which as individuals they were unable to accomplish'.[7] In London the Society of Gentlemen Practisers in the Courts of Law and Equity had been founded in 1739, and law societies had been founded in Bristol in 1770 and in Yorkshire in 1786.

THE REFORM OF THE KING'S INNS

In 1786 work was commenced on the construction of new courts on the property of the King's Inns at Inns Quay, Dublin, the area of the grant of land to the society in 1542. Other sites had been considered and the whole question discussed for decades. In 1772 the Government had decided to concentrate certain public offices, principally those connected with the courts, in one place, and Public Offices designed by Thomas Cooley were constructed at Inns Quay, commencing in 1779. The subsequent court building, which adjoined the Public Offices, was one of the most magnificent edifices in Dublin, providing a grand focus for legal activity, and gave lawyers a handsome and imposing forum for their work. It was designed by James Gandon, and was his second major public building in Dublin, the Custom House having been started in 1781. The first stone was laid on

7 R. Robson, *The attorney in eighteenth-century England* (Cambridge, 1959), p. 35.

3 March 1786. The building was substantially completed in 1796 and was finished in 1802. Subsidiary buildings at the wings were erected, and in due course the area behind came to be filled with other legal buildings, including buildings for solicitors.

While the Four Courts were being constructed, a number of other significant developments affecting the profession took place. One of these was the appointment of John Fitzgibbon as lord chancellor of Ireland on 19 June 1789. (He was raised to the peerage at that time as Baron Fitzgibbon, received the higher honour of viscountcy in 1793 and became earl of Clare in 1795.) He held office until his death in January 1802. He is of course best remembered for his work in the government of Ireland in those years, but as lord chancellor he was also chairman of the Benchers of King's Inns, and during his period of office and under his auspices the society and the government of the legal profession assumed the form it was to hold for much of the nineteenth century. Rules confirming and regulating the admission of barristers and solicitors and solicitors' apprentices were adopted, and fees and 'deposits for chambers' were levied which put the society into a comfortable financial position.

At this time a number of other important if little publicised changes took place which also helped to shape the future development of the solicitors' profession.[8] For instance, the common law courts set out to improve supervision of the attorneys attached to each through a system of registration of names and addresses, and it became more common for attorneys to be admitted in more than one of those courts. The profession also became exclusively 'Irish'. Rules of the court of common pleas in 1671 and the act of 1733 had expressly contemplated the possibility that an apprenticeship might be served with an English master in England, and admission of persons born in England and undergoing training there was both sanctioned and welcomed. The 1773 act and rules made by the Benchers in 1793 required apprentices to attend at the courts in Dublin, however, and also confined the taking of apprentices to practising solicitors.

---

8 W.N. Osborough, 'The regulation of the admission of attorneys and solicitors in Ireland 1600–1866' in D. Hogan & W.N. Osborough (eds.) *Brehons, serjeants and attorneys* (Dublin, 1990).

In May 1792 the Benchers issued draft rules for the government of the profession and a committee was appointed to confer with a committee of barristers and with a committee of attorneys on such of the rules as related to each of them respectively. In 1792 a catholic relief bill was enacted by the Irish Parliament and with effect from 24 June 1792 what the preamble to the act described as 'certain restraints and disabilities' to which catholics were subject and which had prevented them openly joining the legal profession were abolished. No religious bar to entry to the profession then remained for solicitors, and the only continuing restriction was that the act provided that nothing therein contained 'shall extend to enable or qualify any person to hold or enjoy the place or office of King's Counsel',[9] and hence, by extension, prevented catholics from being eligible for appointment as judges, a restriction not removed until 1829.

In November 1791 the Law Club of Ireland was formed. Little is known of this society of solicitors, but like the society formed in 1774 it appears to have been composed of the better educated or more substantial members of the profession. It had premises at 13 Dame Street until 1869 and thereafter at 25 Nassau Street, and was dissolved at the end of the nineteenth century. It is conceivable that one of the reasons for the formation of the club and for the reorganisation which the Benchers had put in hand was to provide for greater supervision of the legal profession, since catholics would now be free to join it.

There is no record of a meeting between the Benchers and a committee of attorneys, although a general meeting of attorneys was held in November that year. On 5 July 1792 the Bar passed resolutions rejecting the draft rules. The Bar had many objections to a charter which the Benchers had obtained (which was soon surrendered) and to the draft rules, but after some delay and controversy the Benchers in November 1793 simply proceeded with their plans and declared that they had

> full power and authority to make and ordain rules and orders for and concerning the business and practice of attorneys and for their admission into the said society, as members thereof; and for and

---

9 32 Geo III (1792) c. 21 (Ir.).

concerning the admission of students into the said society; and for and concerning their being generally admitted into the said society and to ranks and degrees therein; and for the advancement of knowledge in the science and practice of the law.[10]

The rules required each barrister, solicitor, and bar student to be a member of the society and to pay fees to the society, including payments as a 'deposit for chambers', and they made detailed provision for fitness to become a member of the society to be evidenced to the satisfaction of the Benchers.

The rules derived their force from the fact that – as was made clear in various controversies in the following century – the judges were all Benchers (members of the bench, in a confusing phrase often used) and could give effect to the rules adopted by the Benchers. A solicitor or attorney would read in no statute that he should be a member of the King's Inns as a condition of admission to practise in one or more of the courts, but if the judges who decided whether he should be admitted had decided, in their capacity as Benchers, that this would be a condition of admission, there was no opportunity to object. The same was true for barristers, whose call to the Bar was carried out by the lord chancellor.

In this decade also the Benchers took in hand a further project, the building of an Inn of Court – that is, a headquarters for the society which, if it had followed the pattern of the Inns of Court in London, might have been expected to include a dining hall, chapel, library, offices and apartments and chambers for the members of the Inn. Various buildings occupied by the society since 1542 had become ruinous or derelict. Land at Constitution Hill/Henrietta Street, about half a mile north of the Four Courts, was selected for the building. Gandon was appointed as architect and on 5 August 1800 the foundation stone was laid by Lord Clare.

Early in the nineteenth century what came to be regarded as one of the most important privileges of the solicitors' profession, the conveyancing monopoly, was created. Solicitors had to pay stamp duty upon their annual practising certificates, a tax introduced in Great Britain in 1785 and

10 *Rules of Society of King's Inns* (1793), preamble.

extended to Ireland in 1816, the rate of duty initially being £8 for solicitors in London, Dublin and Edinburgh and £3 for country solicitors. The duties were increased to £12 and £8 in 1842 and reduced to £9 and £6 in 1853. This tax came to be resented by solicitors, who believed that no other persons were obliged to pay an annual tax as a condition of entitlement to practise a profession. When it was increased in Great Britain (in 1804) and introduced in Ireland (in 1816) the profession received a monopoly in the preparation of property deeds (conveyancing) as a benefit in return.

In 1821 a bill was read in the house of commons to permit university graduates to be admitted as attorneys and solicitors after a shortened period of apprenticeship, three years instead of the usual five. This proposal gave graduates a concession on the terms of entry to the solicitors' branch of the profession similar to that which they had had for a number of years on entry to the Bar. Although the bill initially referred only to the English universities, Oxford and Cambridge, and the English profession it was changed prior to its enactment so as to refer to Dublin University and the Irish profession also.

Solicitors in London and in Dublin began to work at about this time on means of securing that some tests (in addition to those of the 'moral examiners', in Ireland) should be passed before a person would be accepted as an apprentice and again before he would subsequently be admitted to the profession. Early in the decade a committee of 21 solicitors was set up in Dublin which worked with a group of English solicitors, led by Mr Freshfield, head of a leading firm in London, in preparing drafts of charters for the regulation of the profession in England and in Ireland respectively. Each draft charter provided for the appointment of a council to control the education and admission of solicitors. The English group made more progress than the Irish group. In 1823 they published a prospectus for a Law Institute, which was followed two years later by the formation of the Law Society and by the erection between 1828 and 1832 of a handsome building in Chancery Lane. A royal charter was granted in 1831.

1830: THE LAW SOCIETY OF IRELAND

On 24 June 1830 the Law Society of Ireland was established. Its principal objects were:

(a) to preserve the rights and privileges of attorneys – to promote useful communication and good feeling amongst the members of the profession – fair and honourable practice – and to adopt such measures as may be best calculated to ensure respectability and advantage to the public;

(b) to suggest to the proper authorities such alterations as experience or change in circumstances may require for improving the rules and practice of the courts of law and equity;

(c) to adopt such measures as may be best calculated to prevent the apprenticing or admission of uneducated and improper persons, and to prevent unqualified persons from practising;

(d) to procure or erect a proper hall for the purposes of the society when the funds shall be sufficient or the society otherwise enabled to do so.[11]

The Society was in its initial years (like the Law Society in England) a club for which members had to be proposed and approved by the committee, but it subsequently acknowledged that to restrict membership was incompatible with a claim to represent the profession as a whole and it became simply a voluntary society which, as will be seen, actively encouraged solicitors to join.

It leased rooms at Inns Quay, consisting of a reading room, committee room and office for the secretary of the Society. In November 1830 the committee of the Society submitted a memorial to the Benchers as to the 'necessity and propriety' of erecting chambers, with the funds of the King's Inns, for the use of solicitors, and retained Darley, the Benchers' architect. It wished that the hall and chambers for the use of solicitors should be erected away from the King's Inns, and proposed that the Benchers should acquire property at the back of the Four Courts for this purpose. At a

11 *The Dublin Almanac and General Register of Ireland 1834* (Dublin, 1834), p. 148.

general meeting of the Society on 1 December 1830 a resolution was passed 'that the erection of chambers at Henrietta Street would be altogether useless, from the great distance from the courts, at least so far as respects the members of this society, and therefore we are determined not to take chambers if built in that situation'.

A conference was held between a committee of the Benchers and members of the Law Society in February 1831, following which the Society furnished plans for a building. In April 1834 a new plan prepared by Mr Owen, the architect to the Board of Works, was considered by the Benchers; this plan, according to a minute of a Benchers' meeting,

> secures what appears to be the most convenient site for the erection of the nisi prius court … affords the means of adding to the present library and thus continuing it in the most commodious if not the only situation in which it could be practically useful to the Bar … (and) carries into effect the wishes of the attorneys by giving them an extensive building immediately at the rear and close adjoining the courts, containing apartments such as they require.

The building work was completed in November 1840 and the apartments allotted for the solicitors were put in the hands of five trustees on their behalf in May 1841.

The Law Society was active in pursuing at least two of its other objects during the 1830s namely better control of admission to the profession – with respect to both apprentices and attorneys – and the protection of the rights and privileges of the profession, a question which took its most dramatic form in a first attempt to remove the control which the Benchers exercised over their branch of the profession. These matters will be considered in turn.

ADMISSION TO THE PROFESSION

Irrespective of the activities of the Society the control of admission to the profession might in any event have been an issue of importance in that decade since there was a sharp rise in the number of persons becoming apprenticed. The table below, taken from the records of the King's Inns, sets out the average number of new solicitors' apprentices in each decade from 1801 to 1860:

Decade	Average number of new apprentices per annum
1801–1810	77.2
1811–1820	94.9
1821–1830	104.8
1831–1840	146.2
1841–1850	98.7
1851–1860	46.8

Between 1827 and 1844 the number of apprentices was never less than 100, a figure which was exceeded only in five other years (1802, 1810, 1813, 1819, and 1846). Between 1829 and 1836 the number was never less than 136, and was at its peak in 1833 and 1834 when 172 and 180 new apprentices respectively were enrolled.

Since the new rules had come into force in 1794 the Benchers had taken seriously their duty of considering the suitability of masters for prospective new apprentices. In January 1798 the petition of one William Tomkins for permission to take an apprentice was refused, 'it not being stated to the satisfaction of the Bench that the said Tomkins does now attend His Majesty's Courts of Justice in Dublin'. In May 1800 Arthur D'Esterre was refused permission to take an apprentice, 'the Bench thinking him an improper master', an opinion they expanded the following year into considering him 'a person quite improper to have the care of an apprentice'. The Benchers rigorously applied the letter of the act of 1773 requiring the masters of apprentices to attend the courts in Dublin, rejecting a memorial of solicitors resident in Cork who maintained that adequate experience for apprentices was available in the courts in Cork. Prospective apprentices who did not show a satisfactory knowledge of Latin or who were under the age of 16 years were not accepted.

In any case in which the Benchers had not raised any objection to the acceptance of an apprentice by a solicitor into the King's Inns it was possible for the court or courts in which he wished to practise to refuse to admit him as a solicitor.

The act of 1773 had expressly reserved the right of the judges to examine and inquire into the qualifications of applicants for admission to practise in their respective courts and to admit 'such persons in such manner and with such discretion' as heretofore, and it was a concern of G.E. Howard that 'the dispensing power the judges have by the act be [not] too indulgently exercised' although he himself had benefited from this discretionary power:

> Upon these, my early publication[s], the lord chief justice of king's bench did me the honour to take me by the hands in the hall of the Four Courts and had me instantly sworn an attorney in the court of king's bench, where he presided, without any of the usual preliminary requisites upon such occasion.[12]

In 1836 the Benchers adopted a new rule that henceforth any future applicant to take apprentices had to be not only an attorney admitted in all three common law courts but a solicitor in addition. This marked a most significant stage in the formation of a unified profession out of the attorneys practising in individual courts. When the Benchers had second thoughts about this new rule, in May 1837, they gave notice to the Law Club of their intention to review the rule 'in order to hear what may be offered by them in supporting the existing regulation', an indication that the Law Society had not then been accepted as the principal representative body of solicitors. Finally in 1840 it was enacted that when the practitioner paid stamp duty on securing his admission to practise in any one of the four superior courts (chancery and the three courts of common law) he would be entitled to be admitted to the three others without the payment of any additional duty.

An applicant for admission was required to post notice of his intention in the Four Courts, and in a case reported in 1830/31 the court of common

---

12 G.E. Howard, *Miscellaneous works*, p. xxx.

pleas refused to admit as an attorney an apprentice whose notices had not been posted regularly despite his counsel's urging that 'it was of great consequence, from some business he had lately been promised, that he should be sworn in this term'; the court pointed out that the object of posting notices was to enable objections to be made and considered that there could be no injury in a short delay, remarking 'from the records of the King's Inns there is an average application of 130 persons to be admitted in every year. For their own sakes apprentices should wish the utmost strictness to be attended to.'

In 1827 an application for admission by a person named Bamfield was rejected by the court of common pleas. Seven years previously the moral examiners had rejected him as an improper and unfit person since while he was an apprentice, he had acted in his master's name and had caused a person to be arrested, but they left it to the court whether it would, as the proper tribunal, excuse this. The chief justice said that the court 'held themselves in duty bound as protectors of the public not to permit such a person to be admitted into so high and respectable a profession as that of attorney'.

After the formation of the Law Society the Benchers occasionally referred applications for permission to take an apprentice to it; in May 1832 the Benchers granted permission to four attorneys to take apprentices after the list had been printed, upon notice being given to the Law Society and the Law Club, although a similar late application in November that year was not referred either to the Society or to the Club.

Some reported cases in the 1830s illustrate the practice and procedure followed on application to a court for admission as a solicitor, and are of particular interest in showing the role of the Law Society as holding a watching brief on such applications, and in generally opposing applications for admission before the expiry of the period of apprenticeship or applications seeking the use of the judges' discretionary powers of admission. Within six months of its formation the committee of the Society had objected to the proposed admission as an attorney of the court of the exchequer of a person who had been apprenticed for less than a year, calling it 'an unprecedented indulgence'.

In 1833 a person named Grady who had not been apprenticed in the manner required by law was admitted as an attorney. He was the son of an attorney and had been brought into his father's office in 1824 with a view to him becoming an apprentice, but his father became financially embarrassed and unable to pay the stamp duty and other expenses of having him articled regularly. He continued to work in the office until his father's death made it necessary to regularise the position. There were several family suits and several clients of the father who wished that Mr Grady should continue to conduct their business. An application in the summer of 1833 was rejected because he had not been apprenticed to any person at all, but by November he had become articled to a solicitor, and was admitted. Counsel said that he had obtained certificates of good character from eminent barristers and important court officers, and 'the committee of the Law Society had reported upon his case and in favour of his claim to be admitted an attorney'.[13]

The Law Society was not always so obliging, as two cases in 1834/35 and 1838 show. In the first of those the Society opposed the application to the court of exchequer of one Bernard Dowling, who their counsel maintained 'had been practising as an attorney, in the names of different persons, but it was endeavoured to be so covered and cloaked as having been done by him merely as an apprentice. It also appeared that he had served his time to several members of the profession and that while he was so serving his time he was acting as hired clerk to these very persons.' The court accepted Mr Dowling's explanation and admitted him.[14]

In 1838 applications made by one Timothy Lyons were contested in the court of chancery and in the exchequer. In the course of his apprenticeship Mr Lyons had been a salaried clerk in the office of one of the six clerks of the court of chancery, and the Society argued that a principle should be established that it was not competent for an apprentice to undertake duties, the discharge of which may be necessarily inconsistent with his situation and with the attendance due to the business of his master. They said that against Mr Lyons personally they had no objection, but 'the members of the Society conceiving a very important question, as affecting the respectability of their

13 *Law Recorder* II (n.s.) 1833–34, p. 13, *In re Grady.* 14 *Law Recorder* II (n.s.) 1834–35, p. 198, *In re Dowling.*

profession, to be involved in the present case, are naturally apprehensive lest his admission as an attorney be drawn into a dangerous precedent'.

Mr Lyons's master, testifying to his ability and industry, satisfied the court of chancery that it had not been a 'collusive apprenticeship' and he was admitted by the lord chancellor. Six days later in the exchequer the chief baron thought his case a fit one 'for the exercise of the discretionary power we possess of dispensing with the requisites in strictness imposed by the statute'. He gave weight to the fact 'that another court had thought fit to exercise its like discretionary function'.[15]

For every person whose admission as a solicitor raised some difficult point, there must have been many more whose application to the court would have been a formality, all their papers and affairs being in order. The way was not always completely clear, however, and a case early in the decade illustrated the confusion which might exist in practice. A question arose as to whether a solicitor (properly so called) was obliged to take the oath taken by an attorney, not to permit any person to practise in his name (originally a penal law, but subsequently used to prevent solicitors lending their names to unqualified persons). A Mr Smith claimed not to have taken any such oath and hard words were directed at him in open court by the master of the rolls. Mr Smith investigated the matter, and proved himself to be right, to the surprise of the master of the rolls who thought it would be advantageous if all solicitors in his court had taken the same oath. Mr Smith said that when he intended to become a solicitor he

> adopted a course different from that usually adopted by other gentlemen, whose habit it is to apply for information to some of the subordinate clerks in the master's or six-clerks' offices … who have an interest in making a mystery of the manufacturing of solicitors.

He had examined the rules and satisfied himself that no oath was required, and suggested that the quite unnecessary practice, solemnly followed for a substantial period, had been introduced 'through the ignorance of some clerk who had obtained some hearsay notion of the oath taken by attorneys'.[16]

15 *Irish Equity Reports* 1 (1838–39) at p. 267 and 279, *In re Lyons.* 16 *Law Recorder/Glasscock Reports* (1831–32), p. 351, *Birch* v. *Oldis.*

In 1843 the Benchers agreed to the Society's request that copies of the petitions and affidavits of prospective apprentices should be lodged with the secretary of the Society as well as with the under-treasurer of the King's Inns, so that the Society would have a better opportunity of objecting to the apprenticing of any person they considered unsuitable. In 1854 the Benchers agreed to a variation in the form of the apprentices'/intending masters' affidavit, at the request of the Society. Although the Society shortly afterwards expressed its regret that the practice of the Irish courts in the admission to the profession of persons who had not been regularly apprenticed was not as strict as in England, they were satisfied that since 1841 there had been fewer applications for admission not in proper form (for example, by apprentices before their full term had been served) or by 'persons considered ineligible'.

The Benchers rejected a proposal of the Society in 1852 that only solicitors who were members of the Society should be permitted to take apprentices, scarcely a surprising decision in view of the unrepresentative nature at the time of the Society and the implied interference with the Benchers' own prerogative.

Towards the end of the 1830s the Law Society took up the question of the standing of solicitors in relation to the King's Inns. It believed that the rules regulating the taking of apprentices by solicitors and the various other regulations of the Benchers by which they were bound had no foundation in law, and took the opinion of Mr Serjeant Warren. He advised that

> the Benchers are not entitled to exercise control over the attorneys and their apprentices except so far as attorneys by becoming members of the society have submitted themselves to its rules and orders and so far also as the regulations of the Benchers having been recognised and acted on by the judges of superior courts in their respective courts may have thereby acquired an authority they would not otherwise possess … I am of the opinion that apprentices are of right entitled to have their indentures enrolled without any payments to the King's Inns society and that apprentices who have duly complied with the provisions of [the 1733 act] and [the 1773 act] and who have paid the sums required by the statutes above referred to and any fees of offices established by the courts and who have also complied with the

regulations of the courts as to examinations, etc., are of right entitled
to be sworn attorneys without making any payments to the King's
Inns society and without having become a member of that body. But
although such is my opinion as to the rights of attorneys and their
apprentices I see no way in which such rights can be enforced without
legislative interference.[17]

In November 1837 a committee appointed by the Law Society to consider
the regulation of the profession forwarded a draft bill to the Benchers for
their consideration. The Benchers considered that one of its principal
objects was

> to render attorneys altogether independent of your society and to
> form that profession into a distinct body free from its control and
> interference, and also to diminish to a considerable extent its revenues.
> We do not see any grounds upon which a change affecting so materially
> the interests of the society is required and we think the tendency of it
> so injurious that we think we are warranted in recommending that
> immediate steps should be taken to oppose the further progress of
> the bill.

The scheme of regulation proposed by the bill was that no person
should be admitted as a solicitor unless he had been duly articled and had
served for five years or, in the case of his having taken a degree in one of
the universities, for a period of three years (which would not have changed
the existing position). Under the bill solicitors would not be members of
the society of King's Inns, and the Law Society, with the various attorneys
and solicitors whose names were set out in a schedule to the bill, and such
further solicitors as wished to join, would become an incorporated society.
The Society was to have power to make rules as to articled clerks
(apprentices), subject to the approval of the judges and was to be able to
alter the regulations from time to time, subject to the like approbation.
The council of the Society was to have power to make bye-laws for the

---

17 *Minutes of house of commons select committee on legal education*, 1846, q. 2774.

general government of the whole body. The fees then payable to the King's
Inns by solicitors were to be payable to the secretary of the Law Society.
The judges would appoint twelve attorneys to be the examiners of persons
seeking to be admitted as solicitors, subject to the general supervision of
the judges.

This bill was given a first reading in 1838 and again in 1839 (together
with a further bill to incorporate the society of King's Inns), and was
introduced on each occasion by Daniel O'Connell. The Law Society put
modified proposals to the Benchers from time to time, but as the Benchers
considered that the propositions of the Law Society involved 'not only a
denial of the authority of the Benchers to make regulations for the
attorneys, but also a denial of the legality of the society' [that is, the King's
Inns] no meeting of minds could take place. The bills were not passed and
the solicitors remained bound by the regulations of the Benchers.

In other fields steps were taken by the Society to defend the interests of
the profession. Publishers of directories were requested to omit from the lists
of solicitors the names of persons who had long been dead or who had retired
from the profession. After a meeting with the president of the Society the lord
chancellor directed various works to be carried out in the court of chancery
for the better accommodation and convenience of solicitors. Lastly, foreshadowing something that was to concern the Society for a good time to
come, a resolution was passed and published in 1830, denouncing advertisements by solicitors 'proposing to transact professional business on terms
below the legal and established fees'; 'we cannot too strongly express our
reprobation of a practice which we conceive to be derogatory and degrading'.

1841–1852: A NEW SOCIETY AND A CHARTER

On 29 May 1841 the solicitors took possession of three rooms in the new
building in the Four Courts. Since one of the objects of the Law Society
formed in 1830 had been satisfied, at least in part – the adequacy of the
accommodation in the solicitors' buildings was to be a bone of contention
between the Society and the Benchers for thirty years – it was thought
appropriate for the Society to adopt new rules, and this was done on 17

June 1841, on the basis of a report of a provisional committee of 21 solicitors. This committee considered that among the principal objects of the Society should be:

1. to give lectures and to provide better education in the laws and the practice of the courts;
2. to establish a library;
3. to suggest alterations in laws as may be expedient, and to watch all bills, with a view to protecting the rights of the profession;
4. to preserve the rights and privileges of the profession, and to guard its respectability by a vigilant attention to the preservation of upright and honourable practice; and to prevent the apprenticing of uneducated and improper persons, and their admission to the profession.

Rule No. 1 of the new Society provided that a society be formed for the regulation of the profession of attorney and solicitor in Ireland, for protecting their rights and privileges; and also for the institution and support of a library, for the use of the profession, and for the providing means for the instruction of apprentices; and that such society be called 'the Society of the Attorneys and Solicitors of Ireland'. It was resolved also that the apartment adjoining the Four Courts, allotted for the exclusive use of the profession of attorney and solicitor, be placed under the control and management of such society.

The rise of the Law Society as a spokesman for the solicitors' branch of the profession appears to have been, to some extent at least, at the expense of the Law Club of Ireland, This had had 189 members in 1824, a number which fell to 131 in 1841 and to 95 in 1846. In 1841 the Law Society had 390 members, and 11 of its 31 officers were members of the Law Club. Although, as mentioned above, in the 1830s the Benchers had thought fit to consult the club rather than the Society on a matter affecting the solicitors' profession, the club henceforth appears to have been almost exclusively a social club, playing no part in the direction of the affairs of the profession.

The Society was incorporated by royal charter, dated 5 April 1852. This followed the grant of a charter in 1845 (replacing an earlier charter of 1831)

to the Law Society in England. It recited that the petitioners for the charter
and other attorneys and solicitors 'with a view to the general benefit of
their profession had associated themselves for the purpose of founding an
institution for facilitating the acquisition of legal knowledge, and for the
better and more conveniently discharging their professional duties' and that
they 'conceived that the intentions of the said Society would be carried into
execution more effectually, beneficially, and satisfactorily to the public, if
the petitioners were incorporated by Royal Charter', and then declared that
the members of the Society 'shall be and be called one body politic and
corporate in deed and by law, by the name and style of 'The Incorporated
Society of the Attorneys and Solicitors of Ireland', with perpetual succession.
It was an official acknowledgement of the Society's useful public functions
and, more generally, of the respectability of its members.

The years 1852–1922

DAIRE HOGAN

The principal events with which the Law Society was concerned in the second half of the nineteenth century were the inauguration of a scheme of education for apprentices, the independence of the solicitors' profession from the King's Inns and the achievement of an increasing degree of self-government and of recognition of its position as the representative and regulatory body for solicitors in Ireland, culminating in the Solicitors' (Ireland) Act, 1898. The solicitors' frustration in dealing with the King's Inns on the subject of legal education is one instance of a supervision of the affairs of the profession which the Law Society found both irksome and unnecessary and which in the years after 1864 gave rise to a major controversy which broke the link between the Inn and the profession.

Two general points are of relevance for the whole of the period under review. One is that the Law Society was initially under very consistent direction, having only three presidents in its first thirty-five years, namely Josias Dunn who, having been president of the 'old' Law Society since its foundation in 1830, was elected as first president of the new society in 1841 and held office until his death in 1848, William Goddard (1848–60) and Richard Orpen (1860–76). The practice of electing a president for a single year was adopted in 1876. The first secretary of the Society, Edward Iles, held office from 1841 to 1864. He was succeeded by John Hawksley Goddard for another period of 24 years, up to 1888. His successor, W.G. Wakely, was appointed at the age of 23 and held office up to 1942 and was in turn followed by Eric Plunkett who held office up to 1972. There was a remarkable record of continuity of service in a key position, as further discussed in Chapter 5 by Eamonn Hall.

A second point is that while the Society took it upon itself to speak for the solicitors' profession its membership in the period under review did not extend beyond about a quarter or a third of all practising solicitors. The annual reports of the council of the Society constantly appealed for new members and, in 1857, the council observed that in their dealings with the King's Inns they had been 'taunted' that they did not represent the profession. Membership then consisted of 382 solicitors, little more than a quarter of the 1,250 or so solicitors in practice. It is of course probable that the Law Society spoke for many solicitors who did not join it. One reason why membership of the Society did not expand was that, notwithstanding its national title, it was widely regarded as a Dublin grouping. The council of the Society in 1833/34 had 21 members, all of whom had offices in Dublin and only four of whom also had offices outside the city. The first council of the new Society, elected in 1841, had 31 members, all of whom had offices in Dublin and only six of whom had offices outside the city.

Local law societies were formed in Belfast in 1843 and in Cork in 1859 (the annual report of which in 1872 referred to the Law Society as 'the Dublin Law Society'), and in the Society's campaign in Parliament in 1866, referred to later in this chapter, the council stated that it was supported by 'the active exertions of the Belfast, Cork, Derry and Waterford Law Societies'. The committee of the Northern Law Club, having received a letter from the Law Society in 1862, considered that they would not be justified in urging their members to join the Society, and 'they therefore leave each member to use his individual discretion in determining whether he should do so or not', recording their view that 'those who are seldom in Dublin and consequently seldom enabled to enjoy its [that is, membership of the Society's] most important advantages' might be induced to join if the membership subscription were reduced. They also resolved at that time

> that in order to procure for the Northern Law Club information as to all the proceedings of the Incorporated Law Society of Ireland and to facilitate communication with its officers the treasurer do henceforth pay an annual subscription to that society in the name of the secretary, for the time being, of this society.

At about this time, in 1863 and perhaps under the inspiration of the formation of a similar association in England in 1858, the Solicitors'

Benevolent Association was formed, independently of the Law Society, with the object of giving assistance to poor and necessitous solicitors and members of their families in succession to a similar charitable association that had been formed a few years before.

EDUCATION

At about the time that the Law Society was being re-established in 1841 a much more short lived body, but one which was to have profound effects in the field of legal education, was founded. This was the Dublin Law Institute, set up in 1839 by Tristram Kennedy, a member of both the Irish Bar and the English Bar.[1] Its prospectus comprised courses of lectures in common law, medical jurisprudence, equity, property law and conveyancing and practice at nisi prius. It initially received support and a small financial subsidy, soon discontinued, from the Benchers of King's Inns. Kennedy subsequently interested Thomas Wyse MP in the whole subject of legal education, and in 1846 the house of commons resolved 'that a select committee be appointed to inquire into the present state of legal education in Ireland and the means for its further improvement and extension', the committee's brief being extended four weeks later to the 'state, improvement and extension of legal education in England'.

Wyse had been chairman of the select committee of the house of commons on national education in Ireland which in its report in 1838 remarked that 'the present deficiency of institutions for the regular study of law is generally admitted'. With Wyse as chairman the committee met during the summer months of 1846 to hear witnesses and its report and minutes of evidence were published in August. The committee's principal conclusion was 'that the present state of legal education in England and Ireland, in reference to the classes professional and unprofessional concerned, to the extent and nature of the studies pursued, the time employed, and the facility with which instruction may be obtained, is extremely unsatisfactory and incomplete, and exhibits a striking contrast and inferiority to

1 Colum Kenny, *Tristram Kennedy and the revival of Irish legal training, 1835–1885* (Dublin, 1996).

such education at present in operation in all the more civilised states of
Europe and America'. The committee recommended that courses of lectures
and examinations be provided for apprentices (who should pass a preliminary examination before becoming apprenticed) and for Bar students.

The way of life of a solicitor's apprentice was described by a couple of
witnesses before the 1846 committee. An apprentice 'attends from 10 o'clock
in the morning until 4 or 5 in the evening at his master's office ... he
generally, at the commencement of his profession, is put to write and copy
out documents, and so forth; and afterwards, when he had a little more
knowledge, he gets on by degrees to do the whole routine business of the
office'. Another solicitor stated that in an apprentice's first year 'he is
generally occupied in copying, and by this system of copying he acquires
a habit of drawing legal forms; as he advances he goes through the details
of the business, and he at last comes to be what is called an outdoor
apprentice; that is, doing court business'.

The latter witness considered 'that a young man is perfectly useless for
the first year or two of his apprenticeship'. The former witness thought
more highly of apprentices; 'sometimes they are, and in fact they generally
are, very intelligent young men and very useful'. These observations
perhaps say more of human nature than of apprentices in the first half of
the nineteenth century, but at all events it was clear that the way of life of
an apprentice, even an industrious one, did little more than give him 'an
acquaintance with the practical forms of law'. It was not thought usual for
attorneys to take pains to instruct their apprentices in the principles or
practice of law.

Lectures for Bar students were introduced by King's Inns in 1850 but no
provision was made for the education of solicitors' apprentices, and in 1855
the Law Society presented a memorial to the Benchers calling for examinations to be introduced as a test both for admission to apprenticeship and
subsequently for admission to the profession. The legal education committee
of the Benchers considered the matter and declined to take any action.
There would be little value, they thought, in setting a standard of education for intended apprentices since an advanced standard would 'be
scarcely attainable in practice, especially in more remote parts of Ireland,

and by young men of humble means'. The Benchers were not prepared to permit apprentices to be admitted to the King's Inns' library, since apprentices were not members of the Inn (unlike students for the Bar) and if admitted would more likely read the light literature in preference to law books. They were in any event entitled to use the library of the Law Society.

The Law Society considered that the report of the legal education committee 'seems apparently framed in a disparaging tone towards our profession', and since they conceived that they had no further remedy in Ireland against the Benchers – they could not appeal to the courts because all the judges were Benchers – they resolved to apply to Parliament to investigate the King's Inns, and presented a petition in 1858. This pressure on the Benchers eventually led to them resolving in May 1860 to introduce a preliminary examination (in Latin, history, arithmetic, bookkeeping, geography and English composition) for prospective apprentices and a final examination before admission to the profession. They also instituted a professorship of law 'specially adapted to the wants of that branch of the profession', and thereafter lectures were given to apprentices. The new final examinations were not very difficult – initially almost nobody failed or was 'postponed' – but the principle had been established. In 1866 the Law Society took over responsibility for education of their branch of the profession from the Benchers, under the supervision of the judges.

PREMISES, RIGHTS AND PRIVILEGES OF THE PROFESSION

The Society was in constant correspondence with the Benchers about the state of the Solicitors' Buildings. They wrote in 1843, for instance, asking that the painting of their rooms, as originally intended, should proceed and that proper ventilation and glass panelling be installed. In 1845 the Benchers allotted an extra room for the Society's library, and in 1848 a further room was made available for solicitors' writing clerks. All the books and papers of the 'old' Law Society had been taken over in 1841, and in 1846 the Benchers, having previously allotted £500 for the Society's library, resolved to give surplus books from their library at Henrietta Street to it. The desire for a library had been one of the motives for the formation of the Northern Law Society earlier in 1843. In February a prospectus signed by 28 solicitors 'desirous of establishing a Law Club with a library in connection therewith' was circulated in Belfast, and the Society was established in May, the library being accommodated in the Linenhall Library.

The Society provided other services for its members. It called for the centralisation of all legal offices at the Four Courts, for the greater convenience of the public and of the profession and was gratified by the successive transfers to that location of the office of the accountant-general of the court of exchequer in 1843 'from its very inconvenient locality', William Street, of the law taxing offices in 1849 from Henrietta Street, and of the encumbered estates court also from Henrietta Street in 1853. In 1849 and in 1861 the council of the Society suggested that, following London practice, members of the Society should have a daily rendez-vous at 2 o'clock in the Solicitors' Building for a quarter of an hour so that appointments could be made and members of the profession meet each other 'without the loss of time, trouble, delay and uncertainty involved in calling at their respective residences'.

The Law Society expended a lot of energy in trying to abolish the stamp duty upon solicitors' practising certificates. The increase in duty in 1842 offered it an early opportunity to raise its voice with that of the Law Society of England in protest. In 1854 the campaign for its removal was suspended because the outbreak of the Crimean War made it impolitic to look for a reduction in taxes, and reached a pitch of excitement in 1865 (when the house of commons passed a resolution in favour of its abolition) and again in 1867 (when a bill to abolish it received a second reading in the house but was refused a third reading). From this point on the English Law Society rather lost interest in the matter, apparently considering that the amount of money involved was not material having regard to the other interests of solicitors. In 1871, for instance, the Law Society was advised by its English counterpart that the goodwill of members of parliament would be needed to protect the interests of the profession when the Judicature bills were being debated and that it would be best to wait for a more favourable opportunity before raising the matter again. In 1888 the chancellor of the exchequer offered as a reason for retaining the duty the fact that the profession in England was unworried by it, and in the following year when another bill to remove the duty was introduced in Parliament the Society was aware that the council of the English society did not 'deem the object of the bill advantageous to the profession and consequently declined to support it'.

The defence of the conveyancing monopoly and the work of the profession which consisted in drafting deeds took many forms. The 1816 statute prohibited any person other than a government official, lawyers or licensed conveyancers from preparing 'for or in expectation of any fee, gain, or reward … any conveyance or deed relating to any real or personal estate or any proceedings in law and equity'. Fees of solicitors in the preparation of deeds were traditionally measured by the length of a deed (the number of folios) and had been reduced by the Real Property Act, 1845, and other statutes which simplified conveyancing practice and shortened deeds. A proposal to abolish the principle of determining fees by reference to the length of deeds was opposed by the Law Society in 1850.

Solicitors' incomes were threatened more drastically by the principle of public registration of title which was brought forward in the 1850s and 1860s in Britain and Ireland. Under the system a deed transferring property would become as short and simple as a deed transferring stocks and shares. Robert R. Torrens, who was born in Cork in 1814 and educated at Trinity College Dublin, devised and introduced the system in South Australia in 1858, and it was soon generally adopted throughout Australia. On his retirement Mr Torrens returned to Europe and campaigned for registration of title. He was elected as Liberal member of parliament for Cambridge in 1868 and was knighted in 1872. He addressed a public meeting in Dublin in February 1864 at which the lord mayor took the chair. The duke of Leinster, who also spoke, said that 'land was incumbered by heaps of useless documents', and was supported by a leading businessman, Sir John Gray, who said that as 'the owner of extensive estates, largely encumbered, the mass of deeds I have is appalling to look upon'. A resolution was passed 'that the delay and expense incident to the present system of conveyancing is peculiarly oppressive, as regards the sale of small properties and as regards loans for short periods'.

In January that year the Northern Law Club had received a letter from Mr Torrens canvassing their support for his system. At a meeting of the members his proposals were thought to be inapplicable to the state of property in Ireland and 'highly injurious' to the solicitors' profession. As early as 1855 the Law Society had described registration of title as impractical and objectionable. In July 1865, in the face of opposition from the Society, the Record of Title (Ireland) Act was passed. The act (which recited that 'it is expedient that titles conferred by the landed estates court should be kept free from complication so that subsequent dealings with the estates held under such titles may be more simple and economical') established a registry of title for properties sold through the landed estates court. Purchasers could opt out of this registration procedure, however. The number of titles passing through the landed estates court represented a significant part of all conveyancing business. In the words of a chancery judge, writing in 1874, the court transacted

> the whole mass of the great department which had been the main source of work for the court of chancery when that court was a very great institution indeed. It is not only the sole judicial machine for enforcing sales at the suit of encumbrancers, investigating titles and distributing purchase monies, but it is in constant use as the means of effectuating voluntary sales also, the practice being, where there is any shadow upon a title, to pass it through the landed estates court, as a filter from which it emerges purged of all impurities.

The encumbered estates court, which was preceded briefly by an encumbered estates commission and succeeded by a landed estates court, was established at the end of the 1840s as a mechanism to facilitate transactions in properties the title to which had become hopelessly confused by successive mortgages, limited interests and suchlike. It diminished the cost of conveyancing, although on the other hand it generated at least initially an amount of transactions which might not otherwise have taken place. Its conveyances constituted a good root of title to property, obviating the need to examine deeds relating to previous transactions. Even without registration of title the system of conveyancing of these courts cut costs dramatically.

Solicitors' incomes were affected by matters such as delays in the taxation of bills of cost by the taxing master, about which the Society complained in 1842 and in 1848, and delays in settlement of acceptable schedules of fees and costs in the various courts – something of a perennial concern, but especially in 1845, 1847 and 1851. In 1852 the council requested members having any particularly unsatisfactory experiences of proper costs not being allowed to advise the Society so that, when funds allowed, a test case might be brought.

The Society objected when public appointments for which solicitors were qualified were given to barristers or to non-lawyers. A memorial on the subject was presented to the lord lieutenant of Ireland in December 1841, and the matter was raised again in 1853 when a barrister was appointed as crown solicitor of the Leinster circuit.

Legal work relevant to Ireland was carried out by English solicitors who might be the principal advisers, for instance, to landlords or to British companies, but the Law Society successfully objected on a number of occasions to English solicitors attempting to appear in person before Irish courts, and in 1854 had opposed a bill which, if enacted, would have permitted British plaintiffs to sue Irish defendants in Britain as well as in Ireland. They discouraged Irish solicitors from acting as agents of English solicitors on a profit-share basis, and in 1862 objected to a bill (which did not become law) which would have permitted Irish and English solicitors to practise on both sides of the Irish Sea:

> This bill has on the face of it an apparent reciprocity, calculated to catch the approval of persons ignorant or unmindful of the state of property in Ireland. A large portion of the property of Ireland belongs to absentees resident in England who have their solicitors there; also a great proportion of the articles of commerce consumed here are purchased in England; and the result of this bill, if passed into a law, would be that the absentee proprietor and the English merchant, in case of suits related to their land or to their sale of goods here, will employ an English solicitor to transact his Irish business by a clerk resident here, to the serious prejudice of the members of the profession in this country.

The Society disapproved of Stubbs Trade Protection Office, an association of traders which collected bad debts for its members, the system of
which, according to the council, was that Mr Stubbs 'procures business to
be transacted by some few members of your profession for his subscribers';
members of the Society should have nothing to do with 'this objectionable
practice'.

KING'S INNS AND THE REGULATION OF THE PROFESSION

In July 1862 the Northern Law Club resolved to communicate with the
Law Society 'with a view of co-operating with that society in procuring a
legislative enactment for better regulation of the profession of attorney and
solicitor'. The call for reform was widely shared and in November 1864 a
general meeting of the Law Society passed a resolution to the effect that
the laws regulating the solicitors' profession should be amended and
assimilated to those of England. The statute law of England on the subject
at that time was contained substantially in the Solicitors Act, 1843 (which
recited that 'the laws relating to attorneys and solicitors are numerous and
complicated and it is expedient to consolidate and simplify and to alter
and amend the same') and the Attorneys and Solicitors Act, 1860, of which
the promoter had said on the second reading of the bill in the house of
commons that 'the object of this Bill is to increase the respectability and
education of attorneys'.

The Law Society consequently promoted a bill which was introduced in
the house of lords in 1866 by Lord Chelmsford, lord chancellor of England
in two Conservative Governments, 1858–1859 and 1866–1868, but then in
opposition. The bill ('an act to amend the laws for the regulation of the
profession of attorneys and solicitors in Ireland and to assimilate them to
those in England') in effect consolidated the existing laws on the admission
of solicitors and on the regulation of the profession, but changed them in
certain respects, most importantly by providing that after its passing no
fees other than those authorised therein (payable to the Law Society as
examination fees) were to be payable by any person seeking to be bound
as an apprentice or to be admitted and enrolled as a solicitor. This meant

that membership of, and payment of fees to, the Society of King's Inns would no longer be a condition of admission as a solicitor. Similarly, responsibility for the education of apprentices was conferred upon the Law Society, acting with the consent of the judges, terminating the Benchers' responsibility. The Law Society was appointed as registrar of attorneys and solicitors to work in conjunction with the registrars of each of the separate courts of common law and the court of chancery. The bill became law in August 1866. The King's Inns erected no bar after 1866 to solicitors becoming members of the Inn on the same basis as had existed prior to the passing of the Act (and so informed a solicitor who inquired on the subject in 1893), but in practice solicitors did not join once the obligation to do so had been abolished, and with the death or retirement of those solicitors who had become members before the summer of 1866 the Inn gradually assumed its present character of a society of the Bar and the judiciary only.

One link between the solicitors' profession and the Benchers had been broken, but others remained. For one thing the Benchers were the landlords of the Law Society, since up to 1867 the tenure under which the Society occupied the premises allotted to them at the Four Courts by the Benchers had never been put on a satisfactory basis. In April of that year the Benchers resolved to invite the Law Society to take a lease of the premises at a nominal rent, the Society to accept full responsibility for their upkeep and to discharge the Benchers from any obligation to provide further accommodation. This offer was not accepted, and greater accommodation was requested by the Law Society and refused by the Benchers.

In 1869 the Law Society formally asked the Benchers to transfer to it all moneys received by them from solicitors since 1793 as 'deposits for chambers', less the amount spent by them on the Solicitors' Buildings and certain further apartments then in the course of construction. The Benchers who might at this stage have reflected that not only had their future income from the solicitors' profession been cut off in 1866, but that they were now being asked to account for their pre-1866 income from that source, responded that the Law Society had no claim to those funds which 'have been expended by the Benchers for the benefit of the whole society of King's Inns, including the attorneys and solicitors, and with their assent, and of which the members of the Law Society have enjoyed their full share'. They offered to transfer certain further rooms to the Law Society, but this offer was not acceptable.

The Law Society then took counsel's opinion on how they should proceed, and were advised that they should seek to have the matter investigated by a royal commission or by a select committee of the house of commons. (Since all the Benchers were judges the Society could hardly seek a remedy in the courts.) A resolution for the appointment of a royal commission to investigate the financial affairs of the Benchers, with particular reference to the deposits for chambers paid by solicitors, was passed in the house of lords in April 1870. The three commissioners issued their report in November 1871. No chambers had been erected, of course, but they took the view that in paying for the Solicitors' Buildings and in expending other amounts for the benefit of the entire society of King's Inns, both barristers and solicitors, the Benchers had substantially performed whatever was incumbent upon them towards the solicitors' branch of the profession. Any right to the fund representing the deposits, less the expenditure for which the Benchers were to be given credit, was a personal one vested in each solicitor respectively, and certainly not in the Law Society which at that time represented only 429 of the 1159 solicitors in the country. The commissioners did accept that the accommodation available for the Law Society at the Four Courts was insufficient. The Society had shown, for instance, that the room in which its council 'consisting of 31 members and its secretary are obliged to meet is only 16 feet square, not even affording space for seats for a full meeting of the council'. After some negotiation the Benchers agreed to make a lease of an area comprising both the original accommodation and a further area for a term of 999 years from 1874 at the annual rent of one shilling (if demanded). The Solicitors' Buildings then stood more or less where the Bar Library now stands, at the back centre of the Four Courts complex.

One matter remained on which the Society was to seek redress from the Benchers, namely the payment to the Benchers by the Inland Revenue of £14 out of the £80 stamp duty payable upon the indentures of apprenticeship of solicitors' apprentices. This duty had first been imposed (at a lower rate) by the Stamp Act, 1790. The Society believed that this money was payable to the Benchers for the benefit and education of, or other purposes connected with, the solicitors' profession, whereas the Benchers held that it was a form of compensation or rent for the use of their property at Inns Quay for the construction of the Four Courts.

Since 1866 no connection had existed between new apprentices and the King's Inns, and the Society pointed out that solicitors had received no advantage from the sum of £22,876 which had been paid between 1866 and 1889. After lengthy correspondence and some parliamentary agitation (for which the Society thanked, among others, the recently elected Welsh Liberal MP, and solicitor, David Lloyd George) a committee of three persons was set up by the Treasury to consider the matter, the Benchers nominating Mr Justice Holmes, the Law Society nominating one of their most distinguished members, Sir William Findlater (after an earlier nominee, Thomas Sexton MP, had been withdrawn when the Benchers objected that he was not a member of the Law Society) and the Treasury nominating a member of the English Bar as chairman.

The committee reported in 1891 that the statutory title of the King's Inns to the payment of £14 was complete, that there was no evidence to show on what grounds the grant had originally been made or the purpose for which it was intended to be applied, thus supporting neither the Benchers' nor the Law Society's theory of the object of the grant. The circumstances in which solicitors had ceased to be obliged to be members of the King's Inns gave the Society no right, legal or equitable, to any contribution from the £14 grant, although the Society had a reasonable claim to a grant (either out of the £14 or out of public revenues) to assist it in the performance of its statutory duties. Sir William Findlater in a minority report stressed the existence of a moral duty on the Benchers to do something in return for the money derived from the apprentices. Writing an account of the history of the solicitors' profession in 1921 the president of the Law Society recounted the story of this stamp duty on indentures of apprenticeship and of the committee in detail, and the continuing payment evidently rankled still.[2] The fact that no function or service was performed by the Society of King's Inns for the benefit of apprentices

2 Charles Gamble, *Solicitors in Ireland, 1607–1921* (Dublin, 1921).

continued to be a grievance, giving rise to a parliamentary question in the Dáil in 1950 inviting its abolition, until the payment to the Inns was terminated by the Finance Act in 1970.

THE CONSTITUTION OF THE SOCIETY

At the end of the century, the legal functions of the Law Society were substantially increased by the Solicitors (Ireland) Act, 1898, which repealed the act of 1866 and transferred control of education and important disciplinary functions from the direct supervision of the judges to that of the Society. A succession of bills to give the Society these increased powers had for more than a decade been introduced unsuccessfully in parliament. These were modelled upon statutes passed in 1877 and 1888 which had conferred various powers upon the Law Society in England. The new act provided that the Society would have full control of the examinations and lectures for apprentices, would have custody of the roll of solicitors (that is, the register of solicitors entitled to practise, which had previously been maintained by the chancery division of the high court) and that all allegations of professional misconduct by a solicitor would be heard initially by a committee of members of the council of the Society appointed by the lord chancellor, who would consider reports made by the committee.

In 1888 the constitution of the council of the Society had been changed by a supplemental charter which provided that, in addition to the 31 members elected in the ordinary way, the Northern Law Society and the Southern Law Association would each be entitled to appoint 5 members and the members of the Society resident in each province respectively would be entitled to elect one member. This supplemental charter followed a precedent in England, where a supplemental charter in 1874 had provided that 10 places on the council would be filled by the presidents of provincial law societies, and the Irish council hoped that their own new system of making up the council would 'secure unity of action among the solicitors of Ireland generally for the common good of the profession … and will strengthen the ties of professional feeling among them'. The council retained that composition up to 1960, when provision was made for the appointment to the council of three members of the council of the Dublin Solicitors' Bar Association.

The Northern Law Society was the Northern Law Club under a new name, and at the meeting in 1876 at which the change of name was adopted it was also resolved that membership of the society could be open to solicitors in the whole province of Ulster, not merely the counties of Antrim, Armagh and Down. The Southern Law Association was founded in 1878 to maintain a valuable law library which had been presented to the legal profession in the city and county of Cork, and was more firmly established than earlier ad hoc associations and committees of the local solicitors.

The direct representation of provincial solicitors on the council of the Society was arranged after almost two decades of debate, sometimes heated, about whether it was a proper representative body. All the members of the council were elected for one year only, and up to 1865 not more than 21 of the 31 outgoing members of the Society could be re-elected. In 1868 an attempt to restore this system of rotation was defeated at a general meeting of the Society by the casting vote of the chairman 'after an animated and vehement discussion', in the words of the *Irish Law Times*. Five years later the issue was re-opened at another general meeting which rejected a suggestion that the ballot paper should state how many meetings outgoing council members had attended and also turned down a proposal from the Northern Law Society and from Cork solicitors that the names of each candidate's proposer and seconder should be stated 'as an assistance to country members in the selection of candidates for whom they would vote'.

Provincial solicitors thus continued to treat the Law Society with reserve, sometimes arguing that the subscription fee, 10s. or £1, was excessive and a discouragement to them. The provincial societies co-operated with it on matters of common interest and when in 1878 the Society convened a meeting in Dublin to consider a schedule of fees for work in the new county courts the committee of the Northern Law Society 'deemed it prudent to send a deputation to the meeting', at which their recommendations were largely accepted. In 1881 the Law Society nominated the president of the

Northern Society as the representative of country solicitors on a committee
to consider fees under the new Solicitors' Remuneration Act.

In 1880 the Northern Law Society considered whether 'for the purpose
of obtaining the removal or redress of defects and grievances experienced
by the town agents of provincial practitioners an effort should be made to
secure the representation of your society upon the council of the Incorporated
Law Society' – itself an indication of the limited function which the
Northern Society considered the Law Society might discharge – but 'the
apparent impracticability of compassing the regular attendance of a representative at its meetings' led the society to conclude that its ends might be
achieved in other ways, and soon afterwards the standing of town agents
was raised when increased fees were allowed. In 1883 an invitation to the
Northern Society to nominate a candidate for election to the council was
not accepted as it was deemed impracticable to get a solicitor to attend.

In 1887 a general meeting of the Law Society appointed a committee of
13 to consider how to secure 'an increased number of members of this
Society throughout the country generally' and better representation on the
council of solicitors outside Dublin. The meeting was told that if provincial solicitors were represented on the council 'the Society could count on
their approval', and that of the 100 solicitors in Belfast 70 were members
of the Northern Law Society and 8 of the Law Society, and that of the 65
members of the Southern Law Association only 9 were members of the
Law Society. Further research showed that of the 453 members of the
Society 307 practised in Dublin alone (representing more than 60 per cent
of Dublin solicitors), whereas only 46 of the 315 solicitors in Ulster, 37 of
the 244 in Munster, 18 of the 65 in Connaught and 45 of the 109 in
Leinster were members.

The Northern Law Society suggested that it should be entitled to nominate five members of the council – not three, as the Law Society initially
proposed – and the Cork Society eventually agreed with their northern
counterparts. It was finally settled that there could be five nominees, any
three of whom could attend and vote at council meetings. Those proposals
and the provision mentioned above for additional provincial representation were incorporated in the supplemental charter in 1888. The charter

recited the original charter of 1852 and the fact that 'it has been represented to us that since the date of such charter a greatly increased amount of work has devolved on the council of the Society'. It also changed the name of the Society to the Incorporated Law Society of Ireland, since the earlier name, the Incorporated Society of Attorneys and Solicitors of Ireland, had become inappropriate when the Judicature (Ireland) Act, 1877 had provided that all attorneys would henceforward be called 'solicitors'.

The extension of the membership of the council did not end the debate about how representative the council was, and twenty years later the Society amended its bye-laws to abolish the requirement that candidates for election to the council should have been qualified for at least seven years since only three members of the council in 1907 had been qualified for less than 17 years. The new arrangements were followed by an increase not only in the absolute number of members but also in the proportion of solicitors who became members. In 1888 its membership represented 37 per cent of the solicitors in the country (453 out of 1205), the same proportion it had been in 1872 (429 out of 1159). By 1914 it had 884 members which represented 56 per cent of the total (1587). In addition, 160 solicitors who were members of either the Northern or Southern societies but had not joined the Law Society were to all intents and purposes associated with it, and this would be true also of provincial solicitors who joined local or county bar associations, the formation of which was actively encouraged by the Law Society.

THE SOCIETY AT WORK

Even before the reorganisation in 1888 had put fresh life and authority into the Society it had carried out its work vigorously. In 1880 it was contrasted favourably by the *Law Times* (London) with its English counterpart, saying that the Irish Society, 'usually shows greater vigilance in endeavouring to assert the just claims and protect the rights of the solicitors' branch of the profession than does the sister society in Chancery Lane'.

Considering first the Society's work in conveyancing business, one last statement of its objection to the principle of registration of title was made

in 1879 in a submission to the royal commission on the system of registration of deeds. Thereafter opposition diminished and was eventually
overcome by a new system of remuneration for conveyancing work (see
below) and the fact that the new business created by the Land Acts and the
operations of the Land Commission, both in tenant purchases and in fair
rent adjudications, became by 1891 a large portion of the business of solicitors
throughout Ireland.

The Society, with a view to seeing that the interests of the profession
were protected in the distribution of the new work, protested in 1871 to the
Irish Church Temporalities Commissioners (the body charged with the
disposal of tenanted land held by the Church of Ireland) at the contents of
a circular it had issued to its tenants to the effect that a form of conveyance
and mortgage had been settled and printed by order of the Commissioners
and that their solicitor would prepare and register conveyances at specified
fees if the tenant did not desire to instruct his own solicitor. The council
thought that this circular was 'calculated to take from solicitors their
private clients and was subversive of the ordinary rules which governed the
dealings of professional men with each other'. The Commissioners replied
that in facilitating the operation of the Irish Church Act, 1869 they wished
to minimise the expense to purchasers of small holdings and would supply
copies of the approved form of conveyance on application to any solicitors.
Advice more acceptable to the profession was given in the same year by
J.G. MacCarthy, 'solicitor and land agent', who published *The Munster
farmers' guide to the new Land Act*, setting out 'in the fewest and plainest
words what rights are conferred by the act on Munster farmers. If they
wish to know how to enforce these rights, let them not try any "every man
his own lawyer" dodge. Let them consult the nearest respectable solicitor.'

A point similar to that on the Irish Church Act arose on the subsequent
Land Acts. In 1893 the Land Commission issued a circular to certain
tenants requesting information to enable the Land Commission to take
steps to register the tenants' title. When the Society complained, the Land
Commission referred to their statutory obligation to see that certain
compulsory registration provisions were observed, and said that the
circular was sent to tenants who had stated that they were unable to employ

solicitors because of the cost. The Land Commission was more sympathetic in 1899 when, after strong objections were made by the Society they ceased a practice of sending a printed form of conveyance to persons who inquired how registered land could be transferred, and instead less helpfully told persons making inquiries that they should refer to No. 14 of the forms printed in the rules made under the acts. In 1903 the Society objected to certain provisions in the Land bill before it was enacted (it was known as 'Wyndham's Act') and received assurances that it was not the intention of the Government to establish a state department for the purpose of preparing the titles of vendors under the act; the council was confident that 'it would be found that the act could only be worked successfully with the assistance of the legal advisers of both vendors and purchasers'. The council also constantly complained at the delay of the Government in making adequate funds available for the completion of purchases under the Land Acts.

Protection of the profession from old style unauthorised conveyancing was less of a problem than it had been earlier in the century, although as late as 1898 the Society interested itself in an application by a stockbroker to be appointed a notary public (to transact certain business for the Bank of Ireland) and, on the application, the lord chancellor required an undertaking to be given by the broker that he would not transact any conveyancing business (notaries being one of the permitted classes of conveyancers under the 1816 Act). The secretary of the Society prosecuted illegal conveyancers in a number of cases in the 1880s and the 1890s. In one case heard in the County Court at Killarney the solicitor for the defendant, having made his apologies, said 'this poor fellow had been drawing these deeds for a number of years, and he thought he had got by prescription a kind of right to do so in Kenmare where there was no solicitor located'; the judge spoke scathingly of 'amateur conveyancers' and the confusion they caused.

The Northern Law Society in 1893, after a study of the conduct of sales of property, resolved to settle and adopt a standard form of general conditions of sale, 'each solicitor inserting the special conditions required in each case'. It was common for sales to be conducted by auctioneers without a preliminary investigation of title, which led to vendors suffering loss if they subsequently had to make unsatisfactory compromises.

Standard conditions would, it was thought, reduce the cost of sales and increase public confidence, enhancing the value of the property.

The council was active not only in defending the conveyancing monopoly but in opposing any statutory or other innovations which threatened solicitors' work. When a select committee of the house of commons was appointed to consider the administration of trusts in 1895 the president of the Society gave evidence opposing the appointment of a public trustee, a government officer who would be available for appointment as an executor of a will or a trustee of a private trust. Since he was the only witness from Ireland the committee concluded that 'in Ireland there does not seem to be any widespread desire for change or complaint of the existing law', and pursued the matter no further with regard to this country. The Society had opposed a previous proposal for a public trustee in 1890 (and opposed a further one made in 1908).

The council opposed a bill in 1893 which would have given substantial powers to the official assignee of the court of bankruptcy, permitting that officer to be appointed generally as a liquidator and receiver of companies. In 1908 it corresponded with the Institute of Chartered Accountants in Ireland on amendments to articles of association of companies, pointing out 'that such work should not be performed without the intervention of the solicitor to the company', and its representations were 'reasonably met' by the Institute, which issued a circular to its members drawing attention to the Society's views. It was not until the enactment in 1908 of the Companies (Consolidation) Act that a qualification in accounting was required of company auditors generally, but as early as 1869 the increasing importance of accountants in business life occupied the mind of solicitors, who received a hearing but little sympathy from the *Irish Law Times*: 'with a knowledge of accounts and bookkeeping solicitors are seldom credited ... it is a matter of complaint on the part of solicitors that mere accountants were employed more and more every day to transact business which belongs properly to the domain of the profession. This is a circumstance to be regretted but the best way to prevent its occurrence is for solicitors to qualify themselves to transact the business as well, at least, as their rivals.' Perhaps in that spirit bookkeeping was made a compulsory subject in the apprentices' final examination in 1907.

In 1877 a proposal of a select committee of the house of commons that cases might be conducted in the county courts not only by lawyers but also 'by leave of the judge ... [by] any other person allowed by him to appear instead of the party' was thought by the council to be 'most injurious', and a general meeting of the members of the Society passed a resolution protesting 'in the strongest manner against the unjust invasion of the rights of our profession'. Ultimately the right of audience was confined to the husband or father of the party concerned, excluding 'any other person'.

In 1894 the council objected to a provision in the Finance bill which would have authorised Inland Revenue officers to act in the issue of grants of probate if the value of the net assets of the estate did not exceed £1,000, a variation from the limit then applicable of £300 gross value under a statute of 1881; 'The council considered that this clause, if passed into law would be most injurious to the interests of the solicitors profession', and after a deputation had met the lord chancellor and the chancellor of the exchequer a reduced limit of £500 gross assets was set. In 1899 the Society procured an amendment to be made to the Moneylenders bill then before Parliament (it was enacted the following year) since 'it was not sufficiently clear that solicitors who in the ordinary course of their business advance money to clients would not come within the definition of moneylender in the bill'.

In 1890 the Society obtained an opinion from the solicitor general upon the meaning of the word 'agent' in the Petty Sessions Act, since land agents, stewards and house agents were conducting cases in the magistrates courts. He advised that 'agent' meant 'legal agent', and the council, considering 'that such opinion would be of use to country solicitors and clerks of petty sessions', distributed copies. In 1893, on learning that prosecutions brought in the name of the Secretary for State for War for trespass on the Curragh were being conducted in court by members of the military police, the council took a further opinion (under the same act) and sent copies to the Secretary of State and to the magistrates presiding at the Curragh Petty Sessions 'with a request that the practice which counsel considered illegal should for the future be discontinued, and the council are pleased to report that, owing to their action in the matter, a member of the profession has been appointed to conduct these prosecutions in the future'.

Much of this work is referable to maintaining the income of solicitors, by ensuring that certain classes of work would be reserved for the profession. The Society took a close interest in the Solicitors' Remuneration Acts which were passed in 1870 and 1881, taking an initiative to have the 1870 act extended to this country. In 1881 it successfully proposed that the president of the Society should be a member of the committee which would draw up the approved scale of charges under the act, a first recognition of the right of the profession 'to have a voice in the regulation of their professional charges'.

The rules made under the new act provided for conveyancing work to be charged on an ad valorem basis, a practice which had first become more general in 1874 when the council circulated a draft schedule of fees applicable to loans and sales of properties, varying by reference to the value of property concerned. This was broadly welcomed by the profession, the Cork Law Society thinking it would mark the beginning of 'a system of contract price for professional work'. This was a modification of the opposition of the Society to a bill published in 1850 which would have changed the basis of remuneration from the length of a deed to 'the skill and labour employed and the responsibility incurred in the preparation thereof'. Since 1850, however, not only had the system of registration of title, which involved much shorter deeds of transfer, taken root but also deeds of transfer of unregistered land had been abbreviated by the Conveyancing and Law of Property Act, 1881 which provided that certain covenants of title which it had been the practice to set out at length in deeds would now be implied by the use of short phrases to the effect that the transferor conveyed in his capacity 'as beneficial owner' etc. The operations of the encumbered estates court had similarly simplified conveyancing practice.

The council was vigilant in pressing for higher rates of remuneration under the County Courts Act and Petty Sessions Acts, and also under the Land Acts. In 1905 it issued, at the request of country solicitors, a recommended schedule of fees for work in negotiating the purchase of land under the Land Acts. It financed test cases on certain disputed elements of costs, and in 1902 published a book (of 735 pages) of reported cases on costs.

Other services to the profession included publication of details of the proceedings of the council (in 1886), the publication of a monthly *Gazette* (from 1907), making arrangements for the earlier publication of the daily law list of cases to be heard in the Four Courts the following day ('before solicitors' offices are closed, as this would enable solicitors to communicate with their country correspondents, clients and witnesses as to the necessity for attending on the following day'), a successful request to the Benchers that a meeting which they traditionally held at 11 o'clock a.m. on the eighth day of each term should be put back to 3.30 p.m. so that the courts could sit that day and – reminiscent of the 1830s – discouraging advertising and unfair methods of self-promotion by solicitors and opposing applications of apprentices to be admitted as solicitors before the expiry of their indentures. In one case in 1888 the lord chancellor said that, in the face of the opposition of the Law Society, it was 'quite impossible' for him to grant such an application.

The deprecation of advertising and other unfair practices demonstrated the Society's traditional concern to maintain high standards in the profession, a concern evidenced in a case of professional misconduct in 1900, which suggested that the Society had adopted standards which some solicitors thought unnecessarily high. A solicitor in County Tyrone who had been struck off the roll for misappropriating £100 of a client's money applied to court a year later to be re-admitted, and his application was supported by a petition signed by 56 solicitors from his locality. The Society strongly opposed this application and said that the idea should not go around that all a defalcating solicitor had to do in such cases to be re-admitted was to make restitution to his client.

In the second half of the nineteenth century the Law Society thus established itself ever more firmly not only as the representative organisation of solicitors in Ireland but also as their primary superintending body. In the first decade of the next century it encouraged the formation of local or county bar associations, where they did not already exist, and much of its work at this time, in recommending or setting down minimum fees and in attempting to reserve particular classes of work for its members, is reminiscent of the development of trade unionism around this time. This analogy was explicitly drawn by the president of the Society in 1912: 'In these days of combinations and trade unions it is of the utmost necessity that all solicitors practising in Ireland should become members of the Society. See what powerful influences trade unions have.'

THE FIRST WORLD WAR AND ITS AFTERMATH

The First World War and the political developments and the war in Ireland that came in its train had a considerable impact upon lawyers in Ireland and their professional organisations. Many Irish lawyers joined the forces. When the *Irish Law Times* published a War supplement in February 1916 it listed 110 solicitors, 71 solicitors' apprentices and 126 barristers (a number of whom may not have been practising members of the Bar, of course) who had enlisted (together with 175 sons of solicitors and 166 sons of barristers). The final total of solicitors and of apprentices who joined the Army or Navy was 155 and 83 respectively. The council of the Law Society decided that a period spent by an apprentice in naval or military service during the war should be counted as a part of the term of apprenticeship. This precedent was followed in 1943, when the council decided that time spent by apprentices engaged in service in the defence forces could similarly be reckoned as part of apprenticeship, subject to certain conditions, although in the event only one application for this relief was made. In May 1917 the half-yearly general meeting of the Society passed a resolution acknowledging the war service to date by the solicitors' profession and their apprentices and expressing the hope 'that in view of the extension of the military age to that of fifty a larger number may offer their services to the military forces'. At the November annual general meeting the president read out a list of military distinctions conferred upon solicitors who had enlisted. A memorial to those who had died was erected in the Four Courts by the Society in July 1921.

The Four Courts were occupied by the Volunteers during Easter Week 1916; books and furniture were piled in windows as barricades. The opening of the Easter Term, due to take place on Thursday 27 April, was postponed to 19 May. A number of solicitors' offices in central Dublin were in buildings destroyed by fire in the course of the fighting. The council of the Society passed a resolution assuring the king of their continued loyalty, expressing their 'abhorrence and condemnation of the scenes of outrage and destruction which have taken place' and recommending proper compensation for all who had suffered. It also intervened with the military authorities to obtain permission for solicitors to take instructions from persons arrested in connection with the Rising.

The end of the war was quickly followed by the general election of December 1918. As the Parliament first elected in December 1910 came to an end a remarkable number of its Irish members were practising or qualified lawyers; of the 103 Irish MPs, 11 were solicitors and 20 had been called to the Bar. The council, three members of which in 1918 were members of Parliament, had been prompt in expressing their 'hearty congratulations' to Lloyd George in December 1916 on becoming the first solicitor to hold the office of prime minister. The legal profession was not as well represented in the Parliament elected in 1918, the Sinn Féin members of which refused to take their seats at Westminster and formed the First Dáil. Three of these 69 Sinn Féin TDs (who had been elected in 73 constituencies) were barristers and two were solicitors, and at least three of the Unionist MPs were members of the Bar. When the Second Dáil, consisting of 125 persons, was elected (in Southern Ireland) in May 1921, three barristers and six solicitors were members, two of whom, George Gavan Duffy (originally a solicitor in England, later a barrister and judge in Ireland) and Eamon J. Duggan (a solicitor) were members of the delegation which negotiated and signed the Anglo-Irish Treaty in London later that year.

The enactment by Parliament of the Sex Disqualification (Removal) Act in 1919 permitted women to become members of the legal profession, and the whole subject of the admission of women to the profession is dealt with in Chapter 4 of this book. The act provided that a person should not be disqualified by sex or marriage from the exercise of any public function or from being appointed to or holding any civil or judicial office or post, or from entering or assuming or carrying on any civil profession or vocation and that a person should not be exempted by sex or marriage from the liability to serve as a juror. As the terms of the act suggest, the admission of women to the legal profession was but one part of a general review of their legal position in society occurring in the first part of the twentieth century, an issue brought to head by the social changes caused by the war. Their exclusion from the profession had led to litigation in England against the Law Society in 1914, but does not appear to have given rise to controversy in Ireland. Although women could not practise as lawyers, they had been entitled to appear in court and plead for themselves in cases in which they were concerned.

At the end of the war economic problems took precedence over political issues for the profession. The rise in the cost of living and its effects on their incomes had for some time been a concern of lawyers. In May 1917 the council of the Law Society had said that they had received numerous letters from solicitors throughout the country 'pointing out that while extra wages and war bonuses were given to various trades and businesses, the only business in which the remuneration did not increase in accordance with the increase in the cost of living was the solicitors' profession'. This would not have been completely true, at least so far as conveyancing work was concerned, since the rate of remuneration was generally calculated as a percentage of the price of the land being transferred, and any increases in the price of land being transferred would have been reflected in the fees charged. However it was broadly true, and in May 1918, following representations from the Society, a temporary increase of 25 per cent in fees as measured under the Solicitors' Remuneration Act, 1881 was granted. A permanent increase of 50 per cent was made in 1920 to take account of 'the increased cost of living and the rise in office expenses'.

Solicitors' employees, their law clerks, also pressed for increased remuneration. In January 1919 the council of the Society, following a meeting with a deputation from the Irish Clerks' Mutual Benefit Society, recommended to the profession throughout the country that their employees' claim for an increase in salary of 25 per cent over salaries at August 1914 should be met, taking into account any increase of less than 25 per cent which individual solicitors might previously have made. The Clerks' Society took the view that this recommendation was unsatisfactory (although the council had apparently agreed to all suggestions made by the deputation) but did not indicate what would be satisfactory. Instead they turned to trade unionism and by October the Law Clerks' Branch of the Irish Clerical and Allied Workers union had 250 members. In May 1920 the ICAWU gave notice to the Law Society of new terms of employment required for its members in Dublin, 'terms which', in the view of the president, 'it would be impossible for the Dublin solicitors to comply with and carry on their business with any hope of success'. A strike of the unionised clerks quickly followed. The ad hoc committee which the Dublin solicitors set up to handle the matter declined to recognise or negotiate with the union; the staff of a solicitor's office was a personal one, and in trying to organise it the union was 'going beyond the recognised demands of trade unionism'. Some members of the Society were more sympathetic to the union, one having a guilty conscience that 'he should pay a wage which should make men sit up half the night working overtime as he knew was the case when he looked into the cases of his clerks'. During the strike the opening of the Trinity Term in June had been marked by a demonstration by a large number of clerks who paraded between Grattan Bridge (Capel Street) and the Four Courts.

The reasonably satisfactory economic position which the profession had held during the war quickly deteriorated, as each year brought increasingly disturbed conditions which diminished the volume of legal business. In the summer of 1919 the *Irish Law Times* reported that the High Court and the County Courts were less busy than for a long time. Conditions thus were poor, with an increased number of lawyers sharing a diminished amount of business, before the setting up in 1920 of the Dáil Éireann courts and the associated policy of disruption of the working of the established courts introduced a political element into the conduct of ordinary legal business. The Dáil Éireann courts had their origin in the national arbitration courts set up pursuant to a decree of Dáil Éireann passed in June 1919. These were generally local arbitration tribunals, the pedigree of which might ultimately have been traced back to the land courts set up by the National League in the 1880s. Twelve months later a full structure of parish courts, district courts, a circuit court and a supreme court was provided for by a new decree of the Dáil (Decree No. 5, Session 1–29 June 1920). This was intended to be an alternative judicial system, and functioned most openly in the summer and autumn of 1920 and again in 1921 after the Truce in July.

In 1920 the IRA increased its efforts to disrupt the established judicial system, a task made easier by the fact that the manner of the administration of justice in itself became more open to criticism. Many offences were tried in camera, and court-martials took over a part of the work of the ordinary criminal courts. Magistrates resigned their commissions, some through conviction, others through intimidation. Accommodation was refused to judges on assize and members of jury panels became reluctant to attend court. Following local elections in 1920 Sinn Féin controlled a large number of local authorities. In July the Westmeath County Council decided that all courthouses in the county would be closed, the government officials working there evicted and the Irish Volunteers requested to see that no judges were to enter the buildings for the purpose of holding courts which were not recognised by the Dáil. In August the Tyrone county courthouse was burned, and the Roscommon County Council resolved to serve notice on the landlords of various courthouses throughout the county not owned by the county council stating that in future no rent would be paid as the courthouses were no longer required. The Ballinamore quarter sessions were transferred to Carrick-on-Shannon because the courthouse had been burned down. The business, which chiefly consisted of decrees for non-payment of rent to the Land Commission, was finished in an hour although it usually occupied several days.

In a circular which, while undated, was sent out between the Truce and the Treaty in 1921 (that is, between July and December), Austin Stack, the Minister for Home Affairs, himself a former law clerk, asked the clerks of Dáil Éireann courts to supply regular information both about the work of their own courts and about cases from their districts which had gone 'to enemy courts and what steps were taken to prevent this happening'. The enemy courts were to be 'rigorously boycotted. Public notice by the officers commanding the police should be publicly broadcast stating that any person who takes part in proceedings in an enemy court either as plaintiff, defendant, witness or otherwise unless with a special written permission of the Minister for Home Affairs will be deemed guilty of assisting the enemy in a time of war and will be dealt with accordingly'. Although this circular was issued after the Truce it is reasonable to suppose that it did not set out a new policy, but simply recorded an existing aim.

More generally, political developments associated with the establishment of separate governments in the north and south of Ireland affected the regulation of the affairs of both branches of the profession. The Law Society had commented on an abortive proposal made by the Government in the summer of 1916 that the Government of Ireland Act, 1914 should be brought into operation in 26 of the 32 counties, taking the view that 'whatever division of Ireland for administrative and judicial purposes might be considered desirable the status of the Society as the governing and educational body of the solicitors' profession in Ireland should not be affected, and there should be no division of the solicitors' profession, but all Irish solicitors should continue to have a right to practise in every part of Ireland'. In the event this limited scheme of Home Rule did not get off the ground, but legal issues arose again in 1920 on the new Government of Ireland bill. The council now took the view that the establishment of separate judicial systems in Northern Ireland and Southern Ireland was 'not a necessary consequence of the other proposals of the bill', and they supported an amendment unsuccessfully put forward at the committee stage of the bill to provide for the continuation of a single judiciary.

In May 1920 the Northern Law Society resolved to take steps to secure for itself the same status and powers with respect to Northern Ireland as the Law Society had at that time for the whole of Ireland. This came as a 'great surprise' to the council of the Law Society which had hoped that it would continue to exercise its functions in relation to the profession throughout the whole of Ireland. The Government of Ireland Act, enacted in December 1920, provided that as from the appointed day (1 October 1921) existing solicitors of the Supreme Court of Judicature in Ireland should automatically become solicitors of the Supreme Courts both of Northern Ireland and of Southern Ireland, but thereafter (with an exception in the case of existing apprentices) new solicitors were to be entitled to practise only in the part of Ireland in which they had qualified. In July 1922 the Northern Law Society was granted a charter constituting it as the Incorporated Law Society of Northern Ireland, and in October the Parliament of Northern Ireland passed a Solicitors' Act to give effect in Northern Ireland to the Solicitors (Ireland) Act, 1898, with certain modifications. The Incorporated

Law Society of Northern Ireland continued to be represented on the council of the Law Society and initially, at least, Northern apprentices continued to receive a part of their education in Dublin. The two societies maintained civil relations, the presidents of each respective society being entertained at dinner in Dublin and Belfast in 1926 for instance, and they co-operated in 1929 to procure provision in the Finance Acts in each jurisdiction to ensure that solicitors entitled to practise on each side of the border would not be obliged to pay a separate licence fee in each jurisdiction. Political changes had a limited effect upon the work of the legal profession in Northern Ireland, since even with the constitutional changes consequent upon the introduction of a devolved government the fundamental structure of the court system and of the law remained familiar. It was to be different in the South.

The Society from independence to 1960

DAIRE HOGAN

The end of the Anglo-Irish War, marked by the Treaty in December 1921, gave rise to hopes that the unrest of the previous few years would be replaced by a return to normality in legal business as in other walks of national life. In April 1922, however, the Four Courts buildings were occupied by units of the IRA opposed to the Treaty, and the bombardment and capture in June of the Four Courts by government forces resulted in serious damage to the buildings, including the Solicitors' Buildings. In 1899, in what turned out to be a most useful precaution, a fireproof room for the records of the Society had been constructed after it had become the statutory custodian of the roll of solicitors pursuant to the Solicitors (Ireland) Act, 1898. Despite the destruction of the building in 1922 the contents of the strongroom were afterwards found to be intact. Most of the property of the Society was destroyed, however, including all the furnishings and the library, and for the rest of the decade its offices were at 45 Kildare Street, a building which the government placed at its disposal. Examinations and lectures were held at the Royal College of Surgeons on St Stephen's Green. The Society worked with the Benchers of King's Inns in furnishing a claim for compensation, jointly employing an architect in January 1923 to prepare plans of the destroyed buildings and make an estimate of the cost of reconstruction.

Many changes in the legal system took place in the 1920s, in the introduction of which the Society played a part, although not all of them met with its approval. The challenges faced by the legal profession in those early years of independence were well expressed by Chief Justice Hugh Kennedy in 1929:

> In an old established state in undisturbed times of settled and hum-drum conditions, the practising lawyer finds it no easy thing to keep his

knowledge abreast of ordinary current legislation, but in the epochal
seven years through which we have just passed in the Saorstát, there
has been enacted and put upon the virgin pages of the new statute
book a body of legislation, very large in volume, and quite outside
the current of experience of even the most experienced amongst us,
the experience of a stream of ordinary legislation flowing along
familiar channels of precedent and principle, with here a deviation
generally long anticipated, there a cutting off or an accretion seldom
unforeseen. With the abruptness of revolution the new stream began
to flow, welling out from the new spring, making new channels and
courses as it flowed.

It is not alone the selfish interest of business men which will
compel the members of the legal profession to devour and digest this
mass of legislation. It is a solemn duty resting upon them by reason
of the privilege they enjoy from the State. Lawyers who have not a
full knowledge of the national constitution and a real understanding
of the liberties it secures as well as of its courts and other organisations,
and the constitutional principles upon which they are based, endanger
those liberties and are a menace to the State and its citizens.[1]

THE COURTS

The Society was represented on a committee (the Judiciary Committee)
under the chairmanship of Lord Glenavy which was set up by the
Government early in 1923 to advise on the administration of justice, having
particular regard to 'accessibility, efficiency, expedition and cost'. Its report was
issued within a few months and its recommendation of the establishment of
the system of a Supreme Court, High Court, Circuit Court and District
Court formed the basis of the Courts of Justice Act, 1924. The Circuit
Court system, created by the 1924 Act was initially thought to herald a
concept of 'decentralisation' of the court system 'from the High Court
centre in Dublin to these various and scattered Circuit Courts in which

1 Foreword to Mr Justice Hanna, *The statute law of the Irish Free State, 1922 to 1928* (Dublin, 1929).

the bulk of the business will be done, now that they have such an extended jurisdiction', and took time to be accepted. There was considerable difficulty in settling the rules for the Circuit Court, which finally came into force in 1932, and there was ongoing discontent about the scale of fees.

The impending reform of the courts system led early in 1923 to the formation of an Association of Provincial Solicitors, intended to consist of all practising provincial solicitors, for the conservation and protection of their interests, the association intending to act as far as possible with the council of the Law Society. The inaugural meeting was held at the Law Society's premises, and it recommended that in view of the rumours of far-reaching changes which might most prejudicially affect the interests of country solicitors local bar associations should take an active interest in any reforms of legal procedure. The Law Society's submission to the Judiciary Committee was made jointly with this new association, and contained proposals for the jurisdiction limits of the lower courts. The Society believed that there should be a relatively low limit of £100 for claims for debt or damages for the Circuit Courts, although it reluctantly accepted the views of the provincial solicitors when formulating their joint submission, and was taken aback when the Judiciary Committee in its final recommendation went beyond even what they had suggested, and a limit of £300 was enacted.

The formation of this association at a time of impending fundamental change in the court system was a new manifestation of the traditional perception among provincial solicitors that the Law Society primarily represented the interests of Dublin-based solicitors. The council of the Society had usually contained a higher proportion of Dublin solicitors than did the membership as a whole, presumably because of the greater convenience for such members of attending meetings. In the event no permanent split arose within the profession, and the annual report of the Society for 1925 stated that in the previous year (that is, on foot of the council elections in 1924) for the first time a majority of the ordinary members of the council were provincial solicitors, and it became more common for solicitors outside Dublin to hold the office of president.

At the half-yearly meeting of the Society in May 1924 the president, James Moore, expressed grave fears for the workings of the new courts. He was reported as saying that:

> the Courts of Justice Bill had become law, and they must now do all that lay in them to work the new Act as best they could for the benefit of the community. He was afraid that the procedure laid down was quite unsuitable for a sparsely populated country like Ireland, where facilities for communication between different districts were very inadequate. He believed that the collection of traders' accounts would become very difficult, that consequently credit would be impaired, and that the community would suffer, as trade without credit would not be too feasible in a country not overflowing with capital. The working of the Circuit Courts, he thought, would be a matter of great difficulty and inconvenience. Offices of record would have to be established, with an accountant's office for each circuit. He assumed that the Government did not intend to put the country to the expense of having such an office for each county. He noted that one circuit included Donegal, Leitrim, Cavan and Monaghan; another Roscommon, Westmeath, Leix, Offaly, and Longford; and yet another Louth, Meath, Kildare, Wicklow, and Wexford, and said that he trembled to think of the difficulties that would face the majority of solicitors practising in these circuits. He thought it hardly likely that libraries would be established in places sufficiently convenient to facilitate counsel in arguing serious law points, and that judges would labour under great difficulties in consequence.[2]

The Society remained of the view up to 1936 that the system of circuit courts had proved disappointing and required radical amendment. It had objected to section 62 of the Courts of Justice Act, 1924 which provided that appeals from the Circuit Court would be made on the basis of a stenographer's note of the evidence as originally given, not a re-hearing of the evidence. The Minister for Justice, Kevin O'Higgins, was of the view

2 *Irish Law Times and Solicitors Journal,* 24 May 1924, p. 129.

that the County Court trial in the past was like a preliminary canter before a race, giving the parties an opportunity of mending their hand in terms of evidence, and that the real test had been the hearing on appeal. He was not diverted from this view by a deputation from the Law Society, which pointed out that only a small fraction of cases were the subject of an appeal. The strictness of the original provisions governing appeals was modified in 1928 to give the High Court a discretion to admit additional evidence, either oral or on affidavit, or to re-hear any evidence, and the full principle of re-hearing was provided for by the Courts of Justice Act in 1936. There were also difficulties in framing and adopting rules for the Circuit Court, and these were not ultimately adopted until early in the following decade, following a review by a joint committee of the Dáil and the Seanad. This had been appointed on foot of a resolution moved by Mr J. Travers Wolfe TD, a member of the council of the Society who was an independent deputy for the West Cork constituency.

THE IRISH LANGUAGE

A second innovation which the Society strongly opposed was the requirement for newly qualified solicitors to be proficient in the Irish language. The Legal Practitioners (Qualification) Bill, 1928 was introduced as a private member's bill and enacted the following year. It provided that a person would not be eligible to be admitted to practise as a solicitor, nor to be called to the Bar, without having passed an examination that would demonstrate 'a competent knowledge of the Irish language'. It was government policy to restore the use of the Irish language, and the Chief Justice, Hugh Kennedy, who had a strong personal interest in the language revival movement, remarked at the end of 1928 that regard might be paid to the example of the revival of their language by the Hebrew people, and that if there was to be a revival it would take place only by the people really wanting it, because they felt a real consciousness of their own nation and race.

The bill, as originally introduced, contained a definition of 'competent knowledge' as being 'such a degree of oral and written proficiency in the use of the language as is sufficient to enable a legal practitioner properly to conduct the business of his clients in the Irish language'. As eventually enacted, after representations by the Society, led by Mr Travers Wolfe, it was defined as meaning 'such a degree of oral and written proficiency in the use of the language as is sufficient to enable a legal practitioner efficiently to receive instructions, to advise clients, to examine witnesses and to follow proceedings in the Irish language'. Although the Society remained unhappy at the terms of the eventual obligation the vehemence of its reaction to the bill might best be assessed in the light of the implications of the original much more far-reaching definition.

A special general meeting of the members of the Society was held in February 1929, and it was resolved 'that the Society is opposed to the bill so far as it affects the solicitors' profession, and instructs the council to use every possible effort to secure its rejection'. An amendment that would have recorded an acceptance of the principle of the bill with reservations received the support of only eight out of 118 solicitors present, the vast majority not being prepared to support a text that would have expressed the profession's view as being that

> while recognising the legal status accorded to Irish as the national language with its necessary results in the life and business of the people, and while undertaking to apply the principles enunciated in the Legal Practitioners (Qualification) Bill, 1928, in the spirit as well as in the letter in connection with the professional education of solicitors' apprentices, [the Society] strongly deprecates the fact that this Society was not first asked to apply those principles, the tone of distrust of this Society evinced in the said bill and the tendency in a degree to take the training of aspirants to our profession out of our own hands, and demands that such amendments as shall be in accordance with the dignity of this profession may be made in the bill.

The Society then issued a pamphlet to all members of the Dáil and Seanad, spelling out its view that the bill (a) was not wanted either by the public or by the profession, and was unnecessary; (b) was oppressive; (c) was unworkable; (d) set an impossibly high standard of Irish; (e) must lead to inefficiency; and (f) should not be compulsory. At the half-yearly meeting in May 1929 the president, Edward H. Burne, referred to 'this atrocious measure which in its present form spelt waste of money, brains, energy and time ... which was not wanted, and had not been asked for by any save extreme and foolish idealists, quite ignorant of the necessary high legal education of future solicitors'. The provisions of this 'tyrannical measure ... were impossible and ridiculous'. He also remarked, in words not perhaps best calculated to win support in Leinster House, that 'some of the enormous amount spent annually on compulsory Irish might usefully be employed in bringing the High Court office work to a more efficient standard'.

Politicians from both government and opposition criticised the attitude of the Society. The Minister for Finance, Ernest Blythe, who was a leading proponent of the bill, said at an early stage that if a reasonable attitude had been taken by the Law Society he would have been willing to acquiesce in matters of detail, although he eventually did agree to the amended definition of competent knowledge of the language. In 1930 Seán McEntee TD said that the Society had taken a very partisan attitude to recent legislative proposals and was not representative of the whole profession. The Society believed, more than a decade later, that what appeared to be a decline in the standard of answering in legal subjects in the final examination for apprentices was due to the strain imposed on students who were attempting to pass the final Irish examination at the same time.

The imposition of the Irish language requirement in this way upon an unwilling profession might suggest that at least at that time a rather difficult relationship existed between the government and the Society. The subject of regulation of the profession and its statutory framework was to be a preoccupation of the Society for much of the 1940s and 1950s. However, it might be noted that the profession did have influence at a high level in government in the 1920s and 1930s. Two western solicitors, Patrick Hogan from County Galway and Patrick J. Ruttledge from County Mayo, were prominent members of successive governments, Hogan being the Cumann na nGaedheal Minister for Agriculture and Ruttledge heading different departments, including that of Justice, in Fianna Fáil governments in the 1930s.

THE FOUR COURTS

The Law Society was concerned about the temporary nature of its accommodation, but it was not clear until 1926 that the Government actually did intend to reconstruct the Four Courts. It had been possible for certain legal offices, such as the Land Registry, to be reopened within the complex fairly soon after the destruction but plans for complete reconstruction were not made available to the judiciary, the Bar Council and the Society until May 1926. In 1927 the Government agreed to a suggestion of the Society that an architect be retained by the Society, at public expense, to advise on the plans for the new premises which had been submitted by the Board of Works to the council 'and generally to watch the progress of the building in the interests of the Society'. When the works had been completed the new Solicitors' Buildings gave general satisfaction. These were sited adjoining and slightly to the east of the location upon which the premises formally occupied by the Society had stood. It was a four-storey building, including a basement, and although the usage of various parts of the building changed over the years the principal rooms were those on the first floor, being the hall (subsequently the library), the council chamber, and the president's room. The hall was panelled and floored in oak and the chamber had walnut panelling.

The reconstruction of the Four Courts was a great event for the legal profession as a whole and a symbol of the authority and institutions of the new state. Their re-opening in the autumn of 1931 appears to have been the occasion for the initiation of what are now the traditional religious services in neighbouring churches (and more recently also in a synagogue and in a mosque) to mark the opening of the legal year. The courts were closed for the duration of the Eucharistic Congress in June 1932, pursuant to the Eucharistic Congress (Miscellaneous Provisions) Act. It might be noted that it was at about the same time that the Royal Courts of Justice in Belfast were built, on the same general design as the Four Courts with four courtrooms opening off a central hall. The foundation stone was laid in October 1929 and the building was opened in June 1933. The Incorporated Law Society of Northern Ireland had to take forceful action at this time –

including intimating that it might otherwise be necessary to surrender its charter, and to ask to be released from its statutory functions – in order to secure proper accommodation within the new complex and adequate financial provision for the discharge of its statutory responsibilities.

Negotiations for settling the title of the Society to its new premises in the Four Courts were complicated. The position was summarised in the 1943 annual report of the council:

> Prior to the destruction of the Four Courts in 1922 the Solicitors' Buildings stood approximately on the site of the present Law Library and its precincts. The Society held this property under a lease from the Benchers subject to a nominal rent. Subsequent to the destruction of the Four Courts an arrangement was made between the Commissioners of Public Works, the Benchers and the Society, whereby the Society would acquire and the Benchers would convey to the Society the fee simple of the Benchers' property in the Four Courts, including the site of the former Solicitors' Buildings, and this Society should then lease the said property to the Commissioners of Public Works for a term of 99 years at a nominal rent. In consideration of this lease the Commissioners of Public Works agreed to make a lease to the Society of the present Solicitors' Buildings (which stand on State property) for a term of 99 years at a nominal rent. For reasons which are outside the control of the council the transactions have not yet been completed.

In 1932 the arrangements for completing the transaction had reached the stage of draft conveyances and leases being submitted to the various parties, but, as the 1945 report of the council stated, a difficulty arose over the form in which the Commissioners of Public Works would formally acknowledge the right of the Benchers to the use of certain rooms in the Four Courts for their meetings:

> The Benchers and the Commissioners of Public Works have up to the present been unable to agree as to the adequacy of the assurance proposed to be given to the Benchers. It is understood that the

Benchers require an acknowledgement of their right to continue in possession of their existing chambers in perpetuity, while the Commissioners state that they are precluded by law from giving an acknowledgement for any period longer than 99 years. The matters in issue are entirely outside the control of the council and until such time as the Commissioners of Public Works and the Benchers can come to an agreement the matter will remain in its present unsatisfactory position for the Society.

The next report on the subject was made in 1952, when it was reported that negotiations with the Commissioners had been pursued, the outcome of the issue between the Commissioners and the Benchers having presumably been resolved in some way. The Commissioners had no statutory power under the State Lands Act, 1924, to grant a lease to the Society for a period exceeding 99 years, but, as the council reported, 'the position of the Society has been safeguarded by the arrangement under which the Society has acquired the fee simple of the Benchers' property in the Four Courts and has leased same to the State for the term of 99 years only. This property will be occupied in part by the State and in part by the Bar Council under lease or licence from the State. The Society will thus have security for the renewal of the lease of the Solicitors' Buildings.' In other words, the Society would be in a position to decline to renew the lease of which it was the lessor unless the lease of which it was a lessee was also renewed.

The lease to the Society agreed in 1954 did not entail it being responsible for external portions of the building, and it contributed to the central heating expenses of the premises one-fifteenth of the total cost of heating the Four Courts (apparently on the basis that the cubic capacity of the buildings was one-fifteenth of the cubic capacity of the whole of the Four Courts buildings). The lease to the Society from the Minister for Finance and the Commissioners of Public Works contained provisions for the repairing, servicing and heating of the Solicitors' Buildings in consideration of a yearly charge. This was thought to be a very advantageous arrangement and whether it should be surrendered was one of the considerations borne in mind by the council in 1968 when it was coming to a decision whether to take up the proposal to acquire the historic King's

Hospital building in Blackhall Place, a few hundred yards west of the Four Courts, as described in Chapter 5. The Society's existing premises were very heavily used, and provided inadequate facilities, particularly for the increased number of apprentices who were entering the profession during the 1960s.

The Society was aware that 'on leaving its present premises the society would have but one buyer, the Board of Works', and the proceeds of sale of the building would be an important consideration in determining whether to offer to acquire the King's Hospital. The president, Patrick Noonan, had met the Minister for Finance and asked him if he would interest himself in the matter and pointed out that the attitude of the Board of Works would be of the utmost importance. The minutes of the council meeting record that 'Mr Haughey when he received the president had been very non-committal', and further attempts to persuade the Minister for Finance to make a grant in exchange for the Solicitors' Buildings proved fruitless. The Solicitors' Buildings were sold to the Bar Council in 1977 after protracted negotiations, the Society retaining an office and extensive consultation rooms there.

THE PROSPECTS OF THE PROFESSION

The number of solicitors practising in Ireland increased by about a third in the first decades of independence, rising from 995 in 1924 to 1255 in 1934, 1365 in 1937, 1420 in 1940 and a peak of 1422 in 1943, a number which it did not afterwards attain for almost thirty years. An average of about 70 solicitors practising in Northern Ireland who had been admitted or apprenticed before 1922 maintained a registration also in the South, and are included in the above totals. Membership of the Law Society slowly became virtually universal among solicitors, the proportion who were members growing from two thirds in the 1920s up to 80 per cent in 1948. In 1951 the Society took an initiative to encourage local bar associations to become more active, and to bring about the establishment of a bar association in the four or five counties in which they had not already been set up.

This growth in numbers, in what was generally an economically depressed or stagnant period, put pressure upon the incomes of solicitors. Legal work would traditionally derive from the occurrence of transactions or events requiring legal advice, although there is clearly a close relationship between economic prosperity and the volume of certain types of legal business, in conveyancing and property or mortgage and other financing work, for instance. Legal fees payable by the State were reduced by 5 per cent in 1933 as an austerity measure by the Public Services (Temporary Economies) Act. In 1936 the president complained that situations vacant advertisements recently published in the newspapers showed that a plumber, at two shillings an hour, would earn more than a solicitor in the Land Commission at a salary of £175. In 1944 the president spoke of overcrowding in the profession and warned young people against 'entering a profession in which they might have to endure respectable starvation', and representations were made to the Government later in the decade about the unreasonably low salaries that were paid to solicitors in the service of the State. A more detailed complaint that might have been made at almost any time in these decades had been expressed at the annual general meeting in 1939:

> The outlook for young people at present entering the profession was anything but rosy. Although the number of students seeking to enter the profession was smaller than a few years ago, it was still high, and out of proportion to the opportunities for making a reasonable livelihood for those who succeeded in becoming qualified. The volume of litigation tended to decrease, and scarcity of money tended to restrict enterprise, with resulting diminution of commercial and conveyancing business.

One aspect of the economic pressure on the profession was that the opportunities to practise abroad were not expanded and indeed became more limited after 1922. There had never been reciprocity or mutual recognition of qualifications between Ireland and England, and although provision was made by the Solicitors Act, 1923 to facilitate English and Scottish solicitors in qualifying to practise in Ireland this was not reciprocated by the British government (and would have been opposed by the

Law Society in England) and as mentioned below it was withdrawn in 1947. Prior to 1922 Irish solicitors had been entitled on the same basis as English solicitors to apply for and take up legal positions in territories forming part of the British Empire. The Law Society wished that the Colonial Solicitors Acts would be made applicable after independence in the same way as before, but the government would not agree to take up the matter with the British government.

The Society continued to exercise its statutory function of monitoring and disciplining the profession. An unusual application for admission as a solicitor was made in 1929 by Sir James O'Connor, formerly a Lord Justice of Appeal in Ireland, and an initial member of the Supreme Court set up in 1924. His legal career had followed a complicated course. He had been admitted as a solicitor in 1894, and then struck off the roll at his request in 1900 in order that he might be called to the Bar. He retired as a judge in May 1925 and was called to the Bar in England later that month. In 1929 he was disbarred in England, at his request, and applied to the High Court in Ireland to be re-admitted as a solicitor here, with a view to practising in his family firm in Wexford. The Law Society said that it had no objection, but the chief justice was critical of what he evidently regarded as a complacent attitude to the application. He adjourned the application and asked the Society to consider the matter in more detail, and he also directed that notice be served on the attorney general so that the public interest in respect of the application would be more formally considered. The application was then approved, subject to Sir James O'Connor undertaking not to exercise any right of personal audience in the courts, having regard to the public interest in a person who had held judicial office not thereafter participating in any proceedings in which his judicial decisions might be in issue.[3]

---

3 *In re the Solicitors Act and Sir James O'Connor* [1930] IR 623. See also G.W. Hogan, 'Chief Justice Kennedy and Sir James O'Connor's application', in *Irish Jurist*, XXIII (1988), pp 144–59.

THE CENTENARY OF THE CHARTER

In May 1952 a series of celebrations were held by the Law Society to mark the centenary of the granting of its charter in 1852. A reception was held in the hall of the Four Courts and in the Society's library at which over 1,100 guests and members attended. Religious services were held in the Pro-Cathedral and in St Patrick's Cathedral, followed by a special general meeting of the Society which was addressed by the chief justice, the attorney general, the presidents of other law societies from Northern Ireland, England and Wales, and Scotland and by the presidents of the Southern Law Association and of the Law Society itself, Arthur Cox. A reception was held by the President, Seán T. O'Kelly, at Áras an Uachtaráin in honour of the centenary, attended by the Taoiseach, heads of the churches, representatives from the other law societies, the lord mayor of Dublin, the diplomatic corps, members of the Oireachtas, and representatives of the universities, other professional organisations and of the civil service and courts service. The celebration concluded with a dinner in the Gresham Hotel.

AMENDING LEGISLATION

The passing of the Solicitors Act, 1954[4] was the culmination of efforts extending over more than a decade by the Law Society to amend and update the law on the regulation (more precisely, the self-regulation) of the solicitors' profession. What was soon found to be a constitutional infirmity in its provisions for certain disciplinary measures that could be taken against members of the profession[5] required amending legislation, which was passed in 1960.[6] The two acts were a part of a chain of legislation extending back to 1866 and 1898 and subsequently continued by the Solicitors (Amendment) Act, 1994[7] by which, at intervals of about 40 years or so, the framework of regulation of the profession has been revised and extended. The terms of the legislation were of very great interest and

---

4 No. 36 of 1954. See generally Daire Hogan, 'The preparation of the Solicitors Acts, 1954 and 1960', in *Irish Jurist*, XXXI (1996), pp 266–79.   **5** *In re Solicitors Act, 1954* [1960] IR 239.   **6** No. 37 of 1960.   **7** No. 27 of 1994.

importance to the profession but were not politically controversial, and were dealt with by different governments between 1943, when the Society's proposals were first submitted to a government headed by Éamon de Valera, and 1960. The communications of the Society with the government during this period were generally dealt with by the president for the time being or the long-serving secretary of the Society, Eric A. Plunkett, and in a number of instances by Arthur Cox, one of the most distinguished members of the profession, who also played an important role in 1954 in the approval by the Seanad of the legislation.

In 1937 the Society decided to promote updating regulatory legislation, and the council arranged for the preparation of a draft bill. When this was submitted to the Department of Justice in April 1943 it had three main objects, namely (a) to enforce the keeping in an approved manner of accurate accounts by solicitors of client moneys entrusted to their care, (b) to enforce stricter discipline and (c) to make membership of the Law Society compulsory for all practising solicitors. In June 1946 the government decided that it would adopt or take on the bill as a government measure, subject to provision being made for (i) a fidelity bond to be taken out by solicitors and (ii) the keeping of proper accounts by solicitors, including the auditing of accounts. It would not accept the concept of membership of the Society becoming compulsory. These matters, together with a more general government concern about whether the self-regulating nature of the profession adequately protected the public interest, were to prove stumbling blocks in the way of framing and finalising and ultimately amending the legislation.

The government generally showed a responsiveness to concerns of the Law Society, which succeeded in persuading the government that its views or recommendations should prevail in almost every instance where these were queried. This pattern changed in 1960 when the Society's proposals on the amending bill received a vigorous and determined challenge from Charles J. Haughey, then at the start of his ministerial career. The Society's main complaint against the government, at least until 1960, was not that it was, in the last resort, unwilling to accept the Society's views but that the wheels of legislative drafting seemed to grind very slowly.

The first instance of a (comparatively quick) governmental acceptance of a Law Society proposal occurred in 1947 when the short (one page) Solicitors (Amendment) Act repealed a provision of the Solicitors Act, 1923 which entitled a solicitor in England and Wales or Scotland of three years' standing to be admitted to practise in Ireland without service as an apprentice or any examination. No reciprocal provision had been made by Parliament to facilitate the admission of Irish solicitors in any part of the United Kingdom. A number of enquiries and applications had been made from 1943 onwards (no applications had been made in the previous 20 years) from persons hoping to benefit from this provision, and the Law Society no longer wished this unilateral re-qualification option to be available. Regulations made by the Society under the 1923 act had required any solicitor admitted in England and Wales or Scotland seeking to avail of the section to remove his name from the roll in the relevant jurisdiction before he or she could be admitted in Ireland, and the Act thus had not facilitated any form of dual qualification.

The provisions in the 1923 act had never applied to solicitors from Northern Ireland (at least those who had not been qualified or apprenticed in 1921), and whether the admission of Northern Ireland solicitors to practise in the South should be facilitated along the lines which had existed for British solicitors between 1923 and 1947 would be a constant item of discussion before the 1954 bill was finalised. The government initially decided that facilities for qualifying in the South should be made available to Northern solicitors without requiring a reciprocal facility in the North, but eventually accepted the Society's view, expressed as 'a matter of principle, on which there should be no compromise', that there should be a reciprocal provision in the North before any procedure for expedited admission in the South would become effective, a decision which was represented in due course by section 44(4) of the 1954 act.

The other items of particular controversy between the Department of Justice and the Society were whether proper arrangements could be made for compensation of clients of dishonest solicitors, the form of accounting (particularly for client money) to be observed by solicitors and the nature of the disciplinary powers of the Society. The government was eventually persuaded that to require a fidelity bond or any other form of compulsory insurance of solicitors would be impractical, and that the Society should be allowed a trial period to persuade and encourage solicitors to improve their system of accounting before compulsory auditing ('more drastic provisions') would be introduced. A general meeting of the Society had agreed in 1948 to establish a compensation fund from which, at its discretion, grants might be made in appropriate cases to relieve or mitigate losses resulting from dishonesty of a solicitor or his or her employee (clerk or servant).

The new disciplinary powers of the Society over members of the profession, as eventually set out in Part III (Sections 13–23) of the 1954 act, can be summarised as follows:

1. A disciplinary committee of between seven and ten members or former members of the council of the Society, was to be appointed annually, with the approval of the chief justice.
2. The committee had power, inter alia, to admonish a solicitor, to suspend him from practice or to strike his name off the roll of solicitors and, if satisfied that a prima facie case of misconduct of some kind had been made out, would hold an inquiry, for which purposes 'the disciplinary committee shall have the powers, rights and privileges vested in the High Court' concerning the enforcement of the attendance of witnesses, etc.
3. An order made by the committee would be enforceable as if it were a judgment or order of the High Court.
4. An appeal against any order made by the committee could be made to the chief justice.
5. The Society had power to direct the registrar of solicitors to refuse to issue a practising certificate, without which it was not lawful to act as a solicitor.

The government initially took the view that it would not be appropriate for the committee to have power to strike a solicitor's name from the roll, and that the existing provisions on the subject should be retained or re-enacted. These were contained in the 1898 act, under which the function of the committee was to consider applications to strike the name of a solicitor from the roll and to report its findings to the lord chancellor (or, after 1924, to the chief justice) who could make such order(s) on the report as he might think fit. However upon reconsideration at the request of the Society it decided that the relevant powers should be vested in the committee.

INITIAL LITIGATION ON THE 1954 ACT

A challenge to the constitutionality of the new disciplinary procedure was quickly made and was heard by the chief justice (sitting as a judge of the High Court) in February and March 1956, within fifteen months of the enactment of the act, in relation to a decision of the disciplinary committee to strike two solicitors off the roll. The High Court upheld the power of the committee to strike off, but this decision was reversed by the Supreme Court on appeal.

It was argued on behalf of the two solicitor appellants that the committee was in fact exercising a judicial power, contrary to Article 34.1 of the Constitution, which provides that justice shall be administered in courts established by law by duly appointed judges, and that the limited exception to that principle contained in Article 37 of the Constitution was not applicable. Article 37 provides that 'nothing in this Constitution shall operate to invalidate the exercise of limited functions and powers of a judicial nature, in matters other than criminal matters, by any person or body of persons duly authorised by law to exercise such functions and powers, notwithstanding that such person or such body of persons is not a judge or a court appointed or established as such under this Constitution.'

The High Court had accepted that the disciplinary committee was purporting to exercise judicial powers, but had also held that as these were subject to a right of appeal to the courts they were of a limited nature within the meaning of Article 37 of the Constitution. The appeal on the merits of the committee's actions, as not being supported by the evidence, was dismissed by the High Court, the two solicitors concerned having not participated in any way in the proceedings of the committee, neither filing an affidavit nor appearing in person or by solicitor or counsel.

The approach of the Law Society as advanced at the High Court hearing had been that the committee was exercising not a judicial power but an administrative or ministerial function, in the control of the officers of the court. It had referred to the statutes governing various other professions which entrusted to internal bodies a somewhat similar measure of control of their members. The Society had also drawn attention to the fact that in England since the Solicitors Act, 1919 the jurisdiction to strike solicitors off the roll had been exercised by a committee of the profession. The High Court, while accepting the general tenor of the Society's arguments, had commented that 'one cannot escape the feeling that it was perhaps the provisions of the English act which prompted the Society to attempt to achieve for the profession here the extent of self government granted to the profession in England by that act. It has to be remembered, however, that in England parliament is supreme and there is no constitutional bar to legislation which entrusts persons other than judges with the exercise of powers which ordinarily are entrusted to the courts.' In the Supreme Court appeal the Society further argued that if the actions of the committee were of a judicial nature then the High Court's finding that it was a power of a kind contemplated by article 37 of the Constitution was correct. In support of this contention the Society argued that the powers of the committee were limited to solicitors, who were a comparatively small proportion of the community, and that the powers (not only if exercised to strike a solicitor off the roll, but on other punishments) were subject to an appeal to the court.

Mr Justice Kingsmill Moore, delivering the judgment of the Supreme Court, said that the power to strike a solicitor from the roll was a very severe sanction, which in its consequences might be more serious than a term of imprisonment, and its exercise could only properly be described as the administration of justice. 'It seems to the court that the power to strike a solicitor off the roll is, when exercised, an administration of justice, both because the infliction of such a severe penalty on a citizen is a matter which calls for the exercise of the judicial power of the state and because to entrust such a power to persons other than the judges is to interfere with the necessities of the proper administration of justice ... The existence of an appeal to the courts cannot restore constitutionality to a tribunal whose decisions, if unappealed, amount to an administration of justice.'

The appeal was heard by the Supreme Court in November 1956 and judgment was given on 7 March 1958, on which date a special committee of the council met and considered proposals for legislation to provide a new basis on which the Society could safely exercise disciplinary functions. Representatives of the Society and the Department of Justice met in April 1958, when the Society expressed its concern at the absence of any disciplinary procedure, and requested an indemnity against costs and damages and any civil liability that might arise if solicitors who had been the subject of proceedings of the disciplinary committee now were to allege that its acts had been done without lawful authority. The Society subsequently supplied a confidential analysis to the Department of the cases that had been considered by the committee, showing that twelve solicitors had been struck off the roll in the previous three years, and pointed out that in a number of cases that had come before the court in which the judge had deemed it proper to temper justice with mercy, the excessive leniency of the court had ultimately given rise to further losses.

In June 1958 the government approved the Department's proposal for a new bill which would transfer the striking off jurisdiction to the High Court, restricting the disciplinary committee's role to that of fact finding and the making of recommendations to the High Court as to the appropriate sanction. It also resolved to give an absolute privilege to the proceedings of the committee both past and future, and a qualified privilege (ultimately in the 1960 act, at the behest of the Society, this was made an absolute privilege) for applications to the committee. The progress of the bill was halted, however, by the judgment in a second case on the 1954 act.

THE SECOND CASE ON THE 1954 ACT, AND THE 1960 ACT

In this second case (in which, again, the initial order of the chief justice, sitting in the High Court, in July 1958, was reversed when an appeal came before the Supreme Court),[8] involved a review of the legality of an appeal against a direction of the Law Society to the registrar of solicitors (who was ordinarily the secretary of the Society) to refuse a practising certificate to a particular solicitor, pursuant to section 49(1)(g) of the 1954 act. The High Court held that, having regard to complaints that had been made by clients, the Society had acted reasonably and was justified in giving a direction to refuse the person concerned a practising certificate, but on appeal to the Supreme Court it was held, on the merits, that the order should be set aside. The appellant was represented by John A. Costello SC, who argued that the judgment in the first case brought under the act was applicable to the facts of the case and that sections 49(1) and (2) were repugnant to the Constitution, as involving the administration of justice. (There cannot be many instances in which a counsel has argued (as it transpired, unsuccessfully) that provisions of a law which he had introduced in the Dáil were repugnant to the Constitution.)

The High Court had held that the procedures to be followed by the Society leading to the exercise of their powers to give a direction that a practising certificate be refused were very different from those provided in relation to the function of the disciplinary committee, that in effect the Society merely screened the application, and that the effective decision was that of the court. The High Court had further held that a direction to refuse to issue a solicitor with a practising certificate would entail only that he would be deprived of his right to practise for the year in question and hence was very different from the removal of his name from the roll of solicitors, and that consequently a direction of the Society to the registrar to refuse a practising certificate did not constitute the administration of justice, and that sections 49 (1) and (2) were not repugnant to the Constitution. The High Court judgment had also commented that it was probable that if a question had not been raised as to the repugnance to the Constitution of certain sections of the act of 1954 in the earlier case the Society would most likely have proposed to strike the solicitor's name off the roll of solicitors. Instead they had resorted to the provisions of section 49.

8 *In the matter of the Solicitors Act, 1954* 95 ILTR 60 (1960).

The Supreme Court took a different view of the circumstances of the case, and had regard to the efforts the appellant had made (since 1956, when the Society had frozen his bank accounts) to rectify the confusion in his office affairs, and the fact that the clients whose complaints had grounded the Society's action had been fully compensated by him. In November 1958 the Supreme Court set aside the Society's direction, and concluded that 'having regard to the court's view and decision of the case on the merits it is unnecessary to decide the constitutional issue raised by the notice of appeal'.

The government regretted that the Supreme Court had not decided the constitutional issue that had been raised about section 49 in that case and, despite the urgency associated with the fact that the Society no longer had any effective disciplinary procedures, the Department of Justice and the Society believed it best to take a more considered look at the bill and at associated issues of regulation of the profession – in particular the requirement on solicitors to keep proper books of account, and the financing and operation of the compensation fund which had been set up under the 1954 act.

The Solicitors (Amendment) Act, 1960, which was enacted in November that year, contained thirty three sections and dealt primarily with the new disciplinary provisions, a re-statement of the basis of the compensation fund and provisions to be implemented at a future date for the furnishing by every solicitor of an accountant's certificate of compliance with the Solicitors Accounts Regulations. The financing of the compensation fund was the main difficulty. Charles Haughey, appointed on 6 May 1960 as parliamentary secretary to the Minister for Justice, explained to the Dáil that losses to the fund had been much higher than anticipated, and that no payments had been made to claimants for some time. In its negotiations with the Department of Justice the Law Society reverted to a modified version of one of its original proposals some fifteen years earlier, namely that membership of the Society should become a condition not of entitlement to practise (as originally suggested) but of entitlement to participate in the compensation fund. The Society said that it would thus be less relevant to check whether a solicitor who was not a member of the Society was complying with the Solicitors Accounts Regulations since the compensation fund would not cover any defalcations by him. It pointed out that it would never have agreed to accept the burden of establishing and maintaining a compensation fund unless it had felt assured that simultaneously the new disciplinary procedures, under the auspices of the Society, would allow it to monitor the profession; 'the Society is now unable to discipline its members, while it is committed to the maintenance of the compensation fund. The result is akin to having a safe containing money but without a lock.'

The government initially accepted this approach, although it had second thoughts when it transpired that the Society was not willing to establish a fully financed compensation fund, at a higher level of annual contribution from the profession. However what really terminated that whole line of approach was the fact that, in the words of a subsequent Department of Justice memorandum to government, 'following his appointment the parliamentary secretary decided to examine the whole matter afresh'. The memorandum continued:

> As a result of this examination he was satisfied that the scheme as proposed by the Law Society for the compensation of clients defrauded by solicitors was unsatisfactory.
>
> Firstly, there was no assurance that even if members of the public would be sufficiently aware of the position (and the parliamentary secretary was extremely doubtful if they would) full compensation would be payable in any reasonably foreseeable time to those members of the public who confined their legal dealings to Law Society members.
>
> Secondly, the present fund was bankrupt and could only be salvaged by substantially increasing the annual contribution.
>
> Thirdly, there was the danger that if contributions to a fund confined to the members of the Law Society had to be increased substantially to keep the fund solvent members would tend to leave the Society rather than pay the increased contribution.
>
> Fourthly, it was essential in the interest of the public and of the profession that solicitors be effectively compelled to keep proper accounts.

Mr Haughey then rapidly held a series of meetings with representatives of the council. He accepted its proposal that a reserve amount of the compensation fund should be £25,000 rather than £100,000, did not press 'on an unwilling profession' his view that compulsory annual accountants certificates should be introduced immediately, and intimated that proposals for 'reasonable increases in solicitors' fees would have his goodwill', without committing the government on the subject.

The representatives of the council of the Society found dealing with Mr Haughey to be a novel experience. When the outcome of the negotiations was reported to a special meeting of the council an extended debate on the final proposals took place, during which seventeen members spoke, and they agreed that the debate should not be reported in any detail in the next issue of the Law Society's *Gazette*. They reluctantly agreed to accept what had been put forward as 'the best agreement that could be achieved with the parliamentary secretary'. They resolved to inform him that this acceptance was given 'having regard to the parliamentary secretary's assurance that he would give his full support to an application for a reasonable increase in solicitors costs'.

The bill was introduced in the Dáil in November 1960. The only parliamentary opposition came from a critic of the Law Society, who was himself a solicitor, Richie Ryan TD. One of Mr Ryan's objections related to the reliance placed upon accountants in a matter relevant to the right of a solicitor to practise. He raised the prospect of the public being prejudiced by 'the dishonest solicitor and the dishonest accountant working in collusion', which led to the following exchange in the Dáil:

> Mr Haughey: There is no such thing as a dishonest accountant.
> Mr Corish: Only smart ones.[9]

The bill became law later that month and, with the 1954 act, formed the basis of regulation of the profession for another generation.

9 Dáil Éireann, *Parliamentary Debates*, Official Report Vol. 184 col. 144 (2 November 1960).

1. The Four Courts, Inns Quay, Dublin *(Photograph: Lensmen)*

2. The Solicitors' Buildings, Four Courts, c.1950

3. Supplemental royal charter granted to the Law Society in 1888 *(Photograph: Roslyn Byrne)*

4. The Solicitors' room at the Four Courts, *c*.1860 (*Collection: Peter Pearson*)

5. The Law Society library, on the first floor of the Solicitors' Buildings, *c.*1952

6. The Society's council chamber, on the first floor of the Solicitors' Buildings, *c.*1952

7. Memorial by Oliver Sheppard to the 20 solicitors and 18 apprentices who died in action in the First World War, erected by the Society in the Solicitors' Buildings, Four Courts, in 1921. It now stands in the Society's premises at Blackhall Place. *(Photograph: Lensmen)*

8. Council of the Law Society, 1951/52

Back row, left to right: Thomas A. O'Reilly, Derrick M. Martin, George G. Overend, Ralph J. Walker, John F. Foley, John J. Sheil, John Maher, Cornelius J. Daly, Christopher E. Callan, Maurice Power

Middle row: James R. Quirke, Seán Ó hUadhaigh, Louis E. O'Dea, Eric A. Plunkett (Secretary), Gerald J. O'Donnell (Vice President), Arthur Cox (President), Desmond R. Counahan (Vice President), Patrick R. Boyd, Henry J. Catchpole, William J. Norman, Senator Patrick F. O'Reilly

Front row: Reginald J. Nolan, Dermot P. Shaw, Desmond J. Mayne, John R. Halpin, John Carrigan, Francis J. Lanigan, James J. O'Connor, Niall S. Gaffney, Joseph P. Tyrrell, Joseph Barrett, John L. Kealy

Absent – Roger Greene, Francis J. Gearty, Henry St. J. Blake, Timothy A. Buckley, John J. Dundon, Cuthbert J. Furlong, Edmund Hayes, Charles MacLaughlin, Alexander S. Merrick, Joseph Morrissey, George Murnaghan, John J. Nash, James C. Taylor, John B. McCann

9. Sir Denis Hicks OBE, Chairman of the International Bar Association, addressing the opening session of the IBA Twelfth Conference in Dublin, 8 July 1968. *Seated, left to right:* Tom Stafford, Lord Mayor of Dublin, Micheál Ó Moráin TD, Minister for Justice, Patrick Noonan, President of the IBA and President of the Law Society (the host organisation in association with the Bar Council), Éamon de Valera, President of Ireland, An Taoiseach, Jack Lynch TD, the Hon. Cearbhall Ó Dálaigh, Chief Justice, Gerald J. McMahon, Secretary General of the IBA and the Right Hon. Lord McDermott, Lord Chief Justice of Northern Ireland *(Courtesy: Jo Noonan)*

10. Eric A. Plunkett, Law Society Secretary (*centre*) in 1968, with Thomas C. Smyth, solicitor, who held the post of assistant secretary with the Society from 1963 to 1968 and Joseph Finnegan, solicitor, who succeeded him as assistant secretary from 1968 to 1972. Thomas Smyth and Joseph Finnegan were subsequently called to the Bar and appointed judges of the High Court. Mr. Justice Joseph Finnegan was appointed President of the High Court in 2001. *(Courtesy: Eric Plunkett)*

11. The Law Club of Ireland, formed in Dublin in November 1791, was one of the early associations of solicitors predating the Law Society of Ireland (1830) and the Society of the Attorneys and Solicitors of Ireland (1841). It had premises at 13 Dame Street until 1869, 25 Nassau Street until 1885 and 23 Suffolk Street until 1899 when it was dissolved. After the formation of the later societies it became primarily a social club. *(Photograph: Roslyn Byrne)*

VERITAS·VINCET

12. The Society's coat of arms, granted in 1911, in the register of arms at the office of the Chief Herald of Ireland *(Photograph: Roslyn Byrne)*

13. The president's badge was inaugurated in 1910. It consists of the arms of the Society wrought in gold and enamel and it was executed by jewellers West & Son, Dublin. *(Photograph: Roslyn Byrne)*

14. William George Wakely, Secretary of the Law Society, 1888–1942

15. Eric A. Plunkett, Secretary of the Law Society, 1942–1973

The emergence of women in the solicitors' profession in Ireland

MARY REDMOND

'I would love to offer you my seat, Lady, except I am sitting in it myself.'
Groucho Marx

It is difficult to believe that less than ninety years ago women in Ireland were prohibited from practising as solicitors or barristers or from serving as judges. The story of how women worked to overcome prejudice and to gain equality within the solicitors' profession is summarised in this chapter. It names the early pioneers for the cause of women lawyers. The stories of these women merit research and greater exposition. The praise of these women is long overdue. The chapter[1] celebrates some of the many women who have achieved prominence in the profession and outside it.

In nineteenth-century Ireland and Britain women were effectively excluded from practising law. It was widely accepted that at common law women were under a general disability by reason of their sex to become lawyers. Although no law expressly prohibited female solicitors, it became custom and practice to regard a lawyer's work as not fit for a woman. This was such an established principle that the legislature did not see the need to make specific reference to the unsuitability of women as solicitors in the Solicitors Act, 1843, nor by the same token, in the corresponding legislation applicable in Ireland that was enacted in 1866.

1 The author records her gratitude to Marie-Louise McMahon, solicitor, Shaw Pittman, London, and formerly Arthur Cox, Dublin, whose research and drafting of earlier versions of this chapter were invaluable, and to Conor O'Dwyer and Peter Bredin of Arthur Cox. Thanks also are due to Moya Quinlan, solicitor, Dixon Quinlan, Margaret Byrne, librarian, Law Society, Thérèse Broy, librarian, Arthur Cox, Gerry Whyte, TCD, and Rosemary Vaughan (née Crofts) who made private papers available. As to the women solicitors celebrated in this chapter, the author has offered her choices.

The honour of being the first woman in the English-speaking world to be an accredited lawyer did not fall to a citizen of these islands, where progress was well behind that of other countries. The first female lawyer in the English-speaking world was Arabelle Mansfield. In June 1869, she was admitted to the Iowa State Bar and became the first female lawyer in the United States of America to be granted a law licence. Just under twenty years later, in February 1887, Clara Martin became the 'first woman lawyer in the whole British Empire'[2] when she was admitted in Ontario. In the same year, Ethel Benjamin became the first woman lawyer in New Zealand.

EARLY DAYS

In the nineteenth century, while Irish and English women were able to become members of the medical and accountancy professions and were permitted to hold positions such as mayor, postmistress, insurance commissioner and engineer, they were rigidly excluded from the legal profession. They were also excluded from public office, the professions of parliamentary agent, stockbroking and from the ministry of the church.

Many women who had a connection with the legal profession (through fathers, brothers or husbands) were thought to act as 'shadow lawyers'. It appears, however, that women were entitled to appear in court and plead for themselves in cases in which they were concerned. Some Irish women became well known for this in the late 1800s, one being described when she appeared in the land commission court in Dublin in 1898 as 'a well-known lady litigant from Co. Monaghan, a familiar figure at every Monaghan assizes for years past'.[3] In the famous Yelverton marriage case, where the validity of a marriage was litigated through Ireland, Scotland and England for a number of years in the 1860s, the abandoned 'wife', Theresa Yelverton, argued her case in person when the matter finally came before the house of lords on appeal in 1867. She

---

2 H. Button, 'The first women lawyers' in *Gazette of the Incorporated Law Society of Ireland* (October 1990). **3** *Irish Law Times and Solicitors Journal,* 5 March 1898.

addressed their Lordships in a firm clear voice, which became loud and impassioned when she adverted to the unfortunate position in which she was placed by the conflicting decision that had been given upon her case.[4]

The granddaughter of Richard Brinsley Sheridan, Caroline Norton, made her own defence in *Thripps* v. *Norton* (1853) to the court's applause. In *A letter to the queen* (1855) she wrote succinctly of her status as a married woman:

> I exist and I suffer; but the law denies my existence.

Caroline Norton succeeded in improving the laws affecting married women in several substantial ways, and significantly influenced the Divorce and Matrimonial Causes Act, 1857.

The *Law Times* of 16 April 1904 refers to a case under the Truck Acts in which a Miss Squire, one of the lay inspectors under the Factories Acts, not only issued the summons but also conducted the prosecution of the case herself. This did not please counsel for the defendants. The journal remarked that counsel's objections that the Home Office did not, as a rule, procure legal assistance in the prosecution of such cases, were 'very reasonable' under the circumstances, 'for their own sake as well as his'. At the same time Miss Squire was described as a lady of large experience and great ability.

In the mid-nineteenth century, many judges were prepared to decide that women were mentally inferior and not suited to law or public office. In *Queen* v. *Crosthwaite*,[5] a female applicant successfully contended that she should be eligible for the office of town commissioner. The decision was reversed on appeal. Baron Fitzgerald unapologetically remarked:

> Having regard to every one of the reasons of the common law, the subordination of sex, the inferiority of bodily ability, and the mental inferiority, in the sense explained, as well as to decency and decorum,

---

4 *Irish Law Times and Solicitors Journal,* 22 June 1867. The house of lords ordered the sum of £150 to be paid to Mrs Yelverton to enable her to carry on the appeal. See *Yelverton* v. *Longworth* (or *Yelverton*) (1864) 4 Macq 145; 11 LT 118; 10 Jur NS 1209; 13 WR 235, HL. 5 (1867) 17 1 CLR 157.

> I am not sorry that I am able, on the best consideration I have been
> able to give to the case, to come to the conclusion that this judgment
> ought to be reversed.

In 1879, the first woman applied to the English Law Society to sit the
solicitors' examinations. Her application was dismissed, as was Margaret
Hall's in 1900 when she applied to the Law Society of Scotland. Hall
challenged the decision to reject her application. Her case failed, the judge
ruling that an act of Parliament was required to allow women to become
solicitors.

While women's exclusion from the profession led to litigation in
England against the Law Society it does not appear to have given rise to
much controversy in Ireland. In 1901 a Miss Weir Johnston enquired
whether a lady could become a member of the Irish Bar. The Benchers
replied that a lady could not enter the Inns as a student nor become a
member of the Bar. The *Irish Law Times* of 2 November 1901 recorded that
the Benchers 'felt themselves obliged to follow British precedent'. There is
no record around this time of any application for admission as an
apprentice being made to the Law Society by a woman in Ireland.

Until 1919, the position remained in Britain and Ireland that women
were not permitted to enter the legal profession (although it was possible
to obtain a law degree). There were two main arguments for this. The first
was financial – there was a fear that the admission of women to the
profession would lead to overcrowding. The second was prejudice – in a
circular argument, it was contended that enormous work needed to be
done to address prejudice against women in the profession and such
prejudice needed to be overcome before women could be permitted entry.
Added to these 'public' arguments, females were considered intellectually
inferior and too delicate to work in a profession where they might come
up against such unpleasant matters as murder, rape and grave-robbing.

The movement for the reform of university education in Ireland so as
to guarantee equality of opportunity for women undoubtedly assisted
women in their campaign to open the legal profession. The Association of
Women Graduates, founded in 1902, consistently demanded that women
be admitted to all the benefits and privileges of university education which

were available to men. Trinity College, Dublin (the University of Dublin) admitted women to full membership in January 1904, long before any comparable English institution. The controversy regarding their entry mainly centered on the issue of whether women should be housed in another college of the multi-collegiate university. Women were subject to a 'six o'clock rule' and had separate lunch facilities.

In 1908, the Irish Universities Act established that female students of its three constituent colleges had equal status and could sit for degree examinations of the university.

That there were greater opportunities for the advancement of women lawyers in the United States than in Ireland is illustrated by the story of Mary O'Toole who was born and reared in Hacketstown, County Carlow. She emigrated to America in 1891, aged 16, and set about educating herself by studying at night. She took a course in stenography and for five years was a reporter for the surrogate's court, Steuben County (the first woman to hold that position). She then became the first woman to attain the high post of judge in the municipal court of Washington. The *Irish Law Times* of 8 August 1931 records that Judge Mary O'Toole visited Ireland with the American and Canadian Bar Associations. It is likely that this visit reminded Judge O'Toole that her move to the US had probably served to advance her far more quickly within the legal profession than had she stayed in Ireland.

EARLY PIONEERS – GWYNETH BEBB AND GEORGINA FROST

In December 1912 Gwyneth Bebb (who had had a brilliant academic career) and three other Oxbridge women (Karin Costeloe, Maud Ingram and Lucy Nettlefold) applied to the English Law Society to sit the solicitors' examinations. In the usual manner, they were turned down and their fees were returned. All four issued writs against the Society in what was to become a widely discussed case: *Bebb* v. *The Law Society*.[6]

The action was heard in July 1913 before Joyce J in the Chancery Division. The case turned on whether the intention behind the Solicitors Act, 1843

6 [1914] 1 Ch. 286; see H. Kirk, *Portrait of a profession* (London, 1976), pp 110f.

was to exclude women from becoming solicitors. The act of 1843 provided that any 'person' with the requisite qualifications was entitled to train to be a solicitor. Each of the four applicants had the requisite qualifications. They sought a declaration that a woman was a 'person' within the meaning of the 1843 act and was therefore entitled to be admitted to the preliminary examination of the Law Society.

Counsel for the Law Society argued that a woman was not a 'person', relying on the long-established principle at common law that no woman should hold a public office. Counsel for the women argued that the office of an attorney or solicitor was not a public office but a private profession and that therefore women were not disqualified.

The women's action failed. In due course the matter came before the court of appeal. The Law Society was faced with the problem that the Interpretation Act, 1889, section 1, provided that the masculine pronoun included the feminine and that on that footing legislation about admissions and education applied to women as well as to men. The court of appeal was not prepared to discard a practice of very long standing on the strength of the Interpretation Act. The court, in dismissing their appeal, held that the disability prohibiting women from entering the legal profession had not been addressed by the 1843 act. Cozen-Hardy MR concluded:

> in point of intelligence and education and competency women – and in particular the applicant here, who is a distinguished Oxford student – are at least equal to a great many, and, probably, far better than many, of the candidates who will come up for examination, but that is really not for us to consider. Our duty is to consider and, so far as we can, to ascertain what the law is, and I disclaim absolutely any right to legislate in a matter of this kind. In my opinion that is for Parliament, and not for this Court.

Five years later, a courageous Irish woman, Georgina Frost of Sixmile-bridge, County Clare, challenged the decision of the lord lieutenant not to appoint her clerk of the petty sessions for the district of Sixmilebridge and Newmarket-on-Fergus.

The petty sessions was a court of summary jurisdiction the functions of which were transferred with the establishment of the new courts system in

1924 to the District Court. Frost's father had been clerk of the petty sessions for Sixmilebridge and Newmarket-on-Fergus and she had often assisted him in his duties. In 1915, the magistrates unanimously elected her to succeed her father in office. However, the lord lieutenant would not approve her appointment on the grounds that a woman was not a 'person' within the meaning of the Petty Sessions Acts.

In an unprecedented act of support, the magistrates awarded Frost a temporary contract for one year to allow her to fight her case. Frost's high-powered legal team included T.M. Healy KC (afterwards first governor-general of the Irish Free State). Her case came before Barton J in the chancery division of the High Court.[7] In rejecting her application he commented:

> The reason of the modern decisions disqualifying women from public office has not been inferiority of intellect or discretion, which few people would now have the hardihood to allege. It has been rather rested upon considerations of decorum, and upon the unfitness of certain painful and exacting duties in relation to the finer qualities of women.

The decision of the High Court was upheld by a majority of the Court of Appeal. However, it is discernible from the judgments of the Court of Appeal that the majority felt that while they were precluded by statute from confirming the appointment of women to office, the general disqualification of women at common law no longer existed. In this respect, judges in Ireland displayed greater sensitivity than their English counterparts.

Undaunted, Frost appealed to the house of lords. By the time her appeal was heard on 27 April 1920, the Sex Disqualification (Removal) Act, 1919 had become law and there was no legal bar to Frost holding the office of clerk of the petty sessions. The lord chancellor, Lord Birkenhead, recommended that the lord lieutenant grant retrospective approval and the appeal was decided on that basis. In an unquoted introduction to the decision it is reputed that Lord Birkenhead turned to Frost's counsel and

---

7 *Frost* v. *the King* [1919] 1 IR 81.

said, 'We are going to let Georgie stay.' Frost was the first woman to hold public office in the United Kingdom of Great Britain and Ireland.

The house of lords decision was not officially reported at the time. In the *Weekly Notes* being Notes of Cases heard and determined by the house of lords, an asterisk appears in front of the case denoting the intention that it should not appear in the Law Reports, although in honour of Frost's pioneering work the case was reported in *Irish Law Reports Monthly* [2000] 1 ILRM 479.

SOLICITORS (QUALIFICATION OF WOMEN) BILL, 1914

Buoyed by the unconvincing arguments of the Law Society in *Bebb* v. *The Law Society*, women continued to campaign for legislation to abolish their exclusion from the legal profession. In early 1914, J.W. Hills (counsel in *Bebb*) and two other solicitors in the house of commons introduced a bill to qualify women for admission to the roll of solicitors. The Solicitors (Qualification of Women) Bill, 1914 had one clause as follows:

> A woman shall not be disqualified by sex or marriage from being admitted as a solicitor or from acting or practising as a solicitor under the Solicitors Act, 1843 and the Acts amending the same and the other enactments for the time being in force relating to solicitors.

The *Irish Law Times* of 12 March 1914 records that the bill was not to extend to Scotland or Ireland and questions why, if women were to be admitted to the legal profession at all, they were to be excluded from the Bar:

> One would have imagined that it was in the 'brawling courts' to use Tennyson's phrase, that most of the leaders of the new feminist movement would seek to find a sphere of activity.

The bill was passed by the house of lords in March 1914. A Committee to Obtain the Opening of the Legal Profession to Women was established to progress the bill through the commons. It issued a publication setting out its case in favour of the 1914 bill arguing, among other things, that despite popular belief, the profession was not unsuited to women because of the occasional case which was painful and unpleasant. The committee pointed out that at that time women were engaged almost exclusively in rescue and preventive work and it had never been suggested that contact with social evils contaminated them. Moreover, as prisoners and witnesses, women had to appear in the criminal courts and it surely could not be wrong for responsible women in the solicitor's profession to face unpleasantness in order to help other women.

On 8 March 1914, a deputation from the committee met with the lord chancellor, Lord Haldane, to see if he could be encouraged to use his influence with the Government to secure time for the discussion of the one-clause bill. The deputation, which included the four plaintiffs from *Bebb*, reminded the chancellor that practically every university in England admitted women to the law degree. For thirty years women had practised as lawyers in the United States and other countries including several British colonies. Women could be doctors and accountants, could institute prosecutions as factory inspectors and were commissioners under the Mental Deficiency Act. The chancellor was also informed that women wanted to be solicitors not only because it afforded them the opportunity of exercising their talents, but also because of the advantage that would accrue to other women in being able to consult a member of their own sex in times of distress and difficulty.

The deputation was assured by the chancellor that he was in favour of the principle of the bill and that he had consulted the Prime Minister and the law officers of the Crown who were all in favour of the measure.

However, the City of London Solicitors Company (consisting of 200 practising solicitors) resolved to oppose the introduction of females to the profession. Similarly the council of the Law Society formally resolved that it would not welcome the removal of any existing disabilities which prevented women being admitted as solicitors.

The view of English solicitors at that time seemed also to be the view of their Irish counterparts. The *Irish Law Times* of 11 April 1914 recorded that the deputation had been received by the lord chancellor but noted:

Although the present generation may see lady barristers and lady solicitors, we do not believe any benefit will accrue to the ladies themselves, the profession or the public.

Women fought hard to bring their cause to debate. The *Irish Law Times* of 23 May 1914 noted that a lively discussion was proceeding in the columns of the *Law Journal* on the 1914 bill. The same *Irish Law Times* noted that if women were to be admitted as solicitors, it would be their duty to select 'counsel to whom the affairs of their client should be entrusted'. Foreshadowing *Adam's Rib*, it expressed alarm that if a competent woman solicitor were to be 'happily married' to a competent barrister and the husband barrister was briefed on the other side, the 'domestic arrangements' may not be advantageous. On the other hand, it was conceded that if both were on the same side 'all the points could be thoroughly considered at home'.

Lord Finlay (appointed lord chancellor in 1916) was also against the bill:

I do not believe that the active practice of a profession is compatible with the proper work of a woman which, after all, is that of a wife and a mother attending to her family.

Although the 1914 bill was passed by the house of lords it did not survive the commons. Unfortunately, the law journals and press of that time do not address the passage of the bill in any detail – war and military issues dominated most of the publications.

The Representation of the People Act, 1918 enfranchised all women over the age of thirty who were householders, the wives of householders, or university graduates. Although it did not meet the aspirations of women reformers, the tide had started to turn.

The Woman's Emancipation Bill of March 1919 was a private member's bill introduced with the support of the Labour Party. One of its main objectives was to remove disqualifications based on sex or marriage in relation to 'any civil or judicial office or place of profit on trust under His Majesty …'. The bill suffered a government defeat on third reading.

SEX DISQUALIFICATION (REMOVAL) ACT, 1919

A large number of solicitors and articled clerks in the UK served with the Forces during the First World War. Many members of the Irish solicitors' profession in Ireland were also recorded by the *Irish Law Times* of 22 May 1915 as 'serving in His Majesty's Forces'.

During the war, with the men away, women came forward to fill their roles. R. Verkaik noted in his article 'Girl Power'[8] that while Britain was at war, Lloyd George's government was sensitive to anything that might affect the morale of the largely conscript army fighting in France and Belgium. It was regarded as underhand to pass a law which might take jobs from the soldier solicitors who would have to return to civilian life after the war.

However, due to the valuable work carried out by women, public opinion shifted at the end of the war. As a concession to women's significant war performance, and very likely due to the valiant efforts of pioneers associated with Bebb and Frost, the Barristers and Solicitors (Qualification of Women) Bill, 1919 was published.

Once again, it was intended that this bill would not apply to Ireland. However, the *Irish Law Times* of 14 June 1919 recorded that a letter was sent by the Irish Women Citizens' Association to the Irish members of parliament requesting them to do all in their power to secure the inclusion of Ireland in the measure. Favourable responses were received and appropriate pressure was brought to bear at Westminster.

In the same way that women were seeking admission to the legal profession, they were also calling for equal access to voting, public functions, jury service and civil posts. The prosaically titled Sex Disqualification (Removal) Bill, 1919 was introduced to replace the Barristers and Solicitors (Qualification of Women) Bill, 1919. It was passed by the house of commons and the house of lords and became law in Britain and Ireland in 1919. The act in section 1 provided that a person should not be disqualified by sex or marriage from the exercise of any public function or from being appointed to or holding any civil or judicial office or post, or from entering or assuming or carrying on any civil profession or vocation.

8 *Gazette* 94/48, 17 December 1997.

Section 2 dealt with the admission as solicitors of women who had qualified at universities which did not admit women to degrees. Section 3 removed any obstacle in the statutes or charter of any university to the admission of women to membership or to degrees of that institution, although it did not place any duty on universities to admit women.

The effect of the 1919 act was quickly seen in Britain and Ireland. Women became liable for jury service; they could hold office as justices of the peace; they could be appointed to various public bodies which had formerly been exclusively male preserves; and they gained a right of access to occupations which had hitherto been denied them. As an anti-discrimination statute, the 1919 act had considerable practical impact after it became law although it must be said that as an instrument for challenging sex discrimination it became a dead letter.

The *Gazette* of the English Law Society recorded that six women lodged articles of clerkship for registration immediately on the passing of the act and, within four years, the Society's ruling council found itself having to designate a number of rooms at Chancery Lane, including the coal store, for conversion into ladies' cloakrooms.

Within the legal profession, attitudes towards women began slowly to adapt to their presence. The *Irish Law Times* of 14 February 1920 recorded that the president of the English Law Society spoke at a special meeting on 30 January 1920 to welcome the ladies who had registered articles of clerkship to solicitors. He hoped

> before long to see them fully qualified and their abilities occupied and tried in good practice … helping their sisters and extending a helping hand to their brother men.

For some time the *Gazette* of the English Law Society listed the names of women under the heading of 'Gentlemen Applying for Admission'. At the annual provincial meeting in 1922 the president humorously suggested that women would be better employed at home bringing up future generations of solicitors of the male sex.

The first Irish women students were admitted to the King's Inns in January 1920. In February 1920 a woman sat as magistrate for the first time at Dundrum, County Dublin, and in January 1921 the first woman juror sat in Dublin.

Mary Dorothea Heron, Ireland's first woman solicitor, was admitted in 1923.

A year after the passing of the 1919 act, in an article for *Women's Employment Magazine*, Maud Crofts (née Maud Ingram, one of the applicants in *Bebb* and one of the first women solicitors in the UK) wrote:

> Though there is undoubtedly prejudice still to be overcome, the fact remains that women have at last succeeded in obtaining entrance into a profession hitherto one of the most closely guarded in the world – their future in it, in the last resort, can only depend on the special contribution they are able to make to the public good.

It was not an easy time for fledgling female solicitors and only the wealthy or the well connected were able to consider practice. An article in the feminist newspaper *Women's Leader* in 1923 recognised that it would be foolish for a woman to start a practice alone. However, having won the battle to have access to the legal profession, women struggled to ensure that their presence within the profession would be felt. In 1923, a group of women in the UK formed the 1919 Club to ensure that women lawyers had a collective voice. It was also charged with the more mundane task of considering such conundrums as should women wear hats in court as men did not.

The club was reformed in 1969 to become the UK Association of Women Solicitors, which still flourishes. There is also an Association of Women Solicitors in Northern Ireland.

A DEVELOPMENT TO VIEW WITH 'CONSIDERABLE INTEREST AND CURIOSITY'

The president of the Law Society of Ireland wrote in 1921 that the admission of women to the solicitor's profession was a development which 'will be viewed with considerable interest and curiosity'.[9] This interest and

---

9 C. Gamble, *Solicitors in Ireland, 1607–1921* (Dublin, 1921).

curiosity was kindled early on by the emergence of the first female apprentice solicitor in Ireland in 1920 and the first female solicitor in 1923.

Ireland

Mary Dorothea Heron, the first woman to be admitted a solicitor in Ireland, was a graduate in classics of Queen's University, Belfast. She obtained second place and a special certificate at the final examination for solicitors' apprentices held in January 1923. Her name went on the roll of solicitors on 17 April 1923. She was apprenticed to her uncle, T.M. Heron, Mayfair, Belfast, and was the first woman to pass the final examination for admission as a solicitor in Ireland. Mary Dorothea Heron continued to work in her uncle's firm until around 1946. She mainly did probate work.

It is interesting from today's perspective that Heron was not listed as practising in the Northern Ireland section of the law directory. However, there was a convention which was widely followed, until the Society adopted a stricter practice in 1974, that solicitors who were not principals in a firm and who did not appear in court need not take out practising certificates. There would have been a perception that women solicitors were largely engaged as assistants in conveyancing or probate work and accordingly many of them did not take out practising certificates.

In 1920 Helena Mary Early of Swords, County Dublin, secured first place at the preliminary examination for solicitors' apprentices, having the honour to become the first woman in the United Kingdom under the Irish Solicitors Act to become bound for the short term of three years apprenticeship. During her apprenticeship, she was elected first lady auditor of the Solicitors' Apprentices Debating Society and for her inaugural address in November 1921 she chose the topic 'The Irish Exiles Abroad'. The *Irish Law Times* of 12 November 1921 reported that the lord chief justice of Ireland paid warm tribute to the auditor's address, although he did remark that

> We must always be glad to see Irishwomen taking their place beside Irishmen in the learned professions, but I think that even from what we have heard from Miss Early we must come to the conclusion that the hopes of the happiness and prosperity of the Irish race depend upon the Irish mother.

Helena Early qualified and was admitted as a solicitor on 25 June 1923. She practised with her brother in Dublin and continued for many years to appear in the courts. She was described in the *Irish Law Times* of 28 July 1923 as 'the first lady in Ireland practising as a solicitor'.

It was not until October 1970, almost fifty years later, that there was another woman auditor of the Solicitors' Apprentices Debating Society. Marking an historic event, Helena Early attended a meeting in October 1970 when Elizabeth A. Ryan of Killenaule, County Tipperary, was elected auditor.

England

In December 1922, it was reported by a daily UK newspaper that for the first time the Law Society's list of those who had passed the final examinations for solicitors contained the names of women. The *Gazette* of the Law Society carried no mention of this, a reflection perhaps that prejudice against the entry of women to the profession had not been entirely overcome by the 1919 act.

Maud Isabel Crofts (née Ingram), one of the women pioneers involved in *Bebb*, is widely regarded as the UK's first woman solicitor. She was certainly the first woman to take out a practising certificate. She had considerable experience of social work and industrial conditions and practised until 1955. Many of her clients were members of the women's suffrage movement in which she had been prominent.

Cambridge graduate Carrie Morrison is stated to be the first woman to be admitted to the roll in 1922. The Association of Women Solicitors recorded in its newsletter of 1997 that

> Carrie Morrison was admitted as Britain's first woman solicitor, immediately followed by the three others [Maud Crofts, Mary E. Pickup and Mary E. Sykes] who chased her down Chancery Lane.

In 1997, the Association of Women Solicitors recreated the race at Chancery Lane to mark its 75th anniversary.

Morrison entered private practice with her husband. In 1928, she was the first woman solicitor to handle a divorce under the Poor Persons Rules, a forerunner of legal aid in the UK. In 1931, she was the first woman to read a paper to the Law Society at a provincial meeting in Folkestone.

A slow beginning

Although women had won the right to become solicitors, the number entering the profession in Ireland during the 1920s and 1930s was very small. The requirement that an articled clerk should pay a training premium made it very difficult for women to become solicitors. For many years, most women solicitors came from professional families and most likely from families where their fathers, brothers or husbands were either barristers or solicitors.

A woman who qualified in 1937 was Síle MacBride, niece of Séan MacBride. She won the Findlater Scholarship for property. Poet Paul Durcan is her son.

Eileen Kennedy, the first woman judge in Ireland, was born in Dublin. She qualified as a solicitor in 1947 and entered into partnership with her brother in the family firm (there were four solicitors in her immediate family – father, daughter and two sons). In 1964 she was appointed the first woman judge in Ireland, as Justice of the District Court, and was also appointed Justice of the Metropolitan Children's Court.[10] Chair of the committee which produced the *Kennedy Report* in 1971, she campaigned most effectively for children's rights for many years.

There is little information available regarding female solicitors in the early decades of the twentieth century in Ireland. The *Irish Law Times* of 17 April 1948 included a short article describing Blanaid Ó Brolcháin, solicitor and member of the panel of *Information Please* (a popular radio programme on Radio Éireann at that time). The article remarks that there were 'many' women solicitors at that time, but not many Blanaid Ó Brolcháins. She is described as 'petite and vivacious, having none of the traditional attributes of the blue-stocking' and as being 'the absolute antithesis of what I always imagined a woman solicitor to be'. The article does not expand to give us a more thorough insight into the average female solicitor in 1948.

10 Many Irish women solicitors have been appointed to the District Court since then, among them Maura Roche, Mary Kotsonouris, Mary Martin, Gillian Hussey, Thelma King, Mary O'Halloran, Clare Leonard, Catherine Murphy, Mary Collins and Mary Devins.

Other clearly 'not average' solicitors admitted in 1948 were Carmel Killeen and Frances Mary Callan. Killeen graduated with a BA (Legal and Political Science) and LLB from University College Dublin. She spent most of her professional career in the local government legal service where she became deputy law agent. In 1975 she was elected to the council of the Law Society and was elected junior vice-president for the year 1985 to 1986. Mary Callan from Boyle practised in her father's firm and in McCann White & FitzGerald as it then was. She later entered the religious order of the Sainte Union and went on to become principal of Our Lady's Bower school in Athlone (twice) as well as provincial of the Order. Retired since 1992, Sister Christopher (Callan's religious name) is living in Athlone.

Thelma King, another outstanding solicitor, graduated from Trinity College Dublin in 1949. She started practice in 1950 having obtained a Gold Medal in English composition as an apprentice. King practised in Hayes & Sons, where she became a partner in 1955. In 1989 she was appointed judge of the District Court.

In an essay entitled 'Attorneys and Solicitors in Ireland'[11] the secretary of the Law Society, Eric A. Plunkett, noted that from 1923 to 1953 only 107 women had been admitted to the solicitors' profession. He stated that

> the number, however, is increasing, although in proportions still too small to cause alarm to the advocates of male predominance in the profession.

This comment was made with some justification – a majority of the 107 women who were admitted by 1953 did not take out annual practising certificates.

Plunkett commented that if the trend for women to take out annual practising certificates continued, the proportion would be considerably higher in the next generation. However, the proportion did not start to increase until the mid-sixties. In 1960, no female solicitor was admitted to the roll. From 1961 to 1969, only 39 female solicitors were admitted to the

---

11 *Record of the centenary of the charter of the Incorporated Law Society of Ireland, 1852–1952* (1953).

profession. By way of contrast, 273 men were admitted over the same period.

It was customary at that time for women solicitors to cover their head while in court. Indeed it was not unknown for female apprentices to carry a large white handkerchief to avoid being caught out. Eileen Kennedy was the first woman lawyer to sit in court with her head uncovered.

Numbers begin to rise

The influx in the numbers of women entering both branches of the profession began in the 1970s and early 1980s. This was probably as a result of a combination of the women's movement and the expansion of higher education. It was during the 1970s that a woman successfully impugned the constitutionality of the provisions of the Juries Act, 1927 relating to the preparation of lists of jurors. Women were exempted from jury service although they could apply for insertion of their names on the appropriate list.[12]

Around this time a UK Royal Commission conducted a number of surveys of the legal profession in England, Wales and Northern Ireland. These showed among other things a yearly increase in the numbers of women practising law; that a higher proportion of women than of men left within the first ten years of practice; that few women sat on the governing bodies of the profession; and that the earnings of women in practice for between nine and fifteen years fell behind those of their comparable male colleagues.

It was during the 1970s that Moya Quinlan, later elected first woman president of the Law Society, was appointed chair of the Blackhall Place premises committee. Not only the profession but Dubliners owe her an enormous debt of gratitude for having successfully secured the future of Blackhall Place as the Law Society's headquarters.

Quinlan was elected to the highest office in the Law Society in 1980. She had been admitted as Moya Dixon in July 1946. Like many female solicitors, she applied to the Society for re-admission on the basis of her married name in February 1953. Moya Quinlan is a partner in Dixon Quinlan, Dublin.

12 *de Burca* v. *Attorney General* [1976] IR 38.

In May 1981, at the half-yearly general meeting of the Law Society, President Quinlan took the opportunity to welcome the increased number of ladies graduating into the profession and expressed the wish to see the profession have a more caring image towards the individual client. During her presidency Quinlan addressed many topical issues then affecting the profession such as delay in the administration of estates, outdated court procedures, and the state of courthouses throughout the country. Quinlan is known and respected by many generations of lawyers who have appeared before her at the Employment Appeals Tribunal, of which she is a vice-chairman.

The current president of the Law Society, Elma Lynch, is the second woman to have been elected to this post.[13] President Lynch, who is a partner in Daly Lynch Crowe & Morris, Dublin, took up office in November 2001. She was first elected to the Society's council in 1987. A graduate of University College Dublin, Lynch qualified as a solicitor in 1970. She was apprenticed to Benedict J. Daly, Solicitor, Dublin where she was a partner from 1979 to 1981.

Katherine Delahunt, the first woman solicitor appointed to the Circuit Court, was sworn in on 29 November 2001. Delahunt was apprenticed at Vincent & Beatty, Dublin where she became a partner in 1983. A graduate of University College Dublin, Delahunt specialised in litigation, maritime law, employment law and family law.

The table at the end of this chapter gives a snapshot of the total numbers holding practising certificates and the number of women with practising certificates from 1923 to 2000.[14] In the decade from 1970 to 1980, a total of 1652 solicitors were admitted. Of these 479 were women, amounting to 29 per cent of the total admitted. In the period from 1981 to 1990, 1890 solicitors were admitted. Of these 781 were women, amounting to 41 per cent of those admitted. Although there are no definitive figures available, the majority of the women solicitors admitted in these two decades appear to have taken out a practising certificate.

13 Four women to date have been elected president of the Law Society in Northern Ireland: Thomasina McKinney (1978); Margaret Elliot (1990); Antoinette Curran (1988); and Catherine Dixon (1999).   14 The records do not readily disclose the position as at the end of each year. Figures are from the *Law Directories* of the following year which state a cut off date, or from the annual reports which record the position up to 30 September and, since 1984, from Law Society records which indicate the total number of solicitors holding practising certificates as at 31 December in each year.

Since the mid-1990s, the number of women entering the profession and taking out a practising certificate each year has consistently exceeded the number of men. While the Society's *Annual Report* for 1999/2000 identifies that the current gender profile within the profession is 37 per cent female to 63 per cent male, this profile is expected to balance out and to lean in favour of women over the next ten to fifteen years due to the ongoing increase in the number of women entering the profession.

Within a period of ninety years, women have risen to the highest level of the solicitors' profession. They have contributed a richness and diversity to the profession, and to many facets of life in Ireland and outside. From a time when there were few women solicitors in many areas, e.g. commercial law in the early 70s, women are now found practising in all aspects of the law. Many have developed specialist interests in areas as diverse as maritime law, tax, employment and trusts.

Patricia Rickard-Clarke is a partner in McCann FitzGerald specialising in tax planning and trusts. She worked as a senior executive in the Institute of Public Administration before being admitted as a solicitor in 1982. Rickard-Clarke is a member of the Law Society's taxation committee. She was appointed law reform commissioner in 1997. Another woman solicitor who is a law reform commissioner is Marian Shanley. She received her parchment in 1975 and commenced practice in McCann FitzGerald. Shanley is currently involved in legal education with the Law Society.

Some women like Carol Fawsitt and Cliona O'Tuama have set up their own practices. Whilst apprenticed to her father's brother, Boyle Fawsitt, Carol Fawsitt did her apprenticeship at the offices of Fitzpatricks in Dublin. She was admitted to the roll of solicitors in 1980. In April 1987 she established her own practice, Fawsitt & Company, which specialises in employment law and family law. Cliona O'Tuama set up her own practice in London in 1994 concentrating on tax, trusts, probate and charity law. She is well known for her efforts on behalf of Irish solicitors in England and Wales. Due to her successful lobbying, Irish solicitors became entitled to be readmitted in England and Wales as and from January 1991 without any further formalities. O'Tuama's professional career as a solicitor started in 1977 in Ireland, whence she went to Linklaters and Paines, London, in 1987. She founded the Irish Solicitors Bar Association, London, in 1988.

Other women have moved from practice to private or public corporations. Karen Erwin became the first woman executive in the *Irish Times* in 1996 where she is group general counsel responsible for all legal matters, pensions, insurance and corporate affairs. Before that she had been the first woman apprentice in A. & L. Goodbody, Dublin, and in 1980 the first woman partner. Patricia O'Shea is counsel and company secretary at IBM Ireland Ltd, since 1993. She qualified as a solicitor in Ireland in 1986 and in England and Wales in 1990. Raymonde Kelly is manager and legal consultant, legal unit, at Mercer in Dublin, co-founder and first chairman of the Association of Pension Lawyers in Ireland. She worked at McCann FitzGerald between 1976 and 1983 and then as assistant revenue solicitor from 1983 to 1986. In 1990 Frances Cooke became the first woman to be appointed revenue solicitor and the first woman promoted to the grade of assistant secretary in revenue. Cooke enrolled as a solicitor in 1975 having served her apprenticeship to James Fagan. She joined the revenue commissioners as an assistant solicitor in 1981.

In financial services Clare Connellan is associate director of legal services with Bank of Scotland (Ireland) Limited. She was appointed chairman of the Legal Aid Board in 1995, the first solicitor to be appointed to this position and the first woman since Mella Carroll (the first woman appointed to the High Court in 1980). Connellan qualified as a solicitor in 1969. Anne Counihan is a director of the National Treasury Management Agency with responsibility for legal and corporate affairs. She is also in charge of the State's national savings schemes which form part of the national debt. She holds the professional qualification of solicitor both in Ireland and in England, and has been president of the Corporate and Public Services Solicitors Association since it was formed in 1996.

Outside of Ireland, there are many successful women who qualified as solicitors. Karen Banks is legal adviser in the Legal Service of the Commission of the European Communities. She qualified as a solicitor in 1979 and joined the Legal Service of the Commission in 1983. Since 1998 she has been a member of the business law team. Elizabeth Frances Murray has been working for the court of appeals, State of New York, since 1990. She is currently chief legal reference attorney specialising, among other things, in the derivation of common law principles applicable in New York

State. Murray was admitted in 1971 having been apprenticed at McKeever & Son, Dublin.

Connelly and Hilliard's *Gender and the law in Ireland* (1993) contains an insight into women's progression in the legal profession. Women were asked about their own experience of practice and their perception of the experience of women generally in the profession. The outcome of the study suggests a number of reasons why women choose to become solicitors rather than barristers. Many of the participants viewed a career as a solicitor as a more practicable option than a career at the Bar, 'especially for those women who do not have strong family or other connections in the legal world'. Qualities such as ability, a capacity for hard work and a calm temperament were identified as essential in either branch of the profession.

However, the study noted that 'women were perceived as having certain qualities' which were put forward by participants as being particularly relevant to the work of a solicitor'. To be a good solicitor important traits such as patience, persistence, thoroughness, empathy and communication skills were identified. Women were thought by participants to have these traits more commonly than men.

It would be worthwhile to build on this research by soliciting the views of male solicitors. Solicitors in private practice as well as those who have taken their skills to public or private corporations would no doubt be useful to interview also. It would be interesting to have a profile of women's career paths and aspirations. How many choose to practise on their own, or in partnership with one or more other solicitors? How many are employed by a sole practitioner or by a small or large firm? How many in the latter case have aspired to partnership and how many of these have been successful? How many women have chosen to work for corporations, public or private?

Within the solicitors' profession, issues of equal opportunities, for example, in promotion and in partnership, and of equal pay, continue to be relevant to women. In addition, in the case of women who are trying to balance motherhood with a legal career, there are calls to ensure that women have access to flexible work practices. Although progress is being made in these areas, much has still to be achieved.

Such issues are not, of course, confined to women. Women lawyers are affected by the broader equality debate where the focus is moving from equality to diversity, from a focus on groups to a focus on individuals and the work/life balance is important to men and women alike.

Analogous issues are also relevant for women lawyers who happen to be barristers. Approximately 30 per cent of the members of the Law Library are women. Unlike the current trend in the solicitors' profession the number of women called to the Bar in any one year has never exceeded the number of men.

In 1980 a distinguished woman solicitor was called to the Bar, now a High Court judge: Mary Finlay Geoghegan. She graduated from UCD with a degree in mathematics/mathematical physics. She was apprenticed to John Gleeson[15] then a solicitor in practice with Alphonsus Grogan & Company, Dublin. Admitted in 1973, she practised as a solicitor from that year until 1979 at McCann FitzGerald. She became a partner there in 1976. Finlay Geoghegan was admitted as senior counsel in 1988 and was appointed a judge of the High Court in 2002.

From the ranks of the many distinguished women who practise or have practised at the Irish Bar, including such 'greats' as Frances Kyle, Averill Deverell and Dr Frances (Fanny) Elizabeth Moran, there have been many historic or 'first' appointments. Susan Denham was the first woman appointed to the Supreme Court in 1992; Mella Carroll to the High Court in 1980; Catherine McGuinness to the Circuit Court in 1994 (later to the High Court in 1996 and the Supreme Court in 2000). In 1999 Fidelma Macken was sworn in as the first woman judge of the European Court of Justice in its 47-year history. Most recently Maureen Harding Clark has been the first Irish lawyer to be appointed a judge on the UN International Criminal Tribunal for the former Yugoslavia.

Reference must also be made to two women lawyers who in succession have assumed the highest public office in Ireland. Barrister and academic Mary Robinson secured a role in history when she became Ireland's first woman president in 1990. She was subsequently appointed UN Commissioner for Human Rights. In 1997 Mary McAleese, also a barrister and academic, was elected Uachtarán na hÉireann in succession to Mary Robinson.

The early women lawyers were pioneers, women with a mission. At the time, less than ninety years ago, this was to some their offence. To others,

---

15 John Gleeson subsequently returned to the Bar and was later appointed a Circuit Court judge.

and to us today, the perseverance of these women, their resistance to established convention, is an inspiration. That inspiration is still needed in the profession of the twenty-first century.

Let Moya Quinlan, first woman president of the Law Society and role model for generations of women solicitors, have the last word. At a conference in Dublin in December 2000 ('From Pioneers to Presidents and Beyond – Women and Law from two islands in Europe') she said

> … much remains to be done to ensure that in the future all will come to accept as a fact that women are lawyers who just happen to be women.

TABLE

Practising Certificates

Year	Total number of solicitors holding practising certificates	Total number of women holding practising certificates
1923	1,397[1]	nil
1925	999[2]	2[3]
1930	1,032[4]	9[5]
1940	1,420[6]	27[7]
1950	1,374[8]	44[9]
1960	1,335[10]	62[11]
1970	1,349[12]	71[13]
1980	2,150[14]	359[15]
1990	3,529[16]	907[17]
2000	5,551[18]	2,221[18]

1 This number is stated in the Law Directory and includes Northern Ireland solicitors, who are not included in the figures for later years given in this table.   2 Annual Report to 30 September 1925. 3 Law Directory to 17 December 1925.   4 Annual Report to 30 September 1930.   5 Law Directory to 17 December 1930.   6 Annual Report to 30 September 1940.   7 Law Directory to 17 December 1940.   8 Annual Report to 30 September 1950.   9 Law Directory to 30 November 1950. 10 Annual Report to 30 September 1960.   11 Law Directory to 10 November 1960.   12 Annual Report to 30 September 1970.   13 Law Directory to 2 December 1970.   14 Annual Report to 30 September 1980.   15 Law Directory to 30 September 1980.   16 The Society's figures at 31 December 1990.   17 Law Directory to 1 December 1990.   18 The Society's figures at 31 December 2000. See also footnote 14 on page 115 above.

Note: Until 1974 assistant solicitors, whether women or men, who did not appear in court were not required to hold practising certificates. Up to 1974 there would thus have been women solicitors working as assistants in firms, doing conveyancing and probate work, without holding practising certificates, who would not be included in either column of the table above.

The modern era: Blackhall Place, rights of audience and court dress, delays and reforms in the legal system

EAMONN G. HALL

This chapter and the next chapter chronicle certain legal issues facing solicitors, as individual members of a learned profession, and the Law Society, as the institution representing and regulating solicitors in Ireland.[1] The period under consideration starts from the 1970s and covers a third of a century, a time of profound challenge and change in Ireland. Of course, each generation considers its own era to be a period of change without precedent. But historians will look at the last thirty years in Ireland as a period of heightened and quickened change.

Law and lawyers exist in a time frame. As the late 1960s and early 1970s are a starting point for themes considered in these chapters, it is appropriate, for perspective purposes, to refer to some specific moments of time at the commencement of that period. On 2 February 1967, Donogh O'Malley, Minister for Education, authorised University College Dublin to proceed to build a new arts and administration block on the Belfield campus. In this context, a generational defining point for some (UCD-educated) solicitors may be those who were introduced to formal legal studies in UCD at Earlsfort Terrace, Dublin, rather than on the Belfield campus. On 21 July 1967, J.J. Horgan (of the firm M.J. Horgan & Sons), Cork solicitor and distinguished public figure, died. He had been the coroner at the inquest on the *Lusitania* in 1915 and had significantly influenced the Cork City Management Act, 1929 and the development of the county management system in Ireland.

1 The author is grateful to Jim Ivers, the director general of the Society from 1973 to 1990, who has written a chronological account of the activities of the Society during the period 1973 to 1995; this account is available in the library of the Society.

In 1970, the High Court consisted of the president and six judges, one more judge than in 1925. In 2001, the High Court consisted of the president and twenty-five judges. One word characterises the period under review in terms of law, lawyers and the Law Society: 'growth', reflecting social, economic, educational and cultural change.

During the last three decades of the twentieth century and up to the present, the Society, its presidents and directors general have taken an increasingly prominent role as spokesmen and leaders of the profession. Of course, in the ancien regime, such was the esteem of the office of president that several former presidents received knighthoods from the palace in London for their service to the law. Notable among those presidents were Sir Richard J.T. Orpen (1860–76), Sir William Findlater (1877–78 and 1896–97), Sir Patrick Maxwell (1886–87), Sir William Fry (1895–96), Sir George Roche (1900), and Sir Augustine F. Baker (1902–03). It is apt here to refer to a recent recipient of a knighthood for distinguished services to his fellow man, the solicitor and businessman Sir Anthony O'Reilly.

Some presidents of the Society may even be on a possible beatification list! Arthur Cox, president of the Society during the centenary celebrations in 1952, was ordained a priest by Archbishop John Charles McQuaid in December 1963, and subsequently served on the Jesuit African Missions, before dying in 1965 following a car accident.

A notable feature of secretaries and directors general of the Society has been, in general, their longevity of office. Edward Iles held office from 1841 to 1864; John Hawksley Goddard served for 24 years up to 1888; William George Wakely held the office from 1888 to 1942, a period of 54 years, and incidentally is noted for an act of bravery in rescuing the president's chain of office from the Four Courts in 1922 at grave personal risk. Eric Plunkett served from 1942 to 1973; James Ivers from 1973 to 1990; Noel Ryan from 1990 to 1994 and Ken Murphy from 1995 to the present time. These seven men have straddled a period of almost 161 years.

The presidents and directors general, particularly in recent times, have been ambassadors at large, not only on behalf of solicitors but to a certain extent on behalf of the legal arm of government in Ireland. Such is the demanding schedule of the office that today the presidency is almost a full-time position. The president travels many parts of Ireland, North and South, on official engagements to local bar associations and represents the Society at meetings of lawyers, whether those of our nearest neighbour, Great Britain, or further afield among the chief bar associations of the world.

THE SOCIETY'S HEADQUARTERS AT BLACKHALL PLACE

The story of how the Society acquired its headquarters at Blackhall Place, Dublin, and carried out sensitive refurbishments is worthy of a book in itself. In fact, in March 1990, the Society in conjunction with the Irish Architectural Archive published a book entitled *New lease of life: the Law Society's building at Blackhall Place* written by Seán O'Reilly and Nicholas K. Robinson. The book was published during the presidency of the late Ernest J. Margetson, and provides a record of the history of the building whose original and official title was 'The Hospital and Free School of King Charles, the Second Dublin', shortened to the King's Hospital, whose charter dates from 1671. Maurice Craig in his *Dublin, 1660–1860: a social and architectural history* (1952) described this building as 'one of the most beautiful and, in its way, original' of Dublin's major buildings. Designed by Thomas Ivory (*c.*1732–86), one of Ireland's greatest architects, Blackhall Place (as we colloquially call the headquarters of the Society) was inspired by, and modelled on, the Royal Hospital, Kilmainham.

By the middle of the 1960s, the Solicitors' Buildings at the Four Courts were proving inadequate for the expanding activities of the Society. In fact, outside premises were used for lectures for students. A casual conversation over lunch was to offer a solution, when Kevin I. Nowlan, assistant town planning officer with Dublin Corporation and head of town planning at University College, Dublin, remarked to Peter Prentice, a member of the council of the Society, that professional bodies such as the Law Society should interest themselves in some of Dublin's old buildings as head-quarters citing, as an example, the King's Hospital School which had then been on the market for some time. Interestingly, the prospectus for the building which was for sale by private treaty read: 'The sale of this property gives an opportunity to a government or local authority or to a national or international religious order, institution, commercial or industrial concern to take over an unusually well maintained and unique example of Georgian architecture.'

The council of the Society appointed a committee consisting of Peter Prentice, Desmond Moran, Bruce St. J. Blake, P.C. Moore and Norman Spendlove to investigate the possibility of obtaining additional premises for the Society. The committee recommended the purchase of the King's Hospital. Peter Prentice proposed a motion at a special meeting of council of the Society on 3 July 1968, seconded by John Jermyn, that the Society purchase the King's Hospital for the sum of £105,000. The motion was carried unanimously and a contract was executed on 9 July 1968 following a structural report by Sir Hugh Molony, consulting engineer. Completion date was to be 31 July 1970 allowing the existing school some time to relocate to Palmerstown, County Dublin. The president of the Society, Patrick Noonan, in his address at the ordinary general meeting of the Society in November 1968 noted that the Society looked forward to the day when 'we will find ourselves in the building which will provide within its walls all our needs, organisational, educational, business and social and where at last our president will find a place to park his car'. President Eunan McCarron in his address to the general meeting of the Society in May 1969 in Killarney expressed the desire to have in the new headquarters 'the first non-denominational chapel in the country'. Noting that there would be 'no problem with car parking', he was also pleased to report that future presidents would have 'at their disposal a presidential suite'. According to President McCarron, the 'pleasant grounds' adjoining the building could be used for various sporting activities by apprentices and for 'peaceful contemplation by elderly gentlemen' like himself!

Few great projects run smoothly and the Blackhall Place project was no exception. A special premises committee was set up with Peter Prentice in the chair to plan for the new building. The cost of funding the purchase and alterations was estimated at a committee meeting on 11 June 1969 at £325,000. Many views were expressed by solicitors, apprentices and others on what was required. One practitioner, conscious of the needs of apprentices, wrote to the Society arguing for a function room at Blackhall Place 'where dances and functions could be held of a private nature for the apprentices on a profit-making basis with the view in mind of sending final-year apprentices to the summer law schools throughout Europe. If as anticipated Ireland is to become a part of the common market, then it would be a good thing to plan somewhat in advance and attune the minds of our senior apprentices …'.

Some solicitors expressed concern about expenditure on the proposed new headquarters. Costs escalated on the Blackhall Place project to such an extent that by late 1971 there was strong pressure within the Society to abandon the entire project. Peter Prentice was elected president of the Society in 1973 and Moya Quinlan was appointed chair of the Blackhall Place premises committee in that year. Both continued to explore all avenues of financing and in October 1974 the council of the Society agreed in principle that the Society would 'move by degrees' to the premises at Blackhall Place while still retaining the existing premises at the Four Courts. Protracted negotiations in relation to the sale of the Solicitors' Buildings in the Four Courts to the Bar ended in 1977.

O'Reilly and Robinson in their book *New lease of life* paid a handsome tribute to Peter Prentice and Moya Quinlan on the achievement of securing Blackhall Place as the Society's headquarters:

> It had not been easy; indeed the parallels with the 1770s are striking: it had been necessary for Peter Prentice, Moya Quinlan and their colleagues to demonstrate the same qualities of tenacity and fortitude that had carried the day for Sir Thomas Blackhall and the founding governors. Then, as now, not every compromise forced by financial considerations provided the best solution to aspects of the building; nevertheless taken as a whole they secured the future of Thomas Ivory's great building and the old boys of the school, solicitors and Dubliners alike will be proud of it for generations to come.

The opening of Blackhall Place

Wednesday, 14 June 1978 was an important day in the history of the Society. President Joseph Dundon in his address on the occasion of the official opening of the headquarters of the Society at Blackhall Place stated that the day marked the completion of what must surely be one of the greatest undertakings in the history of the Society. The beautiful premises would provide members of the Society with an administrative head-quarters, a law school and a meeting place for all occasions and purposes.

The president noted that the Blackhall Place premises would provide facilities for a law school run on the most modern lines 'which will fully meet the demands of the Irish people for the services which this profession will continue to provide on an increasing scale during the last decades of the twentieth century and into the next.' He noted that the Society's critics, for their own reasons, chose to ignore the fact that the solicitors' profession was a young, vigorous and growing profession whose number had increased steadily from 1,300 in 1964 to over 2,000 then, with projections, which he said had been published and which remained uncontradicted, of over 3,000 by 1986. He continued:

> The public, quite properly, make new and greater demands on us. Our changing society poses new problems; a wide spectrum of legal problems associated with changing attitudes to the family and marriage; a more sophisticated demand for specialised services arising from a more prosperous agricultural and a larger industrial sector; a whole new dimension of EEC law; complex problems of labour law arising from new legislation and the intractable problem of job creation for our predominately young population. We are ready and willing to play our part in tackling all these problems, and this Society will give all the assistance in its power to its members by providing them with continuing education both in law and in modern business methods.

Joseph Dundon noted that the beautiful building at Blackhall Place, then made new, was a metaphor for what he felt should be the solicitors' view of the legal system and of their profession. Noting that the interior had been modified and improved so as to preserve all that was good and remove all that had outlived its usefulness or had decayed, the president remarked that this was surely the quintessence of conservation where what is old and beautiful could still remain modern and functional. He said that

Patrick Noonan who was president in 1968 and the council deserved special praise. Peter Prentice was specifically praised as one who had the foresight to identify the premises. The president noted that, having taken the initial step of acquiring the premises for £105,000, the members paused for some time when they considered the cost of refurbishment. Moya Quinlan was commended as chair of the premises committee of the council which planned and supervised the completion of the project.

The Taoiseach, Jack Lynch, in his address at the opening ceremony stated that it was 'the beginning of a new epoch in the life of an historical Dublin building'. The Taoiseach referred to one of the main reasons for the move by the Law Society from the Four Courts – the need for more space to facilitate a new education programme for solicitors' apprentices. Noting that it was an important development, the basic aim was to improve the standard of entry into the solicitors' profession.

As the Taoiseach arrived for the opening, he was met with a picket from the union of students in Ireland protesting at what was described as the decision of the Law Society to restrict entry to the legal profession to 150 students per year. Restricting entry to 150 students, according to the president-elect of the union, Peter Davies, meant that a comprehensive system of free legal aid would be impossible to implement from a practical viewpoint.

There was a large attendance at the opening ceremony. The Chief Justice, T.F. O'Higgins, and Mrs O'Higgins were among the guests together with the Minister for Finance, George Colley, the Minister for Justice, Gerry Collins, the Minister for Industry, Commerce and Energy, Desmond O'Malley, the Attorney General, Anthony Hederman, former Taoiseach, Liam Cosgrave, the former Minister for Justice, Patrick Cooney, other members of the judiciary, other public figures and the Rev. G.S. Magahy, headmaster of King's Hospital school, Palmerstown, Co. Dublin. It was a day of celebration for solicitors.

SOLICITORS' RIGHT OF AUDIENCE

Prior to 1971, barristers enjoyed a right of audience in all courts but solicitors had a right of audience in the District and in the Circuit Courts.

With minor exceptions, a solicitor had no right of audience in the High and Supreme Courts: the right of audience in the Supreme Court was confined to barristers. However, High Court judges from time to time permitted solicitors a right of audience in a case to move an adjournment or to seek some other interlocutory order. The right of audience in the High Court and Supreme Court was not based on statute or a rule of law but on usage and practice. It was regarded not as a right but as a privilege given by the court. The long-established usage of the former superior courts in Ireland and Great Britain when solicitors did not have a right of audience was continued in the High Court and Supreme Court at the foundation of the State. The solicitor's right of audience in the Circuit Court was based on usage. The rules of the Circuit Court made no express provision for the solicitor's right of audience as an advocate. The *District Court rules* (1948) did allow any party to any proceedings in any court to appear by his solicitor.

The issue of a solicitor's right of audience was addressed by the Courts Act, 1971, which created a general right of audience. This reform followed the report of the committee on court practice and procedure which issued its thirteenth interim report entitled 'The solicitor's right of audience' in 1971. The committee was chaired by Mr Justice Brian Walsh of the Supreme Court. The other judicial members were Mr Justice John Kenny of the High Court, Judge Charles Conroy of the Circuit Court and Judge Cathal Ó Floinn, president of the District Court. Two senior counsel, E.C. Micks and James McMahon, represented the Bar; Dermot P. Shaw, solicitor, and Brendan P. McCormack, solicitor, represented the Law Society.

Various arguments were submitted by parties in relation to the solicitor's right of audience and are interesting from the perspective of 2002; the arguments reflect the often opposing 'mind sets' of the two branches of the legal profession. The main arguments advanced against solicitors obtaining a right of audience in the superior courts included the argument that advocacy in court was a specialised function which, in so far as the High Court and Supreme Court were concerned, was best left to those whose professional training and experience specifically fitted them for it, namely the members of the Bar. Other aspects of litigation such as ascertaining from prospective witnesses the facts of the case were within the solicitor's domain.

The Bar argued that one of the advantages of confining the right of audience in the High Court to barristers was that it provided an independent and impartial advocacy; the judge's task was made easier when the advocates shared the same professional experience in advocacy as the trial judge had experienced. The exclusive right of audience in the High Court and Supreme Court given to barristers would preserve within that profession the solidarity and understanding which fostered the opportunity for discussions between counsel with a view to the settlement of cases.

An argument in favour of solicitor advocates in all the courts was that the exercise of the solicitor's extended right of audience would eliminate some duplication of work and result in a reduction in costs to litigants. There were many motions and applications which could be competently dealt with by a solicitor which at that time were dealt with by a barrister.

The two senior counsel on the committee, E.C. Micks and James McMahon, dissented. Having set out the role of the advocate and quoting the words of Lord MacMillan in a paper, 'The ethics of advocacy' read before the Royal Philosophical Society of Glasgow in 1916 and from Lawton J in *Rondel* v. *Worsley* (1967),[2] they articulated in the 1971 report their opposition to any extension of the rights of audience of solicitors, doing so in a manner that, even at the time but certainly with the benefit of hindsight, seems somewhat dismissive and patronising as to the relationship between solicitors and the Bar:

> Advocacy is a highly specialised matter and if a lawyer is to practise it in the superior courts he must have training and experience. He must cultivate clarity and order, with commendable brevity, in presenting his client's case. He must have honesty and judgment, a good measure of sagacity and quick discernment. Again he must above all things have courage and independence. Counsel, when first admitted to practice, learn partly from their early briefs in the Circuit Court and also to a great extent from listening to their more experienced brethren doing their cases in the right way. It is only after they have acquired a considerable measure of experience and confidence that

2 [1967] 1 QB 443 at 469.

they are really fit to present a case in the High Court or the Supreme Court. Then again, counsel have the inestimable advantage of the Law Library at the Four Courts, where the solidarity and understanding which exists in the profession gives the fullest scope for discussions of the most confidential nature with a view to settling actions.

The two senior counsel argued that litigation would become more complex and their main concern would be that litigants might suffer by an extension of the solicitor's right of audience since they regarded it as of the utmost importance to the community that nothing should happen which might hinder justice being done as amply and as impartially as possible. They remarked that their observations were not intended to be read as in any way 'forgetful of the great assistance which counsel get from their instructing solicitors when counsel are briefed as advocates'.

The committee on court practice and procedure was of the opinion, by a majority, that solicitors should be granted a right of audience in all courts at least until it appeared that the disadvantages to the public interest of such extension outweighed the advantages. The committee, however, appreciated the force of the submissions in support of the argument denying solicitors a right of audience. The majority view was adopted by the government, and section 17 of the Courts Act, 1971 conferred the right of audience in all courts upon solicitors, by providing that a solicitor who was acting for a party in an action, suit, matter or criminal proceedings in any court and a solicitor qualified to practise (within the meaning of the Solicitors Act, 1954) who was acting as his assistant should have a right of audience in that court.

With some exceptions, solicitors have not exercised a full right of audience in the High Court and Supreme Court since the granting of that right in 1971. The Fair Trade Commission in its *Report of the study into restrictive practices in the legal profession* (1990), which is considered later, queried why solicitors did not generally exercise their right of audience. Some views had been expressed that solicitors might be unwelcome as advocates and that attitudes within the legal system militated against full representation of their clients by solicitors in the superior courts; all judges (except in the District Court) were then drawn from the ranks of practising barristers, and because of the association between the judiciary and King's Inns, judges might not encourage the appearance of solicitors or 'might even refuse to hear a case or ask a barrister to attend'.

The Fair Trade Commission stated it was disappointed at the minimal appearances by solicitors as advocates in courts other than the District Court. It was of the view that greater use of the right of audience could serve to increase competition and it could result in some reduction of costs to clients, though the commission accepted that a solicitor was entitled to be paid a fee for acting as solicitor and another fee for acting as advocate. The commission recommended that the Law Society should encourage solicitors to make extensive use of their rights of audience in the higher courts. While it was envisaged that greater emphasis would be placed on advocacy in the professional training of solicitors, the commission recommended that the Law Society introduce training in advocacy for qualified solicitors as part of the programme of continuing legal education.

The Law Society in its response to the Fair Trade Commission report (October 1990) noted that the Society had already and was continuing to encourage solicitors to make extensive use of their rights of audience in the High Court; advocacy training was an important part of the Society's Law School course and the Society had also organised residential continuing legal education courses in advocacy. There may be too much emphasis placed on experience in advocacy before the courts: what matters most is an understanding of the law and a knowledge of practice and procedure.

COURT DRESS

In general, solicitors have not been greatly exercised by court dress. However, the issue did arise from time to time. For example, the issue of the forensic dress for women lawyers raised 'eyebrows' when women first began appearing in court as advocates. There was a view shared by many (including some women solicitors) even up to the 1960s that a woman, in court as in church, should have her head covered. Judge Mary Kotsonouris, solicitor, writer and former judge of the District Court, in her book *Retreat from revolution*

(1994) having noted that Judge Eileen Kennedy was the first woman judge to be appointed in Ireland in 1963, recounts how Judge Kennedy created another precedent by being 'the first female to sit in a court with her head uncovered'. Judge Kotsonouris, who was a solicitor's apprentice at the time, remembers 'the frisson of excitement at such daring'.

The rules of the superior courts (1986) (Order 119) prescribe that the judges of the superior courts shall on all occasions, during the sittings, including sittings of the Central Criminal Court, wear the following costume, namely, a black coat and vest of uniform make and material of the kind worn by senior counsel, a black Irish poplin gown of uniform make and material, white bands, and a wig of the kind known as the small or bobbed wig. The 1986 rules also prescribe that senior and junior counsel shall appear, when in court, habited in a dark colour, and in such robes and bands and with such wigs as have heretofore been worn by senior and junior counsel respectively, and no counsel shall be heard in any case unless so habited.

In the context of wigs, section 49 of the Courts and Court Officers Act, 1995 provided that a barrister or solicitor shall not be required to wear a wig 'of the kind heretofore worn or any other wig of a ceremonial type' leaving the option open to the individual barrister or solicitor. The Judicial Separation and Family Law Reform Act, 1989 made certain provisions to the effect that neither judges, barristers, nor solicitors appearing in the various family courts should wear wigs and gowns.

The Law Society's *Guide to the professional conduct of solicitors in Ireland* (1988) states: 'A solicitor should appear in court, or at judicial and quasi-judicial tribunals, dressed in clothing suitable to reflect the dignity of the proceedings.' The nature of the clothing is not defined. The present writer remembers solicitors appearing in the District Court wearing gowns but they never wore wigs, at least not wigs of the ceremonial nature worn by barristers and judges.

Court dress was another issue considered by the Fair Trade Commission in its *Report of the study into restrictive practices in the legal profession* (1990). Many who gave evidence were highly critical of the wearing of wigs and gowns by judges and barristers. The practice was stated to contribute to the alien atmosphere of court proceedings as a whole, especially when people were appearing in court usually for the first time. Wigs and gowns were said to be medieval, anachronistic, intimidatory, a harassment and off-putting, and an 'out-moded nonsense'. They were not necessary, but barristers felt strongly about them as they lent a feeling of 'mystique' and that, without them, they would 'not be heard' by the judge. Wigs differentiated barristers from solicitors, and put solicitors at a disadvantage. Others argued that wigs added to the formality and solemnity of the court, and certainly did not intimidate people. If there were no wigs and gowns, there was a danger that multi-coloured casual dress would be adopted for appearances in court. This was not regarded as a prospect to be welcomed.

Mr Justice Niall McCarthy, a courageous and sometimes outspoken judge of the Supreme Court, addressing the MacGill Summer School in 1987 in an attack on 'post-colonial servility' in the Irish courts system, had described the wearing of wigs as quite absurd. He said that he saw the wearing of male wigs by women barristers as 'comic' and the wearing of wigs afforded barristers 'a sense of protection against their clients, as if they were a sort of forensic condom'.

The wearing of wigs and gowns in court was a peripheral issue to the Fair Trade Commission's study. The commission nevertheless considered court dress was important to some people. It did not believe that the wearing of wigs, in particular, added to the formality and the solemnity of court, rather the reverse. It considered wigs to be 'anachronistic, unnecessary and, possibly, intimidatory'. Wigs differentiated between solicitors and barristers in court and might, to a small degree, inhibit solicitors from representing their clients more frequently. Since both judges and barristers wore wigs, this might convey the impression of an association and a community of interest between barristers and judges. The commission considered that it would be a sensible move towards a more modern profession if barristers no longer wore wigs and welcomed the prohibition on the wearing of wigs and gowns in the Judicial Separation and Family Law Reform Act, 1989. No comment was made on the wearing of wigs by judges. The commission had 'no strong feelings' about the wearing of gowns which might be regarded as a kind of court uniform. Noting that a different gown might be worn by solicitors, it was argued that the gown, of itself, did not discriminate between barristers and solicitors, to the possible disadvantage of solicitors. The commission did consider, however, that the dress of solicitors and barristers should be sober and reflect the dignity of the court.

At the time of writing, the lord chancellor in England, Lord Irvine, was considering allowing solicitor advocates wear wigs in the Crown Courts; he conceded that juries and witnesses might make value judgments about advocates on the basis of their court dress. However, the wearing of wigs in the civil courts was described by the lord chancellor as an anachronism. The Crown Court was different, he argued, saying that a greater degree of 'solemnity and anonymity' was required. The issue of court dress in the form of wigs, gowns and sober attire will undoubtedly feature from time to time in the future.

DELAYS AND INEFFICIENCIES IN THE LEGAL SYSTEM

Time is of seminal importance to lawyers and their clients. Delay is an issue of crucial significance; justice delayed is justice denied. Delay has been a constant theme in the history of law. For example, Charles Dickens in his description of the fictional case of *Jarndyce* v. *Jarndyce* in *Bleak House* (1853), having stated in his preface that the case was substantially based on fact, wrote of the 'ten thousand stages of an endless cause', 'the mountains of costly nonsense' in the context of legal papers and the dreary length of the case before the court as being 'perennially hopeless'.

It is appropriate here to refer to a chapter entitled 'Delays in the legal system' from the paper of the National Prices Commission, *Solicitors' remuneration in Ireland*, published in December 1976. The chapter is a snapshot in time, a snapshot of difficulties, in relation to delays and inefficiencies in the legal system. It must be emphasised that this snapshot is obviously limited in time and describes a period in the mid 1970s. The paper was prepared by Dennis Lees, then professor of industrial economics, University of Nottingham, for the National Prices Commission.

The terms of reference of the National Prices Commission inquiry called for, inter alia, an examination of 'delays' in the legal system, particularly those associated with court organisation and practices. Professor Lees stated that the Dublin Solicitors' Bar Association had been 'kind enough to establish sub-committees on the subject' and to let him have their reports. He said that with a little editing, they were reproduced in his report. In the High Court, it was stated that the use of juries in personal injury cases increased the length of time those cases took at hearing. The listing arrangements for cases were unsatisfactory, in that fixed dates for hearings were rare with the result that litigants, solicitors and expert witnesses were required to be 'on tap for sometimes several days' to await a judge becoming free on the termination of an earlier case. The appointment of further judges and fixed dates for hearings would lead to a considerable increase in efficiency since 'the only time that would be wasted would be that of the judge who had nothing to do for an afternoon, occasionally'. Judges would have their own views on a comment of this nature.

The office of the Official Assignee, which administered the affairs of bankrupts, was subject to 'enormous delays' due to shortages of personnel. The Examiner's office, which was responsible for the administration of chancery cases and the making of enquiries and taking of accounts in cases referred by the High Court, was also subject to 'enormous delays not only because of shortage of personnel but because of the outdated procedure in that office'. The office of the Accountant to the High Court, with responsibility to receive lodgments of funds by defendants in court, was 'notoriously slow in making payments out' and 'required complicated documentation'. The procedure before the Master of the High Court was 'unsatisfactory'. Defendants with no genuine defence to claims were permitted 'excessive leniency' by the Master, which sometimes resulted in a plaintiff losing his opportunity to secure his debt.

In the Circuit Court, delays in the hearing of cases at the time of the 1976 report were 'legendary'. Cases which had been properly set down for trial for well over twelve months still had not been allocated a date for hearing. The major cause of this delay was the heavy volume of criminal work in the Dublin Circuit Court to which precedence had been given. While it was accepted that criminal trials should proceed as rapidly as possible, the appointment of additional judges and the provision of additional courts would help to remedy that situation. The rigid method of fixing dates for hearing in the Circuit Court led to an unsatisfactory procedure whereby a case which was not finished on its fixed date might have had to be adjourned for several weeks before the same judge would be free to resume the hearing. It had proved extremely difficult at that time to arrange to get two days set aside for the hearing of a complicated case in the Dublin Circuit.

The location of the District Courts particularly in Dublin in relation to the areas which they were supposed to serve was not 'logical', having regard to the public transport system. The court areas had not been changed from the time when there was a small population in rural areas outside the city boundary which had since become substantial dormitory suburbs. Personal attendance by solicitors was required for far too many formal applications in the District Court, such as applications for the fixing of a date for defended civil claims or the granting of licence extensions to hotels or clubs for particular functions when there was no objection to the extension by the Gardaí.

The principal focus of delay in conveyancing practice related to the Land Registry. The delays in the mapping department were described as 'appalling'. Most cases of transfers of part of folios, seemed to take over twelve months to be completed. This, in itself, would be regarded as highly unsatisfactory, but if there was a further transaction involving that particular property during the twelve months after the first transaction, the solicitors concerned would find themselves involved in repeated applications to the Registry urging the expedition of their particular case. The delays in dealing with first registration cases were 'notable' and were known to take several years to complete.

The Valuation Office suffered from 'very considerable delays' and was 'almost permanently understaffed'; cases had been known to take two or three years to be processed and concluded. This office acted as the official valuer for the Adjudication Office, assessing stamp duties on conveyances and other transfers of property and also acted for the Estate Duty Office in the valuing of estates; consequently there was 'disastrous consequential delay' in the issuing of certificates of discharge from death duties.

Complaints were also made about delays in the Companies Office and in the law departments of local authorities. Lending institutions were also criticised; loan approval process was slow and the consequent effect on investigation of title and delays in the issue of loan cheques were considerable. This involved expensive bridging finance interest and two separate sets of searches and additional expenses.

Professor Lees in the 1976 report was not going to let lawyers themselves off the hook. At the end of the chapter on delays, he stated that comment must be made on delays involving the legal profession itself. Noting that while delays by members of the Bar in dealing with cases sent to them was a contributory factor to solicitors' delays in some cases, still there was no doubt that in the great majority of cases the cause of the delay rested with 'the solicitor himself'. Interestingly, Professor Lees did not suggest that delay was due to individual solicitors but suggested 'institutional' causes. Noting that causes for delays by solicitors may be 'legion', Professor Lees submitted that delays were in part due to the fact that reforms in the training system for solicitors had been greatly delayed owing to the reluctance of the Department of Justice to prepare a new Solicitors Bill to enable fundamental alterations to be made in the training programme for apprentices. The Law Society had been seeking such statutory authority since 1961 and various reports from interested parties had all recommended a change in the educational system. The academic and professional training of solicitors was being squeezed into a four-year period with the result that no proper opportunity was given to a solicitor to learn any of the practical aspects of running solicitors' practices, such as office administration.

Another cause of delay was that adequate back-up staff for solicitors was not readily available. There was no ready supply of law clerks or legal executives so that solicitors were either forced to occupy their time in doing legal work which could satisfactorily be performed at a lower level by a trained or experienced clerk, or delegate legal work to a person who had received no training and had little experience which obviously involved some risk and the necessity of regular constant supervision.

The amount of administrative work which was necessary in connection with the running of any solicitor's practice, in common with all other businesses of equivalent size, had increased dramatically over the years, partly due to the necessity of keeping more detailed records in connection with PAYE, social welfare contributions, VAT accounts as well as the particular concern of solicitors of having to keep accounts in the specified format in accordance with the Solicitors Accounts Regulations.

In his conclusion, Professor Lees in his report to the National Prices Commission (1976) noted that while it must be accepted that there would never be an ideal situation in which no delays would affect the efficiency of the service provided by solicitors, nevertheless, the outside sources of delays then affecting solicitors in their practice were far too numerous which all had a serious effect on the efficient servicing by solicitors of their clients' interests.

The picture painted of legal life for the average solicitor in the mid 1970s appeared to be one of unmitigated gloom. It would be wrong, however, to assume that legal life in the 1970s was all gloom: there were some compensatory factors.

Delays in the legal system, particularly in courts and court offices, have been continuously highlighted over the years. Undoubtedly, the effective operation of a courts system is a critical element in the well-being of any society. The Law Society was represented on the Working Group on a Courts Commission, and is represented on the governing board of the Courts Service and fully supports its objectives.

The establishment of the Courts Service took place on 9 November 1999 pursuant to the Courts Service Act, 1998. It had been recommended in the first report of the Working Group on a Courts Commission, 'Management and financing of the courts', published in April 1996. The Working Group identified a number of shortcomings in the then existing institutional framework: the Irish courts system had remained largely unaltered since its establishment in 1924; there had been an enormous increase in civil and criminal litigation; there was perceived to be an unacceptable delay in the determination of cases; there were instances of overworked and poorly organised staff; there was evidence of a lack of adequate back-up and support services to judges; and there was an absence of adequate systems for communicating information and of modern computer and information systems to support the increasing workload of the courts. In addition, the Working Group identified several factors as contributing significantly to the problems within the courts structure: lack of clear management structures with accountability and responsibility; fragmentation of administrative systems within and between each of the courts; minimal training and development of staff; lack of professional management support; an absence of strategic planning; no annual reports; inadequate information service to the public and limited availability of statistical information in a meaningful format.

The mission statement of the Courts Service is to manage the courts, support the judiciary and provide a high-quality and professional service to all users of the courts. To accomplish its mandate and to fulfil its mission, the service is to be guided by certain fundamental principles which will underpin all its operations: highest quality service to the judges and the public; prompt and effective service which is responsive to the needs of users; public accountability and value for money; equality, fairness and integrity; and public trust and confidence.[3] There is undoubtedly an expectation that the new Courts Service will deliver.

---

3 See, generally, *The Courts Service: strategic plan, 2000–2003* (2000).

Prevailing issues: remuneration, prospects, advertising, restrictive practices, judicial appointments, compensation fund and internal governance

EAMONN G. HALL

SOLICITORS' REMUNERATION

Remuneration of solicitors is a key issue which has occupied the minds of presidents, members of the council, directors general and solicitors over the years. In the context of the timeframe considered in this chapter, the problem associated with just and fair remuneration for solicitors surfaced acutely in the early 1970s. There were several tensions. First, some persons outside the profession accused solicitors of overcharging. The Society had found these complaints were largely based on misunderstandings and misconceptions of what was involved in a solicitor's work. Meanwhile, solicitors themselves continued to complain to the Law Society about particular items of remuneration which needed to be increased.

A critical difficulty was the fact that at the time the State, in one guise or another, had the power to veto any cost increase. Approval for costs was always slow. By the 1970s, it was argued that solicitors' remuneration as a whole had fallen far behind other sections of the community. Some fees were hopelessly low. In 1975, the rules of the Cork Admiralty Court, originally fixed in 1877, still remained unrevised at 10p for various attendances up to a maximum of £4.20 for conducting a case without counsel in court for an entire day.

A general sense of frustration existed in the profession in relation to what was regarded as a cumbersome system of statutory committees touching upon the remuneration of solicitors. The Society held discussions with the Minster for Justice with a view to the establishment of a central costs committee. The Society also initiated surveys to gain information as to the real situation regarding the remuneration of the private sector of the profession. The first survey was carried out in 1970 on a selective basis. Further surveys were carried out in 1972 and in 1975. As indeed in most surveys, the Society cautioned that the results of these surveys must be viewed on the basis that returns were more likely to have come from the most efficient and better organised practices and, as a result, from firms that enjoyed better than average earnings. The 1975 survey conducted by Coopers & Lybrand revealed that the average salary paid throughout the country to qualified staff, other than partners, was £2,938. There were, however, considerable regional variations around this national average figure with the average ranging from £800 in Connaught and Ulster to £4,056 in Dublin. In 1975, the national average income (pre-tax) of partners was stated to be £7,900.

The gross annual income figure of £7,900 was, however, regarded as an unsatisfactory measurement of the true return on a principal's time and skill, since a practising solicitor of partner status was stated to be subject to a number of continuing financial commitments over and above those incurred either by non-partner solicitors in private practice or solicitors in the public service or industry. Of these, the three most important financial commitments were: (i) the necessity to obtain a competitive return on the capital investment which the partner had made in fixed and working capital, (ii) the need to provide (from post-tax income) for the expansion of this capital in order to provide for inflation and real growth of business and (iii) the need to provide the partner with a retirement pension.

The 1975 survey concluded that the gross annual average income of partners of £7,900, adjusted to take account of the factors mentioned in the last paragraph and certain other factors, in fact, became £1,710. Accordingly, as of about March 1974, sole principals and other principals in Connaught and Ulster were actually stated to be in receipt of 'negative adjusted incomes'; partners in these two categories were not, on average, earning sufficient gross income even to meet their commitments for returns on, and expansion of, their invested capital and for provision of a retirement pension. This was indeed a most gloomy scenario.

Several applications were submitted to the National Prices Commission for increases in solicitors' remuneration. The commission engaged consultants in May 1975 to undertake a study of solicitors' remuneration in Ireland with wide terms of reference. The Society made detailed submissions. In the context of factors relating to income such as time, the Society argued that thirty-five to thirty-eight hours constituted 'a reasonable working week'. On this basis, allowing for holidays, including public holidays, professional training, illness and approximately 300 hours per annum for what was called office administration, a solicitor in private practice could count on not more than about 1,200 fee earning hours in the year.

The Society submitted to the National Prices Commission that it was absolutely essential for every solicitor to keep abreast of the rapid changes taking place by virtue of new legislation. To become expert in the new codes of taxation law, employment law, EC law and other complex legislation, a considerable time commitment was required in reading, studying and attending seminars. At an absolute minimum, two to three hours per week were required for continuing education of one description or another or about 5 per cent of a solicitor's normal working week.

Stress is a major factor in the life of a busy solicitor, and ought to be taken into account in relation to remuneration. Although much is written nowadays about the subject, it is not a new phenomenon, and the Society's perception of the causes of stress on solicitors in the 1970s, conveyed to the commission, is of interest:

> [A solicitor] must deal, inter alia, with the moral and psychological difficulties of his client. If he could limit his obligations to a client's commercial problems, a solicitor would thereby undertake only remunerative work. He could refuse to see people with moral or psychological difficulties, people who have created their own emergencies, and refuse to deal with matters outside office hours; he could decline to attend to matters at short notice which result in the frustration of his work programme and the re-arrangement of a busy schedule at very short notice; all of which has a cost in time, effort, nervous tension, pressure on staff and results in disruption of home

and social life. In practice, the average solicitor has to face all of these problems frequently at very short notice and irrespective of the cost.

The Society concluded that it could not over-emphasise the stress and strain on solicitors in private practice: it was difficult to assess remuneration for such stress.

From the perspective of 2002, it is interesting to consider what the Society then regarded as the minimum remuneration of a solicitor. The Society argued that the remuneration of a solicitor in private practice should not be less than the salary paid to a solicitor in full-time employment in the public service. It noted that in addition a solicitor in private practice must be compensated for those facilities which are available free of charge to a solicitor in the public service and these facilities were categorised as (i) working capital; (ii) premises and equipment; (iii) trained staff, and (iv) readily available back-up services. Consideration should be given to certain other factors which a public-service solicitor enjoyed compared with his or her private-practice counterpart. These benefits included: (i) fixed hours; (ii) sick pay; (iii) pension rights; (iv) paid time for training e.g. seminars and lectures; (v) guaranteed client with no element of commercial risk and (vi) absence in a public-sector solicitor ('to a large degree') of the usual stress and strain conditions of private practice due to 'limited area of responsibility' and a 'considerable degree of specialisation in work'. The last point may not have been, even at the time, a fair observation on the demands placed on solicitors in the public sector, and it could not seriously be suggested now that stress was a phenomenon which only affected the private-sector solicitor.

The Society complained about auctioneers being allowed to earn a non-tapering scale of 2.5 per cent of the value of the property in Dublin and 3.5 per cent elsewhere. The Society asked specifically if there was any reason why solicitors should not be similarly paid in respect of work which, compared with auctioneers, involved greater time, training, expertise, skill and responsibility. The Society also asked if there was any reason why a solicitor who negotiated a sale without the assistance of an auctioneer should not be remunerated on the same basis as an auctioneer. The difference between the fees of auctioneers and solicitors in relation to the sale of property, having regard to their respective contributions to such transactions, has been a bone of contention for many years with solicitors.

The consultants concluded in 1976 that increases in solicitors' earnings had fallen somewhat behind those of the community as a whole. Solicitors had fared less well than some of their counterparts in the public sector but were stated to have done better than several groups of management executives in the private sector. The consultants concluded that an increase in solicitors' fees would seem to be justified. The following increases in court costs were recommended: an increase of 150 per cent in District Court costs; an increase of 100 per cent in Circuit Court costs; and an increase of 50 per cent in High Court costs. Increases were also recommended for conveyancing fees. However, the consultants' recommendations caused concern to the National Prices Commission. The commission argued that under the proposed system of charges, the income of solicitors in general would increase by 169 per cent over the period 1970 to 1975. A further 5 to 6 percentage points could probably be added to this in respect of the recommended minimum conveyancing charges and a new negotiation fee. Such an increase, according to the commission, would have been far in excess of 'comparable' income groups. The recommendations made by the consultants would widen the gap even further. The commission refused the Law Society request for a general increase of 150 per cent in certain litigation costs but recommended increases of 50 per cent for certain civil litigation fees and some modification to conveyancing fees.

Subsequently, certain increases in fees were sanctioned. But general dissatisfaction continued to be expressed by the Society in relation to certain aspects of solicitors' costs. The Society in its submission to the Fair Trade Commission, *Report of study into restrictive practices in the legal profession* (1990), expressed dissatisfaction that the relevant rules on fees were only revised infrequently to take account of inflation and rising costs and so were totally out of date. It was argued in 1990 that some fees had not been revised since 1972 or earlier. The Fair Trade Commission noted that the method of determining the fees of solicitors and barristers was 'a matter of some complexity'. The Society argued that the fees as set by the rule-making bodies had largely fallen into disuse by the lack of reviews. What had in fact happened was that various rules committees had proposed fee increases but those fee increases required the concurrence of the Minister for Justice who had not given his approval.

The Fair Trade Commission considered that a prices advisory body should examine all aspects of legal costs and provide the taxing master and county registrars with guidelines and scales. The Society objected because no indication had been given as to who would constitute membership of the prices advisory body and whether the concurrence of the Minister for Justice and the consent of the Minister for Industry and Commerce might or might not be required.

The Society noted that that after a total of almost eighty five pages, the chairman of the Fair Trade Commission was of the view that the high level of legal costs was a result of the unnecessary complexity of many laws and suggested the enactment of a law reform programme. The Society was in complete agreement with the chairman on this issue and believed that the way forward was law reform. However, the Society noted that successive governments had failed to implement the vast majority of recommendations made by the Law Reform Commission to that date.

The Solicitors (Amendment) Act, 1994 dealt, in part, with the issue of charges to clients. Section 68 of the 1994 act obliges solicitors on the taking of instructions, or as soon as is practicable thereafter, to provide the client with particulars in writing of the actual charges, or where this is not possible or practicable, an estimate of the charges, or where an estimate of the charges is not, in the circumstances, possible or practicable, the basis on which the charges are to be made. Section 68 of the 1994 act also prohibits a solicitor from acting in contentious business on the basis that all or any part of the charges to the client are to be calculated as a specified percentage or proportion of any damages. Any charges so made shall be unenforceable in any action taken against that client to recover such charges.

SUPPLY OF SOLICITORS

The 1950s, as a decade, is generally regarded in Ireland as a period of stagnation. Of the small number of solicitors who qualified in the 1950s, some were forced to emigrate and, of these, many joined the British Colonial

Service. In the period 1955 to 1960, the number seeking admission to the roll of solicitors declined. By 1960, the number of solicitors on the roll was at its lowest for several years. In the period 1960 to 1973 there was relatively little growth in the numbers in the profession.

Numbers of solicitors holding practising certificates

Year	Number	Year	Number	Year	Number
1960	1,335	1974	1,548	1988	3,410
1961	1,300	1975	1,655	1989	3,422
1962	1,290	1976	1,750	1990	3,529
1963	1,290	1977	1,780	1991	3,642
1964	1,319	1978	1,944	1992	3,808
1965	1,319	1979	2,075	1993	3,959
1966	1,298	1980	2,150	1994	4,131
1967	1,298	1981	2,340	1995	4,355
1968	1,301	1982	2,674	1996	4,593
1969	1,337	1983	2,788	1997	4,776
1970	1,349	1984	3,010	1998	4,975
1971	1,393	1985	3,188	1999	5,257
1972	1,452	1986	3,292	2000	5,551
1973	1,489	1987	3,360	2001	5,912

Joseph Dundon, solicitor, former president of the Law Society, in his introduction to *The future of the solicitors profession in Ireland,* a report prepared on behalf of the Society by Brendan M. Walsh, Department of Economics, University College, Dublin, and Maurice Roche, Department of Economics, Maynooth College (September 1985) noted that in the period 1973 to 1979 many relatively junior solicitors were able, because of a scarcity of the best talent, to procure advancement to partnership status with a speed that would have been inconceivable a decade earlier. Dundon noted that the growth and supply of solicitors was accentuated by a large influx of apprentices seeking admission in the period preceding the change to graduate entry under the Society's new system of education. By 1985, it was considered that an oversupply of solicitors existed, the extent of which was hard to measure. The 1985 report noted that a difficult market situation had developed in Ireland in the wake of the recession of 1980 to 1983. The dramatic increase in unemployment in general and youth unemployment in particular were causes for national concern.

Based on the available evidence from the records of the Society, by 1985 an average of 20 practising solicitors were estimated to die each year. A further 20 were assumed to retire from practice each year. However, that left a net increase of about 100 solicitors. An increase of 100 solicitors a year on an initial total of 3,000 would result in a total of 4,600 by the year 2000 according to the report, a number, in fact, greatly exceeded in the event.

Reference was made in the 1985 report to international comparisons on the ratio of lawyers to the general population. The ratio of solicitors to population was similar in Ireland, England and Wales, and Scotland. A slightly higher ratio was recorded in Northern Ireland. In the United States, by 1985, there was one lawyer for every 390 persons. This was proportionately over three times the number in Ireland. In Japan, there was only one lawyer for every 10,000 persons.

Law students in Ireland were among the best qualified entrants to higher education, demonstrated by their high average points in the Leaving Certificate. In 1980, for example, 80.2 per cent of students starting university law courses had six or more honour grades in the higher papers in the Leaving Certificate; this was only slightly lower than the percentage for medicine (84.0 per cent) and dentistry (82.9 per cent) and far ahead of the level of attainment of students studying engineering (49.3 per cent), commerce (16.9 per cent) or arts (14.1 per cent).[1]

The then level of intake to the profession would lead to a surplus of personnel relative to the requirements of the Irish economy, according to the 1985 report. This fear had been aggravated by the effects of the recession and the demand for the services of professionals in Ireland and the shrinking number of opportunities for their employment abroad. Concerns were expressed about whether demand for solicitors' services would generate sufficient work for those additional numbers.

[1] See Patrick Clancy, *Participation in higher education: a national survey*, The Higher Education Authority (1982), table A16.

Joseph Dundon in his review of policy options set out as an introduction to the 1985 report noted that the report represented a 'gloomy prognosis'. The report was made in the context of a period of the deepest difficulty in the Irish economy that most had ever experienced. He noted that it would seem quite irrational for those with the highest academic qualifications to continue to commit themselves to entry into the legal profession where the career prospects within Ireland were extremely uncertain and the prospects outside Ireland 'virtually non-existent'. This last factor changed in the late 1980s when a considerable demand arose in London for Irish qualified solicitors.

Dundon noted in 1985 that there was an unknown number of solicitors who were either unemployed or under-employed. He made an estimate that that figure might be around 400. To this would be added each year about fifty more who were likely to find it difficult to obtain employment unless and until the economy started to grow at an annual rate in excess of 3 per cent. On an optimistic note, Dundon noted that the ability of members of the solicitors' profession to respond to the challenge should not be underestimated. The more active and progressive members of the profession would seek to protect themselves by extending their areas of practice. He noted that as far as possible solicitors should ensure that this was achieved by activities in areas hitherto neglected by the profession such as taxation and labour law. He noted that those already in the profession should be encouraged to enhance their skills in areas in which they were weak, for example, taxation, financial counselling, estate planning, employment protection, planning and environmental problems.

Further, a more flexible approach should be adopted in relation to the delivery of legal services. Opening hours might need adjustment to fit in with the life style and working patterns of clients and a solicitor's office situated in a shopping centre, open from 6 p.m. to 9 p.m. on a Friday night, might attract clients who would otherwise not have the opportunity to consult a solicitor. Dundon also noted that solicitors might have to consider other means of communication such as telephone counselling during specified hours. He suggested the Society should consider a pilot project on prepaid legal services – a legal voluntary health insurance as it were – which would be organised and funded by the Society in a particular local area.

Dundon argued the universities should place an increased emphasis on business-related skills, financial analysis, management skills, industrial relations, linguistic skills and knowledge of European institutions with a view to tapping employment opportunities in Europe. In fact, universities to-day provide a combination of law and practical non-legal subjects on degree courses. Dundon concluded that only when it was publicly perceived that there was no guarantee of a rosy future for all those qualifying as solicitors would the pressure to enter the profession be relieved. The task of creating that realisation would remain a difficult one so long as employment prospects at home and abroad continued to be depressed.

Nobody could possibly have foreseen the era of the Celtic tiger, an unparalleled period of growth and considerable demand for services of solicitors in the 1990s. However, the implications of the terrorist attacks on New York and Washington on 11 September 2001, the slowing down in Ireland of one of the longest economic booms in history and the rise in unemployment may affect the employment prospects and income of solicitors.[2]

ADVERTISING

Advertising by solicitors has been a contentious issue over many years. Indeed, for decades solicitors were strictly prohibited from advertising. Under the Solicitors Act, 1954 the Law Society was empowered to make regulations regarding the professional practice, conduct and discipline of solicitors. The prohibition on advertising was contained in regulations made in 1955 and amended in 1971.[3] The prohibition on advertising by solicitors was set out in regulation 5 of the 1955 regulations which read as follows:

> A solicitor shall not obtain or attempt to obtain professional business by directly or indirectly, without reasonable justification, inviting instructions for such business or doing or permitting to be done without reasonable justification anything which by its manner, frequency or otherwise advertises his practice as a solicitor or doing

---

2 See T.P. Kennedy, 'The shape of things to come; a profile of the number of solicitors of tomorrow', *Gazette*, August/September 2001 p. 30. **3** S.I. No. 151 of 1955 and S.I. No. 344 of 1971.

or permitting to be done anything which may reasonably be regarded as touting and it shall be the duty of a solicitor to make reasonable enquiry before accepting instructions for the purpose of ascertaining whether the acceptance of such instructions would involve a breach of this regulation.

Regulation 6 of the 1955 regulations prohibited a solicitor from holding himself or herself out, or allowing the solicitor to be held out, as being prepared to do business at less than the scales of fees fixed by rules or orders. This prohibited the charging or advertising of lower fees. Any breach of the regulations was a breach of professional discipline rendering the solicitor concerned liable to disciplinary action.

From time to time, the council of the Society issued opinions concerning advertising matters. The council determined, for example, that it was permissible to have one insertion in each recognised Irish daily or local newspaper circulating in the district in which the solicitor carried on practice dealing with any of the following matters: change of address or telephone number; commencement of practice; acquisition of another practice; dissolution of partnership and entry of a new partner into an existing firm, provided that in each case the notice had not the form or appearance of an advertisement. The use of block letters or layout of an advertising nature was regarded as unprofessional. There was also a ruling that press notices concerning branch offices should not be published. In 1969, the council ruled that solicitors should not have their names listed in bold type in the Golden Pages classified directory. The inclusion of certain names in bold type in a classified directory would amount, in the opinion of the council, to advertising and unfair attraction of business. The council concluded that the needs of the profession and their clients would be adequately served if all members and firms used the ordinary small type in the Golden Pages directory. Opinions of the council gave directions to solicitors also in relation to lectures, the writing of articles and radio and television broadcasts.

The question of advertising was raised frequently by solicitors and after much research and debate a working party of the council of the Society in 1986 produced a draft statutory instrument which would permit individual advertising by solicitors. The draft instrument was presented to the annual general meeting of the Society in November 1986, but the proposal on advertising was defeated by a majority of two to one. Opposition came from many country solicitors. Following further consideration, a meeting of members in June 1988 voted to allow a postal ballot of all members on a proposal to allow advertising, subject to certain guidelines. The ballot, in which almost two thousand solicitors participated in October 1988, resulted in a narrow majority in favour of permitting individual advertising, subject to specific restrictions. The proposal was that solicitors be entitled to advertise their services, but that the council of the Society, for the purpose of protecting the reputation of the profession, might make regulations prohibiting advertising which was false or misleading in any respect; or which was not in conformity with the principle of ensuring that solicitors' advertising was 'sober and restrained in style and manner' and did not contain material which could be regarded as reflecting unfavourably on the profession; or which indicated the fees at which a solicitor was prepared to conduct business, provided that no regulation was to prohibit a solicitor from advertising that his fees or charges would be made known on application.

In December 1988, a statutory instrument, the Solicitors (Advertising) Regulations, 1988,[4] revoked completely the previous regulations of 1955 and 1971 and permitted advertising by solicitors, subject to certain limitations.

The Fair Trade Commission in its 1990 report commended the Law Society for the adoption of the more liberal regulations because the commission considered that the previous restrictive regulations amounted to unfair practices which were not in accordance with the common good. The commission noted that solicitors were not permitted to obtain business by means of 'cold calling', that is unsolicited direct approaches to potential clients. Subject to the general limitations on the content of advertisements and the rules for protecting the reputation of the profession, the commission in 1990 recommended that any prohibition on direct mailing or cold calling by solicitors or barristers should be removed, the rules limiting content being exercised in a reasonable and equitable manner. The commission argued that the Law Society should delete the prohibition on

4 S.I. No. 344 of 1988.

touting and the attracting of business unfairly. The commission also considered that the Society should be requested to repeal relevant regulations which prohibited advertisements which compared fees with those of other solicitors and which specified a fee for any service.

The Solicitors (Amendment) Act, 1994, section 69 (3) gave statutory recognition to the acceptability of advertising. However, the Society was specifically authorised to prohibit advertising by solicitors which

(a) is likely to bring the solicitors' profession into disrepute, or
(b) is in bad taste, or
(c) reflects unfavourably on other solicitors, or
(d) contains an express or implied assertion by a solicitor that he has specialist knowledge in any area of law or practice superior to other solicitors, or
(e) is false or misleading in any respect, or
(f) comprises or includes unsolicited approaches to any person with a view to obtaining instructions in any legal matter, or
(g) is contrary to public policy.

Notwithstanding (d) above, the 1994 act authorised the Society to provide in any regulations that where a solicitor satisfied the Society of his or her specialist knowledge in a prescribed area of law or practice, a solicitor might be permitted by the Society to designate himself or herself as having specialist knowledge in that area of law or practice. Subsequently, the Society made the Solicitors (Advertising) Regulations, 1996[5] which came into force on 1 January 1997.

Advertising containing the words 'free' or 'no foal no fee' or similar words was specifically regulated in the 1996 regulations. Regulation 5(b) of the 1996 regulations provides:

[A]n advertisement which uses the words 'free' or 'no foal no fee' or other similar words which expressly or impliedly indicate that the provision of legal services would be without obligation on the part of

5 S.I. No. 351 of 1996.

a client to pay professional fees to the solicitor providing such legal services, whether at all or only in circumstances of there being a successful outcome to the issue the subject matter of such legal services, shall be deemed to be an advertisement which is likely to bring the solicitors' profession into disrepute and to be in bad taste and to be false and misleading, unless the advertisement expressly makes it clear –

(i) whether or not the client would be liable for any outlays, disbursements and expenses incurred by the solicitor concerned in the course of providing the legal services; and

(ii) where the legal services provided by the solicitor concerned might involve the taking or defending of proceedings, that the client may be liable for legal costs of another party or parties to such proceedings.

The Solicitors (Amendment) Act, 2002 makes provision for stricter regulation of the content of advertisements, particularly personal injury advertising.

THE 'RESTRICTIVE PRACTICES' INQUIRIES

The consultants' report, commissioned by the National Prices Commission, published as an occasional paper in December 1976, dealt with the issue of solicitors' remuneration. The consultants in that report recommended that the monopoly on conveyancing for gain held by the legal profession should be referred to the Examiner of Restrictive Practices and the Restrictive Practices Commission and that the prohibition by the Law Society on advertising by solicitors should also be similarly referred. The National Prices Commission supported these recommendations in its monthly report of December 1976.

The Minister for Industry, Commerce and Energy asked the Examiner to forward a request to the Restrictive Practices Commission to hold a public inquiry under section 5(1)(a) of the Restrictive Practices Act, 1972 into

(i) the nature and extent of competition in the carrying on of conveyancing for gain with particular reference to the effects on competition of legal requirements restricting the provision of this service; and

(ii) how the prohibition on advertising affects competition by solicitors.

The Minister's request in relation to conveyancing was furnished to the Examiner on 26 August 1977 and that relating to advertising on 2 September 1977. The permanent members of the commission, Nial MacLiam, chairman, Patrick Lyons and Charles McCarthy intimated to the Minister that they would welcome the addition to their number of a temporary member with legal experience to assist them in understanding and evaluating the issues involved. The Minister subsequently appointed Judge William A. Tormey to be a member of the commission for the purposes of the inquiry.

Public notice was given on 15 October 1980 that the sittings of the inquiry would commence on 12 November 1980 in Dublin. The public sittings which extended over twelve days concluded on 5 February 1981. Evidence on oath was taken from twenty-nine witnesses. The witnesses on behalf of the Law Society were (in alphabetical order) Walter Beatty, John F. Buckley, Maurice Curran, Rory O'Donnell, W.A. Osborne and Thomas Shaw. Only fifteen submissions were received expressing criticism of one or other aspect of the existing conveyancing system (apart from a half dozen complaints of inefficiency or delay in individual cases). This surprised the commission in view of the suggestions made from time to time that there was widespread public dissatisfaction with the present position. Some of the criticisms in the past had come from academic lawyers and economists and the commission noted it was a matter of regret that none of these came forward to develop their views at the inquiry.

In its conclusion, the Restrictive Practices Commission in its *Report of enquiry into the effects on competition of the restrictions on conveyancing and the restrictions on advertising by solicitors* (1982) stated that the practice of conveyancing was detailed involving many matters with which the non-specialist would be unfamiliar. It would be difficult but not impossible for a non-specialist to conduct a conveyance. The importance of special expertise, however, lay not so much in the need to be able to find one's way through the intricate procedures as in the need to be able to recognise and deal with the legal difficulties which may arise. These difficulties could arise not only in relation to the law of property but in relation to many other fields of law. A conveyancer without legal training might very well fail even to recognise the presence of such difficulties in a transfer which he or she was handling.

The Restrictive Practices Commission found that the disciplinary machinery of the profession and the availability of its compensation fund provided solicitors' clients with a degree of protection which would not be available to the clients of conveyancers who were not solicitors. The commission suggested to the Society that greater publicity be given to the availability of its disciplinary procedures. The commission in 1982 recommended there should be lay representation on the Society's disciplinary bodies and on its council and that a solicitor should not be entitled to undertake conveyancing unless he or she had suitable professional indemnity insurance in an amount not less than £250,000. A majority of the commission recommended that the reservation to solicitors of certain conveyancing acts required by section 58 of the Solicitors Act, 1954 should in future only apply to documents under seal – and not to documents whether or not under seal. The commission also recommended that the existing requirements to the effect that the registration of transfers in the Land Registry should be effected by a solicitor should be repealed. The commission considered that a non-practising barrister in employment should be empowered to conduct conveyances on behalf of his employer. To ensure that the concept of the scale fees as maxima be preserved, the commission in 1982 recommended that a restrictive practices order be made rendering it unlawful to attempt to induce a solicitor not to charge less than the prescribed scale fees. The commission also recommended that a restrictive practices order should be made making it unlawful for the Law Society or for any body such as a local bar association to impose restrictions on advertising by solicitors, save that the Law Society might make regulations prohibiting advertising by solicitors which would be injurious to the reputation of the legal profession.

Fair Trade Commission Report, 1990

On 25 April 1984, the Minister for Industry, Trade, Commerce and Tourism requested the Restrictive Practices Commission, subsequently known as the Fair Trade Commission, to undertake a wide ranging study under section 12 of the Restrictive Practices Act, 1972 into the rendering of certain professional and analogous services. The Minister was particularly concerned with any practices which led to increased costs to consumers and any practices which curtailed or limited employment opportunities within the professions. It was subsequently proposed that the study, in two stages, would focus on restrictions on advertising and any concerted fixing of fees or charges practised by professionals or providers of similar services.

Reports on the restrictions of advertising and on concerted fixing of fees or charges in respect of accountancy and in the engineering profession were subsequently published. In the case of the legal profession (solicitors and barristers), the Fair Trade Commission considered that it would be more practical to undertake the whole study in a single stage rather than in two stages as originally planned. An advertisement was placed in the press on 19 November 1986 giving notice of the commission's intention to commence the study into the legal profession. The commission stated that in addition to restrictions on fees and advertising, it would pay particular attention to the following matters:

1. educational and training requirements for admission to the profession of solicitor or barrister;
2. division of the legal profession into solicitors and barristers;
3. number of legal representatives required in a particular case;
4. limited right of audience of solicitors before the courts;
5. access to a barrister by the client being only possible through a solicitor;
6. restrictions upon persons with whom solicitors and barristers may join in partnership;
7. limitations upon the form of organisation of solicitors' and barristers' practices; and
8. representation on disciplinary bodies being confined to members of the profession alone.

In all, more than eighty submissions were received from organisations and individuals, including the Law Society, the Bar Council, teachers of law, individual practitioners, non-practising barristers, various interest groups and members of the public. Meetings were held with a large number of parties, representing some forty persons and organisations, commencing on 6 April 1987. Meetings occupied a total of forty days, including four days with the Law Society and six and a half days with the Bar Council. The report of the Fair Trade Commission, entitled *Report of study into restrictive practices in the legal profession*, was published by the Stationery Office in 1990.

In the context of competition in professional services in the legal profession, the commission in 1990 repeated its strong view that competition between the suppliers of professional services, as with suppliers of goods and other services, was desirable as being in the public interest. The commission considered that there was a fundamental requirement that the public should have available an adequate supply of legal services, of sufficient quality, with a wide degree of choice among practitioners, and delivered efficiently at a reasonable price. It was in the public interest that suppliers of legal services should maintain a high standard of competence, conduct, integrity and independence for the protection of consumers. The commission did not consider that there was any fundamental incompatibility between the maintenance of high standards by lawyers and the subjecting of the providers of legal services to the ordinary market forces of free competition. The commission foresaw that the developments in the European Community would provide both major opportunities and challenges for the legal profession in Ireland.

The Society in its response of October 1990 welcomed the Fair Trade Commission Report for the interest it had stimulated in improving the legal system for the benefit of the public and the solicitors working within it. The Society considered that a number of the recommendations in the report would be beneficial although it did not agree with all the conclusions.

The commission set out an analysis of legal costs and stated that solicitors' fees in litigation were generally higher than the combined fees of counsel and considerably higher than those of individual counsel. The solicitor's instruction fees appeared to account for between 80 and 99 per cent of the solicitor's total fees; with specific stated fees averaging only just over 2 per cent of total costs. The Society in its response stated that a considerable element of the costs which the public had to pay for in litigation consisted of the fees of doctors, surgeons, dentists, radiologists, architects and other expert witnesses. Many of these professional witnesses sought and, in some cases, insisted on payment of report and court attendance fees in advance. There was no control whatsoever over those fees. The Society stated that this often created severe difficulties and stress to clients and the Society was disappointed that no reference had been made to this problem in the commission's report.

Noting that the Fair Trade Commission had made an implied criticism of the level of fees charged by solicitors against those of barristers, the Society argued that the commission did not acknowledge or appreciate the fact that solicitors normally did far more work than barristers in any given case. The Society also noted that the report did not deal with the overall impact of VAT and its effect on the general public. Except in very limited circumstances, VAT was charged on legal fees at the rate of 23 per cent.

In its examination on limitations on the provisions of legal services, the commission argued for

(i) the creation of a class of licensed conveyancers and, in the long term, five to seven years, any person should be able to undertake conveyancing for reward (chairman only);

(ii) employed barristers should be able to undertake conveyancing on behalf of their employer's clients as should employed solicitors without a practising certificate;

(iii) lending institutions, especially banks and building societies, should be permitted to provide conveyancing services to clients;

(iv) the lifting of the present restrictions on the drawing or preparing of legal documents, whether under seal or not, with particular reference to grants of probate and letters of administration, and

(v) the allowing of lay persons to speak for a client in the District Court.

The Society argued that the terms of reference of the commission did not include conveyancing on the basis that it had been accepted that the recommendations made by a previous commission in 1982 (*Report of enquiry into the effects on competition of the restrictions on conveyancing and the restrictions on advertising by solicitors*) adequately covered the situation. It was stated that notwithstanding this, the commission commented further, although the two members of the commission did not agree with each other on their recommendations. The Society stated that it was not sufficiently appreciated that domestic conveyancing relied on a system of solicitors' undertakings enforced by the Law Society. For the protection of the client, it would be most unwise for solicitors to accept undertakings from non-members of the profession.

Commission member, Patrick Lyons, stood by his previous view that the introduction of a category of 'licensed conveyancers' was not a practical proposition because of the need to install a governing institution with machinery to regulate admission, training and discipline and the likely cost of this would not be warranted by any significant increase in competition. The Society agreed with the views expressed by Mr Lyons. However, commission chairman, Myles O'Reilly, suggested that 'appropriate measures be taken and the necessary resources invested to simplify the transfer of land and property so that the transfers can be effected by any person'.

The views of the Society on this statement were set out in a 'Viewpoint' in the July/August 1990 issue of the Society's *Gazette* and are quoted, in part, here:

> It is, however, in the area of conveyancing that the chairman [of the Fair Trade Commission] is impossibly optimistic. He envisages that appropriate action to reform the law to reduce its unnecessary complexity and to bring the procedures and methods of the Land Registry up to date 'may take five to seven years'. It is difficult to avoid the conclusion that the chairman has not grasped the size of the problem which exists here.
>
> Even where resources have been devoted on a significant scale, as in the UK or to a more limited extent in Northern Ireland, it neces-

sarily takes a number of years to bring about statutory reform in the area of land law and conveyancing. Equally even if any significant resources were devoted to the improvement of the Land Registry or if it were to be converted into a public corporation, as the Law Society has recommended, it would certainly be a great deal longer than five to seven years before the combined effects of statutory reform and improvement of the registration system could bring about any lessening of the present complexity in the law relating to conveyancing and the registration system. In passing, it may be remarked that the complexity of the law will not be improved if there is to be a continuance of ill-drafted, though socially desirable, legislation. Commencing with the Family Home Protection Act and continuing on to the Judicial Separation and Family Law Reform Act, it has unfortunately been the case that the effects of this legislation on conveyancing practice have been to make matters more difficult for the solicitor and the client and to slow down the process of transfer.

The Society argued that it would like to see all available resources concentrating on improving the Land Registry and converting it into a commercially-motivated public corporation, as already recommended by the Society in 1989, and a programme of reform on land law and conveyancing.

On the issue of employed barristers being entitled to perform conveyancing services, the Society considered that they should only be entitled to do so on the same basis as employed solicitors and they should be subject to the same regulatory control and restrictions in relation to a compensation fund, undertakings, discipline and professional indemnity, where applicable.

The Society argued that the reservation of the taking out of grants of probate and letters of administration to solicitors, as officers of the court, was in ease of the High Court. When a solicitor made an application there was no need for further inquiry by the court regarding the will document itself, the witnesses, executor, administrator or distribution to beneficiaries. The court in making such grants was greatly influenced by the integrity of its solicitor officer. The Society noted that that the element of fraud was thus greatly reduced and the service to the consumer was delivered

16. The Law Society's headquarters at Blackhall Place, Dublin since 1978. Formerly the Blue Coat School or King's Hospital, the building was designed by Thomas Ivory in 1772. The first stone was laid on 16 June 1773 and the building was completed in 1783. *(Photograph: Jacqueline O'Brien; reproduced by kind permission)*

17. The official opening of the Law Society's new headquarters on 14 June 1978. An Taoiseach, Jack Lynch TD, receives the ceremonial key from the architect Terence Nolan of the firm Nolan and Quinlan. Also present is the President of the Society (1977/78), Joseph L. Dundon. *(Photograph: Lensmen)*

18. 'Four provinces' window with the Society's coat of arms, formerly in the Solicitors'
Buildings, Four Courts, and now on the main corridor in Blackhall Place *(Photograph:
Lensmen)*

19. The Law Society council chamber. The ceiling was designed and executed by Charles Thorp about 1778. It was damaged by fire in the 1930s and was restored by the Dublin firm of Sibthorpe and Son. *(Photograph: Jacqueline O'Brien; reproduced by kind permission)*

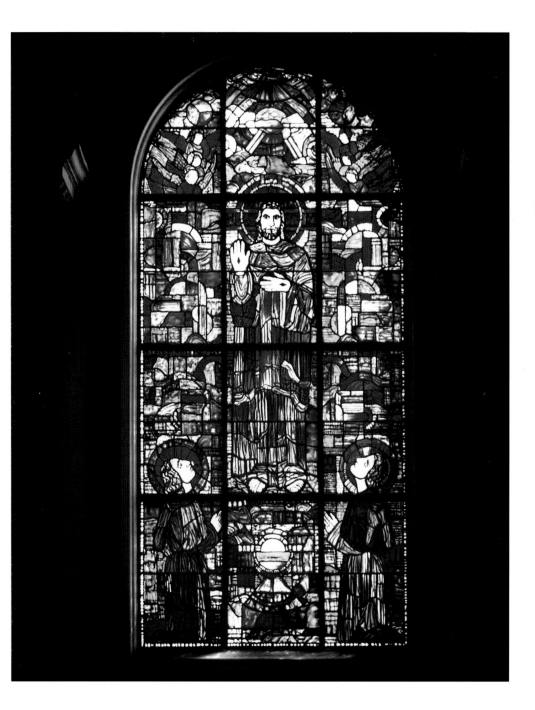

20. Stained glass window executed in 1936 by Evie Hone for the east window of the chapel of King's Hospital, now the President's Hall of the Law Society *(Photograph: Brian Cusack)*

21. First and second women auditors of SADSI. Elizabeth A. Ryan (left) on her election as auditor for the year 1970/71 with Helena Early, the first woman auditor in 1921/22. (*Reproduced from the Irish Times*)

22. Portrait of Peter D.M. Prentice, President of the Society 1973/74 by Thomas Ryan RHA. The portrait, which hangs in the Society's council chamber, was presented to Peter Prentice by the council of the Society in appreciation of his initiative and commitment in the acquisition and refurbishment of the Society's headquarters at Blackhall Place. *(Photograph: Gillian Buckley)*

23. An Taoiseach, Charles J. Haughey TD, unveiling a statue of Stephen Trotter, judge of the prerogative court in the eighteenth century, with Law Society President Donal G. Binchy, May 1991. The statue is attributed to Peter Scheemakers (1691–1781) and was brought from Duleek, Co. Louth, with the assistance of the National Heritage Council. It stands in the entrance hallway of the Law Society. *(Photograph: Lensmen)*

24. James J. Ivers, Director General of the Law Society, 1973–1990 *(Photograph: Lensmen)*

25. Noel C. Ryan, Director General of the Law Society, 1990–1994 *(Photograph: Lensmen)*

26. The first practising solicitors appointed judges of the Circuit Court in 1996 were (*left to right*): Judge Frank O'Donnell, Judge John F. Buckley and Judge Michael White. (*Photograph: Lensmen*)

27. The late Terence de Vere White, admitted as a solicitor in 1933, member of the Council of the Law Society from 1954 to 1961, biographer, novelist, and literary editor. His portrait, by Muriel Brandt RHA, hangs in the offices of McCann FitzGerald, Dublin, where he was a partner for many years. *(Photograph: Lensmen)*

28. David R. Pigot (*right*) (admitted 1951; President of the Law Society 1986/87) and Robin Waters walk out to open the Ireland innings in reply to the West Indies all out 25 at Sion Mills, Co. Tyrone, 2 July 1969. *(Courtesy: David R. Pigot)*

29. Sean Flanagan TD (admitted 1946) leads out the Mayo team against Meath in the 1951 All Ireland football final. Third in line on the Mayo team is Eamonn G. Mongey, Barrister-at-Law, former assistant probate registrar, author of *Probate practice in a nutshell* and contributor to courses in the Society's Law School for many years. *(Courtesy: Dermot Flanagan)*

30. Tony Hanahoe (admitted 1968) played for Dublin in six successive All Ireland football finals from 1974 to 1979, and captained the winning Dublin team in 1976 and 1977. *(Courtesy: Tony Hanahoe)*

31. Tony O'Reilly (admitted 1958) scores a try against the All Blacks during the 1959 British and Irish 'Lions' tour of Australia and New Zealand, under the eye of touch judge Gordon Wood. Tony O'Reilly played 29 times for Ireland and 10 times for the Lions. *(Courtesy: Murray Consultants)*

32. Tony Ensor (admitted 1974; President of the Society 1999/00), Irish rugby full back, avoids a tackle by the Argentinian full back, backed up by Irish hooker Ken Kennedy, in Lansdowne Road, autumn 1974. Tony Ensor was capped 22 times for Ireland in the years 1973 to 1978. *(Photograph: Irish Times)*

efficiently. There already was a facility in the Probate Office to enable individual members of the public extract grants of probate and letters of administration. Any substantial increase in the number of applications by non-solicitors would require far greater personnel and back-up facilities within the Probate Office than existed at that time. If personnel and facilities were not to be increased, the resulting back-log in applications would be 'intolerable'.

On the issue of representation in court, the Society considered it was totally undesirable to allow any person other than a solicitor or barrister to represent a defendant in any court except where a friend or relative appears to explain the absence of a defendant. It was a fundamental principle that the court must have authority over all persons appearing before it, and 'the first duty of a solicitor is to the court'. It was argued by the Society that the suggestion of a person other than a solicitor or barrister representing a litigant in the District Court was contrary to both the interest of litigants and the proper administration of justice. It was likely to lead to the court being misled and to time-consuming speeches and other delaying tactics being adopted by unqualified persons doing their best but without accountability. Apart from these fundamental matters, the implementation of such a suggestion might well lead to a great number of cases being appealed and ultimately higher costs.

The Society submitted that a solicitor was the best person to advise a defendant facing a criminal charge because of his or her knowledge of both substantive law and court procedures. Opening the process to non-legal advisers 'could leave the public and the court at the mercy of persons of dubious credentials'. The Gardaí had publicly stated that behind the scenes, in criminal cases, known criminals were already advising defendants on how to disrupt the course of justice, for example by the making of spurious complaints against Gardaí in order to tie up Garda manpower and delay the progression of a trial. The Society concluded that the commission's proposal in this area of lay representation was not based on a sound knowledge of court procedure.

On the issue of the division of the legal profession into two branches, the commission noted that there was no statutory separation of functions between the two branches of the profession. The two branches of the profession did operate separately in practice and there were lines of demarcation, according to the commission, with varying degrees of rigidity between them. The commission did not consider that a fused profession would result in the dire consequences predicted by its opponents. The commission did not accept that there would be any diminution in standards. Simply fusing the profession, however, would not be a means of eliminating the restrictive practices then in existence, though it might affect some of them, and a fused profession would not guarantee the delivery of more efficient and less costly legal services. Any harms caused, or contributed to, by the fact that the profession was divided were certainly not, in the opinion of the commission, so great as to warrant a recommendation that the two branches should be compulsorily fused into a single profession. At the same time, the commission did not consider that it would be unfair or contrary to the common good if there were to be a single, fused profession. Indeed, it believed that a fused profession might, without being a cause of concern, evolve gradually over time. In its view, nothing should be done to frustrate such a development.

The Society was of the view that any proposal for fusion of the profession could only be justified if it resulted in a more efficient or less costly service to the public. As this had not been demonstrated, the Society did not support the concept of fusion. The view was held by many solicitors that if the two branches of the profession were to fuse then barristers would join large firms and their advice would no longer be available to individual clients advised by a small firm of solicitors. Interestingly, the Society did mention there was a view among some solicitors that some form of fusion should be considered, such view being based on the consideration that there did not appear to be any good reason as to why all lawyers should not have a common vocational education and on qualification be admitted as solicitors and barristers. On qualification, however, the Irish lawyer should have the right to choose to practise as a specialist/advocate if he or she so wished, taking instructions only through other members of the profession. Such a specialist group would provide services to the smaller rural practices on which much emphasis was placed in certain submissions to the commission.

On the issue of education of solicitors, the commission in 1990 noted that the Law Society and the King's Inns exercised effective control over the numbers entering the respective professions. The commission considered there was a great danger arising from such control over entry; the number admitted might be restricted to a level which was believed to match the perceived requirements of the profession and not of the public. The commission considered that such self-protection would amount to both a restrictive practice and an abuse of a dominant position which would be seriously disadvantageous to the common good. In principle, the commission favoured freedom of entry to a profession, consistent with the maintenance of acceptable but not excessive standards, with the market for professional services being allowed to determine the numbers of practitioners. The commission considered there should be a common vocational course for solicitors and barristers with the minimum of separate training and recommended that there should be established as a matter of urgency by the Minister for Justice an advisory committee on legal education and training, charged with reviewing the education and training of lawyers at all stages and with implementing a system of common vocational training, and comprised of a majority of non-lawyers.

John Buckley considers the issue of education of solicitors in the next chapter but it may be stated here that the Society strongly opposed the establishment of such an overall advisory committee on legal education and training. In the Society's view, the structure of the committee proposed by the commission was entirely unsuitable. Due to the initiative of the Society, there was already in existence a joint committee on legal education comprised of representatives of all the universities and the Law Society considering the alignment of legal education and training. The Society considered that a committee of this composition was the correct one with the necessary qualifications and experience to deal with the matter but would welcome representation on the committee from the Department of Justice.

In relation to the Irish language, the commission recommended that the Irish language requirement should be abandoned for both solicitors and barristers and replaced by an obligation on both the Law Society and the Bar Council to arrange representation for persons who wished to conduct legal practice through the medium of the Irish language and consideration should also be given to continuing legal education in this area. The Society endorsed this proposal of the commission.

Views were expressed to the commission concerning deficiencies in the organisation of the courts. The commission was concerned that there appeared to be inefficiencies, but considered also that sufficient resources had probably not been made available for the adequate funding of the court system. It considered that it was essential that the legal process undergo modernising and streamlining, with greater use of modern management techniques and computerisation.

While accepting the onerous nature of the work of judges, the commission was concerned that the courts, particularly the superior courts, apparently operated for 'relatively short hours', and then for not all working days during the year. If a two-month vacation proved necessary, which the commission tended to doubt, it seemed preferable that the months should comprise July and August rather than August and September. The Society welcomed any proposed review of the organisation of the courts. The Society considered that the vacation period should be altered from August/September to July/August in line with school holidays. It was quite unfair to the public involved in litigation that a considerable number of cases listed for July had to be adjourned for three months because expert professional witnesses were unavailable as they had arrangements to take holidays with their children in July.

Other issues dealt with by the commission related to fee determination and advertising, both considered earlier by the present writer.

At the time of writing, the profession faces another inquiry, this time by the Competition Authority. The Taoiseach, Bertie Ahern, made this announcement at the launch of a report by the OECD in 2001 entitled 'Regulatory reform in Ireland' which made passing references to the legal profession. Ken Murphy, the director general of the Society, in the annual report of the Society 2000/01 noted that some of the OECD's recommendations in relation to lawyers appeared to be based 'on ideology rather than information, on prejudice rather than proof'. A great deal of the Society's time and energies have been devoted to the issue with the Competition Authority.

SOLICITORS AS JUDGES

The Society had been pressing for many years for a change in the law so as to permit the appointment of solicitors as judges in the Circuit Court and High Court. The issue had been canvassed in many fora and reference here may be made to the Fair Trade Commission, *Report of study into restrictive practices in the legal profession* published in 1990. Representatives of the Society in submissions to the commission stated that a formal request had been made some years previously that solicitors should be appointed as judges in both the Circuit and High Courts. It was accepted that solicitors generally did not have the same experience in advocacy as barristers, but it was stated to be indefensible that some solicitors, who had an international reputation, could not be appointed as judges.

The Society submitted that a panel of interested and suitable persons for appointment as judges of the District Court should be established and that selection should be made from the panel 'without political interference'. The Society subscribed to the idea that there should be a training period for judges at all levels, except perhaps the Supreme Court. The Society was opposed to the idea of the judiciary being a separate career within the legal profession, with entry as a court clerk and promotion through the ranks of judges. Such persons would not be conversant with the adversarial system, and could not gain the requisite legal experience.

It was accepted that the skills of an advocate were not necessarily the same skills as those required of the judiciary; the Society argued that some persons who had not been particularly good barristers had made excellent judges. The Bar Council representatives stated they had no objection, in principle, to the idea of solicitors being appointed as judges, provided that solicitors availed of the right of audience and obtained training and experience in adversarial procedures, the running of cases, court rules and the rules of evidence. The judge had to be experienced in court practice and procedure. The vast majority of solicitors, it was claimed, did not have the 'slightest notion' of these matters, and academic lawyers would have even less.

The Fair Trade Commission in its 1990 report stated that had the judiciary been within the scope of its study, the commission would have carefully considered whether this restriction upon those eligible for appointment constituted an unfair practice, on the grounds, for example, that it was in restraint of trade and excluded new entrants, and whether it was contrary to the common good. The commission accepted that it was necessary to ensure that only persons of the highest calibre should be appointed judges and that it was arguable that the adversarial system of justice required that judges should preferably be recruited from the ranks of experienced advocates. The commission recommended, however, that consideration be given to the possibility of the appointment of solicitors as judges. A start could be made with appointments to the Circuit Court. The commission in 1990 noted that the skills required of a judge are not identical to those of an advocate, and that experience of court practice and procedure, as well as of the law, were probably more important. While few solicitors had appeared regularly in the superior courts, some had done so, and many solicitors had acted as advocates in the Circuit Court. The commission considered that some solicitors were well qualified for judicial appointment, and that making solicitors eligible for appointment would both widen the pool of available talent from which the choice could be made and increase the level of competition for appointment which would ensure that the highest standards would be maintained. The presence of former solicitors as judges would encourage more solicitors to engage in advocacy since they might very well be partly inhibited from exercising their rights of audience since all judges at that time were former barristers.

In addition, the commission in 1990 considered that advocacy in the courts should not be the only route to an appointment in the superior courts. The commission noted, for example, that judicial experience in the Circuit Court would be an equally appropriate qualification for appointment as a judge of the High Court. The commission stated that consideration should be given, therefore, to the possibility of the promotion of a judge from one court to a higher court, a procedure which is found in other countries; consideration should also be given to part-time judicial service being a pre-requisite for a full-time appointment, and whether some training might be provided for the judiciary, as well as the adoption of a system whereby judicial office should be a separate career, with judges proceeding by promotion from the lower courts to the highest.

The Courts and Court Officers Act, 1995 allowed for the appointment of solicitors as judges of the Circuit Court. In July 1996, the Government announced the appointment of solicitors, John F. Buckley, Frank O'Donnell and Michael White as judges of the Circuit Court. Ken Murphy, the director general of the Society, in a news release subsequently published in the *Gazette* in July 1996, stated that the Society welcomed with particular warmth and pleasure the nomination by the Government of three distinguished solicitors who would enjoy a place in legal history as the first ever solicitors appointed directly from practice to serve as judges of the Circuit Court. Noting that all three judges had 'the qualities of intellect, character, judgment and legal knowledge which made them eminently well qualified to serve the Irish people as members of the judiciary', the appointments represented a breakthrough for which solicitors had been campaigning for decades. Ken Murphy stated that the remaining prohibition on direct appointment of solicitors as judges of the High and Supreme Court was a relic of history which continued to operate against the public interest. If it were dropped, the Government would have available to it a much wider range of candidates with more varied experience both of law and of life from which choices could be made. The increased competition would be beneficial in the High Court and Supreme Court as it had been in the Circuit Court. Subsequently, Patrick McCartan, Professor Bryan McMahon and Katherine Delahunt, all practising solicitors, have been appointed judges of the Circuit Court.

During the Dáil debate on the Courts and Court Officers Act, 1995 the Minister for Justice, Nora Owen TD, indicated she would examine further the issue of the qualifications required to be eligible for appointment as a judge of the High and Supreme Courts. Subsequently, in December 1996, the Minister established a working group with terms of reference 'to consider and make recommendations to the Minister for Justice on the question of qualifications for appointment as judges of the High and Supreme Courts'. Among the solicitor members of the working group were the director general of the Society, Ken Murphy, Geraldine M. Clarke and Ernest J. Cantillon. Garrett Cooney SC, Mary Finlay SC and Turlough O'Donnell SC were the nominees of the Bar Council.

A fundamental difference of opinion existed among the members of the working group as to whether or not experience as an advocate (when used in the traditional sense) should be an essential qualification for appointment to the High Court and Supreme Court. However, the group in its report[6] in 1999 recommended that a solicitor with litigation experience who had significant knowledge and experience of the decisions, practices and procedures of the High and Supreme Courts should be eligible for appointment as a judge of the High and Supreme Courts.

The Government accepted in principle the recommendations of the working group. The subsequent Courts and Court Officers Act, 2002, presented to the Dáil by the Minister for Justice, Equality and Law Reform, John O'Donoghue TD in March 2001 and enacted a year later, provides, inter alia, that a person shall be qualified for appointment as a judge of the Supreme Court and High Court if he or she is for the time being a practising barrister or a practising solicitor of not less than twelve years' standing who has practised as a barrister or solicitor for a continuous period of not less than two years immediately before such appointment. Michael Peart was the first practising solicitor to be appointed a judge of the High Court, in 2002.

The 2002 act also provides that the Judicial Appointments Advisory Board when recommending a person for appointment to the Superior Courts should be of the opinion that the person has an appropriate knowledge of the decisions and an appropriate knowledge and experience of the practice and procedures of those courts and should have regard, in particular, to the nature and extent of the practice of the person concerned insofar as it relates to his or her personal conduct of proceedings in the High and Supreme Courts, whether as an advocate or as a solicitor instructing counsel or both.

THE PROTECTION OF CLIENTS' FINANCES

The Society is obliged by the Solicitors Act, 1954, as amended, to maintain a compensation fund to compensate clients for financial losses arising due

6 *Report of the working group on qualification for appointment as judges of the High and Supreme Courts,* Stationery Office, Dublin (PN 6707) 1999.

to any dishonesty on the part of solicitors or their employees. The fund is maintained exclusively by contributions from solicitors. A noble exposition of the justification for the compensation fund was set out by Ward McEllin, then chairman of the compensation fund committee,[7] in the Society's annual report for 1990/91 and is deserving of being quoted here:

> The true profession of law is based on an ideal of honourable service. It is distinguished by unique responsibilities. The function of the lawyer is to serve the community in the regulation of its social structures, in the conduct of its commerce and the administration of justice … Public confidence in the administration of justice in the legal profession may be eroded by dishonesty or other irresponsible conduct on the part of the individual lawyer. Accordingly, the lawyer's conduct should reflect credit on the legal profession, inspire the confidence, respect and trust of clients and the community, and avoid even the appearance of impropriety.
>
> … As a profession, we must accept that we are different from others in the so-called competitive market place. Integrity for a solicitor is not just a valuable asset – it must be a prerequisite of his make up. If that costs us money – the public trust it generates is worth every penny. In discharging the commission devolved upon it by the council, the compensation fund committee is cognisant of a twofold duty: the vindication of the status and reputation of the profession, by the protection and indemnification of the public against loss occasioned by the dishonesty of solicitors or their employees and the protection and conservation of the assets of the compensation fund.

Unprecedented claims including those relating to the Hunt and O'Toole practices reduced the fund to £36,468 at December 1982, after full provision had been made for all claims. More demands were consequently made upon members of the profession. The contribution per solicitor was £5 for the practice year 1980/81. This was forced to rise to £49 for the following year 1981/82. The per capita contribution of members rose to

---

7 Ward McEllin was president of the Society in the year 2000/01.

£600 per annum in 1994 but was reduced to £400 in 1999 and has remained at that level up to the time of writing. Donal G. Binchy, president of the Society in 1990/91, in the annual report of the Society in November 1991 stated that his year of office opened with headlines in the *Irish Independent* on 16 November 1990 (the morning after his election), publicising two large claims against the fund, one stated to be for £9.2 million and another for £25 million. The president noted that claims such as these could devastate the fund and undermine the protection enjoyed by the public; fortunately claims of such magnitude failed to materialise.

The Jonathan Brooks practice claim in the 1990s made a significant dent in the fund. There developed a widespread view in the profession that honest solicitors should not be required to fund the dishonesty of others. The Society made the strongest representations to Government that the scope of the fund should not extend to persons who are not clients of solicitors and that a cap should be placed on any one claim. Following representations, the Solicitors (Amendment) Act, 1994 provided that the amount of a grant made to any client of a solicitor under the fund should not exceed £350,000 and there was provision for a change in that figure in the future having regard to change in the value of money.

SOLICITORS (AMENDMENT) ACT, 1994

The Solicitors (Amendment) Act, 1994 was regarded at the time of enactment as profoundly important for the future of the profession. The act gave the Society stronger powers to investigate and deal with complaints from the public against solicitors. It also empowered the Society to require solicitors to take certain steps where the Society found that a solicitor had provided inadequate services or had charged excessive fees. The act also provided for a disciplinary tribunal to replace the disciplinary committee and, as mentioned, provided for a 'cap' of £350,000 on grants made to any client of a solicitor from the compensation fund in respect of matters arising from the relationship between the client and the solicitor.

A contentious matter was dealt with in section 68 of the 1994 act which set out provisions in relation to charges to clients. It came into operation on 4 February 1995. From that date, a solicitor was obliged to provide each client with written particulars of the charges to be made for the legal services to be provided. The particulars were to be given on the taking of instructions or as soon as possible thereafter. The particulars must state either the actual charges that would be made, an estimate of those charges, or the basis on which the charges would be made. The remuneration and costs committee of the Society drew up forms of agreements intended to meet the requirements of the section and these were circulated to the profession.

The 1994 act also dealt with the education of solicitors. In the context of apprenticeship, the period of apprenticeship was reduced from three years to two years. In addition, the act allowed solicitors to take two apprentices at the same time with the written consent of the Society and also permitted the taking of one apprentice for every two assistant solicitors in a firm. All practising solicitors were conferred by the 1994 act with the powers of a commissioner for oaths in relation to the administration of oaths and the taking of affidavits. This does not mean that a practising solicitor who was not already a commissioner for oaths could call himself or herself a commissioner for oaths. That separate and distinct category of lawyer called a commissioner for oaths was retained. Statutory offences were created relating to client accounts, client monies and accounting records, the maximum penalty being a fine of £1,500 on summary conviction and a fine of £10,000 on conviction on indictment. The 1994 act also set out a significant number of enabling provisions under which the Society could make regulations providing for compulsory professional indemnity insurance, restrictions on practice after qualification and mandatory continuing legal education.

INTERNAL GOVERNANCE AND THE REVIEW GROUP OF 1994/95

Dissatisfaction with some aspects of the structure of the Society and its governance led to vigorous debates at the annual general meeting on 24 November 1994. A resolution was passed that the Society immediately set up an inquiry to examine the structure of the council of the Society with the objective of better serving the solicitors' profession in modern Ireland

and to examine the administration, finances and accounts of the Society with a similar objective.

The president of the Society, Patrick A. Glynn, appointed a working group under the chairmanship of Donal G. Binchy, Clonmel, County Tipperary. The members of the group were chosen to be representative of urban and rural firms, sole practitioners and partnerships, council members and non-council members. In addition to the chairman, the members of the group comprised Leo Mangan (Dublin), Daire Murphy (Dublin), Ken Murphy, director general of the Society, Pat O'Connor (Swinford, County Mayo), John Shaw (Mullingar, County Westmeath) and Liam Young (Dublin).

Submissions were invited from all practitioners with a notice published in the *Gazette* and the views of local bar associations, committee chairmen and staff members of the Society were canvassed by letter. The first meeting of the group was held on 21 February 1995; the group met on a total of sixteen occasions including eight full-day sessions.

The review group came up with 106 specific recommendations. Among the recommendations was the abolition of the privilege allowing past presidents to attend council meetings except for the immediate past-president. However, a past president who wished to stand for election should be permitted to do so, subject to what was described as a 'quarantine' period.

In the context of election to the council, the review group recommended that the national electorate of solicitors elect 50 per cent of the ordinary council seats annually, with 50 per cent of the council retiring in order to create the necessary vacancies. Once elected, solicitors should serve a term of two years on the council before retiring and being eligible to offer themselves for re-election. The system of election of vice-presidents and the president on the basis of seniority was recommended to be discontinued. However, a minimum of six years' service on the council of which two consecutive years must have been served immediately before candidacy should be required before a council member could offer him or herself for election as senior vice-president. It was recommended that the senior vice-president should automatically proceed to the presidency in the following year.

The group recommended that a balance should be sought in committee membership so as to ensure representation from sole practitioners, small and large firms, both urban and rural, and from particular sectoral interests.

There was to be a five year time-limit on membership of any committee followed by a two-year 'quarantine' period in relation to the committee in question. In special circumstances, this restriction could be waived by the council. There was also to be a two-year time-limit on chairmanship and a minimum 20 per cent turnover of membership on committees every year. The review group recommended that in special circumstances these restrictions could be waived by the council. The then current system whereby committee members and chairpersons were selected by the president and approved by the council should continue.

The review group recommended that the Society should maintain control of the professional training of solicitors in the interests of the profession and the public. The Society should continue its objective of 'producing well-educated, properly trained and skilled professionals conscious of their ethical and professional obligations and equipped with the management and business skills required to provide efficient and high quality legal services'. The existing system of continuing legal education for practising solicitors was recommended to be extended and expanded. However, further efforts were to be made to offer seminars in regional centres and outside office hours. Additional diplomas of benefit to the profession were to be introduced.

The review group was conscious of the Society's role in representing the public interest. The Society was to continue to promote proactively and protect the interests of the public particularly in the area of law reform. The ongoing work of the Society committees in influencing law reform and protecting the interests of the public was to be highlighted; the Society should campaign on issues such as the deficiencies in the courts system, the need for reform of ancient laws and the efficiency of public administration.

In the context of the Society's finances, it was recommended that a cost benefit analysis of expenditure in relation to entertainment, the annual council dinner and council and committee expenses should be undertaken. Attendance by the president and the director general at foreign conferences should require approval, as a matter of policy, having regard to the nature of the event and to the benefit enuring to the Society. The Society's accounts were to be made as user-friendly as possible.

The council set aside a day-long special meeting on Saturday, 10 February 1996 to discuss the recommendations of the review group report. Council members regarded the meeting as one of the best council debates for many years; the 106 recommendations of the review group were analysed and discussed. In what only can be regarded as a great tribute to the members of the review group, the council decided that the overwhelming majority of the recommendations of the review group were viewed simply as common sense and supported unanimously. The overwhelming majority of the review group's recommendations were approved at special general meetings in March and July 1996 and bye-laws were made to give effect to them. The special general meetings were ably chaired in what were described as 'difficult times' by President Andrew F. Smyth. The first special general meeting in March 1996 lasted no less than six hours and in itself must have represented a record.

Accordingly, in 1996, a considerable change occurred in the internal governance of the Society. New bye-laws provided that ordinary members of the council were to be elected for a two-year term and half the council were to step down each year (fifteen in one year, sixteen the next). The same applied to provincial delegates with two stepping down each year and successful candidates being elected for a two-year term. In 1996, a restriction was placed on service on the council so that once council members had served ten years, they were obliged to take a break of four years, referred to as the 'quarantine period', before serving again on the council. The ten-year period started in November 1997 for some members of the council and in November 1998 for others (based on a 'lot' conducted in 1996), so that the earliest application of the restriction would arise in November 2007. The names of the current members of the council of the Society for the year 2001/02 are set out in Appendix 1, on page 225. The 1996 bye-laws provided that any council member who had served on the council for four years was entitled to seek election as junior vice-president; any council member who had served on the council for six years was entitled to seek election as senior vice-president. In both cases, two of those years must be served immediately before seeking election to the office. The outgoing senior vice-president was to be automatically appointed as president for the coming year.

Much of the business of the council is conducted by committees. The incoming president selects the chairman and members of each committee and places their names before the council for approval. In 1999, general guidelines for the appointment of committees were agreed by the council which provided some curtailment on the powers of the president. The incoming president was expected to consult with the chairmen of committees and the executive in relation to the appointment of committees for the forthcoming year; the president was to take great care to create a balance between expertise on a committee and accountability to the council; where possible the chairman or vice-chairman of each committee was to be a council member and a possible chairman was not to be appointed unless he or she had previously served on the committee. The guidelines specified that committee members who had attended less than 50 per cent of committee meetings during the previous year should not be re-appointed to the committee unless the chairman indicated that there were good reasons for the non-attendance and that the member should be re-appointed. The guidelines also provided that at the council meeting before he or she assumes office, the incoming president should seek the council's approval for any proposed dissolutions or amalgamations of existing committees and the establishment of new committees.

The president, council and officers of the Society are always conscious of public relations. Public relations obviously relate to issues pertaining to perception and reputation. The Society as the representative and regulatory body for the solicitors' profession has a number of separate 'constituencies' or 'audiences', some of which from time to time may have directly conflicting approaches to any particular issue. The 'audiences' which impinge on the Society include the solicitors' profession, apprentices, other professional organisations, the Bar Council, the judiciary, the government, the account-ancy bodies, the media and the general public. Understandably, the Society has targeted each of these 'audiences', sometimes all together, in order to communicate and win support and understanding for the Society's position and to influence the attitudes and behaviour of others.

The principal public relations tool used by the Society is the *Gazette*. The *Gazette* is sent on a monthly basis to all members of the profession, the judi-ciary, the media, other professional bodies, apprentices and is on sale to the general public. It aims to be the definitive source of news and information for the solicitors' profession and indeed for all of those with an interest in the law.

During 1999, the Society launched a new corporate image including a full-coloured crest, which is represented on its headed notepaper. A single-colour crest is also used, where appropriate, and examples can be seen on the cover of the Law Directory and on the Society's envelopes.

The Society launched a website in February 1999, www.lawsociety.ie. The focus of the website is to educate and inform the general public about the work of the Society and the solicitors' profession in Ireland and to act as a reference point for all members with regard to activities and functions of the Society. Committees have been allocated their own pages which set out objectives, activities, projects and publications. There is also a profile of the Society, its buildings and personnel and a short history of the Society since its foundation. Included on the website are details of the regulatory and educational functions carried out by the Society, information on the library, details of member services and on-line articles from the *Gazette*. Practice notes published in the *Gazette* since 1986 are available on the website and a number of precedent documents are also published. Frequently asked questions and responses are set out, and other professional information sets out check-lists of fees, tax bands and allowances along with general legal information.

CONCLUSION

Undoubtedly, the profession of solicitor has, over the period since the 1970s, developed a strong cohesion and indeed a powerful advocate in the form of the Law Society. In many ways, the institutional Law Society has been adapted to serve the changing needs of solicitors over the past decades. The law, with Ireland's written constitution, plays an important role in Irish life. With the growth of government, in its many guises, and the complexity in the regulation of business and life in general, solicitors have played a significant role in Ireland in the last decades of the tumultuous twentieth century.

Legal education: a steep curve of learning

JOHN F. BUCKLEY

Very significant changes were introduced into both academic and professional education during the early 1950s. At that time the only law school in the State which offered a primary honours degree in law subjects was Trinity College. University College Dublin, then, as now, the largest of our universities, had discontinued its honours BA degree in Legal and Political Science in the late 1940s and maintained only the pass version of this degree until the middle 1950s. It was not then the norm for apprentices to take degrees. In his address to the 1952 general meeting of the Law Society, the president, Arthur Cox, deplored the decline in the number of apprentices who were taking degrees. The Society required apprentices to take certain courses of lectures in the university law schools, but these did not have to form part of a degree course. Entry to apprenticeship was at school-leaving age and the apprenticeship term coincided with university and Law Society lecture courses.

In 1954 UCD commenced to offer a Bachelor of Civil Law degree at both honours and pass level. This coincided with the appointment of full-time teachers in the law faculty. The course for this degree was more comprehensive and involved longer teaching hours. The degree rapidly gained acceptance and a similar degree was introduced in University College Cork a few years later. University College Galway did not seek to introduce this form of degree at that time and were subsequently refused permission by the Higher Education Authority to offer it.

The structure of the Society's examination system, involving preliminary, intermediate and final examinations had remained unchanged for upwards of fifty years, though there had been changes in the subjects examined. Under the 1954 Solicitors Act the Society was authorised to replace the intermediate and final examinations with first, second and third law examinations. Needless to say the number of subjects to be examined increased significantly as a result of this change. This system was to remain in force for the next twenty years. The overlapping of subjects between the universities and the Society's lectures was ended and the scope of the Society's programme was extended.

One significant change which occurred during the 1950s was the increase in the number of solicitors' apprentices who took degree courses. A comparison of the list of admissions for 1951/52 with that for 1961/62 shows a change from 8 per cent to 50 per cent as having taken degrees. While these figures may have to be treated with caution, an extrapolation of them into the late 1960s certainly shows the majority of apprentices as having taken degree courses. By then the percentage had risen to 62%.

It was not long, however, before the Society was expressing a need for further change. In his address to the general meeting of the Society in 1960, the president, John J. Nash, advocated the splitting of the process into two, an academic course followed by practical training. It had become clear that the changes in the university courses meant that apprentices taking degree courses did not have time to attend their offices during term time and the 'in-office' part of the system had largely broken down. A submission was made to the Commission on Higher Education in 1961, but nothing seems to have come from that. A number of Mr Nash's successors repeated his arguments and the Government was asked to amend the Solicitors Acts to enable the proposed changes to be made. Nothing was to happen until a fresh approach was taken in the 1970s.

The kick-start to these changes was given by a report, 'The Education of a Solicitor', prepared by a committee of the Society of Young Solicitors in 1967. This endorsed the proposal to separate the academic and practical segments of a solicitor's training and made detailed recommendations as to how such a proposal should be implemented. Within six years of the publication of this report, two of its authors, Maurice Curran and the writer, were members of the Society's education committee, then quaintly called 'the court of examiners', and argued for its implementation. A stumbling-block which the Society had always seen, namely the need for amending legislation, was examined critically. The Society's newly appointed director-general, Jim Ivers, a former civil servant and chief executive of a health board, and a veteran of construing statutory powers, suggested that the Society could achieve virtually all of the reforms, save for changing the term of apprenticeship, by utilising its power to make statutory instruments.

The overlapping of the academic and practical courses was to end. The level of the preliminary examination was raised to that of university degree level and exemption from this examination was to be given to university graduates. A full-time law school was to be established, with entry to this school by competitive examination. Research among the common law jurisdictions revealed that the Australian States appeared to have the most developed training programmes. The Society engaged the services of Kevin O'Leary, head of the professional school of the Australian National University, as a consultant and dispatched its newly-appointed education officer, Harry Sexton, to Australia to observe the operation of some of the courses there. It was decided that the optimum way to schedule the practical training in the law school and that in the office was by way of a 'sandwich' system, a six-month period in the law school, the professional course, followed by eighteen months in the office, and then a shorter course in the law school, the advanced course. As the position then was, and still is, that a person on admittance to the roll of solicitors is normally entitled to set up in practice on his or her own account immediately, the policy of the law school was to train apprentices to enter into private practice.

Many members of the profession were recruited to design the individual segments of the courses and to prepare the teaching materials. They and others were invited to join the teaching teams in the new courses. There was a very considerable emphasis on the practical aspects of the subjects. 'Learning by doing' was the philosophy adopted, and so far as possible the teaching was to be done by practitioners. Whatever about the truth of G.B. Shaw's canard, 'He who can, does. He who cannot, teaches', the policy of the school was that only those who could, should teach. Partly because the Society was seen to be enlisting the assistance of many well-known members of the profession in designing and operating the courses, but also because it was abundantly clear that the previous system had virtually broken down, the proposed new system was widely welcomed. The Society proceeded to implement the changes with the appointment of

Richard Woulfe as director of education and Laurence Sweeney as director of training. A key factor in the implementation of the new system was the decision of the Society to proceed to occupy the Blackhall Place property which had been purchased some years earlier. This provided adequate accommodation for the new law school and its opening was co-ordinated with the Society's move there in 1978.

The most vocal opposition to the changes came from the Union of Students in Ireland who took exception to the substantial fees which were being charged for the new courses. While the Society had what it believed was a valid explanation for the charges, the intensive nature of the courses, and was in fact subsidising the courses, this did not prevent pickets being placed on Blackhall Place on the day of the opening of the law school. Another criticism was that the number of places in the law school was restricted to 150 per annum and it was feared that candidates of quality might be excluded by reason of this limitation. There were three reasons for the selection of this figure, as outlined by the Society to the Department of Justice. The first was the capacity of the national economy to provide job opportunities for solicitors, and the second that practical training schemes were the best method of achieving proficiency in the skills and procedures that formed the objectives of the new courses and that 75 students was the limit that could satisfactorily be dealt with in one of the two annual modules proposed. The third was the number of members of the profession available to participate as consultants and tutors in the new courses and the physical limitation of the space available in Blackhall Place.

In fact, during the years in which all candidates were obliged to sit the competitive entrance examination, the number of candidates who passed the entire examination never exceeded 150. The manner in which the Society adjudicated on the results of that examination was to give rise to one of the series of legal proceedings instituted against the Society in the 1980s and 1990s.

One of the side-effects of the 1978 changes was that, while the statutory minimum age at which a person could be admitted a solicitor remained at 21, in practice a person was unlikely to be qualified for admittance until the age of 23 or 24. While this would undoubtedly have increased the cost to the students (or their families) there was a view that the additional maturity which those qualifying would have gained by qualifying at a greater age would be of benefit to them and their prospective clients and employers. In addition the fact that apprentices, who became more useful than before to their masters, would be more likely to be paid, would have offset the cost to some extent.

LITIGATION OVER EDUCATION AND ITS CONSEQUENCES

From 1986 onwards the Society faced challenges in the courts against the education regulations which it had made and the manner in which it had implemented them.

The Gilmer case[1]

In this case heard in 1987 by Mr Justice Hamilton, then president of the High Court, Yvonne Gilmer, an apprentice, who had been informed by the Society that, under the compensation rules which the Society had applied in adjudicating on the results of the final examination-first part, she had not passed the examination, claimed that the compensation rules applied by the Society were devised for the purpose of limiting the number of places. She failed in this claim but the court held that the manner in which the Society had applied the compensation rules in her case amounted to requiring a 51 per cent pass rate and not the 50 per cent published by the Society. In addition the court stated that the Society was required to lay down the compensation rules in advance of any particular examination.

The effect of this case was to introduce a greater degree of inflexibility into the compensation rules, which could no longer be modified to take account of variation in the general standard of a candidate's performance in each individual examination.

The MacGabhann case[2]

In 1987 Frank MacGabhann, an apprentice, sought judicial review of the Society's decision that he had been unsuccessful in his attempt to pass the final examination first part in November 1986 on the grounds that a quota

1 [1989] ILRM 590. 2 [1989] ILRM 854.

of 150 had been imposed on the examination, and that such imposition was ultra vires the Society's powers.

In his judgment, given in 1989, refusing the application Mr Justice Blayney held that as the number of successful candidates at the examination fell below 150, the respondents did not impose a quota. He also held that the Society had no power to impose a quota, nor to hold a competitive examination for entry to the law school. He was satisfied that the education committee was not guilty of manifest arbitrariness, injustice or partiality in adopting its compensation rules and that the pass standard laid down could not be said to be unreasonable.

Following this case the Society decided to give an exemption from the final examination-first part to law graduates of all the universities in the Republic of Ireland, provided that they had passed five of the eight subjects which comprised that examination. This resulted in an increase in the numbers qualifying for entry to the law school – since during the period when all candidates had to pass the examination not all law graduates had succeeded in so doing. The Society's response to this increase was to shorten the length of the professional course so that five courses instead of four could be held in a two-year period, and to shoe-horn 100 students into each course instead of the 75 which had been the norm.

The Bloomer case [3]

The next in the series of cases was brought by a number of students in Queen's University, Belfast, and was heard in the High Court in 1995. The students sought a declaration that the holders of law degrees from Queen's University should receive exemption from the entrance examination to the Society's law school, in the same way as law graduates of the National University of Ireland, Dublin University and the University of Limerick. While the court dismissed that claim, it held that the Society's 1991 regulation, updating one introduced in 1989 following the MacGabhann case, which conferred the exemption, indirectly contravened the prohibition on discrimination on the grounds of nationality contained in Article 6 of the EEC Treaty. A pyrrhic victory indeed for the Society.

3 [1995] 3 IR 14.

The logical consequence was that the obligation on all candidates seeking admission to the law school to sit and pass the entrance examination was revived in 1995. The Society had been considering this course already, given the pressures created by the general exemption given in 1989.

The Abrahamson case[4]

Not surprisingly, those law students who had already commenced their degree courses confident in the belief that, under the 1991 regulations, once they had obtained their law degree, they would have automatic entry to the Society's law school, were greatly upset by the decision in the Bloomer case and the Society's reaction to it, which required them to sit an entrance examination. Once again the Society found itself as a defendant in High Court proceedings in which the plaintiffs, several hundred law students who had commenced their degree courses in October 1995 or earlier, claimed that they had a legitimate expectation that they would be entitled, on obtaining a law degree which included the prescribed subjects, to enter the Society's law school. This action succeeded in the High Court in July 1996.

In his judgment, Mr Justice McCracken held that while the plaintiffs had a legitimate expectation that the regulations would remain in place and that they would be able to benefit from them, once the regulation had been found to be ultra vires the power of the Society, the court could not direct the Society to consider granting exemptions on the basis that the article of the regulations still applied.

The court further held that the Society still had a power under Article 30 of the regulations to grant exemptions in exceptional circumstances and made a declaratory order that the position of the applicants constituted exceptional circumstances and directed the Society to consider modifying the regulations so as to ensure that the applicants would be granted the exemptions.

The effect of this decision was to entitle a large number of law graduates, all emerging from the universities within a very short space of time, to entry to the law school. This 'free ticket' became increasingly attractive as the employment prospects for newly qualified solicitors improved dramatically during the late 1990s. This put significant pressure on the Society's resources,

4 [1996] 1 IR 403.

both human and physical, and the Society's response was later adjudged by the Education Policy Review Group to have been inadequate.

The Portobello case

In 1996, the University of Wales, Raymond Kearns trading as the Portobello College Dublin and twenty-six former students of Portobello College Dublin, who following their studies there had been conferred with degrees in Irish law by the University of Wales, instituted proceedings in the High Court against the Society. These proceedings sought declarations that certain decisions of the Society including the 1995 regulations under which graduates in Irish law from the National University of Ireland, Dublin University and the University of Limerick were to be entitled to exemption from the final examination-first part were invalid and were in breach of the EEC Treaty. In addition there was a claim that the decisions made by the Society as a result of which the twenty-six plaintiffs were refused exemption from the final examination-first part contravened the legitimate expectations of those plaintiffs.

During the hearing of these proceedings in the High Court in Dublin in 2000, the plaintiffs withdrew their claims. These were the only proceedings which went to a hearing which had no consequences for the law school.

THE START OF CONTINUING EDUCATION

The early 1960s saw the introduction of major legislation in the core areas of legal practice, a new Companies Act in 1963, a new Registration of Title Act in 1964, a new Succession Act in 1965, while comprehensive nation-wide planning legislation was introduced in 1963. The developments led to a need for continuing education for practitioners. The Society tried to meet this need by publishing a series of booklets and arranging some lectures. However, this did not meet the pent-up demand as was proved when a new organisation, the Society of Young Solicitors, which had been formed in 1965, under the chairmanship of Bruce St. J. Blake, commenced a regular series of lectures in Dublin, the first of which was given by Thelma

King. That society's major breakthrough came in the spring of 1966, when it organised a week-end meeting in Mullingar at which papers were given on the subjects of land registration, the Succession Act, the impact of the 1965 Finance Act on companies and the taxation aspects of the 1965 Finance Act. There was an attendance of several hundred solicitors of all ages; it soon became apparent that, while the society was administered by youthful solicitors, attendance was confined only to the young at heart.

A key element in the society's successful programme of twice-yearly week-end seminars and its monthly lectures in Dublin was the dissemination of printed texts of the lectures. The society was fortunate in having among its founders Norman Spendlove, who, perhaps because of his engineering background, was willing and able to undertake the process of printing and assembling the texts of the lectures, later proceeding to publish them in bound volumes. The success of the society's seminars and lecture pro-gramme continued for many years, and might be said to have enabled the Law Society not to regard continuing education as a priority but to concentrate during the 1970s on changing its pre-admission educational and training requirements. With the availability of the Blackhall Place premises from 1978 onwards the Society was able to increase the number of its Continuing Legal Education (CLE) programmes in Dublin. At the same time, with the recruitment of a CLE co-ordinator, it was also able to expand the number of seminars held outside Dublin. In later years the Society commenced to organise a number of diploma programmes; the first of which was on property tax. The diploma courses have been expanded to other topics, including legal French (in conjunction with the Alliance Française), currently in its sixth year, commercial law, e-commerce and applied European law. A certificate in legal German is also offered (in conjunction with the Goethe Institut).

The gradual development of CLE programmes continued, including joint seminars with other professions, but there had always been a difficulty in ensuring that members outside Dublin were afforded a proper opportunity of participating in the seminars. Having pursued the possibility of video-linking centres outside Dublin with Blackhall Place for several years, the CLE department was satisfied that the technology required had finally become available and, accordingly, in summer 2000 a seminar on landlord and tenant law was held simultaneously in Dublin and Sligo, with one of the speakers in Sligo and the remainder in Dublin. It was appropriate that the lecture-room in the new law school was used for the first time for this seminar. Much of the success of the continuing legal education programmes was due to the dedicated work of the two solicitors who have successively been co-ordinators, Geraldine Pearse and Barbara Joyce. The expansion of CLE will undoubtedly be more marked with the introduction of mandatory continuing legal education.

THE REVIEW GROUP

During the 1990s considerable discussions took place within the Society and with some third-level educational establishments, with a view to revising the education and training system. The law school had been put under considerable pressure, at least partly due to the increase in the numbers who were entitled to enter the law school, and concern had been expressed in the profession that there had been a decline in the quality of apprentices emerging from the school.

In November 1995 the education committee published a policy document entitled 'Educating and training tomorrow's solicitors: the way forward'. The proposals in this document included one to replace the then current professional course with an academic-year-long professional course to be conducted in a new law school building to be erected on a site at Hendrick Place, adjoining the Blackhall Place complex, at a cost of £3.2m. The Society had already taken an option on the site and had commissioned architects to design the new building. After representations had been received from some bar associations and individual members, it was decided to put the proposals to the members at a general meeting in November 1996. The conclusion of this meeting was that the proposals should be considered by a group representative of a wider cross section of the profession and accordingly fourteen solicitors under the chairmanship of Raymond Monahan, a former president of the Society and a former chairman of its education committee, were appointed to an Education Policy

Review Group. It met for the first time in February 1997, held fourteen meetings and published its main report in July 1998.

It had produced an interim report in September 1997, in which it had expressed concern that the Society had not, in recent years, given the law school the priority it deserved when the allocation of the Society's resources was being determined. It urged that immediate steps be taken to cater for the large number of students awaiting entry to the law school. With a view to eliminating the backlog (apprentices were waiting well over twelve months to gain entry to a professional course) it recommended the running of parallel courses based on a model prepared by two of the law school's fulltime tutors, and the appointment of an additional person at middle-management level to free up the director of education to concentrate on supervising the courses. (The law school had originally had both a director of education and a director of training, but on the retirement of the occupiers of these positions only a director of education was appointed.) It emphasised that action on the interim report should not be delayed until the main report became available. These recommendations were largely implemented, but as is ever the way in the world of education, time passed and it was not until the year 2000 that the last of the backlog could be accommodated in the law school.

The main report did not endorse some of the proposals in the policy document, though it did, by a majority of twelve of the fourteen members, recommend the building of the new law school, at a cost of £5m. The other twenty-four recommendations were adopted unanimously and included the following proposals:

the Society should continue as the direct and exclusive provider of the professional and advanced courses, a reiteration of policy;

it should retain its direct jurisdiction over examinations for apprentices;

the existing 'sandwich' structure whereby the in-office training segment fell between the professional and advanced courses, should continue;

a curriculum development unit should be established to review and monitor on an ongoing basis the curriculum and the materials for the courses;

there should be greater emphasis on the provision of absorption time for the reading of materials and that the number of daily contact hours between apprentices and course contributors should be no greater than four hours and

the performance of apprentices be assessed by a combination of written examinations, performance in tutorial and other interactive sessions and work assignments, and that the structure of the advanced course be revised in order to allow apprentices the option of taking one or more specialised practical subjects.

The proposals were adopted overwhelmingly by the profession in a postal vote and were pursued with determination by the Society. The most visible evidence was the construction of the new state-of-the-art law school building which was completed on schedule and within budget in time to be opened for the professional course which commenced in October 2000. Equally significant was the strengthening of the administrative and teaching staff in the school. The new law school was officially opened by the President, Mary McAleese, herself a former director of the Professional Legal Studies Institute in Northern Ireland, on 2 October 2000. In her speech at the opening she said: 'I am very proud of the fact that the Society's high reputation for leading-edge professional training courses is, and long has been, acknowledged by its counterparts across these islands and much farther afield.' Another major milestone in the history of the Society's involvement in legal training had been reached and it set out into the new century confident that its commitment to the future was well founded.

Legal publishing

JOHN F. BUCKLEY

A young Irish lawyer, practising in the year 2002, regularly bombarded with a stream of brochures and leaflets advertising some new Irish legal tome or yet another specialist journal, would find it hard to credit that his or her counterpart of the 1950s would have been bereft of almost any recent Irish law books and could have only subscribed to three general legal journals. There was a considerable decline in Irish legal publishing in the early years of the Irish State. Whereas during the previous thirty to forty years there had been a steady stream of books emanating from publishers, the flow dried up significantly in the 1920s. As an example the last major work on land law, Strahan and Baxter, was published in 1924, fortuitously, because it crystallised English and Irish land law immediately before the enormous changes brought about by the English 1925 property legislation. It was to be fifty years before the next such work, John Wylie's seminal *Irish land law* appeared.

Why this was so is not easy to explain. Of course the establishment of two separate legal jurisdictions on the island, leading to two smaller pools of prospective purchasers and authors, may have been a factor, and a perception that Irish law at least in the early days of independence did not differ significantly from English law and that therefore English texts could be used, another. A reluctance on the part of publishers to take a risk with a book in the very difficult economic times of the 1920s and 1930s may have been critical. At any rate, what had previously been a comparatively healthy flow of Irish legal books and annotated editions of statutes slowed to a trickle, and by the early 1950s the number of law books published solely for the Irish market in the previous twenty years would not have half filled a modest bookshelf. True, the size of the market would not have seemed attractive to authors or publishers. There were only 1200 practising solicitors and 200 barristers in the State in 1952 and there was only one third-level institution offering a primary honours law degree. The Government was persuaded to establish a fund for the publication of legal textbooks, but little use was made of it. The Incorporated Council of Law Reporting was given the task of arranging the publication of law books and duly published four over a period of sixteen years.

Successive presidents of the Law Society in their annual addresses bemoaned the situation, and the Society offered to sponsor textbooks, but there is no record of these offers having been taken up. In the late 1950s and early 1960s there was an impetus for law reform and an increase in legislation which had a significant effect on the solicitors' profession. The Society commissioned the publication of a series of booklets on the Married Women's Status Act, 1957, the Civil Liability Act, 1961, the Planning and Development Act, 1963, the Administration of Estates Act, 1959, the Statute of Limitations, 1957, Stamp Duty Legislation 1890–1962, the Registration of Title Act, 1964 and Town Agency and general practice. The Society also published *The Succession Act: a commentary* by W.J. McGuire. At about the same time the Society commenced to run what would become known as continuing legal education lectures, but its role in this area was for a time taken over by the Society of Young Solicitors which from 1965 onwards produced a constant series of printed texts of lectures given to that society. The lectures covered a wide range of subjects but useful, or indeed essential, as they were, they did not serve the need for major works. In 1969 the Law Society established a textbooks publications committee, with a view to sponsoring and encouraging the writing of textbooks on various areas of law.

A project which originally failed to come to fruition was to provide a welcome new source of finance for book publishing. Arthur Cox, probably the leading company law solicitor in Ireland, having retired from practice, joined the Society of Jesus, went to work in Africa and was killed there in a road accident in 1965. A group of his lawyer colleagues and friends decided that a suitable memorial to him would be a book on Irish company law and a substantial amount of money was raised to fund its publication. The work was to be a collective one, with different authors contributing a chapter each. Regrettably the project was not realised and the organisers decided to donate the funds which had been collected to a foundation whose principal object would be the publication of textbooks on Irish law. The Law Society is now the surviving trustee of the foundation. Its general method of operation has been to provide funding to enable authors to carry out research, to have their texts prepared for publication and to meet other initial costs of the work. It has normally required authors to refund advances out of royalties. A list of the publications supported by the foundation appears at Appendix A to this chapter.

The availability of funds from the Arthur Cox Foundation and the initiative of the Society's textbooks publications committee dovetailed neatly and the Society was able to commence publication of a series of works under its own imprint, and to commission the publication of John Wylie's *Irish land law* by Professional Books. From the middle of the 1970s and throughout the 1980s the Society was the premier legal publisher in the jurisdiction. Given the great increase in the numbers both of the practising profession and of law students during this period, and the fact that it had been demonstrated that there was a commercial market for legal textbooks, it was hardly surprising that commercial publishers began to enter the market in a significant way. The Society welcomed this development and was happy to retreat to a position where it did not seek to publish major titles save for second or further editions of its own publications, but would confine itself to monographs or booklets on subjects which would not warrant a major work. A list of the Society's book publications appears at Appendix B to this chapter.

Over the years proposals to publish in more permanent form the materials which were being produced in the Society's law school were considered. The texts of the lectures given by the consultants on the Society's continuing legal education programme were normally made available to the profession. No attempts were made to either update the text or upgrade the form in which the lectures were produced, normally duplicated or xerox copies, stapled together. From time to time suggestions were made that the lectures should be edited and polished up with a view to their being formally published, but no enthusiasm was shown by the lecturers to whom this proposal was made. The Society did not have the resources to take on the task of editing and it was accepted that lecturers, who had agreed to provide a text for those attending CLE courses, could not reasonably be expected to devote further time and attention to upgrading the material. Accordingly this project did not come to fruition.

The handbooks produced in the Society's law school from the inception of the new courses introduced in 1979 were widely seen as being of great value, not only to the apprentices to whom they were distributed, but also to other people in the offices to which they were apprenticed. With the availability of greater resources in the law school in the late 1990s arrangements were made with Blackstone Press for the publication of a series of practitioner manuals in an attractive format. Five volumes have been published to date, which are listed in Appendix B under the heading 'Law School Texts'.

THE GAZETTE

Over the last 50 years the Society continued to publish legal writing through the medium of its *Gazette*, in addition to playing the critical role in the revival of the publication of textbooks and commentaries on the law described above.

In the 1950s there were only three legal periodicals regularly published in the State; two of these were the weekly *Irish Law Times and Solicitors' Journal*, established in 1867, and the *Irish Jurist*, which appeared for various periods between 1865 and 1965, when it changed into a learned journal. Each of these contained articles of legal interest and reports of cases. The third was the Society's *Gazette* which was first published in 1907. That first issue which announced a publishing schedule of ten issues a year, unchanged in 2002, contained minutes of council meetings, notes of professional interest, a report of a successful prosecution of an unqualified person for preparing an assignment of property and announcements of future debates by the Solicitors' Apprentices Debating Society, 'Should women have the franchise?' and 'Are the present methods of reviving the Irish language likely to succeed?'

The *Gazette* of the 1950s did not differ greatly from that first issue, and bore little resemblance to its present successor. Printing technology had not yet made colour printing widely available, so the publication bore a sombre black-and-white appearance and, of course, there were no photographs and virtually no advertising. Rationalisation of paper sizes had not been introduced so it was similar in shape to, but smaller than, the A4 format which would now be regarded as the norm. Its content, necessarily, was different, opening as it did with the proceedings of the last meeting of the council of the Society and continuing with news of developments in the legal world culled from many sources. In addition there would normally be one or two short articles on some aspect of the law. In the absence of a supply of Irish legal textbooks or an adequate system of reporting cases, such information was badly needed by the profession and the *Gazette,* the *Irish Law Times* and the *Irish Jurist* provided an essential lifeline of information. The *Gazette* was edited anonymously until 1969 when Colum Gavan Duffy, the librarian to the Society, was formally appointed as editor and it was not until 1978 that an editorial board was put in place. Under the advice of the Society's public relations consultant, Maxwell Sweeney, a journalist of wide experience, changes were introduced not only to the format of the publication but also to its focus. Colour printing became affordable while contributors were found to ensure a steady supply of articles. Summaries of recent cases (known as 'the green pages') were provided while, with the co-operation of the Bar Council and the Incorporated Council of Law Reporting, quarterly and annual indexes ('the pink pages') of all unreported High and Supreme Court written judgments were issued with the *Gazette.* Photographs first appeared in an advertisement in 1971. Most appropriately the first featured the best-loved member of the Society's staff, Willie O'Reilly. In 1972 a drawing of the Four Courts in colour made its appearance as the front cover and remained a feature for several years. The first president of the Society to have his photograph appear in the *Gazette* was T.V. O'Connor in 1973. The first photograph to appear on the front cover was in August 1976 when a group of the members involved in planning the Society's new education programme and their Australian consultant Kevin O'Leary were featured. Over the next ten years or so various experiments with photographs on the front cover were tried and the magazine went to full colour in 1985, thus enabling photographs of social and other events to be carried.

After 1978 there were a number of part-time editors but from 1980 to 1991 the executive editor was the Society's assistant librarian, Mary Gaynor, acting in a part-time capacity. With the appointment of Barbara Cahalane as the Society's public relations officer in 1991, the post passed to her. She in turn was succeeded by Catherine Dolan and by Mary Kinsella, each again in a part-time capacity. It was clear that if the magazine was to expand, much greater resources would be required and accordingly Conal O'Boyle was appointed as a full-time editor in late 1996. Under his stewardship the *Gazette* has been transformed, not only in its visual aspects, but in the variety of its contents. Its designer Nuala Redmond won the 1997 *Irish Independent* Award for best design of a magazine, and in the same year Conal O'Boyle was named editor of the year. It now has the appearance of a glossy magazine, and sits appropriately on the shelves in major newsagents.

APPENDIX A

PUBLICATIONS ASSISTED BY THE ARTHUR COX FOUNDATION

J.S.R. Cole, *Irish cases on evidence* (Cork & Dublin, 1972)

W.N. Osborough, *Borstal in Ireland* (Dublin, 1975)

J.C.W. Wylie, *Irish land law* (London, 1975)

A. Kennedy & H. McWilliam, *The law on compensation for criminal injuries in the Republic of Ireland* (Dublin, 1977)

J.C.W. Wylie, *Irish conveyancing law* (Abingdon, 1978)

B.M.E. McMahon & W. Binchy, *Irish law of torts* (Abingdon, 1981)

R. Clark, *Contract* (London, 1982)

J.S.R. Cole, *Irish cases on evidence* (2nd ed., Dublin, 1982)

G. Golding, *George Gavan Duffy, 1882–1951: a legal biography* (Dublin, 1982)

R. Keane, *The law of local government in the Republic of Ireland* (Dublin, 1982)

D. Gwynn Morgan, *Constitutional law of Ireland: the law of the executive, legislative and judicature* (Dublin, 1985)

M. Forde, *Cases on Irish company law* (Cork & Dublin, 1986)

W. Binchy, *Irish conflicts of law* (Dublin, 1988)

M. Forde, *Extradition law* (Dublin, 1988)

R. Keane, *Equity and the law of trusts in the Republic of Ireland* (Dublin, 1988)

B.M.E. McMahon & F. Murphy, *European Community law in Ireland* (Dublin, 1989)

M. Reid, *The impact of Community law on the Irish Constitution* (Dublin, 1990)

R. Byrne & W. Binchy, *Annual review of Irish law, 1990* (Dublin, 1991)

B.P. Dempsey, Irish company law database, 1991 (Dublin, 1991)

Law Society of Ireland, *The Companies Act, 1990: a summary* (Dublin, 1991)

E. McGarr, *Deadly wages: Irish work hazards* (Dublin, 1992)

R. Byrne & W. Binchy, *Annual review of Irish law, 1991* (Dublin, 1993)

A. Connelly (ed.), *Gender and the law* (Dublin, 1993)

A. Whelan (ed.), *Law and liberty* (Dublin, 1993)

J. Brady & A. Kerr, *Limitation of actions* (2nd ed., Dublin, 1994)

M. Kotsonouris, *Retreat from revolution: the Dáil Courts, 1920–24* (Dublin, 1994)

G. Whyte, *Social welfare law in Ireland: a guide to its sources*, 2nd ed. (Dublin, 1994)

M. Cousins, *Irish social welfare system* (Dublin, 1995)

B. Dickson, B. Collins & D. Madden, *Concordance of Irish, English and Northern Irish legislation* (Galway, 1997)

BAILII (British and Irish Legal Information Institute) web site project

G. Whyte, *Social inclusion and the legal system: public interest law in Ireland* (Dublin, 2002)

APPENDIX B

BOOKS PUBLISHED BY THE LAW SOCIETY

W.J. McGuire, *The Succession Act, 1965* (1st ed., 1967; 2nd ed. by R.A. Pearce, 1986)

R.W.R. Johnston, *Wealth tax* (1976)

K.I. Nowlan, *A guide to the Planning Acts* (1st ed., 1978; 2nd ed., 1988; 3rd ed., 1999)

E.M. Walsh, *Planning and development law* (1st ed., 1979; 2nd ed. by R. Keane, 1984)

J. O'Reilly and M. Redmond, *Cases and materials on the Irish Constitution* (1980)

A.G. Williams, *Principles of corporation tax in the Republic of Ireland* (1981)
   (3 supplements published.)
Garda Síochána Guide (5th ed., 1981; 6th ed., 1991)
J.S.R. Cole, *Irish cases on evidence* (2nd ed., 1982)
R. Keane, *The law of local government in the Republic of Ireland* (1982)
M. Redmond, *Dismissal law in the Republic of Ireland* (1982)
V. Grogan, T. King and E. Donelan, *Sale of goods and supply of services: a
   guide to the legislation* (1983)
Bound volumes of the Acts of the Oireachtas 1922–1976 (reprint; 1983)
J.C. Brady and T. Kerr, *Limitation of actions* (1st ed., 1984; 2nd ed., 1994)
H.M. Fitzpatrick, *Trees and the law* (1985)
D. Hogan, *The legal profession in Ireland 1789–1922* (1986)
P. Lynch and J. Meenan (eds.), *Essays in memory of Alexis Fitzgerald* (1987)
Law Society of Ireland, *A guide to professional conduct of solicitors in Ireland*
   (1988)
S. O'Reilly and N. Robinson, *A new lease of life: the Law Society's building at
   Blackhall Place* (published jointly with the Irish Architectural Archive)
   (1990)
Law Society of Ireland, *Conveyancing handbook* (1st ed., 1990; 2nd ed., 1998)
Law Society of Ireland, *Solicitors Acts, 1954–1994: a compendium* (1995)
B. Bohan, *Capital acquisitions tax consolidation* (1996)
M.W. Carrigan, *Handbook on arbitration in Ireland* (1998)

LAW SCHOOL TEXTS

D. Cahill, T.P. Kennedy and V. Power (eds.), *Applied European law* (2000)
G. Brennan and N. Casey (eds.), *Conveyancing law* (2000)
G. Brennan, M. Linnane and D. Soden (eds.), *Landlord and tenant law* (2000)
S. McNeece (ed.), *Commercial law* (2001)
G. Shannon (ed.), *Family law* (2001)

All the above law school texts were published by Blackstone Press.

The Law Society library

MARGARET BYRNE

Solicitors have had access to a library of their own for over 160 years. This chapter traces the development of the library from a small collection of books to an information service with the printed text still at its centre, but using a variety of paper-based and electronic materials to access legal information.[1]

The earliest reference to a solicitors' library appears in the rules adopted on 17 June 1841 at 'the general meeting of the profession at large':

1. That a society be formed for the regulation of the profession of attorney and solicitor in Ireland, for protecting their rights and privileges; and also for the institution and support of a library, for the use of the profession, and for the providing means for the instruction of apprentices; and that such society be called, 'the Society of the Attorneys and Solicitors of Ireland'.

The rules of the new society were based on a report of a provisional committee of twenty one solicitors, one of the objectives of which was 'to procure a library of elementary and other law works, including the statutes before and since the Union'.

The Society of the Attorneys and Solicitors of Ireland was a successor to the Law Society of Ireland, established in 1830, and was formed on the occasion of the profession moving into new premises at the Four Courts provided for them by the Benchers of King's Inns. The solicitors' profession and the education of solicitors were governed by the King's Inns.

---

1 Sources for the historical part of this chapter include the Law Society annual reports, the *Irish Law Times and Solicitors Journal*, 1867–1980, the Law Society *Gazette* 1907–, and an article by my predecessor, the late Colum Gavan Duffy, 'The library of the Incorporated Law Society of Ireland' published in *An Leabharlann*, March 1957.

Solicitors were members of King's Inns until 1866, and would have had access to its handsome and well stocked library, but this may have served primarily as a resource for members of the Bar and the judiciary, and the desire for a library to service the solicitors' profession was at the core of the foundation of the Society.

It seems that the earlier Law Society of Ireland may have held some form of library but as there were no annual reports published prior to 1842 there is very little information available. The annual report of the new Society for 1842 acknowledged 'the valuable donation to this Society, by the late Law Society, of all the books, papers, etc., etc., collected from the institution of that body, until it ceased on the formation of the present Society'. The committee[2] also acknowledged various presentations of books to the library and the accounts for the year ending 1 May 1842 show that £39. 4s. 5d. was spent on books purchased for the library, and £40. 14s. 6d. was spent on newspapers, periodicals, etc. supplied for the solicitors' room.

In the early years of the Society the focal point of the Solicitors' Buildings appears to have been the solicitors' room, a reading and writing room with desks and presses, where the Dublin, London and provincial newspapers were made available, as well as the votes and proceedings of the houses of lords and commons and all acts of parliament. Only members with the paid up annual subscription of £1 and apprentices of members on payment of 10s. annually had access to the solicitors' room and the library. Strict rules for the solicitors' room provided that 'being intended solely for professional purposes, no noise, nor any discussion upon political or other subjects, not professional, nor refreshment of any kind, or smoking be permitted in the room'.

The membership was very largely Dublin based and the annual reports contain many exhortations to solicitors to join the Society and avail of the facilities, for example 'to make appointments to meet and transact business at the solicitors' room in preference to the hall of the Four Courts where there is constant interruption'. The suggestion was also made that it 'would be of assistance and also increase membership if a practice were adopted of members assembling each day at the solicitors' room at a fixed time to give each other messages'.

2 The 1852 charter changed the name of the governing body to 'council'.

By 1844 there still did not appear to be adequate accommodation for the library. The annual report states that the committee had applied to the Benchers of King's Inns for permission for apprentices to be admitted to the library in Henrietta Street but had received a negative reply. The report also stated that they had presented a memorial to the Benchers to obtain a suitable room in the new building in the Four Courts, adjoining the solicitors' room, for the purpose of a library which was still awaiting a response.

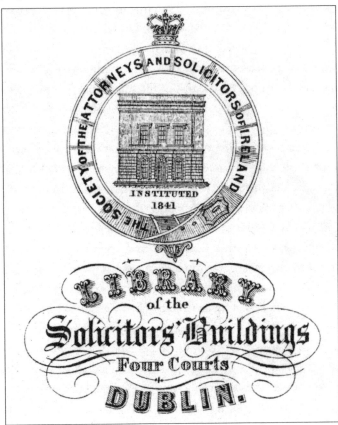

An early library book plate

Meanwhile, the library collection was being built up. During the 1840s several presentations of books were acknowledged. It had a complete set of the patent Rolls and Records of Ireland, a set of the Ordnance Maps of Ireland, presented by the lord lieutenant, Lord Heytesbury, and it had also received, on application, a copy of Griffiths' *General valuation of Ireland*. A subscription fund was set up for the binding of the maps at a cost of £200. In 1846 there is a reference to 'a spacious and suitable apartment having recently been fitted up as a library' and in 1847, following an application by the Society, the Benchers of King's Inns allocated a sum of £500 for the purchase of books for the library and the committee acknowledged receipt from the King's Inns Library of several duplicate editions of works held in that library. The charter of 1852 refers to the Society as already being in possession of a library and valuable maps and surveys of Ireland.

The state of the library seems to have fluctuated in the following years. The 1858 annual report refers to a better arrangement of the library 'with an improved classification of the works which it contains having been recently effected' but goes on to say that 'having regard to the nature and limited extent of such a library as the Society required, as well as to their funds, the library is sufficient for all practical purposes bearing in mind that the profession have access to a copious and extensive library at the King's Inns for such information as the Society's library may not be able to supply'.

The finances of the Society were a critical factor, the main source of income being the £1 membership subscription. There were 379 members listed for the year ending 1 May 1858 and in 1859 it was a reason for congratulation that there was an increase of sixty members. In 1861 the state of the library was found to be unsatisfactory. Books were out of date; new books were needed. There were no funds for the purchase of books. A special subscription would be required. A long circular was addressed to solicitors who had not yet joined the Society. It was a subject of much regret that out of 1,250 practising attorneys and solicitors so many did not become members of the Society though reaping the benefits which its work conferred on the whole profession. Again in 1864 the annual report stated that the library could not be maintained for want of necessary funds, and the council suggested that a subscription list should be opened 'for the purpose of providing means for supplying this important department of your Society with the modern textbooks and works of practice'.

In 1866 one of the long-standing aims of the Society was achieved with the passing of the Attorneys and Solicitors Act (Ireland). This act removed the control of the education, admission and regulation of the profession from the Benchers of King's Inns and placed these functions under the control of the Society subject, in the case of the education of apprentices, to the supervision of the judiciary. This was a turning point for the library as well as for the Society as a whole. Quite apart from the powers which the act conferred on the Society, more sources of income would now be available. The annual reports for 1868 and following years refer to considerable purchases of new books and greater use of the library, and by 1870: '... your library will now be found to contain a most valuable collection of works on nearly every subject connected with your profession; and in order to increase facility of reference to these books, your council intend to appoint a competent person to take charge of the library, and assist generally in that department'. A library clerk was appointed in January 1871. A book to be signed by members visiting the library was introduced, as well as a book for recording books borrowed. In 1873 a new index of all the books was prepared. The system adopted by the Society in 1841, similar to that found in Trinity College Dublin and in colleges of English universities, was that the secretary of the Society was also officially registrar and librarian, hence the title 'library clerk' for the person actually in charge of the library.

The Society continued to rent its by then insufficient accommodation from the King's Inns and following long negotiation and the report of a royal commission of inquiry the Benchers provided additional accommodation for a new library, lecture hall and council chamber. In 1876 the library moved into its new, more spacious, premises that would have been on the first floor of where the Law Library now stands.

In 1877 the library received a gift from an anonymous donor of 155 volumes of Dublin Directories dating from 1692. To assist members in their practice the Society in 1881 negotiated a special price for a bulk purchase of the Chronological Table and Index to the Statutes, and 250 copies were ordered and distributed to members. In the same spirit, over a century later the Society was to purchase the CD-ROM of the Irish Statutes and Chronological Index at a special price for issue to each practice.

In 1884 the library was re-organised and catalogued by Messrs Hodges & Co., booksellers. Two new rooms were added in 1885, one for parliamentary papers and the other for files of newspapers. In 1886, in order to improve study facilities for apprentices the library was opened free of charge to apprentices of solicitor members of the Society. Apprentices of non-members continued to pay the annual 10*s.* subscription. The size and use of the library were increasing steadily, though it was still disappointing for the council that only one-third of practising solicitors were members – 453 members out of a total of 1,205 practising solicitors in 1888. By 1889 the annual report noted that 'the library was fast becoming a place of constant resort to members and their apprentices' and 4,006 visits were recorded. This number rose to the record figure of 4,751 in 1898. At this time a system of three-day loans for Dublin members and six-day loans for country members was introduced.

Samuel Evans, barrister-at-law, was appointed library clerk in 1891. By then there was a book stock of 2,000 volumes. His main task was to prepare an alphabetical author and subject catalogue which was first published in a volume of 184 pages in 1895; a second edition extending to 228 pages appeared in 1909. From the 1890s to 1921 the library enjoyed a great period of growth: over 2,000 volumes were purchased at an average annual expenditure of £172. It was a well stocked library and held all the core Irish legal textbooks being published at the time. From 1896 to 1921 the average number of visits a year to the library was 3,618 and the average number of books lent per year was 3,062. These visit and loan figures for a membership of less than 800 (though with approximately twice as many Dublin as country members) may seem surprisingly high, even by today's standards. But one has to bear in mind that practices were small, mainly run by sole practitioners, and were unlikely to have had large collections of reference books; it was a pre-photocopying age and the books lent included law reports and statutes. The use of signed dockets for borrowing books was introduced in the early 1890s to record loans more efficiently. It also allowed members borrow books without personally coming to the library, and encouraged country members to borrow books. Members were constantly reminded 'to return books within the times mentioned or to intimate their request for an extension of time, and thus save repeated applications for the return of the books lent' – which is certainly as apt today as it was a hundred years ago!

Samuel Evans retired in 1916 and was succeeded by Thomas B. Cooley, who had joined the Society's staff in 1908. During the 1916 Easter Rising the Solicitors' Buildings were occupied on 24 April and for the five following days. Damage was done to furniture, fittings and windows but not to the records, books and pictures and more valuable property. This was a mild forerunner to the losses the Society was to suffer during the civil war.

On 10 April 1922 anti-Treaty forces seized and occupied the Four Courts, including the Solicitors' Buildings. The Society's secretariat and staff had to move to temporary headquarters at 33 Molesworth Street. On 26 June the army of the provisional government began to take the premises by force, and on 28 June after heavy firing and explosions the entire Four Courts building was destroyed, including the Solicitors' Buildings. The secretary, George Wakely, as a result of negotiations, had been able to remove some of the Society's records before the destruction of the building, including minute books, the roll of solicitors, a complete set of the Society's *Gazette* and other books relating to the affairs of the Society, but the books in the library were not allowed to be moved. The only portion of the Society's premises to survive intact was the strong room built in 1899 which contained the charters of the Society, original deeds of trust, registers and roll books, most of the records relating to apprentices and the council and Society minute books. The library of 3,000 books was destroyed with the exception of eighty books out on loan. A list of these books was published in the *Gazette* of July/August 1922 with a note to the effect that they might now be borrowed on application to the secretary at 33 Molesworth Street. A search was recently carried out in the library to see how many of the fifty-five textbooks on that list (the others being volumes of law reports and statutes) were still held in the library. Fourteen were tracked down (plus a *Smith's probate practice* of 1891 not on the list, which must have been on an unauthorised loan!) and they have been shelved together in a special collection as a tribute to their survival.

The council very quickly set about purchasing books in frequent demand and appealed to members for donations. Appeals were also regularly made for particular years of the law reports, the law directory and annual reports to make up complete sets. Members and, indeed, non-members responded very generously and all donations were individually acknowledged in the *Gazette*. When looking through the 19th and early 20th century books in the library, it is remarkable how many of them bear the names of previous owners. A very high proportion of the collection was replaced by purchase and gift within six years – 876 volumes by the end of 1924; 2,017 volumes by the end of 1925; 2,247 volumes by the end of 1927.

While the lending of books continued from the Society's Molesworth Street office and, after 1925, from its larger premises at 45 Kildare Street, the service must have been operating under considerable difficulty. During this period the courts were sitting at Dublin Castle. There was a decrease in membership of the Society from 798 members in 1922 to 714 members in 1923, largely due to the fall-off in membership of Northern Ireland solicitors but also, as was pointed out at the November 1923 half-yearly general meeting, due to the lack of accommodation and the loss of the library.

In September 1931 the Society was able to move back to the Four Courts, to the rebuilt Solicitors' Buildings on a site adjoining the one it had formerly occupied. The library was located on the ground floor, as was the secretary's office, examination and lecture hall and consultation room. The hall, which was available to members as a reading and writing room, the council chamber, and president's room were on the first floor.

After this significant re-constitution and relocation of the library, the annual reports of the Society in the 1930s and 1940s are relatively silent on the subject, merely stating that textbooks were bought and the law reports kept up to date. There was a large expenditure in 1934 on sets of old law reports – *Law Journal Reports, Law Times Reports* and twelve of the missing volumes of the *Times Law Reports*, totalling 461 volumes. In 1937 a new catalogue of the library compiled by Thomas Cooley was printed and a copy sent to each member.

Having worked in the Society for forty-two years, thirty-four of them as librarian, Thomas Cooley resigned in 1950 and was succeeded by Colum Gavan Duffy, who was a solicitor and held the Diploma in Librarianship from UCD. In 1952 the library moved upstairs to what had been formerly the hall and the former library was converted into a general office. The new library was a fine room, the width of the building, with windows at both ends and a glass dome in the ceiling letting in light. It was also equipped with a raised platform at one end and a piano, and being the Society's largest room it was used for functions. Lectures, occasional receptions and dinners, and debates were held there and for a time in the 1950s, provided the books were covered by wooden boards, the council sanctioned the holding of six apprentices' dances in the library each year. Writing in the article on the library in *An Leabharlann* in 1957, the librarian commented dryly that it would seem to be rare to find a library that fulfilled such diverse functions.

Many solicitors who qualified in the 1950s, 1960s and 1970s will have their own memories of Colum Gavan Duffy[3] or 'the Gav' as he was affectionately referred to. A courteous and kindly man, he had an extensive knowledge of law and legal bibliography and was always ready to tease out an enquiry and direct a member or apprentice to the leading case or the most appropriate text on a subject. As a new recruit to law librarianship I received a great grounding from him in legal materials, at a time when there were no relevant manuals on law librarianship, nor much written on legal research. During his time as librarian Colum Gavan Duffy built up a very impressive collection, and added a great deal of material relating to newly developing areas of law, particularly European law, reflecting his great interest in European affairs. He ensured that the library received copies of all available written judgments of the Superior Courts in this jurisdiction and in Northern Ireland, and as a result the library, today, has a very good collection of unreported judgments, some dating back to the 1950s. From 1969 he also edited the *Gazette*, contributing much to it himself in the way of book reviews and case notes. With hindsight, it could be said that the library was run on slightly unconventional lines. A reader arriving in the middle of the day expecting to do some quiet research might have had the added bonus of the lunch-time radio news at a high volume in the adjoining library office or an animated political or legal discussion on the floor of the library. Colum Gavan Duffy put his own inimitable mark on the library, and he is recalled with fondness by all who had the pleasure of knowing him.

3 Son of Mr Justice George Gavan Duffy, former President of the High Court and one of the Irish plenipotentiaries who signed the Anglo-Irish Treaty of 6 December 1921. Colum retired as librarian in 1978 and died in 1999.

I came to work in the library in the summer months of 1974 to catalogue new books and index the unreported judgments and, as I soon
discovered, to take charge when the librarian went on annual leave. I was
subsequently appointed assistant librarian in October 1974. The pace of
life in the library was certainly very different in the mid 1970s to that of
2002. A small number of requests for photocopies and loans would be
received by post. More usually, law clerks from various Dublin firms would
come in with lists of cases that they required. They would be assisted in
locating the material and would take the books downstairs to the photocopying service run by Willie O'Reilly. Members would come in to consult
materials, often combining a visit to the library with other business in the
Four Courts, and a small number of apprentices preparing for examinations
would study there quietly and enjoy the atmosphere. There was very little
placing of requests by phone. The 1975 annual report records 20 volumes
a week borrowed and 40 volumes a week taken for photocopying in term
time.

The Law Society administration moved to Blackhall Place at Easter
1977, the library remaining at the Four Courts for a further year until it
moved in June 1978. The new library was located in the south wing of the
building in what had been the former dining hall of the King's Hospital.
Colum Gavan Duffy retired the same year, and I was appointed librarian.
The new law school and the new system of education were launched in
1979. Mary Gaynor, née Buckley, was appointed assistant librarian and
subsequently deputy librarian. In 1980 the Society installed a computer
system for financial and practising certificate data. The exciting concept of
computerised legal information retrieval became a reality in 1980 with the
launch in the UK of Lexis and Eurolex, two on-line legal databases.

The level of requests for materials received by phone increased steadily.
To an extent, this may have been initially due to the fact that the library,
no longer based in the Four Courts, was not quite as accessible as before;
but it was mainly due to the changing nature and pace of legal work and
the growing range of legal information sources, both publications and
electronic products. There was also a great increase in the number of
reserved written judgments of the superior courts and an increase in the

volume of legislation being enacted. The installation of a fax machine in the library in 1989 allowed for an almost instant response to a request, if required. By 1993 the annual number of requests for copy materials and bibliographic and case searches, dealt with by the library staff was over 2,800; in recent years this figure has levelled out at around 4,000 and around 2,000 textbook loans. The role of the library staff expanded from the more traditional work of selecting, purchasing and organising the collection to providing an information service. The photocopier, the computer and the fax machine revolutionised work practices, but the greatest change in library and information work has to be the development of the Internet and the possibility of accessing legal information world wide.

The library catalogue was computerised in 1997. The database contains catalogue records of books, court judgments (since 1992) and acts and statutory instruments (since 1997). It is intended that on a redesign of the Society's web site members will have on-line access to the catalogue. Manual indexes and other sources are available in the library for locating older cases and legislation.

Through personal contact and through membership of the British and Irish Association of Law Librarians (BIALL), the library maintains close relations with a wide network of law libraries/legal information units in these islands. The number of Irish law libraries now stands at over thirty, including professional, academic, law firm and government libraries. The library subscribes to the inter-library loan scheme and the information and document supply services offered by Trinity College Dublin, the Institute of Advanced Legal Studies, London and the British Library.

The library made one further move, in August 2000, in conjunction with the building of the law school's new education centre for the new professional practice courses. The education centre and the new library were officially opened by President Mary McAleese on 2 October 2000. The newly designed library, on ground floor and mezzanine level, is located at the front of the south wing in what was formerly the student lecture hall. It is a very pleasant environment with light oak shelving and plenty of natural light through the high windows. It has provided some much-needed extra space and the new lay-out includes a mixture of study tables and computer workstations. Twelve networked pcs provide access to the Internet, two on-line legal databases Lexis and Westlaw, various CD-ROMs, as well as word-processing and email.

Today, the library has a staff of five, two with library qualifications, one with legal qualifications and a fourth who is completing a degree in library and information studies. It is both a members and a students library. It services a potential user population of almost 6,500 solicitors in 1,956 practices. The small to medium-size firms are the heaviest users of the service, though the largest firms who in recent decades have developed their own in-house information services are also regular users. It is also used extensively by the students on the professional practice courses. The new courses place more emphasis than before on legal research and writing, and students are required to complete a number of written assignments. A student multiple copy collection of core textbooks has been set up, and these along with the main collection of textbooks and reference materials are heavily used, and the pcs and printer/photocopiers are in continuous use. Further networked pcs are available in the study room above the library and in the IT room in the education centre.

In the 161 years since the library was established, there has been continuity in much of its collection coupled with enormous, and on-going, change in the ways in which legal information is sourced – much of it not within the library itself, but electronically on on-line databases. The library has adapted over the years to the changing needs of the solicitors' profession: it must continue to develop to keep pace with the speed of change in the provision of legal services and legal information at the start of the twenty-first century.

Where were we then? Where are we now?
What are the issues today and for the future?

KEN MURPHY

The purpose of this chapter is to review briefly the Society and the profession as it exists today and to draw some comparisons with the Society and the profession fifty years ago, at the time of the centenary of the charter. Finally the chapter will review a number of the issues facing the Society today and tomorrow.

The chapter is written following a review of the Society's annual report for 2001, together with all of the council minutes and issues of the *Gazette* of 1951. In fact, the *Gazette* of 1951 largely comprises the full text of minutes of the Society's council, with a number of statutory notices attached.

THE SOCIETY IN 1951

The most striking difference is in scale. In 1951 the Society was a tiny organisation for a much smaller profession. The size of the profession was not the only reason for the tiny organisation, however. The Society served a much less complex and demanding profession in a much less complex and demanding world. For example, it must be remembered that in 1951 the Solicitors Act, 1954 still existed only in the Society's drafts and as an aspiration of the profession. The statutory obligations and powers which that act created in relation to education, complaints handling and the establishment and maintenance of a compensation fund, with their major implications for the scale of the Society's operation, did not yet exist.

Although figures always have the potential to mislead, it is worth looking at the annual accounts and reports presented to the general meeting of the Society held in the Solicitors' Buildings, Four Courts, at half past two o'clock on Thursday, 22 November 1951. The income and expenditure account of the Incorporated Law Society of Ireland was in the sum of £8,731. 10s. and 1d. The same audited accounts give the balance sheet figure, balancing liabilities and assets at £37,608, 17s. 8d. The membership of the Society in 1951 was 1,114 as against 1,103, the number in the previous year; there were 467 Dublin members who paid £1 per annum; 573 country members who paid £1 and 74 were members admitted to the profession within three years who paid 10s. per annum.

By contrast, the audited accounts published in 2001, fifty years later, show income and expenditure for the Society at £8,176,316, with a balance sheet figure of £6,473,731. The compensation fund, which is treated separately in the accounts, has an additional income and expenditure amount of £3,751,075 with healthy reserves on the balance sheet of £18,400,033. The Society had 6,478 members at the end of 2001. The annual membership subscription with practising certificate fee (including £400 compensation fund contribution) is £1,395 for members qualified more than three years.

One of the main items on the Society's agenda in 1951 was the draft Solicitors Bill. This, remarkably, had been drafted by the Society and submitted to Government no less than eight years previously, in 1943. It was a source of repeated and bitter complaint in council minutes and in annual reports of the early 1950s that the Department and successive Ministers for Justice would not make good their repeated promises to bring forward this piece of legislation which was regarded as being of such importance both to the public interest and to the interest of the profession.

Other constant concerns of the Society in the period generally and reflected again in the minutes of 1951 are the level of solicitors' remuneration, delays in public departments (in particular the Land Registry), persons not qualified as solicitors performing solicitors' work for fee or reward, the need to encourage the development of local bar associations and the severe shortage of legal textbooks both for solicitors and solicitors' apprentices. In addition there is frustration at the lack of progress in completion of negotiations for the granting to the Society by the Commissioners of Public Works of a lease for the Society's premises in the Four Courts. There is much pride, however, in the Society's new library.

In the council year to 22 November 1951, there were sixteen meetings of the council. The court of examiners held thirteen meetings and the statutory committee (established under the Solicitors (Ireland) Act, 1898, to deal with complaints of misconduct) held sixteen meetings.

By far the most interesting item to appear, serialised over a number of months, in the *Gazette* in 1951, is the very detailed and readable report by the president, Roger Greene, of his representation of the Society at the annual meeting of the American Bar Association in New York. Mr Greene and his wife travelled to New York on the *Ile de France* in September 1951 following an earlier visit to the State of New Jersey Bar Association in June. Mr Greene reports comprehensively on the great welcome he received and hospitality he was shown in New York, where he stayed at the Waldorf Astoria Hotel. His meetings with many American dignitaries, including New Jersey Chief Justice Vanderbilt, Cardinal Spellman and the President of the United States, Harry S. Truman himself, are all carefully recorded.

THE SOCIETY IN 2001/02

Five decades later, Ireland, the solicitors' profession and the Law Society are all very different.

Ireland's stagnant economy and repressed, inward-looking society of the early 1950s have been utterly transformed by half a century of ever-accelerating change. In 2002, Ireland is still enjoying the fruits of an unprecedented economic boom, albeit now at a much slower pace of development, following half a dozen years in which the country's economic growth rate was among the highest in the world. The labour shortage, ameliorated by substantial immigration from poorer countries in Eastern Europe, Africa and elsewhere, could hardly form a greater contrast with the endemically high unemployment and emigration which characterised the Irish labour market of the early 1950s.

Almost thirty years of membership of what is now the European Union, together with ease of foreign travel, global commercialisation, the information technology revolution and, notoriously, television, among other things, have produced an outward-looking, confident and sophisticated Ireland which is very much at ease with the wider world and with itself.

The profession is like the country. In economic terms, in 2002 there has never been a better time to be a solicitor in Ireland. The profession (like almost everyone else) is enjoying the economic good times while they last. The problems of too much, rather than too little, work and how best to balance work and leisure have been, for a happy few years at least, unaccustomed issues for the profession to deal with.

One of the most striking differences between the solicitors' profession in 1951 and today is its size. At the end of 2001 there were 6,478 members of the Society (in contrast to the 1,114 members in 1951) 5,912 of whom had practising certificates. Another striking contrast with fifty years ago – even with fifteen years ago – is that today 40 per cent of the Society's members are women and almost half, 47 per cent to be precise, are under 40 years of age.

The profession's clients also are much more sophisticated and diverse. In addition, the nature of legal services has become more varied with the development of new fields of practice which were largely or completely unknown fifty years ago. New specialist areas have emerged such as family law, employment law, administrative law and, in the commercial law area, competition law, intellectual property law, financial services law, information technology law and so on. All now operate under a vastly more developed constitutional law jurisprudence, together with the all-pervasive influence of EU law.

New legal textbooks of great length and learning are published constantly – one of the most striking contrasts with fifty years ago – and powerful computer search engines have transformed legal research. The volume of new legislation and daily court decisions provide a seemingly endless supply of wheat for this relentlessly grinding legal millstone.

The world for the solicitors' profession is increasingly complex and fast moving. It is very difficult to both maintain a practice and keep up with all the legal changes that occur daily either through new legislation or case law.

This is the modern world and modern solicitors' profession. The Society must meet the ever-growing demands of both.

Fortunately, as Ireland and the solicitors' profession have changed, so has the Law Society. The Society in 2002 is a substantial and sophisticated organisation with total staff numbers (combining full and part-time staff) exceeding 140 and a total annual turnover (combining Society and compensation fund) of nearly €16 million. An organisation of this size must be, and in this case is, managed in a modern, efficient, manner employing the most up-to-date information technology and human resources management. The staff of any organisation is its greatest single asset and that is particularly true of an organisation as complex and unique as the Law Society. The Society's staff exhibit on a daily basis levels of professional skill, specialist knowledge and dedication to the ideals of the Society and of the profession which are deeply impressive.

The next greatest asset acquired by the Society over the last fifty years is its premises in Blackhall Place. The vision of those who led the Society's acquisition of Blackhall Place in 1968 has proved of enormous benefit to the profession. Not merely has one of Dublin's most gracious eighteenth-century buildings been preserved for the future, but the prestige of the profession itself has grown immeasurably from its ownership of such a beautiful, historic, headquarters located conveniently close to the two other green-domed edifices of the law, the Four Courts and the King's Inns.

In Blackhall Place the Society's council, committees and general membership have a meeting place both for work and, when desired, for recreation. The Society's administrative staff, which had already outgrown the cramped quarters in the Four Courts by the time of the move to Blackhall Place in 1978, have sufficient space for a few more years at least. Of equal importance, however, is the fact that the acquisition of Blackhall Place allowed the Society to realise its dream of establishing its own professional training course. The strategic importance of this act, for the success of the profession since then and for the future, cannot be overstated.

A second giant step in this regard was the decision – based on the report of the Education Policy Review Group and adopted ultimately by the membership as a whole (in a poll with 76 per cent of voters supporting it) – to construct a new £5 million state-of-the-art Education Centre at Blackhall Place. When the President of Ireland, Mary McAleese, formally opened the Centre on 2 October 2000, she described it as 'a statement about the future, the shape of that future and what lies at the heart of it for the legal profession'. The modern lawyer must be very comfortably adapted to the changed and changing environment, she continued. 'He or she must be out in front, not lagging behind'.

Of more importance than the physical accommodation in the new Education Centre, of course, are the education and the training courses which are delivered within it both by the Society's staff and by the five hundred or more members of the profession who give unstintingly of their time and expertise to train their future colleagues. The year 2001 saw the first of the fully redesigned professional training courses, with the most modern course materials and teaching methods, delivered to courses comprising as many as 360 apprentices. In addition, extensive use has been made of the Education Centre by continuing legal education seminars which are now routinely transmitted by video-link to solicitors in other venues around the country.

ISSUES OF TODAY

One of the main policy debates in the Society at present is on the proposal that every practising member of the profession should undertake a minimum number of hours of continuing professional development each year. At its meeting in September 2001 the council voted by thirty-two votes to one to approve in principle this recommendation. The intention is that the profession should embrace the concept of 'lifelong learning' whereby every practitioner would spend at least a minimum number of hours every year improving their legal skills (practice management skills, in particular) and keeping their legal knowledge up to date in their field of practice.

The commitment to constantly improving both the pre-qualification and post-qualification education and training of solicitors has a fundamental strategic purpose. In a highly competitive marketplace for professional advice of all kinds, the best guarantee that the solicitors' profession can have of its continuing success is that it is, and ever-improvingly continues to be, simply better than all of the competition in terms of quality, cost and speed of service to the public. Education also improves the practitioner's ability to deliver a wider range of services, together with services of higher value. Although the final decisions on the continuing professional development proposals are yet to be made, if adopted both practitioners and their clients should benefit greatly over time.

The single most significant change actually introduced by the Society in 2001 was on the regulatory side of the Society's activities with the adoption by the council (also at its meeting in September) of the new Solicitors Accounts Regulations, 2001. The purpose of the regulations is to update, extend and repeal the Solicitors Accounts Regulations, 1984, reflecting a number of new policy provisions, together with new definitions and terminology, primarily to reflect the wording of the Solicitors (Amendment) Act, 1994.

The principal policy change prevents a solicitor from keeping his or her own money in the client account. In the Society's experience, some solicitors had used a general 'float' of their own money to mask deficits in the client account. A series of other provisions in the new regulations ensures a complete trail of moneys received.

The new regulations represent a major strengthening of the Society's regulatory regime which will more effectively protect clients' moneys in the interest of the public generally and, of course also, in the interests of the solicitors' profession which must make up deficits.

The Society's handling of clients' complaints against solicitors – in many respects the essence of self-regulation of the profession to the limited extent that this exists – was again under scrutiny by the media in 2001. The long-established presence of a series of layers and levels of external oversight of the Society's role in this regard, however, can give the public full confidence that the system is both scrupulously fair and efficient. Non-lawyer members of the registrar's committee have been in place for almost ten years. In addition we have had the Independent Adjudicator since 1997 and it was particularly heartening to hear him describe the Society's complaints handling to the Minister for Justice, Equality and Law Reform as 'extremely satisfactory' and 'a fully-resourced, state-of-the-art operation, well ahead of its counterparts in Northern Ireland, Scotland, England and

Wales'. Perhaps the biggest threat to self-regulation would result if the Society began to fail in this area of its activities. For the present, at least, complaints handling is one of the Society's main strengths, not least because of the public transparency with which, quite rightly, it is suffused.

Two major new challenges were placed on the Society's agenda by government in 2001. In March the government accepted the recommendations of the Special Working Group on Personal Injury Compensation which had been established under the auspices of the Department of Enterprise, Trade and Employment. The chief recommendation was that a Personal Injuries Assessment Board should be established to which every person suffering bodily injury in a road traffic accident or in the course of employment who wishes to make a claim for compensation must apply for an assessment before the claim can be brought to a court. The declared intention of those who framed the proposal is to have such claims disposed of by the board rather than through the courts with, it is assumed, a consequent reduction in the 'delivery cost' of the personal injuries compensation system. The unstated aim, in the view of the Society, is to reduce the compensation paid to the victims of negligent employers.

The Society is fundamentally opposed to this proposal on public interest grounds. There are two major objections. The first is the inherent anti-claimant bias of both the composition and proposed method of operation of the board, as recommended. The second is the dubious economics whereby, ironically, the establishment of a Personal Injuries Assessment Board could well introduce a new layer of bureaucracy, cost and delay where none exists at present. The Society recognises that the system is over-costly and in need of reform but it doubts the fairness and value of this proposal. It is seeking to persuade anyone who is prepared to listen that, where defects exist in the current system, they can be resolved in other ways. The Society's campaign on the issue is ongoing.

A campaign by vested interests such as the insurance industry, employers' representatives, public authorities and others, has relentlessly criticised Ireland's personal injuries compensation system for many years. Although previous campaigns, such as those which led to the abolition of juries in personal injuries actions and the end of the 'two-senior' system, did not lead to any reduction in insurance premiums, this campaign once again has the ear of the media and politicians. Change seems to be inevitable. The Personal Injuries Assessment Board proposal, unfair to victims and economically senseless as it may well prove to be, has huge political appeal. The legal profession is strategically vulnerable through over-dependence on this area of work.

Following hot on the heels of the government's announcement in relation to a Personal Injuries Assessment Board came the announcement by no less than the Taoiseach himself that the Competition Authority would undertake a study of certain professions in Ireland. The Taoiseach was speaking at the launch of a report by the OECD entitled 'Regulatory Reform in Ireland' which made certain passing references to the legal profession. Some of the OECD's recommendations, such as the one that the control of education and entry of legal professionals should be removed from the self-governing bodies, appear to be based on ideology rather than information, on prejudice rather than proof. The all time record number of 476 new solicitors who came on the roll in 2001, well surpassing the number for the previous year which was also a record, together with the general trend in this regard, gives the lie to any suggestion that the system is being used to suppress numbers entering the profession. The Society accepted as far back as the 1980s that it has no role to play in controlling the numbers entering the profession. The market for legal services reigns supreme in this.

The Society made contact with the Competition Authority and received assurances that the authority does not accept the OECD recommendations as 'given' but will approach matters with a genuinely open and objective mind. If this is so, and if there is also a recognition that wider public policy interests rather than simply competition policy must inform the regulation of the legal profession, then perhaps the Society and the profession should not be overly concerned with the likely outcome of a study by the Competition Authority. Nevertheless, it seems likely that a great deal of the Society's time and energies will be absorbed in its dealings with the Competition Authority over the next year or, perhaps even, years. Undoubtedly some changes will result.

Could it be that in the future the legal profession and even the legal system will be increasingly dominated by competition policy? In many other countries around the world a tension has emerged between the values of lawyers and the legal system, where the emphasis is placed on justice and the rights of individuals, and the values of competition policy, with its emphasis on economic efficiency in the delivery of goods and services to consumers. It seems that competition is becoming the card which trumps all others and may be accorded a superior social value to what the legal profession has traditionally held dear.

This clash of value systems is well illustrated in the world-wide debate as to whether lawyers should be allowed enter into multi-disciplinary partnerships (MDPs) with non-lawyers. There are traditional 'core values' of the legal profession – values believed to protect the interests of clients rather than of the profession – such as always putting the client's interest first, acting at all times with the utmost integrity, the avoidance of conflicts of interest, the maintenance of confidentiality in relation to clients' affairs (with the associated 'cornerstone of the justice system', legal professional privilege) and the independence of the profession protecting the rights of citizens against an over-reaching State. How can these be maintained in a multi-disciplinary partnership between solicitors and others who do not share these values?

The Law Society of Ireland, in keeping with most national bars and law societies in Europe, the United States and elsewhere in the world, has a policy of opposition to MDPs involving lawyers on the basis that they are contrary to the interests of clients and of lawyers. The drive for MDPs seems to come, almost exclusively, from a handful of global accounting/ consultancy firms who wish to integrate not just legal services but the prestige of the lawyer's brand to their portfolio of services.

The judgment of the European Court of Justice in the NOVA case early in 2002, upholding the compatibility with EU competition law of the Dutch Bar's rule prohibiting MDPs between lawyers and accountants, was a major blow to MDPs. The judgment confirmed the special value to all citizens of the legal profession's independence, confidentiality and avoidance of conflicts of interest.

Two pieces of legislation affecting the solicitors' profession in Ireland have been enacted in 2002. The Solicitors (Amendment) Act, 2002 will severely restrict advertising by solicitors in the area of personal injuries claims. The government is, in effect, turning its previous policy on its head in this regard in the wake of the army deafness controversy of a few years ago. The Society fully supports the government as it believes that this type of advertising, engaged in only by a very small minority of the profession, has tended to diminish the standing of the profession and the public esteem in which it is held. Such advertising has encouraged a false 'ambulance chasing' image of the profession just as was predicted by the Society when advertising was effectively forced on a reluctant profession by government in 1988. It is, accordingly, with a certain pleasure that in this instance the Society can tell the government that 'we told you so'.

The Courts and Court Officers Act, 2002 has made provision for a historic breakthrough for the solicitors' profession in that solicitors are for the first time eligible for appointment as judges of the High Court and Supreme Court. Indeed, in July 2002 Michael Peart became the first ever practising solicitor in Ireland or Britain to be appointed a judge of the High Court. This is the culmination of literally decades of campaigning by the Law Society and results from government acceptance of the recommendations of an independent working group, on which both the Law Society and the Bar Council were represented, which reported early in 1999. This report finally put an end to the fallacy that experience as an advocate was required in order to be a judge. A solicitor's experience of litigation is every bit as valuable as a barrister's experience of litigation as a preparation for appointment to senior judicial office. The Society has viewed this as a parity of esteem issue between the two branches of the profession and has overcome enormous opposition to achieve the ending, in the public interest, of the Bar's monopoly of senior judicial appointments.

THE SOCIETY'S RELATIONS WITH THE BAR, JUDICIARY, PUBLIC, GOVERNMENT AND MEMBERS

For a period the opposing views on the judicial eligibility issue was a source of considerable tension between the Law Society and the Bar Council. For a couple of years in the mid to late 1990s relations between the two representative bodies were poor. Thankfully that is now far behind us and in 2002 relations between the Law Society and the Bar Council are particularly warm, cordial and co-operative.

Relations between the Law Society and the judiciary are also excellent and have probably been improved by the appointment of no less than eight solicitors as judges of the Circuit Court since this first became possible in 1995. There can be little doubt that the judiciary themselves have changed much in recent years and are now very considerably more open and approachable in their relationship with the solicitors' profession. Indeed, particularly through the new Courts Service, the judiciary are warmly embracing all manner of change and improvement in the courts and the administration of justice.

A perennial source of concern to the solicitors' profession is its public image. Image is hugely important in the modern world. Surveys show that solicitors are held in high esteem by their own clients but that the profession as a whole is not held in high esteem. This is not something which is unique either to Ireland or to the current era. Throughout the world the image of the legal profession leaves a lot to be desired. At international conferences lawyers from every continent on the globe complain about their low standing with the public. However, there is evidence that the low public standing of lawyers has existed throughout history. Even in ancient Greece lawyers were the subject of criticism on grounds similar to those on which they are criticised today.

The only conclusion that can be reached is that lawyers' relative unpopularity results from the nature of their work. As one American put it, if citizens have their property, their family, their good name or even their liberty at risk they will want the lawyer in their corner to fight on their behalf with the ferocity of a rottweiler, not the docility of a labrador. In society generally, however, rottweilers are not loved. It is a simplistic analysis but there is an element of truth about it. Lawyers will never be popular. It is in the nature of the work.

In Ireland in the 1990s the phenomenon of the tribunals of inquiry caused further deterioration in the image of the legal profession. The first of these major tribunals, the Beef Tribunal, was disastrous for the legal profession in

Ireland in terms of a perceived discrepancy between a time consuming and expensive process and an ultimate report which did not satisfy the public. The profession as a whole paid the price in terms of public cynicism at the perceived ineffectiveness and legal costs of that tribunal and some of the subsequent tribunals have added to this cynicism.

It is to be hoped that the solicitors' profession in Ireland is becoming less thin-skinned, particularly about the manner in which it is depicted in the media. The media's all-pervasive scepticism, not to say cynicism, nowadays applies to everything and everyone and it is no more unfair to the legal profession than to many other elements in society.

Relations between the Law Society and government have been good in recent years, both with the elected government and the so-called 'permanent government' of the civil service. There seems to be a greater understanding of what the Society is trying to do and an acceptance of its bona fides. There is a high level of accessibility to government and the Society's views are listened to even though they are by no means always accepted. It is in the nature of the relationship between the Society and government, however, that there will always be a level of tension. If there was none then one or other would not be doing its job.

The most important relationship which the Society has, of course, is with its members. This is the key to everything. Without the support of its members the Society can do nothing. There will always be some degree of distance but great efforts have been made, with evident success, in recent years to close the worryingly wide gap of distrust whereby the Society was perceived to be significantly out of touch with its members in the early 1990s. This dissatisfaction came to a head in the difficult AGM of the Society in November 1994.

The work of the Review Working Group established following that meeting and the implementation of that working group's subsequent recommendations helped to return to many members the sense that the Society was their organisation and on their side. A renewed emphasis on communication with the members and, in particular, on fighting the profession's legitimate corner with the government and in the media has helped to cement this. The combination of a number of successful political and court battles on the one hand and the 'feel good' factor from the developing economic boom on the other hand, brought a very much warmer and more supportive attitude of most members towards the Society in the late 1990s which still continues. That being said, there must never be complacency in the Society in this regard.

ISSUES FOR TOMORROW

It is said that to make the Gods laugh you have only to tell them your plans. Or, to put it another way, predictions are always difficult – particularly where they concern the future! To amuse readers of the future (if readers there will be) this chapter will now peer myopically into the fog that hides what is to come.

As the Society celebrates in 2002 the 150th anniversary of its first charter (although solicitors and attorneys existed as an organised group in Ireland long before that date) it is worth questioning, even briefly, what the future may be for the idea of a 'profession'. Is it essentially a Victorian concept unlikely to survive for very much longer in the third millennium? Will its, perhaps rather quaint, altruistic values and ideals of service to a higher goal than pure profit ultimately succumb to the values and morals of the business world where profit reigns supreme?

Will the legal profession at some time in the future either formally or informally split, as some international thinkers believe it will, with, perhaps, the large commercial law firms, driven by transactional business and increasingly dominated by the values of their corporate clients, drifting further and further away from the small private client firms who remain dominated by the values of the courts? Or will it remain the case, as the great majority still seem to wish and believe, that the solicitor visiting a client in custody in a police station at 2.00 a.m. will continue to be a member of the same profession with the same basic purpose, identity and core values as the solicitor sitting in a boardroom at 2.00 a.m. advising a multinational corporation about a merger?

Can the Law Society continue to effectively represent and be relevant to both small and larger firms of solicitors? Indeed, to raise again a question which must be around for at least 150 years, can the Law Society as a single organisation both regulate and represent the profession effectively? Is there a conflict between the two roles? The best answer to this question, incidentally, remains the same as it has always been. There is no conflict in the objectives of the Law Society in both regulating and representing the profession. The ultimate objective of both activities, serving simultaneously the interests of the public and of the profession, is the same. It is to maintain the integrity and reputation of the solicitors' profession. How frail and vulnerable reputation is was demonstrated by the collapse of the Arthur Andersen firm early in 2002 in the wake of the Enron debacle.

As to the other questions about the future of professionalism and of a unified legal profession, the enormous US and UK-based international law firms, where the trends referred to above are much more pronounced in terms of scale than anything seen in Ireland, to-date at least, have retained a sense of common identity with the remainder of the legal profession from which they have grown. No hard evidence exists of any likely split in the profession, at least in the near future.

A great strength of the legal profession – one of the reasons why it continues to thrive in just about every country in the world – is its adaptability. Despite its reputation for conservatism, the legal profession has been very good at responding to change both in developing new areas of work and embracing the tools of the modern world such as information technology. The two pieces of technology of the last fifty years which have contributed most to the mass of legal work, vastly increasing the length and volume of documentation in almost all forms of legal work, have been the photocopier and the word processor.

In addition, information technology in the widest sense of the term has been a particularly powerful tool transforming the speed at which a knowledge-based activity like the provision of legal services can (and is increasingly expected by clients to) be delivered. By making the law itself accessible to the non-lawyer it is compelling the profession to focus not on legal knowledge, in which it will no longer have a monopoly, but in the increasingly sophisticated ways in which legal knowledge can be applied to solve clients' problems. Constantly to increase specialist knowledge and skill, with a view to providing ever more sophisticated and high value services, appears to be the best strategic response for the profession.

So, what is the future for the solicitors' profession? No one would be foolish enough to attempt to predict the next 150 years but what of, say, the next fifteen years? Based on the experience of the last fifty years, the future seems bright. The raw material of legal work is law. It seems inevitable that Irish society will grow more and more complex and, hopefully, prosperous and that the law will grow to reflect this. Both the Oireachtas and the European Union seem intent on producing ever-greater volumes of new law every year. Courts and tribunals are likely to produce lengthier and more complex interpretations and applications of this law. Increased education brings increased consciousness of rights and the confidence to assert them. Accordingly, more and more lawyers will be required to advise clients, both private and commercial, of their rights and responsibilities as the law continues to change on a daily basis. Some traditional areas of practice will decline but many new ones will emerge. The only constant will be change. We should hardly be surprised at this. The constancy of change was remarked on by Heraclitus in the fourth century BC. However, today's pace of change would undoubtedly astonish him.

What of the Law Society whose 150th birthday is celebrated in 2002? Although the President of the High Court recently described it as 'a thriving concern', it cannot stand still. It faces an increasingly complex and demanding world which it must grow in size, skill and sophistication to meet. It will have to become ever more transparent and accountable for the discharge of its public interest responsibilities in relation to solicitors. In addition it must constantly increase the quality of its service to its members, to its prospective members and to the public. It must do all of this while remaining true to the twin values of excellence and integrity which have so characterised the work of the Society and of the solicitors' profession in Ireland over the last 150 years.

It seems well placed to meet its challenges and responsibilities tomorrow, as it has always done.

33. An Taoiseach, Bertie Ahern TD, laying the foundation stone for the Law Society's new education centre in July 1999, with Law Society President Patrick O'Connor and Director General Ken Murphy *(Photograph: Lensmen)*

34. Directors of education past and present
Left to right: Dr Albert Power, Director of Education 1993–1999, Professor Richard Woulfe, Director of Education 1978–1993, T.P. Kennedy, current Director of Education since 1999, and Professor Laurence G. Sweeney, Director of Training 1977–1992 *(Photograph: Lensmen)*

35. President of Ireland, Mary McAleese, formally opens the new education centre on 2 October 2000, with Law Society President, Anthony H. Ensor *(Photograph: Mac Innes Photography)*

36. The first students attending a professional practice course in the new education centre, autumn 2000 *(Photograph: Lensmen)*

37. The new Law Society education centre, Blackhall Place, designed by architects Brian
O'Connell Associates *(Photograph: Lensmen)*

38. Newly admitted solicitors who received their parchments from the President of the High Court at a ceremony in December 1999. *Back row, left to right:* Garrett Doherty, Conor Bunbury, John Black, Justin Cody, Gerard Ryan, Mark Byrne. *Middle row:* Louise McNabola, Carmel Cahill, Susan Canty, Anne-Marie Daly, Margaret Ahearn. *Front row:* Sarah-Jane Maguire, Joyce Compton, Eimear Collins, Maeve Carbin, Helen Harnett and Rob Corbett *(Photograph: Lensmen)*

39. Opening of the new library on 2 October 2000
Left to right: Deputy Director General Mary Keane, President Anthony Ensor, Mary McAleese, President of Ireland, Director General Ken Murphy, and Librarian Margaret Byrne. *Back row, left to right:* Library Assistant Eddie Mackey, Deputy Librarian Mary Gaynor and Library Assistant Aoife O'Connor *(Photograph: Mac Innes Photography)*

40. Ken Murphy, Law Society Director General, opening the first video link continuing legal education seminar to be held in the new education centre in September 2000. The subject was landlord and tenant and the speakers were Judge John F. Buckley, chairman, Gabriel Brennan and Marjorie Murphy in Dublin and Michelle Linnane in Sligo. *(Photograph: Lensmen)*

41. Elma Lynch, President of the Society, 2001/02 *(centre)*, with Moya Quinlan, President 1980/81, and Geraldine Clarke, Senior Vice President, 2001/02 *(Photograph: Lensmen)*

42. Ken Murphy, Director General of the Law Society *(Photograph: Roslyn Byrne)*

43. Council of the Law Society, 2000/01, at the commencement of the council meeting of 7 September 2001.

Seated, left to right: John Dillon-Leech, Francis D. Daly, Michael Irvine (Junior Vice President 2000/01), Mary Keane (Deputy Director General), Ken Murphy (Director General), Ward McEllin (President 2000/01), Elma Lynch (Senior Vice President 2000/01), Martin McAllister (President, Law Society of Scotland – visitor), Douglas Mill (Secretary General, Law Society of Scotland – visitor), Patrick O'Connor, David Martin, Eamon O'Brien, Orla Coyne, Stuart J. Gilhooly, Hugh O'Neill, John B. Harte, Owen Binchy, Philip M. Joyce, Moya Quinlan, Gerard J. Doherty, John P. Shaw, Sean F. Durcan, James B. McCourt. *Standing, left to right:* Anthony H. Ensor, Kevin D. O'Higgins, John O'Connor, David Bergin, Patrick Casey, John D. Shaw, Simon Murphy, Anne Colley, James MacGuill, Patrick Dorgan, John E. Costello, Keenan Johnson, Michael D. Peart and Edward C. Hughes. Absent from this photo are: Peter M. Allen, Donald P. Binchy, Geraldine M. Clarke, John G. Fish, Gerard F. Griffin, Thomas Murran, Brian J. Sheridan, Laurence K. Shields, James Sweeney, Eamonn Fleming and Patricia Harney, and the Law Society of Northern Ireland nominees, Catherine Dixon, V. Alan Hewitt, John I. Meehan, John G. Neill and Alastair Rankin *(Photograph: Mac Innes Photography)*

44. P.J. Connolly, Registrar of Solicitors *(Photograph: Mac Innes Photography)*

45. Past presidents and officers of the Society for the year 1997/98 who attended a dinner to honour outgoing President, Frank Daly, in December 1997. *Seated, from left*: Officers Patrick O'Connor (Senior Vice President 1997/98) and Geraldine Clarke (Junior Vice President 1997/98), Frank Daly (1996/97), Laurence K. Shields (1997/98), Joseph L. Dundon (1977/78), Moya Quinlan (1980/81) and Bruce St. John Blake (1976/77). *Standing, left to right*: the late Gerald Hickey (1978/79), Raymond T. Monahan (1992/93), Andrew F. Smyth (1995/96), Judge Frank O'Donnell (1983/84), the late Ernest J. Margetson (1989/90), Thomas D. Shaw (1987/88), Donal G. Binchy (1990/91), Patrick A. Glynn (1994/95), Laurence Cullen (1985/86), Michael V. O'Mahony (1993/94) and Maurice R. Curran (1988/89) *(Photograph: Lensmen)*

46. Solicitors who are government ministers in the 29th Dáil (2002–). *Left to right*: Dermot Ahern TD, Minister for Communications, Marine and Natural Resources, Brian Cowen TD, Minister for Foreign Affairs, and John O'Donoghue TD, Minister for Arts, Sport and Tourism. They served as Minister for Social, Community and Family Affairs, Minister for Foreign Affairs and Minister for Justice, Equality and Law Reform, respectively, in the 28th Dáil. (1997–2002)

47. Celebrating 150 years. President Elma Lynch shows the royal charter of 1852 to the Minister for Justice, Equality and Law Reform, John O'Donoghue, in February 2002. *(Photograph: Lensmen)*

48. Mr Justice Michael Peart, the first practising solicitor to be appointed a judge of the High Court, in July 2002. (*Photogragh: Roslyn Byrne*)

Council of the Law Society of Ireland
for the year ending 7 November 2002

President Elma Lynch

Vice Presidents
Senior Geraldine M. Clarke   *Junior* Philip Joyce

Donald P. Binchy
Owen M. Binchy
Michael Boylan
Anne Colley
Angela E. Condon
John E. Costello
Orla Coyne
Andrew Dillon
Gerard J. Doherty
John G. Fish
Stuart J. Gilhooly
Gerard F. Griffin
Edward C. Hughes
Michael G. Irvine

Keenan Johnson
James B. McCourt
James MacGuill
Simon J. Murphy
Thomas Murran
John O'Connor
Patrick O'Connor
Kevin D. O'Higgins
Hugh O'Neill
Michael D. Peart
Moya Quinlan
John D. Shaw
John P. Shaw
Brian J. Sheridan

Provincial delegates

Ulster James Sweeney
Munster Eamon O'Brien

Leinster John B. Harte
Connaught Rosemarie J. Loftus

Dublin Solicitors' Bar Association

John P. O'Malley
Michael Quinlan

Boyce Shubotham

Southern Law Association

Patrick Casey
Patrick Dorgan
Eamonn Fleming

Patricia Harney
Fiona Twomey

Law Society of Northern Ireland

Catherine Dixon
Joseph A. Donnelly
V. Alan Hewitt

John G. Neill
Alistair Rankin

Past Presidents entitled to sit on Council pursuant to the Society's Bye-Laws.

Francis D. Daly
Anthony H. Ensor

Ward McEllin
Laurence K. Shields

Presidents of the Law Society of Ireland

1842–48	Josias Dunn	1904–05	Edward D. MacLaughlin
1848–60	William Goddard	1905–06	Sir John P. Lynch
1860–76	Sir Richard J.T. Orpen	1906–07	William S. Hayes
1876	Edward Reeves	1907–08	George H. Lyster
1876–77	William Roche	1908–09	William J. Shannon
1877–78	Sir William Findlater	1909–10	Richard A. MacNamara
1878–79	William Read	1910–11	Frederick W. Meredith
1879–80	Henry A. Dillon	1911–12	Gerald Byrne
1880–81	John H. Nunn	1912–13	James Henry
1881–82	Henry J.P. West	1913–14	Henry J. Synott
1882–83	Henry T. Dix	1914–15	Arthur E. Bradley
1883–84	William D'Alton	1915–16	Charles St. George Orpen
1884–85	John Galloway	1916–17	John W. Richards
1885–86	Henry L. Keily	1917–18	William V. Seddall
1886–87	Sir Patrick Maxwell	1918–19	Richard Blair White
1887–88	Richard S. Reeves	1919–20	Robert G. Warren
1888–89	John MacSheehy	1920–21	Charles G. Gamble
1889–90	W. Burroughs Stanley	1921–22	Patrick J. Brady
1890–91	Francis R.M. Crozier	1922–23	Joseph E. MacDermott
1891–92	Thomas C. Franks	1923–24	James Moore
1892–93	Edward FitzGerald	1924–25	Arthur H.S. Orpen
1893–94	John Alexander French	1925–26	Thomas G. Quirke
1894–95	Trevor T.L. Overend	1926–27	William T. Sheridan
1895–96	Sir William Fry	1927–28	Basil Thompson
1896–97	Sir William Findlater	1928–29	Edward H. Burne
1897–98	William Henry Dunne	1929–30	Peter Seales
1898–99	Hugh Stuart Moore	1930–31	Alexander D. Orr
1899–00	Richard S. Reeves	1931–32	Laurence J. Ryan
1900–01	James Goff	1932–33	W. Gordon Bradley
	Sir George Roche	1933–34	James J. Lynch
1901–02	Charles A. Stanuell	1934–35	Charles Laverty
1902–03	Sir Augustine F. Baker	1935–36	Michael E. Knight
1903–04	Robert Keating Clay	1936–37	John J. Duggan
	Edward D. MacLaughlin	1937–38	Thomas W. Delaney

1938–39	Daniel J. Reilly	1970–71	Brendan A. McGrath
1939–40	Henry P. Mayne	1971–72	James W. O'Donovan
1940–41	J. Travers Wolfe	1972–73	Thomas V. O'Connor
1941–42	G. Acheson Overend	1973–74	Peter D.M. Prentice
1942–43	John B. Hamill	1974–75	William A. Osborne
1943–44	Louis E. O'Dea	1975–76	Patrick C. Moore
1944–45	Patrick F. O'Reilly	1976–77	Bruce St. John Blake
1945–46	Daniel O'Connell	1977–78	Joseph L. Dundon
1946–47	Henry St. John Blake	1978–79	Gerald Hickey
1947–48	Seán Ó hUadhaigh	1979–80	Walter Beatty
1948–49	Patrick R. Boyd	1980–81	Moya Quinlan
1949–50	William J. Norman	1981–82	Brendan W. Allen
1950–51	Roger Greene	1982–83	Michael P. Houlihan
1951–52	Arthur Cox	1983–84	Frank O'Donnell
1952–53	James R. Quirke	1984–85	Anthony E. Collins
1953–54	Joseph Barrett	1985–86	Laurence Cullen
1954–55	Thomas A. O'Reilly	1986–87	David R. Pigot
1955–56	Dermot P. Shaw	1987–88	Thomas D. Shaw
1956–57	Niall S. Gaffney	1988–89	Maurice R. Curran
1957–58	John Carrigan	1989–90	Ernest J. Margetson
1958–59	John R. Halpin	1990–91	Donal G. Binchy
1959–60	John J. Nash	1991–92	Adrian P. Bourke
1960–61	Ralph J. Walker	1992–93	Raymond T. Monahan
1961–62	George G. Overend	1993–94	Michael V. O'Mahony
1962–63	Francis J. Lanigan	1994–95	Patrick A. Glynn
1963–64	Desmond J. Collins	1995–96	Andrew F. Smyth
1964–65	John Maher	1996–97	Francis D. Daly
1965–66	Robert McD. Taylor	1997–98	Laurence K. Shields
1966–67	Patrick O'Donnell TD	1998–99	Patrick O'Connor
1967–68	Patrick Noonan	1999–00	Anthony H. Ensor
1968–69	Eunan McCarron	2000–01	Ward McEllin
1969–70	James R.C. Green	2001–02	Elma Lynch

Auditors of the Solicitors' Apprentices Debating Society of Ireland

1884–85	William M. Byrne	1913–14	Arthur Cox
	Thomas B. Moffat	1914–15	Conor A. Maguire
1885–86	Edward N. Greer		John O'Hanrahan
1886–87	Robert Dickie	1915–16	John Foley
1887–88	Guy B. Pilkington	1916–17	Patrick J. Ruttledge
1888–89	John Robert O'Connell	1917–18	Barry I. Sullivan
1889–90	William A. FitzHenry	1918–19	William Devoy
1890–91	William H. Geoghegan	1919–20	James J. Stack
1891–92	Joseph J. Dudley	1920–21	Michael J.C. Keane
1892–93	John H. Walsh	1921–22	Helena M. Early
1893–94	Peter L. Macardle	1922–23	Edward A. Cleary
1894–95	James Tench	1923–24	John S. O'Connor
1895–96	Edward P. O'Flanagan	1924–25	Patrick J. Loftus
1896–97	Edwin N. Edwards	1925–26	Patrick Byrne
1897–98	William Ireland Good	1926–27	John J. Nash
1898–99	Robert N. Keohler	1927–28	Gerald M. Counahan
1899–00	John J. McDonald	1928–29	Herman Good
1900–01	Patrick J. Masterson	1929–30	Daniel J. O'Connor
1901–02	Henry A. Drennan	1930–31	Eric A. Plunkett
1902–03	James O'Brien	1931–32	Patrick J. O'Brien
1903–04	Patrick Donnelly	1932–33	Charles J. Holohan
1904–05	Laurence J. O'Neill	1933–34	William Walsh
1905–06	James J. Hayden	1934–35	James F.G. Kent
1906–07	James C.B. Proctor	1935–36	Francis A. Gibney
1907–08	Henry Shannon	1936–37	Andrew G. Sheedy
1908–09	Enda B. Healy	1937–38	Peter L. Gibson
1909–10	Charles B.W. Boyle	1938–39	Anthony J.F. Hussey
1910–11	John J. Molloy	1939–40	Michael J. Egan
1911–12	Thomas Arkins	1940–41	Dominic M. Dowling
1912–13	Ambrose Davoren	1941–42	Patrick P. O'Sullivan
	Christopher Crozier Shaw	1942–43	Louis V. Nolan

1943–44	Patrick J. Brennan	1973–74	Michael Staines
1944–45	Frank Martin	1974–75	Brian P. O'Reilly
1945–46	Sean M. Flanagan	1975–76	Niall Sheridan
1946–47	George J. Colley	1976–77	Ciaran A. O'Mara
1947–48	John Edmund Doyle	1977–78	Michael D. Murphy
1948–49	James P. Woods	1978–79	Liam T. Cosgrave
1949–50	Edmund S. Doyle	1979–80	John J. Reid
1950–51	Richard Ryan	1980–81	Richard Grogan
1951–52	Patrick C. Kilroy	1981–82	Laurence W. Ennis
1952–53	Charles Hennessy	1982–83	William F. Holohan
1953–54	Walter Beatty	1983–84	Aislinn M. O'Farrell
1954–55	Desmond P.H. Windle	1984–85	Terence McCrann
1955–56	John F. Buckley	1985–86	Francis Hackett
1956–57	T. Michael Williams	1986–87	Brian J. O'Connor
1957–58	Laurence F. Branigan	1987–88	Gavin Buckley
1958–59	Richard M. Neville	1988–89	Paul D. White
1959–60	Michael J. Hogan	1989–90	Eileen A. Roberts
1960–61	Bruce St. John Blake	1990–91	Joseph N. Kelly
1961–62	Thomas C. Smyth	1991–92	Edward T. O'Connor
1962–63	Dermot Loftus	1992–93	Paula E. Murphy
1963–64	Michael V. O'Mahony	1993–94	Philippa M. Howley
1964–65	Thomas W. Enright	1994–95	Fergal P. Brennan
1965–66	Fergus F. Armstrong	1995–96	Paul A. Murray
1966–67	James F. O'Higgins	1996–97	Matthew McCabe
1967–68	Donough H. O'Connor	1997–98	John Cahir
1968–69	Michael C. Larkin	1998–99	Louise Gallagher
1969–70	Michael S. Roche	1999–00	Keith Walsh
1970–71	Elizabeth A. Ryan	2000–01	Claire O'Regan
1971–72	Laurence K. Shields	2001–02	Martin Hayes
1972–73	Bryan C. Sheridan		

Solicitors admitted to the Roll of Solicitors of the Courts of Justice, 1952–2001

(The names in the following list, arranged alphabetically by year of admission, are shown in the form in which they were entered on the roll.)

1952

Bourke, Eileen
Brennan, Eileen Anne
Brilley, Daniel C.
Burleigh, Henry Walter
Callanan, Fionnbar Francis
Carey, Patrick Joseph
Comer, Simon Diarmuid Joseph
Conway, Patrick J.
Cusack, Patrick James
Cussen, Kathleen Elizabeth
Devlin, Dermot Joseph Anthony Joachim
Dey, Arthur
Downes, Patrick Noel
Flanagan, Michael F.
Gearty, Enda C.
Geary, Francis Brian
Greene, John A.
Griffin, Joseph
Keane, Francis G.
Kelly, Ivan William Peter
Kelly, John Vincent
Kelly, Thomas P.
King, Edward Patrick
Lavery, C. Arthur
McCloughan, Edwin Russell
Mackey, James Herbert
Markey, Patrick O'Rorke
Meade, Felim Henry
Molloy, Daniel Mary Francis
Moore, Mary
Noone Mary
O'Brien, William Sylvester
O'Connor, Patrick Desmond
O'Flynn, John Brendan

O'Gara, Patrick Joseph
O'Higgins, Una Mary
Phelan, John Anthony
Price, Colm
Punch, David
Spendlove, Eunice Deborah Jebb
Thornton, Patrick E.
Walsh, Francis A.
Warren, John David Wellesley
Whelan, Teresa Bernadette
White, William Reginald

1953

Boushel, Brendan Edward
Colbert, Norbert Paschal
Corrigan, William Michael
Courtney, Daniel J.
Dockery, Joseph M.L.
Fairbrother, George Berford
Gallagher, Donal Paul
Gallagher, Peter D.P.
Glackin, Joseph
Henderson, Kenneth Burgess
Johnston, Francis
Johnston, Gordon William Kerr
Keaney, Edith E.M.
Kelly, Henry
Kilroy, Patrick C.
Lafferty, Henry James A.
Lee, Frans Hendrik van der
Loftus, Leo Joseph
MacCarthy, Finbarr Patrick Joseph

McEvoy, John Michael
McNally, John P.
Magan, Margaret
Maguire, Bryan
Minogue, Edward
Mullaney, Thomas J.
Murphy, Nora
O'Byrne, Thomas Niall
O'Connor, Ernan Rory
O'Meara, John Anthony
Ó Raghallaigh, Labhrás Concubhar
Overend, Brian Kingsbury
Price, Brian
Riordan, Cornelius
Ryan, Timothy
Taylor, Mervyn H.
Woulfe, Eileen Mary Bernadette
Wright, Elizabeth Marie

1954

Baily, John
Boland, John Killian
Branigan, Ignatius Francis
Buchalter, Mathias
Cody, Patrick J.
Crawford, George Hellyer
Davies, Esmond
Diamond, Alec
Donegan, James Daniel
Fay, Charles W.R.
Flynn, Kieran T.
Gantley, Nicholas Joseph
Gaynor, John Aidan

Goff, Owen Brendan
Hennessy, Charles
Johnston, Denis H.
Kelly, Sean
Kirby, John Bernard
McDonough, Donough B.
Maguire, James
O'Connell, Donal Brendan
O'Connor, John Michael
Reihill, Mary Elizabeth
Smyth, Patrick
Spelman, Dominic B.A.
Sweeney, Francis T.D.
Walker, Raymond M.

1955

Abrahamson, Max William
Beatty, Walter
Breen, Desmond Thomas
Brennan, Bernard Matthew
Carolan, Patrick J.
Carney, Valentine P.
Clancy, Fintan Patrick
Colfer, Patrick
Cooke, John Joseph
Cooney, Patrick Mark
Crowley, Thomas
Cussen, Cliodna Mary
Delap, John Joseph
Dillon, Edward J.C.
Dillon, John Paschal
Donnelly, Michael P.
Early, Kevin J.
Gardiner, Patrick Jeremiah
Harpur, William Francis
Haughton, Gabriel Francis
Henderson, Gordon Alan
Hughes, Nicholas S.
Keaveny, Martin Stephen
Kelly, Patrick Calpurnius
Kennedy, Richard Desmond
Kenny, James Flannan
Knight, Richard
MacCurtain, John Edward
McGinley, Monica
Mac Giollarnath, Seán F.
MacMahon, Patrick P.
Maloney, George Vincent

Moore, John Laurence
Moylan, Anthony Gerard
Murphy, Timothy
O'Connor, Brian Joseph
O'Connor, Patrick J.F.
O'Connor, Patrick Joseph
O'Connor, William A.P.
O'Dea, Albert Louis
O'Donnell, Aidan
O'Gorman, John A.
O'Leary, Arthur J.
Owens, Thomas Patrick
Phelan, Maurice J.
Powell, P.J. Gerard
Quirk, Gerard M.
Rogers, Brendan O'Rahilly
Russell, John E.
Smith, Noel Thomas
Staines, Michael A.
Studdert, Hallam John Cecil
Treacy, Patrick Francis

1956

Binchy, Owen (Jnr.)
Blood-Smyth, William
    Whitton
Bourke, Maureen
Buckley, John Francis
Clifford, John P.
Coulter, Gerald Bernard
Coyle, Peter Joseph Cyril
Devine, Dermott J.
Drum, Matthew P.
Duffy, Edward J.
Fallon, William John Bosco
Farrell, John C.
Fogarty, Michael G.
Garavan, John F.
Gleeson, Michael John
Gleeson, Noel M.
Glynn, Patrick A.
Gordon, Daphne Mabel
Halpenny, Michael Clement
Halpin, Brenda Mary
Hegarty, Dermot
Irwin, William Anthony
Jones, Brendan John
Kelleher, Humphrey Patrick

Kelly, James Joseph
Kelly, Patrick B.
Kennedy, Iseult Clare
Kenny, Kenneth Matthew
    Samuel
Kiernan, Joseph John
Lane, Edward Arthur Guest
McCormack, Anthony
    Francis
McEniry, Timothy Bernard
McGonagle, Alan
McGonagle, Robert W.
Maloney, Dermot John
Meredith, Charles R.M.
Molan, John
Murray, Mary Margaret
Nicholl, William Thomas
Noonan, Michael Anthony
O'Carroll, Michael Aiden
O'Connell, Carmel
O'Donoghue, Walter Brian
O'Dwyer, Albert Columbanus
O'Gorman, Patrick R.
O'Keeffe, Nicholas
O'Leary, James Brendan
O'Mahony, Frank
O'Malley, Gerard
O'Sullivan, James J.
Phillips, James V.C.
Plunkett Dillon, Francis J.
Purcell, Michael Philip
    Osborne
Regan, Michael Augustine
Ruttledge, Mairead F.
Tracey, Patrick L.
Williams, Terence Michael

1957

Bowler, Susanna
Burke, Ann M.A.
Charlton, Gerard
Claffey, Brian J.
Conroy, Julia M.
Crehan, Gerald J.
Cullen, Laurence B.
Derham, Ann M.B.
Dorrian, Patrick A.
Downing, Charles F.C.
Fagan, Patrick

Fitzpatrick, Francis A.
Foley, John M.A.
Gearty, Patrick J.
Gibbons, Niall C.
Goff, John Paul C.
Grogan, Alphonsus
Hodgins, William D.J.
Hoey, Brian V.
King, Donal M.
Lawson, John B.
Lynch, Gregory A.
McArdle, Denis A.
McClenaghan, Kevin P. St.
    George
McGrath, Edmond J.K.
Macken, John Raymond
McKnight, John
Maher, Austin V.
Murphy, Gerard A.
Powell, Patrick Collins
Quinlan, Peter H.
Rigney, Alban B.
Russell, Brian W.
Rynne, Sean Cormac
Smyth, Andrew F.
Tighe, Thomas E.
Twomey, Thomas A.
Ward, Patrick P.
Waters, John Joseph
Windle, Desmond P.

1958

Bowman, Michael J.
Branigan, Richard Joseph
Crowley, Timothy H.
Downes, Francis X.
Ellis, Donal J.
Foley, Margaret M.
Hayes, John Laurence Francis
Holmes, Gordon A.
Hooper, John P. A.
Hussey, Gillian M.
Jellett, Thomas Barrington
Kealy, John F.
Keane, Michael P.
McGowan, Joseph Murray
MacHale, Liam
Mackey, Desmond J.

MacNamee, Patrick M.A.
Marren, Martin E.
Martin, James Kevin
Moore, Michael J.
Moylan, Peter F.
Murphy, Clive Hunter
Neville, Maurice A.
Nugent, John Dillon
O'Brien, Patrick J.
Ó Cleirigh, Michael Brendan
O'Connor, James P.G.
O'Connor, Thomas P.
O'Donnell, John M.
O'Donoghue, Michael N.M.
O'Reilly, Anthony J.
O'Sullivan, Franklin J.
Read, Mary P.
Redmond, John P.
Smithwick, Peter A.
Taaffe, Fergus P.
Tanham, James Noel
Temple Lang, John Keller
Wynne, Henry J.
Young, William A.

1959

Armstrong, Kenneth L.
Ballagh, Thomas I.
Black, Richard J.
Branigan, Laurence F.
Buckley, Thomas Christopher
Cahill, James E.
Casey, Margaret T.C.
Clancy, Conal J.
Connellan, Michael P.M.
Cusack, Thomas F.
Dempsey, Fionnbarra F.
Donnellan, Marie T.
Duane, Fionnuala
Fahy, Fergus L.
Farrell, Patrick J.
Felton, David R.
Fitzgerald, Adrian F.J.
Fitzsimons, Michael J.
Furlong, Thomas J.
Gannon, Francis G.M.
Gannon, Thomas J.N.
Gibbons, Maire Neasa

Greensmith, Jill
Hogan, Michael J.
Kirwan, Valentine J.D.
Lane, Thomas Joseph Derek
MacCarthy, James F.
McGilligan Kevin C.
Maguire, Noelle
Masterson, Edward M.
Mockler, Dominic
O'Callaghan, Mary M.
O'Connell, Gertrude Louise
O'Dwyer, John A.
Pratt, Donald M.
Quinn, Francis C.
Ringrose, Ronald T.
Shaw, Thomas M.D.
Walsh, Gerrard A.
Walsh, Rosaleen

1960

Binchy, Michael E.
Blakeney, Robert E.
Bouchier Hayes, Dermot F.
Cody, Michael G.
Coonan, Charles E.
Devine, James J.
Doyle, John B.M.
Egan, John L.
Fish, John G.
Haythornthwaite, Robert B.
Houlihan, Peter F.B.
Jackson, Thomas
Kingston, Charles B.
Lee, John O.
Lyons, Brian O.
McDonald, Godfrey F.
McGuire, William J.
McMahon Patrick G.
Madigan, Patrick J.B.
Morrissy-Murphy, Dermod
O'Brien Butler, Pierce
O'Connell, Thomas F.
O'Connor, James J.
Pierse, Richard R.
Reidy, Jeremiah A.
Stuart, Donald O.
Teevan, Diarmuid P.
Warren, Edward J.W.
Young, Cathal N.

1961

Allen, Michael J.P.
Berkery, Mary P.M.
Binchy, Mary
Browne, Michael J.
Conlon, Oliver J.
Creed, Michael B.
Cresswell, John V.P.
Curran, Maurice R.
Dennison, James J.
Farrell, Iain R.
Gibbons, Áilín A.
Gilmartin, Joseph
Hogan, Rory M.
Jay, John
King, Michael F.S.
Lavelle, John N.M.
McHale, Maire
Macken, Thomas J.
Mulholland, Owen
O'Donnell, Roderick D.
O'Donohoe, James A.
O'Mahony, Francis J.
O'Sullivan, George J.P.
Sexton, James I.

1962

Blake, Bruce F. St. John
Chapman, Colin A.
Cussen, Robert McC.
Dickson, Michael G.
Dillon-Leetch, Thomas A.
Downes, Robert A.
Dundon, Jospeh L.
Earley, Fintan M.
Geraghty, William S.
Glover, Edward R.A.
Goldberg, Lewis J.
Gore-Grimes, Anthony C.
Hanna, Mary G.
Kiely, David O'N.
Lanigan, John G.
Lynch, Bryan F.
McDowell, Denis M.
Matthews, Neil M.
Monahan, James
Nic Shiomóin, Máire
O'Donnell, James R.
O'Flynn, Francis J.

O'Keeffe, James L.
O'Malley, Desmond J.
Orange, James G.
O'Shea, Patrick J.
Potterton, David A.
Smith, Thomas K.
Woods, Peter J.
Yaffe, Malcolm

1963

Bourke, Sean
Butler, Michael J.
Callery, Peter J.
Comerford, Henry Owen
Concannon, Malachy Francis
Connellan, Patrick J.
Dudley, James Nicholas
Gardiner, Brian J.
Gleeson, Francis Patrick
Glynn, James Concanon
Golding, Graham M.
Hamilton, Daniel J.
Harte, James Alexander
Houlihan, Michael Philip
Kelly, Delphine A.C.
Kirwan, Helen M.
Kirwan, William J.P.
Leahy, William E.
Loftus, Dermot
Lombard, Garrett P.
McMahon, Peter Joseph
Ó Brolcháin, Blanaid D.
O'Callaghan, Margaret J.
O'Connell, Michael G.L.
O'Donoghue, Thomas J.M.
O'Halloran, Carmel M.
Purcell, Michael F.
Riordan, Sylvester W.
Smyth,Thomas C.
Spendlove, Norman Thomas Jebb
Tynan, James Gregory
Walsh, Daire

1964

Barry, Henry C.P.
Bergin, Charles J.

Black, John G.J.
Boyle, Thomas O.
Buckley, Michael A.
Byrne, Brendan
Cahir, William M.A.
Carroll, Brian Anthony
Collins, Anthony E.
Cosgrave, Stuart L.
Daly, Michael G.
Fagan, Peter B.
Fanning, John
Farrell, Laurence A.
Glynn, John F.P.
Hegarty, Michael Basil
Holland, George B.
Kelliher, Daniel
Liston, Patrick
MacGrath, Patrick John
McMahon, Bryan M.E.
Malone, Michael Brendan
Montgomery, Giles F.
Murnaghan, Denis M.
Murrin, Brendan A.J.
Nestor, James J.
O'Donnell, Patrick Francis
O'Driscoll, William F.
O'Flaherty, Bryan L.
O'Mahony, Michael V.
O'Neill, Niall Patrick
Prentice, David W.
Reynolds, Michael
Rochford, John J.
Turnbull, Austin
Veale, Edmond M.

1965

Barrett, William S.
Callanan, Arthur Finbarr
Colgan, Thomas Joseph
Crivon, Ian Quentin
Deane, Joseph T.A.
Dolan, Michael N.
Durcan, Thomas D.
Enright, Thomas W.
Fagan, Yvonne
Farrell, Patrick John
Flynn, Bartholomew J.
Foley, Finola M.
Gallivan, Sarah M.

Glynn, John Vincent
Glynn, William Brendan
Gore-Grimes, John
Griffin, Thomas P. (Jnr.)
Hayes, John P.
Hunt, Eugene P.
Keating, Francis B.
Keogh, Paul W.
Lacy, John B.D.
Lavan, Patrick J.
Lehane, Donnchadh D.
McDowell, Robert
McMahon, Brian M.
McMahon, Michael P.
Menton, Thomas A.O.
Murphy, Colm C.
O'Donovan, Dermot G.
O'Meara, Christopher T.N.
O'Reilly, Thomas J.
Osborne, Cyril M.
O'Shea, Anna
Raleigh, Mary
Ross, Gordon J.
Scott, Ian A.
Sweeney, John R.
Sweeney, Rebecca
Walsh, Brendan D.

1966

Armstrong, Philomena
Boland, Marguerite Joyce
Casey, Denis Joseph
Coady, Anne
Daly, Francis David
Darley, John Frederick
    Michael
Dockrell, John Henry
Doyle, Catherine P.V.
Farrell, Michael
Finnegan, Joseph G.
Fitzpatrick, John Mary
Foley, Felicity Mary
Harte, John Bernard
Harvey, Mary Margaret
Hayes, Anthony Gordon
McArdle, Oliver D.G.
McDermott, Kieran
McGuinness, Francis
    Joseph O.

McMahon, Patrick Joseph
Magee, Brian Joseph
Mitchell, Matthew J.
Moloney, Joseph Patrick
Morrin, Vincent O.
Mullan, George Gerrard
O'Carroll, Enda Patrick
O'Donnell, Elizabeth M.J.
O'Donnell, Thomas Anthony
O'Meara, Josephine Mary E.
O'Rourke, Eleanor A.
O'Toole, Anne
Sheedy, Gerald Brendan
Taylor, Brian George
    McDougall
Tighe, Mary Pamela
Tully, John James

1967

Armstrong, Fergus F.D.
Aylmer, John P.
Baily, John Benedict
Bradshaw, Eric H.W.
Brunker, Eric
Burke, Albert Derek
Connolly, Niall P.
Cox, David
Figgis, Thomas Fernsley
Fry, William O.H.
Greenlee, Derek Hall
Guinness, Paul D.
Hoey, Raphaeline A.E.
Hussey, Pamela Mary F.
Kelly, Alan V.
Kelly, Michael
Kevans, Patrick James
Kirwan, Gerard
Lovegrove, Richard Victor
Lucas, Michael A.
McAuliffe, Donal T.
McCarthy, Cornelius Leo
McDonnell, Brendan Joseph
McLaughlin, Paul M.
Montgomery, William James
Murphy, Peter F.R.
Noonan, Maire
O'Donnell, Hugh B.J.
O'Donnell, John C. (Jnr.)
O'Driscoll, Michael

O'Higgins, James F.
O'Mahony, Brendan
O'Shea, Michael J.
Quick, Simon C.K.
Ruane, Martin J.
Somerville, William B.R.B.
Strong, Stephen Thomas
Sweetman, Angela Miriam
Thompson, Jonathan Piers

1968

Ballagh, Roger P.
Baylor, James S.
Blake, Henry C. St. J.
Branigan, Patrick D.M.
Cafferky, Patrick
Cronin, Cornelius
Durcan, Rose Mary
Fallon, Patrick D.
Farrell, Thomas F.
Finan, Cairbre
Fitzgibbon, Patrick
Fleming, T. Desmond
Flynn, Robert Michael
Foley, Conor C.
Gaffney, John Patrick
Gartlan, Brian
Geraghty, Brian G.
Gill, Garrett
Gleeson, John
Glynn, John N.R. McM.
Hanahoe, Anthony T.
Harrington, Avice M.A.
Harrington, Catherine M.L.
Hayes, John F.
Heffernan, Elizabeth
Heney, James
Houlihan, Desmond
Houlihan, James W.
Howley, Declan J.
James, William A.
Kirwan, Anthony M.D.
MacCarthy, Owen A.
Malone, Francis P.
Martin, Michael
Matthews, John H.
Mulhern, James P.
Murphy, Kieran M.F.
Murphy, Timothy A.

Neilan, John F. (Jnr.)
Neville, Richard M.
Ó Buachalla, Donnchadh
O'Donoghue, Maeve Thérèse
O'Dwyer, John Thomas D.
O'Kane, Malachy J.
Rice, Richard J.
Seery, Edmund F.
Sheedy, John Anthony
Smith, Aveen M.J.
Staunton, Charles de Lacy
Walsh, Valerie J.M.
Woodcock, Brian

1969

Anderson, David R.
Appelbe, Fergus E.
Brooks, Jonathan P.T.
Byrne, Hugh P.J.
Cahalan, Denis P.
Carrigan, Michael W.
Cavanagh, Colm A.
Courtney, Mary H.
Crawford, Brian V.
Cusack, Clare T.
Cussen, John McCartan
Daly, Joan
Dargan, Deirdre
Deane, Kevin P.A.
Delaney, Michael J.
Dixon, Terence E.
Donaghy, Patrick C.
Egan, Laurence R.
Farrell, Ernest B.
Fitzpatrick, Geraldine Mary
Fleming, Patrick G.
Foy, Michael
Gahan, Daniel M.
Galvin, Barry St. John
Gavin, Edmund
Gleeson, Michael
Glynn, Cormac P.
Halley, Gerard Maxwell
Hamilton, Blayney C.
Healy, Andrew William
Hickey, Matthew
Hipwell, Denis G.
Hogan, Desmond P.
Hurley, Caroline M.E.

Keating, Margaret T.N.
Kelliher, Deborah
Kelly, Mary C.
Kennedy, Martin A.
Kieran, Robert
Lavery, James Dermot
Linnane, Michelle M.
McCarthy, Patrick J.
MacGinley, Roger William
  Anthony
MacKenzie, Stephen John
Maginn, Terence W.
Maguire, Peter Martin
Malone, Paul L.
Mangan, Michael J.D.
Mathews, John P.
Matthews, Oliver G.
Molloy, James M.
Muldoon, Orla M.
Mulligan, Herbert William
Murphy, James A.A.
Murphy, John Joseph
Murphy, Patrick L.
Murtagh, Patrick H.
Neville, Grattan
O'Connor, Donough H.
O'Connor, Roderick C.J.
O'Driscoll, Fachtna
O'Dwyer, James M.
O'Hanrahan, Timothy N.
O'Keeffe, Gerard M.F.
O'Leary, John J.
O'Neill, Raymond M.
O'Regan, Rose M.
O'Rourke, Anthony F.
Peilow, Robin A. W.
Potter, Dudley
Purcell, Elizabeth Anne
Reilly, Esmond
Roche, Mary M.E.
Shee, Nicholas P.J.
Sheehan, Garrett F.X.
Sheehy, Niall
Tobin, Thomas
Waterman, Harold

1970

Baily, Mary J.
Beausang, Paul N.

Berrills, Brian
Bourke, Adrian Patrick
Burke, Anthony T.
Burke, Patricia
Cassidy, Damien F.
Clarke, David James
Clarke, Martin M.J.
Comyn, Arthur R.
Comyn, Nicholas G.
Connellan, Murrough
Conroy, Maxwell McD.
Curtin, Christine McAuliffe
Cusack, Michael E.
Cusack, Patrick J.
Cusack, Peter J.
Donnelly, Andrew J.O.
Doris, Francis R.
Dowling, Oonagh M.
Doyle, Eileen
Egan, Martin N.
Fleming, Una
Gannon, J.D. Berchmans
Hanahoe, Michael E.
Hannon, John
Harrison, Peter S.
Harte, Ciaran
Jermyn, John L.
Keenan, Helen M.E.
Kelly, Charles A.
Lacy, Elizabeth
Larkin, Michael C.
Liston, William T.
Lynch, Ellen M.E.
McArdle, Brendan D.
McArdle, Francis G.
McKenna, Peter J.G.
McVeigh, Derek A.
Mannin, Colm P.
Minch, Mary
Mohan, James M.
Moran, Desmond Carroll
Moynihan, Patricia R.
Murphy, Eugene M.
Murphy, Henry
Murray, Michael D.
Nugent, Ann M.
O'Brien, Bernadette
O'Connell, Mary N.G.
O'Connor, Caroline M.
O'Connor, Daniel E.
O'Driscoll, Timothy
O'Hanrahan, Michael

Ó Loingsigh, Amhlaoibh
O'Neill, Edward
O'Reilly, Garrett
O'Reilly, James D.
Ó Síocháin, Ronan
Peart, Michael D.
Quinn, Mary Rose Adele
Reidy, Patrick J.
Reilly, Michael C.
Ryan, Louise
Ryan, Mary
Ryan, Oran
Sexton, John M.
Shaw, Denis F.
Smithwick, Paul B.
Sowman, Francis E.
Taffee, Anthony J.
Tighe, Henry
Toomey, Miriam S.

1971

Binchy, Owen M.
Brady, Anthony P.
Brophy, Bryan C.
Burke, Patrick F.
Burnell, Margaret P.
Callanan, Francis O.
Carey, Katherine
Carroll, Donald V.
Casey, Deirdre M.
Chambers, Daniel C.
Citron, Lewis E.
Clarke, William H.
Conway, Rory
Corcoran, John J.
Corkery, Michael M.T.
Corrigan, Sean Patrick
Daly, George F.
Dawson, Helen C.
Dempsey, Aidan R.
Desmond, Jeremiah
Donnelly, Susan L.
Duncan, Brian P.J.
Eustace, Joan M.
Feighery, Ciaran
Fitzgerald, David M.
Fitzgerald, Gerald A.T.P.
Frost, Raymond A.
Gallagher, Brian M.

Gavin, William C.
Gaynor, Colm R.
Geraghty, Patrick J.
Gleeson, Michael F.
Gordon, John J.
Gordon, Joseph P.O.
Grant, Terence V.
Green, Michael
Groarke, Patrick J.
Hanley, Aine M.
Haughton, Gerard J.
Hegarty, Anna E.
Hussey, Anthony F.
Kelly, Eugene
Kelly, John
Kilcullen, Diarmuid A.
King, John M.T.
Lanigan, Alice M.
Leonard, Clare
Lucey, Timothy
Lynch, Geraldine
Lyons, Daniel E.
McBratney, Richard J.
McCormack, Paul T.P.
McGillion, James J.
McMahon, Owen
McMorrow, Patrick
Maher, Patrick J.
Mahon, Brian J.
Malone, James H.
Malone, Leo J.
Martin, Nigel H.
Meehan, Christopher G.J.
Millett, Carol A.
Millington, Kenneth
Monahan, Raymond T.
Moran, Helen
Murphy, Francis J.
Murphy, Thomas B.
Murray, Elizabeth F.
Neilan, Edward B.
Ní hUadhaigh, Grainne
O'Byrne, Neville R.
O'Connor, Jeremy Blake
O'Connor, Michael T.
O'Donohoe, Michael A.
O'Flynn, Kevin P.
O'Herlihy, Kevin B.
O'Keeffe, Nicholas
O'Mahony, Joan
O'Neill, James P.
O'Reilly, Paul T.

O'Riordan, Rory
Peart, Gylian Imelda
Purcell, Francis J.
Redmond, Mary P.M.
Roche, Michael S.
Ross, John D.
Shaughnessy, Margaret A.
Williams, Ernest F.
Williams, Robert P.C.

1972

Anderson, David K.
Barker, Michael C.P.
Bates, Siubhan A.M.
Bonner, Geraldine
Brady, Peter P.
Brooks, Thomas J.
Brophy, David M.
Burke-Staunton, Margaret
Carroll, Patrick C.
Carty, John
Cassidy, Maurice J.P.
Cassidy, Raymond P.
Chambers, Joseph G.M.
Clancy, Niall B.
Coffey, John J.
Collier, Michael
Comiskey, Brendan
Connolly, Anthony J.
Corrigan, Donal J.
Cresswell, David S.
Crowley, Finbarr J.
Crowley, William E.
Cruise, Carolyn M.
Cullen, Helen Jeanne
Cunniam, Hugh
Curran, Joseph D.
Daly, John J.
Deane, John W.T.
Deeney, Desmond G.
Doyle, Lewis C.
Dunne, Austin
Farrell, Caren
Feran, John P.
Fitzpatrick, Thomas A.
Gallagher, Declan J.
Gaughran, Bernard L.
Glackin, John
Gleeson, Denis A.E.

Hassett, Matthew
Heffernan, Geraldine
Hill, Brendan E.
Jackson, Frederick A.C.
Keane, Joan
Kearney, John F.
Keys, Ciaran
Lanigan, Francis D.
Lavelle, Cyril J.
Lee, Robert M.D.
Lysaght, Liam T.
McCarthy, Roderick F.
McDonald, Noel
McDonnell, Sean E.
McNulty, Aidan
McPhillips, Ellen
Maher, Noel G.
Mangan, Leo A.
Matthews, Vivian C.
Moran, Patrick T.
Moran, Raymond G.
Morris, Dermot H.
Morrissey, John
Moylan, Declan M.B.
Murphy, John N.
Murray, Jacqueline
Neligan, Patrick C.J.
O'Beirne, Eamonn M.
O'Brien, Eamon P.
O'Brien Kenney, Brian
O'Connell, Michael
O'Connor, Patrick J.
O'Donnell, Hugh J.
O'Flynn, Patrick J.
O'Grady, Anne P.
O'Meara, Mary H.
O'Meara, Thomas D.
O'Neill, Charles F.
O'Neill, Finbar
O'Reilly, Vincent M.
O'Rorke, Andrew
O'Shea, John
Owens, Michael
Pierse, James D.
Polden, Stanhope P.
Power, John J.M.
Pyne, Kieran A.C.
Quinn, John J.
Roberts, Richard G. d'E.
Sadleir, Justin
Shields, Laurence K.
Silke, Leonard F.

Steen, Brendan
Tarrant, David A.
Timon, Reginald I.V.
Tracey, Mary
Wallace, Brian
Walsh, David A.
Ward, Francis O.
Woods, Alan
Wright, George C.

1973

Bannon, Maurice
Barrett, Robert P.
Barror, Denis J.
Bolton, Robert
Bowman, Barry St. John
Burke, Francis V.
Cahill, James F.
Carroll, Declan C.
Clyne, Patrick F.
Coffey, Robert J.
Coonan, Edward A.
Crowley, Angela E.
Crowley, Mary E.A.
Curran, Patrick
Daly, Patrick J.
Desmond, Paula
Diamond, Gerard D.
Dillon, Andrew
Doherty, Gerard J.
Douglas, Peter M.G.
Doyle, Gerard A.
Durcan, Patrick J.M.
Earley, William M.J.
Enright, Michael
Ensor, David
Farry, Patrick J.
Finlay, Mary E.
Finn, John William T.
Fitzsimons, Nessa
Flanagan, John P.
French, Bertrand G.
Fry, Edmund
Gallagher, Eamon P.D.
Gill, George J.
Glen, Brian
Hamill, William G.J.
Hanby, Paul
Hanna, Rosalind E.

Harman, Rory
Harnett, William
Hayes, Jean F.
Hayes, Karl E.
Hayes, Peter C.
Healy, Louis A.
Hickey, Gorettie
Hickey, Margaret G.
Hogan, Daire
Horan, Michael J.
Hughes, Anne
Hunt, Harry P.
Hurley, Patrick M.
Hussey, Barbara
Keane, Michael J.
Kelly, Catherine
Kelly, Damien J.
Kelly, Edward A.
Kelly, Raymonde
Kennedy, Sean T.
Kiely, Rosalind
Kirwan, Agnes S.
Kirwan, Laurence P.
Lappin, Henry
Lawler, Mary E.
Lynch, Cyril P.J.
McDwyer, Thomas J.E.
MacGeehin, Colm M.C.
McKeown, John C.
McLoughlin, Brian R.
Maguire, Charles J.
Malony, David A.
Matthews, Brian D.
Mills, George D.R.
Moriarty, Patrick C.
Morris, Paul
Mullan, Elizabeth
Mullins, Thomas
Mulvey, John L.
Nagle, Joan E.
Nolan, Michael F.
Noonan, Jacinta
O'Boyle, James P.A.
O'Brien, Kieran E.J.
O'Driscoll, Nancy
Ó Floinn, Seán M.
O'Gorman, Kieran
O'Halloran, Thomas J.
O'Neill, Dermot
Osborne, James
O'Sullivan, Mary R.
Powell, Michael Collins

Price, Alvin F.M.
Quinn, John B.
Rooney, Aideen A.
Ryan, Elizabeth A.
Seery, John J.
Smyth, Noel M.
Twomey, Patrick J.
Wall, Francis A.
White, Patrick St. John

1974

Ashe, Donald
Bergin, Catherine
Boland, Denis P.M.
Bolger, Rosemary P.
Bouchier-Hayes, Timothy P.W.
Butler, Patrick J.
Byrne, Eamonn B.
Byron, Dermot G.
Carlos, John J.
Carroll, John
Carroll, Raymond
Ceillier, Martin D.
Coughlan, John
Crowley, Peter O'Neill
Delaney, Anne M.
Devins, Philomena M.
Devitt, Sheila M.G.
Devlin, James M.
Dillon-Leetch, John G.
Dolan, Mary Catherine
Dunne, John D.
Durcan, Ivan J.
Dyar, Orlean
Earley, Ciaran
Ellis, David
Ensor, Anthony H.
Fagan, Daniel
Fanning, Eugene P.
Ferris, Paul A.
Finucane, Raymond
French, Grace M.
Gaffney, Kevin J.
Garvan, William J.B.
Gaughan, Mary G.
Gaynor, John
Gormley, Daniel
Griffin, John M.M.
Hall, Edward G.

Halley, Caroline
Hamilton, Stephen C.
Haugh, Joseph D.
Hayes, Michael
Hickey, Edward
Hutchinson, Mary
Irvine, Michael
Jolly, William
Keane, Colin
Kelly, Charles
Kelly, Eimear O'Brien
Kelly, Jean
Kennedy, Patrick T.
King, Alan J.
Liddy, Richard
Ludlow, Hugh F.
Lynam, Ronald J.
McAllister, Brian
MacCarthy, Justin J.G.
McCrann, Roderick V.
McDonnell, Petria K.
McEntee, Rory G.
McGahon, Esther
MacGinley, Deirdre
McGrath, George C.M.P.
McGrath, Madeline
McGuire, Fiona
McLaughlin, Peter V.
McMahon, David F.
Matthews, Kevin
Miley, Stephen
Minogue, Patrick J.
Molloy, Michael
Muldowney, Brendan T.
Mullaney, Desmond D.
O'Brien, Brian D.
O'Brien, David C.
O'Connell, Daniel J.
O'Connor, Patrick
O'Daly, Carroll
O'Donnell, Hugh
O'Donohoe, Matthew
O'Dwyer, John M.
O'Gorman, Martina
O'Grady, Leonie M.M.
Ó hUadhaigh, Donal
O'Kane, Margaret M.
O'Malley, Michael J.
O'Neill, Michael
O'Regan, Anne P.
O'Reilly, Brian Patrick
O'Reilly, Felim M.

Ormond, Anne
O'Shaughnessy, Michael
O'Sullivan, Eugene
Quigley, Michael T.
Quinn, Thomas P.
Redmond, Peter J.
Regan, Anne M.
Regan, Mary J.
Reidy, John C.
Robinson, Nicholas K.
Roche, Brian
Rowan, Patrick D.
Ryan, Rosemary A.
Scales, Linda M.
Sheehan, Edward M.
Sheridan, Bryan C.
Sherry, Michael
Shields, Vincent M.
Stafford, Thomas J.
Steen, Ambrose J.
Sweeney, Patrick J.
Sweetman, Roger
Tormey, Philip F.
Traynor, Michael H.
Traynor, Paul D.
Treacy, Michael C.
Walsh, Michael P.
Wood, John H. V.

1975

Brady, John G.
Brazil, Marian N.
Breathnach, Eithne
Brennan, Michael G.M.
Brophy, John P.
Buckley, Daragh
Burke, Anthony
Butler, Nicholas A.
Butler, Patrick A.
Cantrell, Mary
Carty, Hugh
Casey, Terence F.
Clear, Eoghan P.
Collins, Marie C.
Connellan, Marie
Cooke, Frances
Courtney, James P.
Crilly, Martin
Crowley, Donogh

Crowley, Vincent
Cunningham, Anne
Daly, James M.
Davy, Geraldine
Devine, William B.
Dolan, Roderic
Dowd, Thomas
Elliott, Jennifer
Emerson, Vivian M.
Farrell, Patrick J.
Finn, Denis
Fitzpatrick, Hugh M.
Gallagher, Seán
Geraghty, Sylvia
Gillan, Sheila
Griffin, Mary
Hanahoe, Bernadette
Hayes, Thomas
Healy, Henry Nathaniel
Heffernan, Helen
Hegarty, Declan
Hewson, Dermot V.
Hipwell, Liam
Hughes, Edward
Hughes, Seamus
Keane, Caroline
Kennedy, Anne E.
Kennedy, Niall D.
Kennedy, Simon
Kiersey, Gillian K.M.
Lennon, Martin
Levins, Doreen
Linnehan, Maurice J.
Lowney, Francis J.
Lucey, Helen
Lucey, Margaret
Lynch, John Richard
Lysaght, John B.
McAuliffe, Sarah Anne
MacBride, Sean
McCartan, Patrick J.
McCarthy, Michael J.
McCrea, Alan D.
MacDermot, Dermot M.
McGartan, Patrick J.
Maher, Stephen P.
Malone, Noel
Moran, Arthur D.S.
Morris, David
Morris, Deirdre
Morton, Joseph B.
Mulcahy, Thomas K.

Murphy, Paul
Neilan, Dermot J.
Nolan, Susan
O'Brien, John J.
O'Callaghan, Kieran
Ó Catháin, Ross A.
O'Connell, Isolde A.
O'Connor, Declan P.
O'Connor, Mary
O'Connor, Thomas V. (Jnr.)
O'Doherty, Anthony J.
O'Donnell, Michael
O'Donovan, John
O'Dwyer, John V.
O'Gorman, Adrian Patrick
O'Hanrahan, Michael J.
O'Hanrahan, Richard
O'Herlihy, John B.
O'Keeffe, William F.
O'Leary, Kathleen
O'Sullivan, Brian
O'Toole, Francis J.
Pearse, Geraldine M.
Philpott, Joseph
Prentice, Hilary J.
Redden, Brian P.
Richards, Graham C.
Riordan, James T.
Roche, Margaret
Rochford, Odran
Shannon, John V.
Staines, Michael
Strahan, Bryan
Sweeney, James D.
Sweeney, Joseph R.
Sweeney, Terence D.
Synnott, William
Traynor, Orlath M.
Tyndall, Rosaleen
Walsh, Catriona M.
Walsh, Ronan P.
Walshe, Roderick St. J.
Ward, Mary T.P.
Whelehan, Richard
White, Michael

1976

Adams, Brian
Agnew, Robert H.D.

Ahern, Dermot
Ahern, Michael Christopher
Armstrong, Bernard
Barry, Diarmuid
Beirne, Vincent Paul
Bergin, David
Binchy, James
Brady, Patrick L.
Branigan, Ciaran Jude
Brosnan, Cornelius Donal M.
Browne, David
Browne, Geoffrey
Bruen, George Patrick
Buckley, Roderick B.J.
Burke, Francis X.
Byrne, Paul
Campbell, Marion
Carroll, Patricia
Casey, Brian Declan
Casey, Laura M.
Casey, Niamh F.
Caulfield, Joseph
Clarke, Thérèse
Collins, Aidan D.
Collins, Helen M.
Comyn, Joseph A.
Condon, John F.
Coughlan, Terence
Cush, Eugene
Doherty, Randal
Dowling, Dominic Michael
Dunne, Andrew
Dunne, Cormac Donal
Ensor, Beatrice
Erskine, Janet Alexandra
Erwin, Karen Margaret
Fair, Jospehine
Flanagan, Peter
Fleming, Paul
Gleeson, Margaret Mary A.
Goold, Patrick G.
Graham, Alan Gordon
Grogan, Christopher
Hallissey, Timothy Gerard
Hanahoe, Terence
Harvey, Ita M.
Hayes, John Joseph
Hayes, Michael
Hederman, Mary
Horan, Paul Gerard
Howell, Eileen Marian
Huggard, Veronica

Hyland, Brendan Francis
Jacobson, Denis
Jordan, Andrew Bernard
Jordan, Joseph
Joyce, Philip
Judge, Patrick
Kehoe, Ellen Mary
Kelly, Patrick
Kilrane, Kevin P.
King, Thomas
Langwell, Joseph F.
Larkin, Mary
Lawless, Neasa Aine
Lawlor, Florence Ciaran
Leyden, Joseph P.
Liston, Kevin D.
Lucey, Margaret Elaine
Lynch, Sheila Farrelly
McCafferty, Patrick
McCanny, Gerard
MacCarthy, Cathal
MacCarthy, Jeremiah
  Christopher
McCarthy, Lorna
McCormick, David Paul
  Simon
McEvoy, Michèle
McGlynn, John Joseph Mary
McGovern, Raymond
McGuire, Michael L.P.
McMorrow, Laurence
McMullin, Patrick Ernan
McNally, Patrick J.
Mathews, Derek Joseph
Meagher, Aedin
Moore, Michael
Mulvey, Patrick Francis
Murphy, Fionnuala M.R.
Murphy, James T.
Murray, Anthony J.
Nally, Thomas
Neary, Sheila
Neilan, Gerard
O'Beirne, Bernard
O'Connor, Sylvia
O'Connell, Margaret V.
O'Doherty, Catherine
O'Doherty, Niall K.
O'Donnell, Brian
O'Donnell, Thomas E.
O'Donoghue, Hugh Vincent
O'Dwyer, Stephen Patrick P.

O'Gorman, Anthony
O'Hagan, Donal P.
O'Keeffe, David
O'Leary, Constantine G.
O'Leary, Mona
O'Neill, Raymond St. John
O'Reilly, Anne
O'Riordan, Francis
O'Sullivan, Irene Kathryn
O'Sullivan, Mary Clare
O'Sullivan, Thomas Valentine
Pattwell, Michael
Rogers, Patrick
Rossiter, Brendan
Roundtree, Henry C.J.H.
Ryan, James J.
Ryan, Patrick
Scally, Sharon
Scully, Paula Elizabeth F.
Shatter, Alan
Sheehan, Joanne
Sherry, Charles Colman
Smith, Peter Joseph
Sweeney, Anne
Swift, Brian
Territt, John
Toher, Vincent
Tomkin, David N.N.
Turnbull, Valentine
Turner, David Malcolm
Twohig, William Christopher
  Malcolm
Tyrrell, Michael
Walsh, Gerard
Ward, Henry
Watchorn, Veronica Ann
Weston, John
Whelan, Brian O.
Whitaker, Brian S.
Wren, Margaret Teresa

1977

Allen, Michael Edwin
Barror, Michael Aidan
Baynes, Marian
Beale, Sheena
Becker, Monica
Beresford, Marcus Hugh
  Tristram de la Poer

Blackwell, Noeline M.
Bolger, Michael Anthony
Bourke, John M.
Boyle, Peter
Bradley, Vivienne
Brogan, Enda
Brosnan, Aidan Robert
Bruton, Elizabeth
Byrne, Garrett Vincent
Callinan, John Gerard
Canney, Jarlath A.
Carey, Eugene
Carey, Margaret
Casey, Fionnuala Marian
Cleary, Kieran William
Clinton, Evanna
Collins, Helen Mary
Collins, John Kieran
Condon, Michael
Corrigan, Jean Elizabeth
Costello, John E.
Craig, Catherine
Crowe, Vivienne
Cullen, Mary
Cummiskey, Gerard
Cunningham, Michael J.
Curran, Kevin
Curtin, Bryan F.
Davidson, Andrew James
  Lloyd
Davy, Eugene
Debeir, Heather Kathleen
Diamond, Paul Francis
Dodd, Ian A.
Doherty, Kevin A.
Doyle, Pauline
Duane, Sylvester
Dudley, Jane
Duffy, Bridget Josephine
Duffy, Patrick
Duffy, Thomas Oliver
Duncan, Anthony
Duncan, Dermot
Egan, Frances
Elder, Shaun
Fanning, Gerard P.M.
Farquharson, Elizabeth
Farrell, John Marcus
Fetherstonhaugh, John R.
Fingleton, Sheila Mary
Flynn, Désirée
Friel, Francis

Gallagher, Avril
Garahy, John
Gleeson, John
Gleeson, William Francis
Greene, Michael Arthur
Griffin, Anne
Grogan, Martin Pius Brian
Halley, Robert Emmet
Hanley, Daniel Joseph
Hanna, Barbara
Hartmann, Caitriona
Hickey, James
Hogan, Richard
Houlihan, Kevin Michael
Jordan, Catherine
Joyce, James Hugh
Keenan, June
Kelleher, Eric Olann
Kelly, Mary
Kelly, Philip
Kelly, Thomas J.
Kennedy, William Joseph
Killeen, Conor
Lee, Muriel
Levine, Laurence
Linnane, Martin
Loomes, Thomas
Loughnane, Gemma
Louth, Cathal
Lucey, James
Lynch, Maeve
McAlinden, Gavan
McCarthy, Gerard Michael
McCarthy, John W.
McCarthy, Patrick
McDonnell, Peter Francis
McElligott, Mary
McEllin, Edward
McGovern, Patrick Joseph
  Conor
McInerney, Michael A.
McKenna, Anne M.
McMahon, Denis
McNamara, Barbara
McParland, Mark
McPhillips, Edward
Malocco, Elio
Mangan, Mary
Marshall, Robert D.
Meagher, Pierce Maolmhaire
Mellotte, Margaret Mary
  Michele

Molloy, Denis
Moran, Michael
Moran, Terence
Morley, Roger
Morrissey, Daniel
Moylan, John
Muldoon, Fiona Maire
Mulvihill, John
Murphy, Joseph
Murphy, Mary
Murphy, Miriam
Murran, Thomas Anthony
Mylotte, Mary
Nagle, John C.K.
Nagle, Matthew
Naughton, John
Nicholas, Stephen
Nolan, Ann
O'Boyle, Terry
O'Callaghan, Maurice
O'Carroll, Seamus Patrick
O'Connor, Deirdre Anne
O'Connor, Kevin
O'Donnell, Clifford
O'Donovan, Irene Ann
O'Driscoll, Clara
O'Driscoll, John K.
O'Dwyer, Ursula
O'Gara, Yvonne
O'Gorman, Michael F.
Olliffe, Ann
O'Loughlin, Geraine
O'Mahony, Brian
O'Malley, Anthony
O'Malley, Michael P.
O'Neill, John
O'Reilly, Niall
O'Reilly, Peter
O'Shee, John
O'Sullivan, Patrick P.
O'Tuama, Cliona Mary
Quinn, Noel Anthony
Reilly, Celine Roisin
Reilly, Peter T.
Robinson, Barbara A.
Rooney, Kevin
Ryan-Purcell, Oliver
Scally, James
Sexton, Henry A.
Shanley, Colman D.
Shannon, Robert Vincent
Sheppard, Pamela Jean

Sparks, Conor
Stewart, Jane
Stokes, Adrian
Toale, Mairead
Toolan, Brian
Tounley, Deirdre
Twomey, Mary
Tynan, Dorothy
Wallace, Patrick
Walsh, Ann Catherine
Walsh, Anne Rebecca
White, William Xavier M.K.
Woods, Ann P.

1978

Aitken, James
Alexander, David William
Archer, Martin D.
Archibald, Valerie Florence
Arigho, Henry Joseph
Barrett, Mary
Barry, Sheena
Beausang, Hilary
Beechinor, Richard Owen
Bennett, Richard
Boland, Helen
Bourke, Kevin
Bowe, Helena Maria
Brady, Bríd
Brady, Padraic
Brady, Paul
Brady, Philomena
Brennan, Patrick Gerard
Breslin, Clare
Burke, Helen
Burke, Margaret Mary Hilary
Butler, Gerard William
Cahill, Bernadette
Carroll, Michael
Carter, Michael Joseph
Casey, Katherine E.
Casey, Niall Gerard
Clancy, Joseph
Clarke, Geraldine
Clayton, David
Cleary, Ronald J.
Coghlan, Michael
Coleman, Thérèse A.M.
Colfer, Niall P.

Collins, Thomas D.
Connolly, Carol
Corbett, Cornelius
Coughlan, Stephen
Cronin, Mary Lou
Daly, Stephen
Dargan, Margaret
Davies, Joseph Patrick
Dawson, Patrick
Deacy, John Pius
Dillon, David William
Dillon, Mary
Dobbyn, Paul Robert
Doody, Michael
Doolan, Mary
Dorgan, Mary
Doyle, David
Drumgoole, Patricia
Duffy, Margaret Winifred
Duffy, Paula
Duggan, Raymond
Dunne, Daniel William
Eagar, Robert John
Egan, Eanya
Ellis, Gerard J.
Evans, Richard A.
Fagan, Ann
Fitzgerald, Ann
Fitzpatrick, Michael
Flanagan, Clare
Flanagan, Eithne M.
Fleming, William Patrick S.
Flynn, Desmond
Flynn, James
Fogarty, Gerard
Fox, Bryan Francis
Geraghty, Donal
Gibbons, Conal
Gillece, Geraldine
Gray, Catherine
Grennan, John
Griffin, Gerard Francis
Griffin, Joseph
Griffin, Mary Paula
Halpenny, Padraig
Hanahoe, Anthony Thomas
Harnett, Emer M.
Harney, Patricia
Harrison, Alan
Harte, Nicholas
Harvey, Martin A.
Haughey, Stephen

Healy, Jeremiah F.
Heffernan, Catherine Patricia
Henry, Mary E.
Hickey, Desmond Gerard
Higgins, Michael
Hollwey, Caroline Jane
Horgan, Pauline Mary
Johnson, Brendan Louis
Jones, Peter H.
Joyce, Emer
Kean, John P.
Keane, Miriam R.
Keller, Mark
Kelly, Mary Patricia
Kelly, Michael Kieran
Kennedy, Giles Joseph
Kennedy, Patrick
Kerrigan, Paul
Killeen, Ruadhan
Kilrane, Mel
Lamb, Neal
Larkin, Denis
Lavelle, John D.
Lawler, Ann Mary
Lee, Michael
Lindsay, John B.K.
Linehan, Mary
Long, James
Lynsky, John Edward
McAllister, Rowena M.
McArdle, Paul
McBride, John Gerard
McCarthy, Mary
McCarthy, Philomena
McCourt, Henry
McDermott, Moya
McDermott, Patrick
McDonnell, Patrick
McEvoy, Keyna
McGovern, Helen
McGuinn, Hilary Marie
McLaughlin, Ciaran F.
McLoghlin, Brian
MacMahon, Brian Harold
McMahon, Patrick J.
McNally, Paul
McSweeney, Denis
Maguire, Joseph F.
Maguire, Richard William
Mahon, Raymond
Manning, Barry Edge
Marren, Thomas Gerard

Martin, David
Martyn, Michael Damien
Mathews, Raphael Mary
Mays, Kevin Michael
Meagher, Mary
Meaney, Gerald Joseph
Moran, Charles
Mullane, Michael
Mulloy, Sheila Monica
Mulryan, Patrick
Murphy, David M.
Murphy, James Patrick
Murphy, Kate Ann
Murphy, Stanislaus
Nagle, Elizabeth
Noonan, Joseph
Nowlan, Francis B.
Nyhan, Francis Gerard
O'Boyle, Helen Mary
O'Brien, Ronan
O'Brien, William Mark
O'Connell, Deirdre
O'Connell, Owen Francis
O'Connell, Patrick
O'Connor, Brendan D.
O'Connor, John B.
O'Connor, John Gerard
O'Connor, Michael Francis
O'Donoghue, John Anthony
O'Duffy, Kiran
O'Dwyer, Thomas Seán
O'Farrell, Orlagh
O'Grady, William Francis
O'Hagan, David
O'Herlihy, Gerard
O'Higgins, Mary Brenda
O'Keeffe, Peter J.
O'Keeffe, Terence G.
O'Kelly, Séamus
O'Leary, Cornelius
O'Leary, John
O'Mahony, Deirdre Mary
O'Malley, John Patrick
O'Mara, Ciaran
O'Neill, Gregory Francis
O'Reilly, William
Parkinson, Kenneth
Petty, Michael
Potter-Cogan, Robert
Power, Patrick
Purcell, John P.D.
Quinlan, Barbara

Quinlan, Mary C.
Raftery, Winifred A.
Roche, Luke Enda
Rooney, Desmond Patrick
Rooney, Fergal
Ryan, Christina
Ryan, Kieran
Ryan, Margaret Veronica
Ryan, Michael
Ryan, Michael Joseph
Sanfey, David
Schutte, John
Scott, Mary
Sharpe, Ambrose Anthony
Shee, Peter
Sheehan, Robert
Sheridan, Thomas
Sherlock, Declan
Simpson, Thomas
Sowman, Jennifer Hazel
Spillane, Maurice Timothy
Stack, Nora
Sweeney, James M.
Sweeney, Mary
Synnott, David
Tighe, Miriam
Tormey, Eugene Thomas
Twomey, Brendan Joseph
Vahey, Valerie
Walker, Andrew Philip
Walley, William David
Walsh, John G.
Walsh, Róisín
Walsh, Rosamond Thérèse-
    Marie
Whelan, James C.
White, John William
Wilson, Owen Gerard
Wiseman, Anne P.

1979

Allen, John Gerard
Anthony, Denise
Anthony, Elaine
Ashe, Robert
Baker, Elizabeth Anne
Banks, Karen
Berkery, Patrick Colm
Blake, John Victor Patrick

Boohig, Malachy
Bradley, Brendan Gerard
Brennan, John Kieran
Brennan, Laurence A.
Broderick, Eileen
Buggy, Paul
Buttimer, Francis Anthony
Byrne, Jane Catherine
Byrne, Kevin
Cahill, James
Callanan, Claire Mary
Callanan, Patrick
Campbell, Hugh James
Carroll, Christian Mary
Carroll, John P.
Carter, Martha
Carton, Hélène Olivia Mary
Carty, Owen M.
Cashin, Mary
Cawley, Cyril
Chambers, Marion
Chesser, Brian Joseph
Clissmann, Alma
Cloonan, Stephen Paul
Clune, Paul
Collins, Jeremiah
Comiskey, Kevin
Connolly, John Brendan
Conway, Bernadette
Copplestone, Henry Grahame
Corr, Niall Gerard
Cosgrave, Liam T.
Costello, Fidelma
Cotter, Frances
Courtney, Mary Cliona
Cowhey, William Kieran
Creavin, Bernard
Creedon, Dominic
Cronin, Patricia
Crowley, Daniel
Crowley, Patrick A.
Cullen, William
Cunningham, William John
Daly, Donal
Daly, James Gerard
Deasy, Thomas A.
Delahunt, Katherine
Delahunty, Michael Eamonn
Dempsey, Dermot Mary
Dillon, Nuala Miriam
Donaghy, Thomas
Donoghue, Barry

Dowling, Elizabeth
Drumgoole, Bernadette
Duff, Monica Mary
Duggan, Frances Mary
Dunne, James Brian
Durand, Maria A.
Ebrill, Paul
Egan, Colette
Egan, William Joseph P.
English, Mary Ita
Eustace, Paul
Fahy, Declan Laurence F.
Fahy, Lucille
Farrell, James Edward
Field, Rena Margaret
Finlay, Peter
Fitzgibbon, William
Fitzpatrick, Shaun Ivor
Fleming, Susan
Foley, Charles J.
Foley, Declan
Garty, Vincent P.
Gillespie, Carol Lorna
Gilvarry, Emer
Gleeson, Irene
Glendon, Eugene
Glynn, Raymond P.
Gogarty, Bernard
Goodbody, Fergus Erik
Griffin, Vincent T.
Guilfoyle, David
Harrington, Vincent P.
Hegarty, Nancy Mary Marie
Horgan, Daniel Vergilius
Horgan, Rosemary Nuala
Hynes, Rose
Johnston, William F.R.
Keane, Paul M.
Kearney, Veronica Patricia
Kelly, Padraig Joseph
Kelly, Paul Patrick
Kelly, Paul V.
Kenny, Denise
Keogh, Matthew Gerard
Kiely, Joan
King, John Gordon
King, Michael
Kinsella, Morette
Kirwan, Brian
Lacy, Nathaniel
Lavery, John Linton
Law, Peter Michael

Leahy, Maurice
Leeman, Deirdre Anne
Leggett, Terence
Linehan, Philomena
Lombard, Niall
Loughnane, William
Love, Joseph Clayton
Lydon, Elizabeth M.
Lynch, Brendan G.T.
Lyons, William Joseph
Lysaght, John Anthony
MacBride, Edward
MacBride, Margaret Mary
McCarthy, Fachtna James
McCarthy, Nora
MacEvilly, Walter
McEvoy, Clodagh
McGarr, Edward Patrick
McGonagle, Patrick William
McGuinness, Richard
McKenna, Justin
MacKenzie, Stephanie
Macklin, Patrick
McMullan, Theresa May
  Francesca
McMyler, Patrick Joseph
Madden, Thomas K.
Maguire, Cliona
Maher, Daniel T.
Mahon, Anne-Marie
Maloney, Jacqueline
Mann, Patrick Pius
Mannion, James
Manny, Patrick Joseph
Margetson, Stuart
Martin, Patricia Anne
Matthews, Brian John
Matthews, Henry Joseph
Moane, Caroline
Monahan, Patrick
Moran, James F.
Morris, Kenneth Damien
Murphy, Anthony
Murphy, Denis
Murphy, Edith
Murphy, Fintan J.
Murphy, Frank
Murphy, John Gerard
Murphy, John Noel
Murphy, Linda
Murphy, Margaret M.
Murphy, Michael D.

Murray, Domhnall F.
Newell, Patrick
Ní Shuibhne-Hynes, Maire
Noonan, Margaret
O'Beirne, David Peter
O'Brien, Kevin
O'Brien, Mary G.
O'Connell, Brian
O'Connell, Padraig J.
O'Connor, Julie Geraldine
O'Connor, Niall
O'Donnell, Eleanor
O'Donohoe, Cathal
O'Donohoe, Ciaran
O'Donovan, Denis Anthony
O'Donovan, Marian
O'Donovan, Thomas J.
O'Driscoll, Gearoid Denis
O'Grady, Thomas
O'Hagan, Niall Joseph
O'Hanlon, Cormac Redmond
O'Higgins, Anne Sara
O'Kelly, Donal
O'Mara, Catriona
O'Regan, Redmond D.
O'Reilly, John J.
O'Reilly, Michael Joseph
O'Reilly, Pauline
O'Riada, Philip Martin
O'Rourke, Anthony Patrick
  Murrough
O'Rourke, Dermot Joseph
O'Sullivan, Eugene F.
O'Sullivan, Maebh Brid
O'Sullivan, Mary
O'Sullivan, Maurice B.
O'Sullivan, Niall Timothy
  Pius
O'Sullivan, Timothy Patrick
O'Sullivan, Timothy Robert
Parker, Liam
Pearson, Mark
Petty, Marian Jacqueline
Prendergast, Norman
Punch, Patrick
Quilty, Maigread Maire
Quinn, James A.
Quirk, Jacqueline
Regan, Ursula
Rohan, John Gerard
Scales, Amanda
Shannon, Elizabeth V.E.

Sheehan, Donal Gerard
Sheil, Anthony Francis
Sheil, Michael Joseph
Sheridan, Niall Gerard
Shiel, John
Sisk, Noel Martin
Smyth, Bryan Cornelius
Stapleton, Susan
Steen, Laurence
Sweeney, Manus
Tansey, David
Thornton, Fiona
Tierney, Celine Mary
Timmins, Edward Gerard
Toal, Ann
Tobin, Mary F.
Treacy, John J.
Turley, John David
Turley, Patrick Michael
Tynan, Edward
Walsh, James Vincent
Walsh, John Stephen
Walsh, Mary
Walsh, Maurice
Walsh, Miriam
Walsh, Robert
Walsh, Thomas Anthony
White, Kevin John
Williams, Thomas W.J.
Winston, James
Wolfe, Ernest Michael
Wrafter, Agnes Ann

1980

Aird, Caitriona Mary
Allen, Finbarr
Allen, Peter M.
Anderson, Lavinia
Anderson, Robert G.
Ashe, Christine
Baldwin, Thomas Gerrard
Binchy, Frederic J.
Boland, William M.
Bourke, Michael
Bourke, Michael Patrick
Bradley, Mary
Breen, Patrick
Brennan, Gerard Michael
Brennan, Michael James Noel

Broderick, Simon
Brooks, Kevin John
Buckley, Máire
Buckley, Neil
Buckley, Patrick
Burns, John Gerard
Byrne, Colin Michael Marcus
Caldwell, John
Campbell, Joan M.
Cantillon, Ernest
Carolan, Ruth
Carroll, Maeve M.T.
Carton, Catherine
Casey, John
Chambers, Joseph A.
Clarke. Joan P.
Collins, Barry
Condon, Anne
Condon, Justin
Connolly, Ann
Connolly, Darach Laurence
Connolly, Denis Vincent
Connolly, Margaret M.P.
Corrigan, Diarmuid
Costello, Francis Gerrard
Counihan, Katherine Anne
Cranwell, Peter
Crawford, Alice
Creed, Eamon T.
Crowe, Michael Joseph
Cuddigan, Joseph S.
Culhane, Philip Joseph
Cullen, Michael John
Curneen, Michael James
Curran, Isabelle
Dalton, Patrick Joseph
D'Alton, Thomas
Daly, Rosemary
Davis, Dermot Francis
de Feu, Fearghael
de Feu, Liam Mary
Derivan, Patrick A.
Diamond, Anthony T.
Doherty, Janet
Dowling, Michael Anthony
Doyle, Finnian Gerard
Duffy, Fiona Mary
Duffy, Patrick
Duke, Brendan
Dungan, Fiona
Dunne, David Michael Hugh
Dunne, Michael

Early, William
Egan, Mary Kate
Elliott, Katherine Anne
Fawsitt, Carol Mary
Fetherstonhaugh, Paul Henry
Fielding, Lucia Anne
Fitzpatrick, David J.
Fitzsimons, Dennis
Fleming, Eamon Anthony
Flynn, John Gerard
Flynn, Mary Agnes
Flynn, Paul Michael Liam
Foley, James P.
Foley, Paul
Fullam, Dermot
Gallagher, Gerard John
Gallagher, Jerome B.
Galloway, Charles
Gearty, Conor A.
Gearty, Francis
Geoghegan, Joseph T.T.
Gill, Paul Anthony
Gilmartin, James Raymond
Gilsenan, Joseph
Gleeson, Edward Gerard
Gleeson, John
Glynn, Miriam
Goodman, Mimi
Gormley, James David
Grace, John Raymond
Grealis, Margaret
Grehan, Duncan
Griffin, Maurice M.
Groarke, Lorna
Gunn, Brendan
Halligan, Thomas B.
Hanlon, Edward Joseph P.
Hannigan, Brenda Mary
Hart, Denis A.E.
Hayes, Plunkett
Heather, Douglas
Heffernan, Francis
Hegarty, Deborah Georgina
Hegarty, Deirdre
Hegarty, Joseph Gerard
Hickey, Paul P.
Hickson, John H.
Honan, Thomas E.
Horan, Margaret
Houlden, Noel William
Hughes, Mary
Hughes, Michael J.

Jones, Maeve
Jones, Peter D.
Joy, John M.
Joy, Maurice Patrick
Joyce, Michael Thomas
Judge, Aidan Joseph
Kealy, Conleth W.F.
Kean, Gerald
Keane, Patrick M.
Kearon, Rosemary
Keenan, Eamonn
Kelleher, Nora Mary
Kelly, Jane Mary
Kennedy, Mary
Kennedy, Michael J.
Kennedy, Paula Maria
Kennedy, Pauline Mary
Kennedy, Richard T.P.
Kenny Boyd, Ian
Kiely, Brian C.
Lane, Henrietta Mary F.
Lankford, Padraig
Lardner, James
Lavan, Joseph
Ledwith, Adrian
Lee, Philip P.
Lennon, Peter M.
Leyden, Evelyn
Linehan, Denis
Looby, Brendan
Lowry, Pauline
Lynch, Brian Robert
Lynch, John M.
Lyons, Michael Terence
Lysaght, Oonagh
Lyster, William George
McAuley, Christopher
   Michael
McCabe, Kathleen
McCarthy, Audrey
McCarthy, Orlaith
McCarthy, Richelle
McCarthy, Timothy, Gerard
McClean, David
McCormack, Francis O.
McCrann, Mary Valerie
MacDermott, Laura
McDonnell, Peter Gerard
McDowell, Lonan
McGartoll, Hilary
McGoldrick, Marina
McGrath, Terence B.

McGreevy, Margaret
McHenry, Pauline
McMahon, Colette M.
McManus, Brendan Richard
   Barré
McMorrow, Jim
McMullin, John
McMullin, John Joseph
MacNamara, Anne Mary E.
McNulty, Seamus Gerard
McPoland, John
MacQuaid, Maeve M.P.
McRory, Philomena
Madden, Declan Thomas
Maguire, Damien
Maguire, Gabriel
Mallon, James Joseph
Mangan, Ciaran
Mannion, John J.
Mannion, Thomas
Martin, Rossa
Martin, William Colin
Meade, Oonagh
Meghen, Michael John
Mernagh, John Anthony
Miley, Mary
Molloy, Mary
Moore, Nicholas
Moran, Enda
Morris, Jacinta E.
Morrissey, Peter
Murphy, Anthony Michael
Murphy, Colm
Murphy, Daire
Murphy, Daniel
Murphy, Daniel F.
Murphy, Finbarr
Murphy, Fionnuala
Murphy, Helen Teresa
Nash, John
O'Brien, Cathy
O'Brien, Jeremiah G.
O'Brien, Marie
O'Brien, Richard E.
O'Callaghan, Francisco P.
O'Connell, John K.
O'Connor, Charles
O'Connor, Denis John
O'Connor, Geraldine
O'Connor, Niall
O'Doherty, Claire
O'Donnell, Catherine

O'Donnell, Patricia
O'Donovan, Cathal P.
O'Halloran, Mary
O'Mahony, Susan M.
O'Neill, Hugh
O'Neill, Hugh Francis
O'Neill, Hugh Gerard
O'Reilly, Frank
O Riain, Colm S.
O'Shea, Mary
O'Shea, Paul Francis
O'Sullivan, Denis Gerard
O'Sullivan, Dominick Gerard
O'Sullivan, Edward James
O'Sullivan, Michael
Paul, Mary Vincent
Peart, Valerie
Phelan, Fintan Gerard
Power, Una Mary Thérèse
Quigley, Rory John
Quinn, Terry
Rabbitt, Murtagh Brian
Redmond, John
Reidy, Gerard
Rice, Ailbhe
Richardson, John Henry
Roche, Donal
Rooney, Niall R.
Rowland, Anne B.
Ryan, Justin
Ryan, Michael Gerard
Sandys, Gerard William A.
Scally, Romaine
Scott, Tressan
Shanley, John Oliver
Shannon, Audrey
Sheehan, Maurice
Sheehan, Patrick John
Sheehan, Ronan
Sheridan, Avril
Sheridan, Brian
Shields, Emer M.
Shubotham, Boyce
Sills, Martin
Simms, Charles Dermot
   Munster
Smalle, Patrick Liam
Smith, Ronan
Spencer, John
Stephens, Robert
Sweetman, David M.
Taaffe, Plunkett

Tansey, Damien Martin
Thomas, Patrick Joseph
Tierney, Laurence J.
Tipping, Anne
Walpole, Hilary
Walsh, James
Walsh, John C.
Walsh, Niall John
Walsh, Thomas J.
Whelan, Patrick J.
Woods, Mary R.
Yelverton, Gerard P.

1981

Ahern, Timothy
Alken, Gillian
Allen, Sean
Baker, Laetitia
Beattie, David H.
Binchy, David Gerard
Black Barrett, Mary
Bohan, Brian
Boyle, Owen
Breen, Michael T.
Britton, Ernan T.
Burke, Robert
Butler, Fedelma
Callanan, Martin
Campbell, James
Canny, Raymond D.
Carr, John Martin
Casey, Mary
Cody, Peter G.
Cogan, Catherine
Cogan, Edmond
Coleman, Bernadette
Colley, Henry Patrick
Collins, Catherine M.
Collins, Catriona
Connellan, Paul Edward
Copeland, George
Costello, Joan
Courtney, Breda
Cunniffe, Geraldine
Curran, Colman P.
Curran, Joseph
Daly, Anne Patricia
Dennehy, Marie
Dennehy, Richard

Doherty, Brian
Donnellon, James Michael
Downes, Daniel
Downey, Brigid
Doyle, Isolde Mary
Dunn, Edwina M.
Durcan, Sean
Egan, Frank
Egan, Paul
Egan, Ronald J.
English, Edna
Farrelly, Donal
Fitzgerald, Pamela
Fitzpatrick, Hilary
Fitzpatrick, Michael
Flynn, Michael John
Folan, Mary Margaret
Foley, Jennifer
Foley, Oliver
Forde, Aidan C.
Gallagher, Joseph D.
Gallagher, Noel
Gallogly, Errol
Gartlan, Peter V.
Geaney, Sheila
Gormley, Mary
Griffin, Catherine Maria
Grogan, John Gerard
Guerin, Denis
Hally, James
Halpenny, Gerard
Hanley, Aideen
Hanley, James
Harrington, Patricia
Harris, Anthony S.
Harris, Olivia Mary Pacelli
Harris, Patrick Thomas
Hayes, Ian
Heffernan, Caroline Ann
Heffernan, Jacqueline
Heffernan, Jacqueline
Hegarty, Michael Jarlath
Hewetson, Ann
Hickey, James Brian
Hogan, Edmund
Horgan, Anne
Houlihan, Colm
Hughes, Catherine
Hughes, Noel
Ireton, Caitriona
Jones, Eamon Joseph
Jones, Gerard

Joyce, John Francis
Keane, Geraldine M.M.
Keane, William
Kearney, John F.
Keaveney, Mary
Kelly, David
Kelly, Eugene
Kennedy, Brain Matthew
Kiernan, Kieron Desmond
Killalea, Katherine
King, Niall Patrick Thomas
Larkin, Nora
Larkin, Patrick Joseph
Lynch, William Francis
McCourt, James B.
McDarby, Michael
MacDermot, Ruth
McGowan, Ciaran F.C.
MacGowan, Eamon
McGrath, Thomas J.
McNeilis, Neil
McSparran, Patricia
McTernan, John
Martin, Catherine
Meehan, Gerard Joseph
Mehigan, Pearse
Millar, Hugh
Moloney, Gerald
Monahan, Michael B.
Mooney, Michael P.
Moore, Michael
Moran, William Thomas
Moriarty, Brendan
Morrissey, Patrick J.
Mulcahy, Rowena
Murphy, Eugene
Murphy, John Gerard
Murphy, Kenneth
Murphy, Sarah Teresa
Murtagh, Noel
Nash, James Martin
Nelson, John Peter
Ní Leighin, Mairéad Áine Bríd
Ní Mhuimhneachain, Bríd
Ní Shuibhne, Padraigín Nuala
Nolan, Bernadette Mary
Nugent, Clodagh
O'Beirne, Anthony
O'Brien, Anne Margaret
O'Brien, James David
O'Brien, Owen
O'Brien, Patricia

O'Carroll, Martin Dermot
Ó Catháin, Diarmuid
Ó Cearbhaill, Seán
O'Connor, Bernard Michael
O'Connor, Laurence
O'Connor, Michael John
O'Connor, Peter
O'Connor, Thomas Patrick
O'Donnell, John G.M.
O'Donovan, Carole
O'Donovan, Sheila Mary
O'Flynn, Gerald A.J.
O'Higgins, Kevin
O'Keeffe, Charles
  Terence
O'Keeffe, Michael P.
O'Leary, Edward Shaun
O'Regan, John P.
O'Reilly, Ronan V.
Orr, Caroline Mary
O'Shea, Eileen Mary
O'Shea, Michael
O'Sullivan, Anna Maria
O'Sullivan, Donal
O'Sullivan, Oliver
O'Sullivan, Philip J.
Prendiville, John
Prentice, William Peter
  Maziere
Quinlan, Michael
Quinn, Peter N.
Reidy, John
Riordan, Mary Theresa
Rowley, Brendan Francis
Ruane, Bláthna
Ryan, Katherine Mary
Ryan, Patrick Joseph
Ryan, Thomas F.
Sadlier, Michael
Scully, Geraldine
Shanahan, Thomas A.
Shaw, Duncan Crozier
Shaw, Jennifer Violet
Shields, Vivienne
Smith, Deirdre
Smyth, Sean
Spelman, Brian P.
Sweeney, Elizabeth
Sweeney, Kathy
Taaffe, Francis
Timmons-Kiely, Mary
Torsney, Gerard F.

Walsh, Elizabeth Clare
Walsh, Michael Patrick
Waters, John Joseph
Watters, Paul
Whelan, Barbara

1982

Arnold, Gillian
Bannon, Edward
Barker, Claire J.
Barrett, Niall M.
Bennett, George M.
Bergin, Mary Catherine
Binchy, Mary Rose
Bohan, Gerard Martin
Boland, Lucy
Boland, Marie
Boylan, Michael
Bracken, Timothy
Brandon, Liam
Brannigan, Finian
Breen, Patrick Declan
Brennan, James
Brennan, John
Brown, Aidan
Brown, Léonie
Browne, Niall
Buckley, John Joseph
Burke, Colm
Burke, Julia Mary
Byrne, Ken J.
Byron, Yvonne
Caffrey, Francis
Cahill, John Patrick
Caldwell, Jennifer
Callan, Ciaran Robert
Campbell, Attracta
Campbell, William Martin
Cannon, John Ignatius
Carey, Thomas Joseph
Carlos, William Paul
Carroll, Colm
Cashman, Liam
Caulfield, Patrick
Celmalis, Heather
Coakley, Conor
Coakley, Mary
Coll, Gerard
Collins, Noreen

Collins, Peter
Coolican, Carol Anne
Costello, Colm
Coyne, Dermot Peter
Crawford, Valery
Creed, John
Cregan, John Patrick
Crimmins, Risteard M.
Crowley, Gillian
Culhane, Thomas Patrick
Cunningham, Ann
Curran, Barbara
Curran, Declan
Cusack, Patrick James
Cuthbert, Joseph
Dalton, Timothy Charles
Dalton, Thomas Anthony
Davis, William J.
Devaney, Brian
Devlin, Mary
Dineen, Kathleen
Donovan, St. John
Dorgan, Patrick
Dowling, Barbara
Doyle, Mark Edmund
Doyle, Susan
Duff, Mary P.
Dunlea, Michael
Dwyer, Mary A.
Elliott, Stephen
Ennis, Laurence William
Ensor, Roderic
Etchingham, Brendan
Fahy, Siobhan
Farrell, Edward J.M.
Ferris, Elizabeth
Finnan, Keith P.
Fitzgerald, Alexis Kyran
Fitzgerald, Ann
Flanagan, Charles
Flood, Thomas
Flynn, Peter
Foley, Owen
Forde, Noel Patrick
Fox, John B.
Fox, Michael
Furlong, Alan
Gahan, Aideen
Gallagher, Eunan
Gallagher-Sherlock, Mary
Galvin, John
Galvin, Mary Elizabeth

Geraghty, Kevin P.
Gibbons, Bernadette
Gibbons, Mary
Glen, Jeremy
Gordon, Anita
Grant, Adrienne
Grogan, Richard
Halpin, Richard John
Hegarty, Catherine
Hennessy, John Raymond
Higgins, Josephine Mary
Higgins, Peter
Hogan, Felicity
Hogan, Marie Philomena
Hogan, Michael
Hollis-Mayne, Susan
Hurley, John G.
Hynes, Bridget Mary
Johnson, Keenan
Joyce, Jennifer
Joyce, Richard
Joyce, Richard
Kavanagh, Art
Keane, David Anthony
Kearns, Martin J.
Keenan, Carol
Kelleher, Diarmuid
Kelleher, Francis Colman
Kelly, David
Kennedy, Patrick James
Kennedy, Thomas
Killoran, Aidan
Kingston, Rosemary Ann
Kyne, Joseph M.
Lambe, Gerard
Ledwith, Catherine M.
Linehan, Denis Martin
Lloyd, Alexandra
Long, Daniel Fergus
Long, Ian Joseph
Long, Patrick Mary
Lord, Patricia
Lucey, James M.
McCague, Eugene
Mac Cana, Liam
McCann, David
McCarthy, James
McCarthy, Justin Gerard
McCartney, Mary Monica
McCullagh, Gerard
McDonnell, Richard Edward
McEnroe, Philip Anthony

McEntee, Carol
McErlean, Caroline
McErlean, Gerard Patrick
McEvoy, Bernard
McEvoy, Mel
McGlinn, Noel Anthony
McGonagle, Catherine
McGrath, Joseph
McKeever, Anne Marie
McKenna, John
McMichael, Deirdre
MacNamara, John
McNulty, Denise
McSweeney, Ursula
McTiernan, Felix
Madigan, Adrian
Mannix, Joseph B.
Meagher, James Joseph M.
Meenan, Frances Mary Pia
Meghen, Patrick Joseph
Moloney, Louise
Moore, John Brian
Moriarty, Catherine Emer
Morley, Laurence Joseph
Morris, Barbara M.F.
Moylan, Louise
Murphy, Gerard
Murray, Edward
Murray, Eugenia
Neary, Anne
Nic Craith, Maire
Ní Ghallchobhair, Máire
  Seosaimhín
O'Brien, John
O'Brien, Michael A.
O'Brien, Michael A.
O'Brien, Olive
O'Callaghan, Brian G.
Ó Conchubhair, Donal
O'Connor, Anne E.
O'Connor, Charles Joseph
O'Connor, Cornelius
O'Connor, Elizabeth Anne
O'Connor, Francis
O'Connor, Gillian B.
O'Connor, Michael M.J.
O'Doherty, Adrian
O'Donoghoe, Jeremiah Paul
O'Donoghue, Martin Joseph
O'Donoghue, Shane
O'Donovan, Brendan
O'Driscoll, Terence

O'Dwyer, Dermot Barry
O'Dwyer, Roger
O'Dwyer Durkan, William
O'Gorman, Macarten
O'Grady, Thomas
O'Hanrahan, Ellenore
O'Keeffe, Kevin
Ó Laoide, Phil Browne
O'Leary, Cornelius Pacelli
O'Mahony, Una
O'Malley, Mary
O'Meara, Ruth
O'Neill, Gillian
O'Neill, John J.
O'Neill, Mary
O'Neill, Mary
O'Neill, Michael
O'Reilly, Conor F.
O'Reilly, Patrick
O'Rorke, Ciaran
O'Shea, Niall Patrick
O'Sullivan, Celine Hilary
O'Sullivan, Michael Anthony
O'Toole, Geraldine Mary B.
Pearson, David Jonathan
Pery-Knox-Gore, Mark
Plunkett, John O.
Prendiville, Michael
Punch, Anne
Quigg, Douglas
Quigley, Peter
Quill, Kieran
Quirke, Joseph
Ramsay, David
Reid, John J.
Rickard-Clarke, Patricia
Riordan, Nora Mary
Rogan, James A.
Rogan, Vincent
Ryan, Christopher William
Ryan, Denis
Ryan, James Gregory
Ryan, Mark Bernard
Ryan, Philip
Russell, Philip J.
Ruttledge, William John
Scully, Lorraine
Scully, Paul Dermot
Scraggs, Maurice F.W.
Shanley, Geraldine
Shannon, Tim
Sheehan, Jeremiah

Sheridan, Hugh D.
Sheridan, James Anthony
Sheridan, Noel P.
Sherlock, John
Sisk, Joan M.
Slattery, John Mahon
Smith, Jim
Smith, William
Smyth, Paul R.
Smyth, Shane
Spring, Daniel
Stewart, Derek
Sullivan, Clifford G.E.
Sullivan, Daniel
Sweeney, Ellen
Teahan, Mary
Tighe, James V.
Timon, Victor
Tobin, Eva
Tracey, Paul William
Twomey, Marie
Twomey, Neil
Walker, Richard Garrett
Wallace, John Edward
Walls, Susan
Walsh, David
Walsh, Gabriella M.
Whooley, Ann
Young, Bernadette

1983

Agnew, Brenda
Agnew, Elizabeth Murphy
Ahern, Grainne
Ahern, Stephen
Allen, Breda
Allen, Yvonne
Anderson, Moira
Bacon, Anne
Barr, Nicola K.
Barrett, Jean E.
Barriscale, H. Patrick
Barry, Kevin
Barry, Thomas
Behan, Margaret
Bermingham, Terence C.
Blunden, Jennifer
Bourke, James
Bowe, Joseph

Boyce, Connell M.
Brennan, Bridget A.
Buckley, Lorcan
Burke, Finola
Burns, Gerard
Butler, Neil
Cahill, Patrick J.
Canning, Roger
Carey, Denis
Carthy, Gerard E.
Carty, Padraig Pearse
Carvill, Colm
Casey, Emer
Clarke, Brendan
Coffey, Nessa C.
Coleman, Catherine C.
Colgan, Roy
Collins, Carmela E.
Conlon, Julian D.
Conlon, Paula
Connolly, Roisin
Conroy, Mary
Cooke, Richard
Corbett, Margaret T.
Corcoran, Francis
Coughlan, William
Cowen, Brian T.
Cox, Sarah
Crawford, Anne
Cronin, Jeremiah Martin
Cuddy, Peter A.
Daly, Gabriel C.
Deasy, Catherine M.
Delap, Antoin C.
Dillon, John P.
Doherty, John B.
Dolan, Cathleen B.
Dolan, Daniel J.
Donnelly, Grainne
Doyle, Karina A.
Duffy, James
Dunleavy, Fergus
Dyar, Patrick
English, Philip
Fenelon, Mary
Fennell, Marguerite
Fitzgerald, Finbarr B.
Fitzgerald, Niall
Fitzpatrick, Maura
Flanagan, Joan
Fogarty, William
Forde, Christopher

Fortune, Garrett
Fortune, Peter M.
Foy, Sean
Frawley, Adrian
Gahan, Catriona M.
Garrick, Mary
Gearty, Deirdre
Gleeson, Catherine
Hayden, Rory
Hayes, Mary
Heffernan, Austin
Hegarty, Kevin
Hegarty, Laurette
Hogarty, Christopher
Holohan, William F.
Honan, Mary
Horgan, Anne
Hughes, Sean
Irwin, Brendan
Jennings, Ann
Jordan, Mary C.
Kearney, Deirdre
Kearney, Katherina M.
Kearney, Miriam
Kelleher, Mary
Keller, Niall
Kelly, Gerald
Kelly, Henry
Kelly, Noel
Kelly, Phelim J.
Kelly, Thomas J.
Kennedy, Ann
Kennedy, Patrick J.
Kenny, David P.
Kent, Edmund M.
Kerr, Elizabeth
Lawless, Linda M.
Lawless, Mary
Liddy, Brendan
Lonergan, Donal G.
Loughlin, Christina
Lynch, Patrick
Lyons, Maurice G.
Lysaght, Eoin J.
McCarthy, Paul
McCormick, Peter G.
McCourt, Kieran
McDermott, Deirdre
McDwyer, Denis Francis
MacFadden, Dairine
McGarry, Hugh
McGartoll, Ruth

MacGrath, Elizabeth
McGreevy, Mary
MacGuinness, Rosemary
McIntyre, Patrick C.
McKenna, Isolde
MacKenzie, Nuala
MacKenzie Smith, Evelyn
McMahon, James Vincent
McMorrow, Mary C.
McNamara, Patricia
Madden, Andrew D.
Madigan, Kieran
Maher, Patrick J.
Meade, Margaret B.
Meaney, John
Molony, Ronan
Moore, Catherine Anne
Moore, Paul
Morahan, John
Moran, Joseph K.
Moran, Olive E.
Morgan, James
Morgan, Kenneth
Morris, Nora F.
Morrow, Andrew G.
Mullery, Paschal G.
Mulrine, Margaret M.
Murphy, David
Murphy, Helen
Murphy, Michael J.
Murray, Graeme
Murray, John F.
Nic Dhonncadha, Meadhbh
Nolan, John
Nolan, Joseph
Nolan, Mary
Noone, Brigid
O'Brien, Eamon
O'Brien, Maria B.
O'Callaghan, Declan
O'Callaghan, Miriam
O'Connor, Eoin J.M.
O'Connor, Tony
O'Donnell, Mary
O'Donoghue, James J.
O'Donohoe, David
O'Donovan, Michael
O'Driscoll, Patrick
O'Flaherty, Michael
O'Hanlon, Aisling
O'Hanlon, Yvonne
O'Herlihy, Ian

O'Leary, John G.
O'Rafferty, Hugh Bernard
O'Reilly, Hugh G.
O'Malley, Mary
O'Shea Diarmuid S.
O'Shea Thomas J.
O'Shea, Timothy
O'Sullivan, Anne
O'Sullivan, Carl
O'Sullivan, Henry
O'Sullivan, Peter T.
Perrin, Heather
Powell, Stephanie
Power, Albert
Power, Eithne
Quigley, Helen
Quinn, James K.
Quinn, Peter
Rackard, Helen
Randles, Michael
Riordan, Michael
Roche, Jean M.
Rowan, John P.
Rowe, Margaret
Ryan, Finula M.
Sadlier, Julia M.
Scanlon, John D.
Sexton, Maura
Simons, Caroline
Smith, Jacqueline M.
Stapleton, Aidan
Sweetman, Patrick
Synnott, Alan
Taylor, Patricia M.
Tobin, John A.
Treacy, Patricia C.
Turley, Mary
Twomey, Patrick
Wallis, Fintan
Walsh, Anthony
Walsh, Elizabeth
Walsh, Kevin
Walsh, Margaret Rosari
Walsh, Walter John
Walters, Mortimer
White, Nora
White, Philip Brendan
Williams, Leon James
Woods, Alanna M.
Woods, Ann B.
Woods, Donncadh J.
Wynne, Fiona

1984

Ahern-Millar, Bernadette
Ainscough, Mary
Barnicle, John
Barrett, Paula
Barron, Kevin
Benville, Rory
Berney, Catherine
Boyle, James
Breen-Walsh, Fionnuala
Breheny, Neil J.
Breslin, John G.
Brophy, Kevin
Brophy, Patricia
Buckley, Cliona
Buggy, Brian D.
Burke, Olive
Burke, Padraig A.
Burke, Patrick A.
Butler, Edmund
Butler, Michael F.
Byrne, Elaine F.
Cafferky, Hugh
Cahill, Mairead
Callanan, Maeve
Campbell, Colm
Carroll, Gerard
Carroll, John
Carroll, Paul J.P.
Carroll, Thomas J.
Christie, Cedric R.S.
Clinch, Richard
Collins, Damian
Collins, Kathleen
Colthurst, Charles St. John
Comyn, Philip
Corbett, James
Corduff, Noel
Cosgrave, Terence
Cotter, Kevin
Coughlan, Finbar
Coughlan, Geraldine
Counihan, Michael
Courtenay, Niall
Crawford, Michael
Cronin, John
Crowley, Catherine
Cullen, Shea
Curtin, Pauline M.
Curtis, Deirdre
Derham, Paul D.

Dooley, Frances E.
Dooley, Kieran
Donoghue, Mary P.
Dowling, Vincent J.
Downey, Siobhan
Doyle, Aisling
Doyle, Miriam
Drinan, Mary M.
Dundon, Edward
Durcan, Sheila M.
Egan, Noel M.
Fahy, Benen
Fahy, John
Ferry, Padraig Colm
Finlay, Margaret
Finn, Orla M.
Fitzgerald, John
Fitzmaurice, Robert J.
Flanagan, Mariea
Flynn, John
Fogarty, Geraldine
Foy, John M.
Gallagher, Liam Anthony
Gallagher, Michael E.
Galvin, David
Gannon, Lorraine
Gavin, Gerard
Geraghty, Anita M.
Gibbons, Anne G.
Gill, Colm E.
Gillard-Curtin, Clare
Gills, Maria
Gilvarry, Myles
Given, James
Glynn, Emmie B.D.M.
Glynn, Gregory
Golden, Bernadette
Gould, Denis P.
Griffin, Gerard
Guckian, Aengus T.
Guidera, Liam
Hanifin, Michael B.
Hannon, Brian
Harrington, Eugene
Harrison, Brendan
Hayes, Declan C.
Heavey, Michael D.
Hehir Mulryan, Christina
Henry, Edmund
Higgins, William J.
Hinkson, Michael
Holohan, Martina G.

Hughes, Peter Nicholas
Hurley, Conor
Hutchinson, Brian
Johnston, Patricia
Joyce, Barbara
Kavanagh, Dermot
Keane, Annmarie
Keane, Frank
Kelly, Jacqueline
Kelly, John C.
Kelly, Michael F.
Kenny, Assumpta
Kenny, Sean M.
Landy, John
Larkin, John D.
Larney, David
Lee, John
Liston, Nuala
Lockhart, Geraldine
Loughran, Mary
Lynch, Brian M.
Lynch, Patrick V.
McCarthy, Ann
McCarthy, Michael
McConnon Wallace, Mary
   Gerard
McCudden, Brendan
McCullough, J. Jacinta
McDonald, Claire
McDonnell, Eileen
McDonough, Louis
McGarry, Joseph P.
McGreevy, Conor
MacKenzie, Patricia Jane
McLoughlin, Thomas
McMahon, Katherine
McNally, Patrick
MacSweeney, Gerard
Maguire, Brid
Mahon, Dermot
Mee, Walter
Meyler, Gary
Molan, Kenneth F.
Molumby, Ronan John
Morris, Mary
Moynihan, John Francis
Mullan, Teresa
Mullaney, Michael
Munnelly, Ian G.M.
Murphy, Catherine
Murphy, Cornelius V.

Murphy, John P.
Murphy, Simon
Murray, John
Myles, Thomas
Ní Aodha, Maire
Ní Choigligh, Mairéad
O'Brien, Anne Lucia
O'Brien, Desmond
O'Brien, Finbarr J.
O'Brien, Maura
O'Brien, Michael J.E.
O'Callaghan, Mary
O'Connell, Michael
O'Connell, Sheelagh M.
O'Connor, Eugene
O'Dea, Thomas
O'Donnell, Dudley M.A.
O'Donnell, Gerard
O'Donoghue, Vincent
O'Donohoe, James G.
O'Dowd, Dominic
O'Flaherty, Dermot
O'Gorman, Daniel
O'Hanlon, Mary
O'Hara, Joseph N.
O'Herlihy, Gerard
O'Higgins, Derval
O'Mahony, Edward P.
O'Mahony, James
O'Meara, Joseph
O'Neill, Fiona
O'Neill, Gerard E.
O'Reilly, John Joseph
O'Reilly, Michael
O'Reilly, Thomas P.
O'Shaughnessy, Robert
O'Shea, Christopher
O'Shea, Eoin
O'Sullivan, Denis T.
O'Sullivan, Oliver
O'Sullivan, Seamus T.
Owens, Bernadette
Pasley, Lynne
Pendred, Anthony Conleth
Plunkett, Oliver Randall
Quigley, Michael
Quinn, Raymond J.
Rae, Brendan Michael
Reynolds, Mary E.
Rickard, Elizabeth
Riordan, David

Roche, John B.
Russell, Nicholas
Ryan, Anne G.
Ryan, Martin
Sainsbury, Colin
Scott, Kathleen
Shanahan, Raymond
Shaw, John
Sheedy, Brid Frances
Shields, Stephen L.
Silvester, Peter
Smith, Patrick J.
Staunton, Angela
Stokes, William A.
Swan, Oonagh
Swords, Joseph M.
Timmons, Veronica
Toale, Brendan
Toomey, Louise
Tracey, Esther
Twomey, David
Wall, Daniel N.
Walsh, Christopher B.
Waters, Emilie
Young, Rose-Ann

1985

Aufochs-Ilan, Helen
Bambury, Patricia
Barry, Anthony
Bennett, Eamonn
Benson, Michael
Bergin, Adrienne
Blayney, Ann
Bodenham, Helen
Boner, John
Bourke, Roderick
Branigan, Imelda
Breen, Conor G.
Breen, Susan
Brennan, Barbara
Browne, Donal G.
Buchalter, Richard L.
Buckley, John J.
Buckley, Kieran
Burke, Patrick
Butler, Maura
Byrne, Catherine

Byrne, Michael J.
Byrne, Peter
Caira, Rocco
Campbell, Gavin
Carey, Louise K.
Carolan, Eamonn M.
Casey, Patricia
Cawley, Niall T.J.
Clandillon, Margaret
Cleary, Nollaig
Cogan, Enda
Coleman, Niall
Compton, Lorraine
Connell, Mary
Cooke, John
Corcoran, Neil
Crean, Peter G.
Creed, Mary M.
Cullinane, Patrick M.
Cunningham, Brendan
Daly, John F.
Deane, Bernadette
de Hall, Coilín
Devereux, Declan G.S.
Devereux, Richard J.
Dillon, Linda
Dinan, Mary
Dore, Robert
Doyle, Helen
Duggan, Colm G.
Durcan, Deirdre
Eames, Aidan B.
Egan, Kieran
Farrell, Noel
Flood, Geraldine
Foley, Isabel
Furlong, E. Gerard
Gallagher, Ruth Ann
Govender, Sivalingum
    Purushothaman
Gunn, James
Gunning, Lorraine
Hand, Mary
Hanley, Eamon
Hayes, Margaret
Healy, Angela
Henry, Maoiliosa
Hickey, Anne
Hickie, John
Higgins, Rosemary
Hutchinson, Francis

Hyland, Michael G.
James, Anne Marie
Keane, Mary C.
Kenny, Thomas P.
Kingston, Paul G.
Larney, Brendan
Lavelle, Michael
Lawlor, Martin G.
Leahy, Brian
Leon, David B.
Linehan, Barbara
Lohan, Siobhan
Lynch, Irene C.
McClafferty, Manus
McCormack, John F.
McCormack, Paul F.
McDonagh, Niall
McDonald, John F.
McGann, Gearoid
McGlade, Jennifer
McGovern, Ailbhe
McKeown, Anna
McLoughlin, Denis J.
McNeice, Patrick
Madigan, Pamela
Maher, Stephen F.
Mallon, Patricia A.
Manifold, Brid
Marshall, Brian
Martin, Gerard J.
Meagher, Paul
Moore, Paul A.
Moran, Marie
Moran, Martin D.
Moran, Orla
Mulchrone, Mary
Muldowney, Margaret
Munnelly, Patrick J.
Murphy, Kieran
Murphy, Peter D.R.
Murphy, Sharon E.
Murphy, Timothy
Nestor, Michael
Ní Charltain, Gearóidín
Noonan, Mary
Noonan, Thomas
O'Brien, Clare
O'Brien, Joseph C.
O'Brien, Martin
O'Brien, P. Brian
Ó Conaill, Cathal T.

O'Connor, Adrienne E.
O'Connor, Elizabeth
O'Connor, James
O'Connor, Patrick F.
O'Donoghue, Theresa
O'Donovan, Pauline
O'Dowd, Michael
O'Farrell, John A.
O'Kelly, Niall
Olden, John
O'Leary, Aisling
O'Leary, Philip
O'Mahony, Grainne
O'Mahony, Thomas
O'Meara, David
O'Neill, Helen
O'Reilly, Aideen
O'Reilly, Mary
O'Riordan, Rory
O'Rourke, Fiona
O'Shaughnessy, Conor
O'Shea, Linda M.P.
O'Shea, Mary Rosario
O'Toole, Declan
O'Toole, John
Pigot, David Richard
Power, Elaine
Proctor, John F.
Purcell, Maeve
Quinn, Donal P.
Quinn, Mary B.D.
Quinn, Michael J.
Quirke, Kevin
Reid, Madeleine
Reilly, Mary
Robinson, Victoria M.
Ronayne, Mark
Sheehy, Helen M.
Sheerin, Niall C.
Sherry, Brian C.
Sless, Tania
Smith, Grace S.
Soden, Peter
Spence, Deborah A.
Stephenson, Anne
Thornton, Alfred
Timoney, James
Toner, Edward
Twomey, Jacqueline
Tynan, Lucy
Walsh, Margaret

Whelan, Regina
Whooley, Rosemary

1986

Barrett, Richard
Barry, John Declan
Boylan, John
Brophy, Joseph
Buggy, Michael J.
Byrne, Maurice
Campbell, Anne Marie
Campion, Michael
Carley, Damien
Carmody, Patrick
Casey, John Gregory
Casey, Patrick B.
Clancy, Anne
Clancy, Diarmuid
Coleman, David
Collins, Anne Frances
Corcoran, Claire
Cotter, Barbara
Crewe, Donald
Croasdell, Etain
Crosbie, Suzanne
Cummins, John
Cummins, Mary L.
Curran, Rachel Ann
Cusack, Michele
Dalton, Gabrielle
Daly, Eamon P.
Deale, Julian
Deane, Dermot
Delahunt, Brian A.J.
Dempsey, Peter
Devlin, Caroline
Dineen, Elizabeth
Dolan, Niall Francis
Dooley-Kelly, Tressan
Duggan, John
Durkan, Joseph
Egan, Martine
English, Terence
Enright, Patrick
Enright, Patrick G.
Fallon, Paula
Farrell Quinn, Bridget
Feeney, Fergus A.
Fitzgerald, Eithne
Fitzpatrick, Francis

Fitzpatrick, Patrick D.
Flynn, Raymond M.
Foley, Nora Judith
Foy, Oonagh
Fraser, Emma
Furlong, John
Garahy, Marie
Glynn, David K.
Goodwin, John
Halpenny, Susan M.
Hannigan, Ronan
Hanrahan, Sandra
Harrington, Bryan
Healy, Audrey
Healy, James
Henchy, Gráinne
Heneghan, Brendan
Holland, Ronan
Horgan, Mary
Howlin, Elizabeth
Hughes, Martin B.
Hughes, Thomas E.
Judge, Barbara
Kane, Vivienne
Kealy, Michael
Keating, Ann
Kelly, Catherine
Kelly, Edward
Kelly, Evelyn
Kelly, Kieran
Kelly, Nicholas
Kenny, Padraig
Lanigan, Michael
Loftus, Peter A.
Lynch, Paul
McAleese, Don
McAllister, Mark
McCaffrey, Brigid
McCartan, Noel
McCarthy, Marion
McCrann, Terence
McDonagh, Niall M.
McDowell, Derek
McElhinney, Paul
McEvoy, Yvonne
MacGuill, James
McGuinness, Peter
McKeown, Anne Orla
McLoughlin, Michael
McMahon, Finnuala
McNulty, Thomas
Maher, Susanna

Marren, Robert B.
Martin, Andrea
Martin, Elaine
Martin, Peter M.
Meany, Gerry
Minogue, Carol Ann
Moran, Deirdre A.
Moran, Michael
Moriarty, Siobhan
Murchan, John F.
Murphy, Eugene
Murphy, Florence
Murphy, John C.
Murphy, Niall G.
Ní Fhloinn, Aoife
Nolan, Anne
Noone, Raymond
O'Brien, Michael
O'Byrne, Gearoid
O'Callaghan, Maurice
O'Connor, Mary
O'Connor, William D.
Ó Deasúna, Ciarán
O'Donnell, Martin K.
O'Donnell, Nuala
O'Donoghue, Patrick M.J.
O'Donovan, Kevin
O'Dowd, Rory
O'Driscoll, Grace Louise
O'Driscoll, Kathryn D.
O'Dwyer, Michael
O'Farrell, Aislinn M.
O'Flaherty, Catherine
O'Gorman, Noel
O'Kelly, Niamh
O'Mahony, Anne
O'Malley, Paul
O'Neill, Joan
O'Neill, Patrick J.
O'Reilly, Helen
O'Reilly, Kieran P.
O'Riordan, John M.
O'Rourke, Colm
O'Shea, Patricia
O'Sullivan, Ambrose
O'Sullivan, Cathal
O'Sullivan, Michael
Overend, Rodney
Phelan, Sarah
Powderly, David
Putt, Rosemary
Quigley, Michael M.

Quinn, Charles
Redmond, Noleen
Reidy, Dermot P.
Rice, Gerard
Rowan, Francis Xavier
Ryan, Robert
Ryan, Sylvia
Scott, David
Scully, Cecilia
Seale, Roseann
Singleton, Mary
Soden, David
Stokes, Isabell
Swords, Mary
Tuohy, Paul
Ward, Hugh J.
Woulfe, Richard A.

1987

Ahern, Mary P.
Armstrong, Sandra
Aylmer, Elizabeth
Bambury, Yvonne M.
Bermingham, Matthew
Binchy, Donald Patrick
Boland, Mark J.
Boyle, Vincent Adrian Joseph
Brady, Edward M.
Browne, Helen
Browne, Maria
Burke, Niamh
Burke, Oliver
Byrne, Brendan
Byrne, Carmel
Cadogan, James
Cantrell, Noelle
Carton, Brona
Casey, John
Casey, Mary T.
Coary, Nora
Collins, Rory W.
Comiskey, Christine M.
Connolly, Diana
Cox, David A.S.
Creedon, Eileen
Crotty, Martin
Cullen, Augustus John
Cullen, Elizabeth Mary
Cunningham, Carolanne
Daly, Bridget

Daly, Deirdre
Daly, Marie
D'Arcy, Madeleine
Deane, Catherine
Dennis, Marie-Christine
Desmond, Frank
Dillon, Sheila M.
Dineen, Caroline M.
Doogan, Orla A.
Doyle, Leonora
Doyle, Miriam
Duff, Peter
Ennis, Catherine A.
Fahy, Deirdre M.
Fay, John
Ferguson, Marianne
Finlay, Ruth
Fitzpatrick, Joseph
Flanagan, Brendan
Flanagan, Michelle
Flynn, Patrick G.
Foley, Emer
Ford, Nuala
Gallagher, Nora
Gibbons, Una
Gillen, Fiona
Gillespie, Brian
Gilroy, Maureen P.
Gordon, Thomas C.
Greaney, David M.
Greene, Jeffrey
Gubbins, Maire
Hanley, Gerard A.
Hennessy, Gemma
Hickey, Cliona M.
Hoy, Kevin
Hughes, Thomas E.
Jamieson, Diana B.
Johnston, Karl
Johnston, Robert Shane
Kane, Luan
Keane, Anne
Keane, Liam
Kearney, James B.
Kelleher, Mary Paula
Kelleher, Mortimer
Kelly, Joseph
Kelly, Joseph P.
Kennedy, Michael
Kenny, Patricia
Keys, Joseph M.
Kilfeather, Dermot A.

Kinsella, Denise
Larkin, Deirdre
Larney, John
Lavelle, Christine
Lawlor, Clare
Layng, Michael
Linnane, Howard
Lynch, Paula G.
Lynch, Sinead
Lyons, Carole
McArdle, Bronwyn M.
McCann, Neill J.P.
McCarthy, Brendan Gerard
McCarthy, Ellen Anne
McCarthy, Helena Anne
McCarthy, Timothy
McCauley, Owen
McDermott, Mary
McGinley, Margaret
McGlynn, Sean
McGovern, Patricia
McGrath, Adolphus
McGuinn, Elaine
McLernon, Ann
McLoughlin, Aidan
MacLynn, Adrian
McShane, Peter
Maguire, Noelle
Meehan, David
Molan, Declan G.
Mulligan, Martin
Murphy, Miriam
Murphy, Niall
Murray, James
Murray, Thomas K.
Mylotte, Nora
Nelkin, Carl
O'Brien, John
Ó Caitháin, Cian M.
O'Callaghan, Malachy
O'Connell, Cornelius F.
O'Connell, Helen
O'Connor, Brian
O'Connor, David
O'Connor, James George
O'Connor, Philip P.
O'Connor, Ruth Anne
O'Herlihy, Josephine C.
Olden, John M.
O'Leary, Elizabeth
O'Mahony, James G.
O'Mahony, Owen Richard

O'Neill, Anne
O'Riordan, Sheila
O'Scanaill, Domhnall
O'Shea Gerard
O'Shea, Karen
O'Sullivan, Owen F.
O'Sullivan, Paul
O'Sullivan, Pierce Donal
O'Sullivan, Tom
Phelan, Niamh
Phelan, Orla
Power, Della M.
Reynolds, Aidan
Reynolds, Imelda
Ruttle, Fiona
Ryan, Patrick
Smyth, Kenneth
Staunton, Anne
Stein, Stuart Norman
Tarrant, James Kirby
Taylor, Adam
Troy, Patrick
Turley, Anne
Twomey, John
Wade, Declan Joseph
Walsh, Robert
Whelan, Anne
Whelan, John P.
Williams, Derek P.
Wiseman, Andrew Paul
Woods, Damien
Woods, Thomas

1988

Ahern, Patrick M.
Allen, Kevin P.
Armstrong, Owen
Barr, Mark W.
Becker, Angela M.
Bourke, Robert A.
Boyd, Patricia M.
Branigan, Leo F.D.
Buckley, Fiona T.
Byrne, Shane M.
Byrne, Sharon A.
Callan, Christopher J.
Campbell, John A.
Cantrell, David J.
Carroll, Edward M.

Casey, David
Cassidy, Pamela M.
Coady, Gemma
Colbert Sharon M.
Coleman, Siobhan
Collins, Veronica
Connellan, Patrick M.
Conway, John M.
Cooney, Timothy M.
Corcoran, Gerard M.
Cosgrove, Martin P.
Counihan, Brendan
Crowley, Caroline
Cuddihy, Margaret
Culhane, Bridgetta Audrey
Daly, Fiona A.
Daly, Niall D.
Deegan, Denis R.
Devereux, Finbarr H.
Dolan, Eileen
Donegan, David P.
Doyle, Andrew B.
Doyle, Helen M.
Doyle, Rona
Dunne, Gerard
Fanning, James
Farrell, Niall P.
Feeney, Sheila M.
Fitzgerald, Bridget R.
Fitzgerald, Catherine M.C.
Fitzgerald, Jane M.
Fitzgibbon, Anne
Fitzjohn, Elizabeth
Fox, Thomas Joseph
Gallagher, Elizabeth A.
Gardiner, John L.
Garrett, Myra
Gibbons, Patrick A.
Giblin, Deirdre
Gill, Caroline
Gleeson, Maeve
Gleeson, Patricia
Glynn, Michael G.
Grennan, James G.
Griffin, John G.M.
Grogan, Fiona M.
Guilfoyle, Declan M.
Guiness, Mary-Paula
Hackett, Francis
Hally, Johanna
Harrington, Eamon G.

Hassett, Myles P.
Healy, Marion
Heffernan, Paul
Holihan, Sarah M.
Hutchinson, Mary Ann
Hyland, Anthony M.
Irwin, Katherine M.
Jones, Patrick
Joyce, Declan M.
Keane, Deirdre M.
Kearney, Paul
Kelly, Brian V.
Kelly, Geraldine
Kennedy, Sinead A.
Kennedy, William P.
Kinirons, John
Lambe, B. Verona
Lappin, Siobhan
Larkin, Hilary
Leahy, Patricia
Lydon, Karen
Lysaght, Dara A.
McCarthy, John G.
McDaid, John A.
McDonagh, Joseph
McDonnell, Kevin Conor
McEvoy, Thomas M.T.
McGennis, Paul
McGinley, Fionnuala
McGrath, Gerard
McHugh, Fiach C.
McInerney, Jarlath
McKeon, Jane
McKinney, Gerard
MacNamara, Adrian W.
McNamara Dermot F.
McQuillan, Peter
Malone, Deirdre A.
Maloney, Brendan
Mitchell, W. Alan J.
Mockler, Fiona F.
Molloy, Hilary P.
Molloy, Matthew J.
Mooney, Joseph T.
Muckian, Andrew J.
Murphy, Daniel M.
Murran, Niamh
Nally, Monica M.E.
Nolan, John V.
Nugent, Michael
O'Brien, Deirdre M.B.

O'Brien, Grainne T.
O'Brien, Michael J.
O'Brien, Patricia N.
O'Brien, Paul
O'Brien, Sean M.
O'Connell, Daniel
O'Connor, Catherine
O'Donoghue, Catriona
O'Driscoll, Elaine M.
Ó Dúlaing Feargal D.
O'Flynn, Emer
O'Gara, Aishling
O'Hagan, John B.
O'Hanlon, Peter J.A.
O'Hara, Michael D.
O'Leary, Patrick J.
O'Mahony, Patrick N.
O'Reilly, Aine
Pierse, Risteard J.
Pigot, Janet B.
Powderly, Niall
Power, David
Power, Stephanie M.
Price, Tracy M.
Quirke, Marie K.
Reedy, John J.
Reynolds, Anthony M.
Reynolds, Margaret C.
Reynolds, Miriam
Rochford, Catherine T.
Ronayne, Mary T.
Ryan, Peter
Ryan, Thomas M.
Scully, Margaret M.J.
Shannon, James
Sherlock, Mairead
Shields, Daniel J.
Stanley, Joseph P.
Stephenson, Ultan
Tierney, Ronan
Tooher, Catherine J.
Traynor, Joseph Arthur
Trueick, James G.J.
Twomey, Enda D.
Twomey, Frances
Walsh, Aileen M.G.
Walsh, Martina B.
Walsh, Michael J.
Ward, Mary T.P.
Warde, John D.
Watson, Stanley G.

Whittle, Fachtna J.
Wilkie, Richard Alan
Williams, Rory J.

1989

Allen, David B.
Barry, Pauline A.
Bergin, Mark M.
Binchy, Paul G.
Blaney, Neil M.
Bohan, Michael G.
Boland, Kieran P.
Brennan, D. Maria
Brennan, Patrick J.
Browne, David A.
Canning, Mary A.
Casserly, Peter
Coen, John G.
Coman, John J.
Connolly, Ronan A.
Conroy, Caroline P.
Conway, Jean
Corrigan, Michael P.
Cosgrove, Michael G.
Courtney, Orla L.
Cowhey, Patrick J.
Crawford, Alison J.
Cronin, Rosemary P.
Crowley, Deborah
Daly, Sharon A.
Donnelly, Peter F.
Dowling, Mary
Downey, John M.
Drummond, Stella T.
Duncan, John A.
Earley, Ursula M.
Farrell, Anne T.
Farrelly, Patrick G.
Feaheny, John E.
Fehily, Henry M.
Fennell, Justin F.
Finucane, Kevin G.
Fitzgerald, Helen T.
Fitzgerald, Norman P.
Fitzgibbon, Aisling M.
Fitzgibbon, Marc D.
Flynn, Ian M.
Fox, Sunniva E.
Geary, Michael A.

Gibbons, Alexander M.
Goff, John P.
Grace, Eleanor
Hanly, Elaine M.
Hatton, Catriona B.
Hayes, Loraine A.
Hegarty, Stephen
Hennessy, Robert P.
Hurley, Patrick A.
Hussey, Marc J.
Igoe, Patrick J.
Joyce, Elizabeth M.
Judge, Gordon V.
Kearney, Sinead M.
Keenan, Fiona E.
Kelleher, Katherine M.
Kelly, Edward A.
Kelly, Kevin
Kilcullen, Mary T.
Kilroy, John S.
Kissane, Deirdre M.
Leahy, Ann
Leahy, Bill
Loftus, Cliona M.
Lynch, Aidan J.
Lynch, David F.
Macaulay, Dylan M.
McDermott, Dermot G.
McDonnell, Sarah A.
McDonough, John A.
McGonagle, Patrick J.
McGonigle, Bernadette M.
McGovern, Gerard P.
McGrath, Rhona
McGroddy, Hugh V.
McKeever, Elizabeth A.
McKenna, Justin M.
McMahon, Brian P.
McMahon, Olive
McMahon, Patrick C.
MacNeill, Eoin
Maher, Peter V.
Malone, Leonora F.
Maloney, Patrick D.
Marren, Paul V.
Martin, Mary L.
Mee, Claire M.
Mehigan, Bartholomew M.
Minihan, Karen E.
Mooney, Henry A.
Mooney, Maxwell S.

Mulcahy, Fiona E.
Murphy, Angela
Murphy, John C.
Murphy, Thomas J.
Nagle, Eileen M.
Nolan, Caroline T.
Noonan, Stephen T.
Nuding, Michael R.
O'Connor, Angela B.
O'Connor, Una M.
O'Donnell, Muriel A.
O'Donnell, Una
O'Flaherty, Brendan T.
O'Hegarty, Diarmuid C.
O'Keeffe, Dolores
O'Keeffe, Susan M.
O'Meara, Kevin P.
O'Reilly, Deirdre A.
O'Sullivan, Owen D.
O'Sullivan, Terence J.
O'Sullivan, Timothy C.
O'Toole, Laurence N.
O'Toole, Patrick
Pearson, E. Roy
Prendergast, Eileen
Prendergast, Jacqueline A.M.
Quinn, Christopher J.
Rafferty, David J.
Reid, Colette J.M.
Roddy, Helen E.
Roe, Maura
Scully, Dermot J.
Shaw, John D.
Sheehan, Patrick C.
Shelly, Bairbre A.
Shipsey, Ruth E.
Smyth, Sinead M.
Spain, Edward O.
Tarpey, John R.
Tierney, Bridget M.
Toolan, Gabriel A.
Treacy, Timothy P.
Walker, Ciaran F.
Walsh, Bernadette
Ward, Elizabeth C.
Whelan, Paula M.

1990

Barr, Daphne A.
Barrett, Anna Marie

Barry, Colm C.
Barry, Gillian A.
Beatty, Walter
Beirne, Nola M.
Blake, Finola A.
Bolger, Ciaran D.C.
Booth, Laura B.
Bourke, Mary G.
Boyce, Richard P.
Brady, Michael P.
Branigan, John M.
Brooks, Eileen M.
Browne, Robert F.
Buckley, Gavin S.
Burke, Marie G.
Cadell, Patrick J.
Cahill, Brendan M.
Casey, Kenneth M.
Casey, Mary B.
Cashman, Mairead M.
Cassidy, Francis H.
Cody, Andrew J.
Cogan, Anna B.
Collins, Caoive M.
Coonan, Hilary
Coyne, Ursula M.
Creaton, Donal M.
Cronin, Finola K.
Cronin, Mary N.
Crossan, Anna G.
Crowley, Anne-Marie
Crowley, Margaret M.
Crowley, Mary J.
Cuffe, Mary M.
Curran, Sheila V.
Curtis, Mary Rose
Deane, Gregory J.
Dee, Alice M. (Alma)
Dempsey, Paul P.
Dillon, Brendan J.
Doggett, Sheena M.
Dolan, Maureen P.
Donaghy, Edel L.
Donovan, St. John
Dorrian, Francis
Duffy, Marguerite M.
Dunne, Deirdre M.
Dunne, Geoffrey J.
Dwyer, John A.
Fagan, Joan F.
Farrelly, Mary B.
Fennelly, Loraine J.

Foley, David E.T.
Foy, James J.
Furey, Dermot T.
Gantly, Rosemary
Gardiner, Patrick D.
Garrett, Kathleen
Gilmer, Yvonne R.
Gleeson, Gillian M.
Gleeson, Susan
Halpenny, Conor M.
Hanley, Donal P.
Hanley, Mark E.
Hanley, Melvyn
Hawkshaw, Mary
Hennessy, Grainne
Heslin, Mary M.
Hickey, James C.
Howard, David C.
Hurley, David F.J.
Keane, Aine M.
Kelly, Fiona N.
Kelly, J. Denise
Kelly, Redmond E.
Kenny, Deirdre M.
Kenny, Siobhan E.
Keohane, Jacqueline T.
Kirrane, Keelin B.M.
Lee, Richard P.
Lynch, Katherine D.
Lynch, Maria B.
Lyng, Toni
McAleese, Simon C.
McCann, Margaret A.
McDermott, Brian W.
MacDonnell, Louise
McDonnell, Seamus R.
McEntee, Joan T.
Mac Fhearadhaigh, Padraic C.
McGeough, David J.
McGillycuddy, Miriam B.
McGuinness, Donough
McIver, Frances M.
McKnight, Paul A.J.
Maguire, Sheila
Maher, Ailish A.
Marren, Hilary A.
Meagher, Gerald P.
Meenan, Anne C.
Molloy, M. Jean
Moloney, Patrick
Mooney, Micheal G.
Moore, Alison P.

Moran, Margaret M.
Moran Truetzschler, Roslyn
Morrissey, Daniel J.
Morrissey, Patrick S.
Muldoon, Eamonn P.
Mullen, J. Fergus
Murphy, Brendan A.
Murphy, Catherine L.
Murphy, Eimear V.
Murphy, Michele G.M.
Nally, Kieran P.N.
Ní Ghloinn, Grainne N.
Nugent, Peter J.
O'Brien, Andrew
O'Brien, Eva M.
O'Callaghan, Conor P.
O'Connell, Anne P.
O'Connor, Philip J.
O'Donovan, Christine M.
O'Hanlon, Gerard E.
O'Hanrahan, Eamon F.
O'Leary, Timothy F.
O'Neill, Siobhan C.
O'Reilly, Conleth M.
O'Reilly, Margaret A.
O'Riordan, Stephen A.
O'Shaughnessy, Nevan J.
O'Sullivan, Jerome P.
Parker, Roy W.
Plunkett, Peter F.
Power, Peter J.
Quirk, Catherine M.
Quirke, William A.
Rainsberry, Linda G.
Rainsford, Caroline M.C.
Reynolds, Fiona V.
Rice, Nora
Riordan, Thomas C.
Robinson, Evelyn
Ryan, Catherine A.
Ryan, Denise V.
Simon, Ian W.
Skinnader, Anne
Smyth, Ivan F.
Stack, Catherine M.
Stone, Valentine W.S.
Sweeney, Bridget M.
Taylor, Gideon
Turner, Beverly F.
Twomey, Fiona M.A.
Twomey, Michael
Upton, Mary B.

Waddington, Rebecca E.
Walker, Stephen A.D.
Walsh, Mary B.
White, Paul E.

1991

Ainley, Jonathan N.
Austin, Anna
Beegan, Paul
Black, Niall P.
Black, Terence R.W.
Blake, Madeleine R.
Bradley, Raymond J.
Branigan, Patrick
Brooks, Kathryn E.
Brophy, Grainne C.
Burke, David R.
Burke, John J.
Burke, John P.
Burke, Paula E.
Butler, Isobel
Byrne, Thomas
Cahill, Matthew P.
Callan, Margaret
Carney, Michael
Carroll, Fiona
Carroll, William T.F.
Casey, Rory
Clancy, Niall J.
Colbert, David
Collins, Daniel F.
Comerford, Joseph M.
Compton, Alicia
Conlon, James P.
Connolly, Kieran G.
Connolly, Norville J.
Connolly, Seamus C.
Conroy, Marie
Conway, Barry T.
Cooney, Patrice
Courtney, Deirdre M.
Coyle, Peter
Crean, Geraldine M.
Crowley, C. Kevin
Cunnane, Bernard P.
Cunningham, Niall
Dee, Marianne
de Foubert, Sarah
Delaney, Miriam

Dillon, Kieran
Donnelly, Mary M.
Donovan, William P.
Downes, Seamus P.
Doyle, Terence M.
Doyle, Una M.
Duffy, Catherine
Egan, Aiffric M.
Egan, Caroline M.
Elliot, John B.
Evans, Edward N.
Faherty, Cormac
Falconer, James
Farrell, Alison
Farrell, Angela C.
Fenton, David
Fitzpatrick, Aidan
Flynn, Margaret
Forwood, William G.L.
Foskin, Paul N.
Fraser, Malcolm
Galvin, Brian
Gavin, Mary Teresa
Geraghty, Gearoid C.
Giles, W. Michael
Gowan, Frances Melissa
Greaney, Adrian
Guy, Catherine M.
Hackett, William
Halpin, Lilian
Hammond, David J.
Hanley, Agnes M.
Hargaden, Edel H.
Harlow, Conleth G.
Hegarty, James (Séamus) M.
Heron, Robert
Hickey, Kevin J.
Hodgins, Duncan
Hogan, Denis
Howard, Lynda H.
Hughes, Brian D.
Hughes, Margaret Magdalen
Hussey, John
Keane, Michael
Keaney, Ciaran J.
Kelly, Concepta B.
Kelly, Thomas S.
Kennedy, Eamonn
Kennedy, Francis
Kennedy, Margaret M.
Kidney, Anne Marie
Kilroy, Helen C.

Kinahan, Harriet J.
Kinsella-Leavy, Carmel
Kirwan, Catherine
Kirwan, Noirin A.
Kirwan, Valentine Alan
Lane, Eimear M.
Lawless, Patricia H.
Leech, Anne
Lennon, Cynthia M.
Leonard, Oliver J.
Linehan, Anne-Marie
Loftus, Rosemarie J.
Lynch, Fiona
Lyons, Marcella
Lyons, Stephen
McCarthy, Catherine A.
MacCarthy, Finbarr
McCleery, Samuel M.
McDonald, Paul A.
McEvoy, Declan J.
McEvoy, Dermot F.
MacGabhann, Frank
McGinley, Laura T.
McGovern, Mary Rose
McGowan, Conor J.
McGreevy, Kevin D.
McGuinness, Donal H.
McHale, Marion Anne
McKeague, M. Patricia
McKenna, Mary P.
McKnight, John D.
MacNamara, Michael D.
Madigan, Maria T.
Maher, Daniel J.A.
Martin, Richard
Martyn, Thomas A.
Millard, Alan E.F.
Miller, Peter S.
Moloney, Aoifean M.
Muldowney, Edel
Mulholland, Liam J.
Murphy, Alan G.
Naessens, Paul F.
Neary, Barbara M.
Neville, Richard
Nolan, Sean C.
Noonan, Michael H.
Nunan, Jean Marie (Sinead)
O'Beirne, Fiona M.
O'Brien, Miriam
O'Connell, Julia C.
O'Connor, Columba M.

O'Connor, Jeremiah J.
O'Connor, Kieran
O'Connor, Michael J.
O'Dea, Elizabeth
O'Doherty, Moya J.
O'Donnell, Michael M.
O'Donoghue, Kevin
O'Donovan, Aine B.
O'Driscoll, Neil
O'Hanlon, Ursula
O'Keeffe, Eugene A.
O'Keeffe, Sarah
O'Mahoney, Ruth I.
O'Regan, Fergus
O'Reilly, Aideen
O'Scanaill, Mairéad
O'Sullivan, Franklin D.
O'Toole, Gerald
O'Toole, Padraig
Phillips, Marguerite
Prendiville, T. Gerard
Quinn, Niall J.
Reardon, June
Roberts, Eileen A.
Ruane, Brian
Ryan, Gabrielle
Ryan, Mary S.
Ryan, Tionette
Salmon, Helen
Sarney, Jon M.
Scanes, Roland P.
Scanlon, Timothy
Sheehan, David
Sheils, Theodore J.
Simms, Maurice H.
Smalley, Edward J.
Smith, Philip Howard
Staines, Catherine A.
Stelfox, John B.
Stewart, Brian J.C.
Stuttard, John J.
Sweeney, Theresa M.
Sykes, James P.
Thomas, David
Trainor, Gerard
Twomey, Robert
Tynan, Barbara A.M.
Varley, Martin J.
Walsh, A.C. Elizabeth
Walsh, Anne T.
Walsh, Marianne E.
Walsh, Mary

Walsh, Rosalind M.
Warren, Niamh M.
Williams, Anthony
Wolsey, James S.
Wood, David Henry Charles
Woods, Michael P.

1992

Bannon, Dominic F.
Barker, Gary L.
Bates, Andrew J.
Bergin, M. Patricia
Boland, Dympna
Bourke, Mairead
Bowen, Adrienne
Boylan, Helena A.
Bradley, Patrick J.
Brazil, Liam P.
Breen, Eithne S.
Brennan, Adrian T.
Brennan, Orla M.
Brennan, Paul D.
Breslin, John
Butler, Liam J.
Byrne, Daragh M.
Cahill, Dermot V.
Campbell-Crowley,
   Margaret M.
Carney, Hannah F.
Carney, Liam
Carolan, Brian F.
Cass, Kathleen A.
Cassidy, Susan P.
Cawkhill, Fionnuala
Cawley, Cormac T.
Christie, David H.
Clancy, Brian P.
Clarke, Andrew G.
Clarke, David
Coffey, Geraldine M.
Coffey-Moylan, Helene
Coggans, Stephanie M.
Collins, Denise A.
Collins, John J.
Collins, Michael J.
Collins, Michael W.
Collins, Stella C.
Condon, Ursula N.
Confrey, Anne
Courtney, Thomas B.

Crean-Lynch, Andrew
Cremin, Rose
Cronin, Helen M.
Crowe, Brian P.
Cuff, Thomas
Curran, Mary Lorraine
Daly, Daragh B.
Daly, Sharon C.
Davis, Alan P.
Davis, John M.
Day, William B.C.
Dennehy, Fergal T.
Derby, Brian M.
Devine, Joseph R.
Diggin, Patrick J.
Dineen, Peter G.
Dockry, James V.
Dodd, Fiona E.
Dolan, C.M. Majella
Donnelly, Timothy P.
Donohoe, M. Therese
Doody, James G.(Séamus)
Dooley, Shane N.
Doran, Sharon A.
Dowd, Lorcan P.
Dowling, Shane
Downey-Monaghan, Anne
Doyle, John F.
Duffy, C. Sinead
Duggan, Declan H.
Dundon, James St. John
Dunne, Eugene P.
Dwane, Aonghus M.G.
Eberl, Walter
Fahy, Peter F.J.
Falvey, Diarmaid F.
Feerick, Rita A.
Felton, D. Mark
Fennell, Garrett J.
Fitzgerald, Anne N.
Fitzgerald, John G.
Fitzgerald, Vanessa J.
Flynn, Declan F.
Foley, Emily M.
Freehill, Finola M.
Furlong, Patricia F.
Gallagher, Ailbhe M.
Gallagher, Ann M.
Gallagher, John
Gallagher, Joseph
Galligan, Claire B.
Gannon, K. Alan P.

Garvey, Grace A.
Garvey, Hugh P.
Gearty, Liadhan G.
Geraghty, Patrick J.B.
Giblin, Aileen M.
Glenfield, Paul E.
Gogan, Lorcan
Goodwin, Patrick M.
Gormally, Edel M.
Griffin, Patrick B.
Hallinan, Thomas P.
Hamilton, Patricia M.
Hamilton, Rita M.
Hannon, Michael Philip
Hardy, Thomas G.
Harte, Stanislaus V.
Hassett, Mark
Hayes, Edmund (Eamonn) P.
Hayes, John G.
Healy, Fiona M.
Healy, Timothy G.
Heatherington, Paul
Hennessy, Maura E.
Hession, David P.
Higgins, Benjamin J.
Hill, Suzanne P.
Hogan, Stephen P.
Holland, John D.
Hutchinson, Florence M.
Hyland, Mark L.
Hynes, Carmel M.
Irwin, Richard A.
James, Michael H.
Johnson, Mary J.
Joyce, Anthony J.
Keane, Catherine M.
Keane, David P.
Keane, Shane F.
Kearney, Carmel C.
Kearney, Matthew H.
Kearns, Eugene P.
Keating, David G.M.
Kelleher, Ann
Kelly, Anne D.
Kelly, Joseph N.
Kelly, Patrick F.
Kennedy, Owen R.
Kennedy, Thomas P.
Kent, Anita G.
Kinane, Caitriona A.
Lacy, William M.
Laffan, David

Larkin, Sile M.
Lawless, Judith A.
Leahy, David S.
Leech, Monika M.
Little, Paul M.
Loftus, Claire G.
Loftus, Sheelagh M.
Loughlin, Ambrose D.
Loughrey, Hugh R.
Louth, Edmund F.
Lowry, Eleanor
Lydon, David J.
Lynch, John K.
Lyons, Deirdre A.
Lyons, Linda A.
McAleenan, Fiona T.
McArdle, Sharon E.
McCann, Olivia M.
McCarthy, Annette T.
McCarthy, Brian L.
McCarthy, Manya E.
Mac Cinna, Siona
Mackey, James H.M.
McCormack, Vincent J.
McCourt, Ciaran G.
McCrystal, Anne Marie
MacDonagh, Sean
McDonald, Daragh F.
McGahon, Conor O.
McGeever-Glynn, Bernadette
Mac Giollarnath, Sean R.
McGovern, Anthony
McGrath, Daniel G.
McGuire, Colm S.
McHugh, Paula
McKay, Fiona E.
McKeever, Thomas A.J.
McKeogh, Margaret M.
McMahon, Ralph A.
McManus, Francis J.
McMullin, Brian J.
McNally, C. Una
McShane, Patrick Rory
Madigan, Paraic T.
Maguire, Barbara M.
Maher, Patrick J.
Maher, Thomas F.
Mangan, Ann B.
Manley, Helena M. (Linda)
Markey, Mary-Claire
Mascarenhas, Alexander
  G.F.A.

Maume, Jerome J.
Meehan, Bridgette
Moloney, James P.
Moore, Cornelius William
   (Liam)
Morris, M. Lorraine
Morris, Michelle M.
Moylan, Olivia P.M.
Mulhern, Ann Fiona
Mullany, Conor P.
Murphy, James A.
Murphy, John F.
Murphy, Kevin J.
Murphy, William James
Murray, Robert G.
Nealon, Ann E.
Neary, Kevin J.P.
Newman, Thomas P.
Ní Cruadhlaoich, Máire E.
Ní Dhuinnín, Mairéad T.
Ní Ghallchóir, Máire Áine
Nolan, Margaret A.
Noone, Angela M.
O'Boyle, Dervilla M.
O'Boyle, Michele A.
O'Brien, Niall G.
O'Brien, Nicola M.
O'Byrne, Michael J.
O'Carroll, John A.
Ó Céidigh, Muiris P.
Ó Céidigh, Pádraig J.
O'Connell, Declan J.A.
O'Connell, John A.
O'Connell, Michael Louis
O'Connell, William Kieran
O'Connor, Kevin F.
O'Connor, Marie Benedicte
O'Connor, Michael J.
   (Séamus)
O'Connor, Nora T.
O'Dea, Orla B.
O'Donnell, David E.
O'Donnell, Maria M.
O'Driscoll, Catherine M.
O'Driscoll, Maeve R.
O'Driscoll, Margaret Ann
O'Dwyer, Sharon B.
O'Farrell, Rosemary
O'Grady, M. Carmel
O'Leary, Timothy G.
O'Malley, Catherine A.
   (Karen)

O'Malley, Thomas P.
O'Meara, Finbar (Barry) G.
O'Neill, Anne M.
O'Neill, Karen M.
O'Neill, Maria C.
O'Neill, Orla A.
O'Neill, Ronan G.
Ong, Michele S.
O'Regan, Thomas A.
O'Reilly, Brendan P.G.
O'Reilly, Gerard J.P.
O'Reilly, J. Fintan
O'Reilly, Kevin E.
O'Riordan, Patricia M.
Osborne, Peter J.
Oscroft, Stephen G.J.
O'Sullivan, Declan
O'Sullivan, Joseph M.F.
Pendred, Aideen M.
Plunkett, Cliona R.
Potter, William Mark
Purtill, Mary C.
Quinn, Dervla M.
Quinn, John M.
Quirk, Michael J.
Redmond, Patrick J.
Rennick, Brian A.
Roberts, Colm L.
Robinson, Dara
Roche, Paul M.
Ryan, Donal T.
Ryan, Pearse T.
Salmon, Orla B.
Scott, John (Seán) P.
Sexton, Aoife A.
Shiel, Michael G.
Small, Lucy A.
Smith, Donal S.
Smith, Sinead O.
Spillane, Michelle A.
Staines, James
Stelfox, Fiona M.
Sweeney, James P.
Taaffe, Donal J.
Tansey, Margaret E.M.
Thornton, Benedict Hugh
Tiernan, Thomas E.
Tobin, Mary E.
Tucker, Suzanne M.
Turner, Seamus G.
Vaughan, Caroline P.
Vollans, Timothy

Wallace, Thomas P.
Walsh, Canice M.
Walsh, John F.
Walsh, Mary A.
Walsh, Maurice A.
Ward, Denis E.
Ware, Dorothy M.
Waters, David G.
Whelan, John
Williams, David J.H.

1993

Ahern, John C.
Austin, Margaret M.
Barron, Frances E.
Barton, John (Seán) E.J.
Battles, John J.
Baynes, Michael J.
Beausang, Nora B.
Begley, Maura D.
Begley, Stephen G.
Bell, David A.
Berry, Conleth A.
Black, Declan J.
Black, Maureen P.
Blaney, Anne-Marie
Bothwell, Elizabeth R.
Bourke, Bryan W.
Boyce, Paul
Boylan, Ronan E.A.
Boylan, Suzanne F.
Boyle, Mary W.
Brady, Helena M.
Brehony, Mary T.
Brennan, Fiona
Brennan, John Gerald (Seán)
Brosnan, Julie A.
Budds, Conan P.
Burke, M. Bernadette A.
Burke, Pauline M.
Butler, Grainne M.
Byers, David J.
Byrne, Thomas G.
Callan, Elaine
Cantwell, Patricia E.
Carney, Thomas F.
Clarke, Philip A.
Clinch, Brendan P.
Coldrick, A. Mary B.

Coleman, Carina
Coleman, John P.
Colgan, Louise M.
Collins, Bridget (Brid) H.
Collins, M. Yvonne
Collins, Margaret B.
Connolly, Brian M.
Connolly, Enda J.
Connolly, Maura C.
Cooney, Mary A.
Cooney, Thomas A.
Corcoran, Jennifer A.
Corry, Mary H.
Costello, Gerardine C.
Cottle, Philippa J.
Courtney, Ian P.J.
Cronin, Andrew Aidan
Cronnelly, Patricia M.
Crowley, Emma L.
Crowley, P. Aidan
Crowley, Patrick A.
Cullen, David
Cunneen, Brian F.
Cunningham, Diarmuid P.
Curtin, Jennifer
Curtis, Neil G.
Cussen, Deirdre
Cussen, Robert A.
Daly, Frances Siobhan
Danaher, Mairead T.
Deale, Kenneth E.
Deasy, Orla M.
Dodd, Ronan P.
Donnelly, Maura C.
Donohoe, James M.
Downey, Conor W.
Doyle, Timothy M.
Drury, Carol M.
Edwards, Carol Ann
Egan, Majella M.
Eustace, Nuala M.
Evoy, Geraldine M.(Bernice)
Fahey, W. Joseph
Farrell, Michael F.
Fish, Derek J.
Fitzgerald, Emmet B.
Fitzgerald, Paul E.N.
Fitzgibbon, Bronagh L.
Fitzpatrick, Josephine P.
Fitzpatrick, Paul G.
Fitzsimons, Cora M.G.
Foley, Veronica B.

Forde, Siobhan M.
Fox, Deirdre
Gallagher, Maire B.
Gargan, Noel J.
Geaney, Patrick P.
Geoghegan Conway, Kevin
Geraghty, John L.
Gibbons, David F.
Gibbons, Thomas G.
Gilmartin, Charles
Gilvarry, Ailbhe M.
Gleasure, Michael F.
Glendon, Conor J.A.
Glynn, Tara J.
Goggins, Mary B.
Gohery, Anne M.
Gollogley, James S.
Greene, Bernadette M.
Greene, Michael G.D.
Griffey, Hilary M.
Hannon, Francis M.
Harhen, Geraldine M.
Harty, Sandra M.
Hasson, William J.
Hayden, M. Aideen
Heaney, Terence F.
Hederman, Wendy
Heneghan, Thomas P.
Hennessy, Andrew P.
Hennessy, Yvonne C.
Henry, Donna S.
Hickey, Caroline A.
Hilliard, Barry M.
Hoare, M. Aileen
Hoey, Aisling M.
Horgan, Mary
Horrigan, Christopher W.
Huey, Thomas E.W.
Hughes, Damien J.
Hunter, Katherine J.
Hurley, Daniel P.
Hynes, Geraldine A.
Jameson, C. Raymond
Johnston, Paul J.
Kahn, Julian Max
Keane, Daragh M.
Kearns, Shauna M.
Keeler, Michael
Keenan, Padraig G.
Kehoe, Ciara B.
Kehoe, John A.J.
Kelleher, Anne

Kelleher, Denis N.
Kelly, Eileen M.
Kelly, Mary P.
Kennedy, Daniel T.
Kennedy, Joseph E.
Kennedy, Liam A.
Keogan, Aileen D.
Keogh, Bernard W.
Kiely, Brian D.
Killoran-Coyne, Mary C.
Kilraine, Anne M.
King, John G.
Kingston, Garrett F.
Kirwan, Ciaran S.
Lambe, Shiela Felicity
  (Aoibheann)
Landers, Nora M.
Lawlor, Mary T.
Leahy, Deirdre C.
Leavy, Louise
Leech, Michael C.
Lennon, Aidan D.
Lennon, Maire
Leufer, Mary Ruth
Liston, Patrick T.
Loftus, Katherine P.
Long, Michael David
Lord, Mark P.
Louth, Pauline M.
Lowe, Nicholas A.
Lupton, Aisling M.
Lydon, Fiona M.
Lynch, William (Liam) J.
McCarthy, Aeneas
McCarthy, Fergus P.
McCarthy, Finola H.C.
McCloughan, D. Marshall
McCluskey, Dara M.J.
McConnell, Seamus P.
McCormack, Brendan J.
McCoy, Brigid (Brid) M.
McCrann, Donal M.
McDowell, John Paul
McErlean, Kevin H.P.
McFadden, Grace
McGarry, Rory M.
McGovern, Sheila M.
McGowan, Donagh P.
McGrath, Helena J.
McGreevy, Gerard J.
McKnight, Peter
MacMahon, Dara

McMahon, Paul G.
McNamara, Yvonne A.
McNeece, Sylvia M.
Madden, David M.
Maguire, Deborah M.
Maher, James J.
Mahon, Frances M.
Mahon, John A. (Seán)
Malone, Grainne
Matthews, Peter E.
Meade, John J.
Mee, Michael D.
Molloy, Patrick J.
Moore, Helen Marie
Moore, Rosemary B.
Moran, Deirdre M.
Moriarty, Susan
Morrin, Robert Joseph
Morrison, Richard K.M.
Morrissey, Laura B.
Mullan, Peter T.
Mullooly, Paula F.
Mulroe, Jacqueline A.
Murphy, Anthony S.D.
Murphy, Dermot J.
Murphy, Mark R.
Murphy, Padraig L.
Murphy, Patrick
Murphy, Robert F.
Murphy, Sandra
Murphy, Siobhan M.
Nagle-Casey, Lillian M.
Nagle, Maria Ann
Nic Aodha Bhui, Colma
Ní Cheallaigh, Antoinette
Ní Mhuineacháin, Moirín
Nolan, Paul K.
Norton, Therese F.
O'Beirne, Patricia M.
O'Brien, Anthony J.
O'Brien, Edel M.
O'Brien, Mary M.
O'Brien, Mary S.
O'Brien, Patrick J.
O'Carroll, Donal G.
O'Connell, Kevin J.
O'Connell, M. Deborah
O'Connell, Orla M.
O'Connor, Deirdre C.
O'Connor, Eamonn
O'Connor, Edward T.
O'Connor, Francis E.

O'Connor, John C.
O'Donnell, Finola W.
O'Donnell, Sally-Ann B.
O'Donoghue, Brídín
O'Donovan, Jacinta Karen
O'Driscoll, Niamh M.
O'Dwyer, Maire P.
O'Gorman, John A.
O'Gorman, John F.
O'Gorman, Sean L.
O'Grady, Anthony G.
O'Grady, Michael J.
O'Halloran, Rosalind C.
O'Hanlon, Finola B.
O'Loughlin, Michael D.
O'Mahony, Anne P.
O'Reilly, Caroline M.
O'Riordan, Helen Margaret
O'Shea, David G.
O'Shea, Linda A.
O'Shea-Grewcock,
    Margaret M.
O'Sullivan, Catherine Claire
O'Sullivan, Donal J.V.
O'Sullivan, James G.
O'Sullivan, John J.
O'Toole, Conor P.
Palmer, Nicola M.
Pheifer, Nicholas J.
Pierse, Riobard A.
Poole, Edel E.
Power, Margot M.
Power, Patrick
Power, Vincent J.G.
Prior, John P.
Quinlan, Ursula M.
Quinn, Colm B.
Quinn, Joan E.
Quirke, Niamh M.
Rafter, Carmel M.A.
Reedy, Niamh M.
Ring, Margaret M.
Roe, Seamus G.
Rogan, Estella M.
Rogers, Paul A.
Ryan, Niamh P.
Scanlon, James
Shaw, Matthew V.
Sheahan, Aine
Sheehan, Eileen P.
Sheeran, Denis
Sheridan, Eithne C.M.

Sheridan, Maurice H.
Sheridan, Patrick J.
Shinnick, Michael J.
Slattery, Maeve A.
Stokes, Amanda R.
Toolan, David P.
Travers, Deirdre M.
Treacy, Michael M.
Turner, Andrew N.
Twomey, Lynda M.
Twomey, Sean A.
Tynan, Rita B.
Tyrrell, Roderick P.
Wall, Pamela
Wallace, James A.
Walsh, Aidan P
Walsh, Annelie
Walsh, David M.
West, Andrew
Whittle, Declan M.
Wolfe, Gabrielle
Young, Catherine M.

1994

Acton, Louise A.
Ainscough, David P.A.
Allen, Nigel D.
Aylmer, William L.J.
Baird, Ronan P.
Behan, Sinead A.
Blake, Kieran
Blanchfield, Yvonne E.
Bleahene, Eleanor J.
Bohan, Daragh B.
Bolger, M. Yvonne
Bourke, Jacinta M.
Bourke, John H.
Bourke, W.M. Louise
Bowen, Gwendolen M.
Brady, Danella J.
Brady, Pauline E.
Breen, Garrett P.
Breen, Renate B.
Breslin, Matthew J.
Burke, Karl E.
Burke, Lorraine M.
Burke, Senan P.
Byrne, Tracy H.
Caldwell, Martin
Callanan, Daniel J.

Campbell, Brenda M.
Canavan, Aidan Anthony
Canty, Jeremiah M.
Carney, Eamonn V.
Carney, Karl M.
Carnson, George Andrew
Carolan, Paul G.
Carroll, Sharon
Carter, Ann C.
Carty, Hugh Gavan
Clarke, Ann-Marie
Clarke, Hilary N.
Classon, Jessica M.
Coady, Brian D.
Coffey, A.M. John
Coleman, Claire R.
Collier, Joseph T.
Collins, Dorothy
Comyn, Brendan T.G.
Conlon, A.M. Dariona
Connellan, Ann Marie
Connellan, Patricia M.
Connolly, Marlene A.
Conway, Brian L.
Cormack, Meriel J.
Cosgrave, Patrick F.
Costello, David
Cotter, Barbara
Cotter, Margaret (Mairead) A.
Coughlan, Noel Kieran
Courtney, Padraic E.
Crawford, Anne I.
Cregan, Niamh C.
Cromie, Caroline Sharon
Cronin, Padraig J.
Cryan, Geraldine M.
Cullen, Claire A.
Cunningham, Maire G.
Curran, Sara C.
Daly, Charles C.
Daly, Jacqueline A.
Daly, Philip D.
Dawson, Christine
Dempsey, Angela R.
Devitt, Anne E.M.
Dolan, Angela M.
Donnellan, Isabel F.
Donnelly, Ann M.
Donnelly, Anne
Doyle, Alan S.
Doyle, Jeremiah J.M.F.G.
Doyle, Olive A.

Duffy, Sighle M.G.
Duffy, Siobhan M.
Dunleavy, Cormac P.
Dunne, Donal M.
Durcan, Jacqueline M.
Dwyer, Joanne M.
Enright, Elizabeth A.
Eustace, James P.
Farrell, Michael P.
Feddis, Maria Clare
Finnegan, Emer M.
Fitzgerald, John F.
Flanigan, Annetta J.M.
Flannelly, Joan M.
Fleming, Aileen G.
Fleming, Bridget M. (Breda)
Flynn, James C.
Flynn, William Gerard
Foley, Fiona M.
Foley, John G.
Foley, Patrick G.
Foster, Caroline M.
Gaffney, John P.
Gallagher, Conor B.
Gannon, Patrick A.
Gardiner, Caterina
Geary, Johanna M.
Gillespie, Patrick J.
Glasgow, Sinead F.
Graham, Mark F.
Greene, John William
Greene, Mary B. (Brid)
Griffith, Geraldine M.
Hall, Mary B.
Hamer, Philip C.
Hanglow, James J.
Hanlon, Graham D.N.
Harrington, Sinead A.M.
Harte, John G.
Hartnett, Cormac J.
Haughey, Caoimhe M.
Healy, Fergus
Healy, M. Connie
Heenan, Brona M.
Heffernan, Lorraine C.J.
Heneghan, Ann M.
Heneghan, Nuala M.
Herity, Bairbre M.
Heverin, Bronagh A.
Higgins, Orla M.
Higgins Whelan, Helen M.J.
Hodgins, David W.

Holroyd, W. Andrew M.
Horan, Raymond J.P.
Horan, Sara A.
Houlihan, Ann M.
Houlihan, Sinead M.
Hourihane, Anne Marie
Hughes, Cora F.
Hughes, Kimberley G.
Hunt, Emer C.
Hunter, Hilary Ruth
Hurley, Raymond T.
Hyde, Joanne P.
Hynes, June E.
Jackson, Joanna L.M.
Jackson, Michael G.
Johnston, Brian J.
Joyce, Oliver David
Keane, Marie A.
Keenan, Neil E.
Kelliher, Edward B.
Kelliher, Eileen P.
Kelliher, Simon T.
Kelly, Anne M.
Kelly-Martin, Mary M.
Kennedy, Dorothy A.
Kennedy, Patrick C.
Kennedy, Shane R.
Kennedy, Una M.
Kenny, Teresa B.
Keogh, Anthony P.
Kidney, Judith M.
Kiely, Helena M.
Kilraine, John J.
King, Nicola M.
Kirrane, Michael J.P.
Kirwan, Denise M.
Lally, Fiona M.
Lanigan, Katherine (Jane)
Lawlor, Declan J.
Leader, Kathleen M.
Leahy, Frances M.
Lee, Fiona M.
Lee, Gearoid (Gary) E.
Leonard, Grainne M.
Leonard, Michelle (Shelley) A.
Lett, Paul G.
Logue, Anne Marie
Lordan, Anne E.
Lucey, John Douglas
Lynch, Catherine M.
Lynch, Gillian G.
Lynn, Michael T.

McArdle, M. Elizabeth
McCarthy, John J.A.
McCarthy, Stephanie M.
McCarthy, Thomas J.
MacCormack, Finbarr N.
McCourt, Declan G.
McDermott, John C.
McEvoy, Peter J.
McFarren, Elizabeth A.
McGeever, Jeanette M. (Jenny)
McGettigan, Anthony
MacGinley, Catherine A.
McGlynn, John B.
McGovern, Niamh M.
McGowan, Deirdre E.
McGrane, Brian S.
McIntosh, Jennifer P.
McMahon, Desmond L.
McMahon, Mary G. (Mai)
McManus, Lisa M.
McPartland, Henry P.
McPartland, Patrick
McWalter, Claire A.
Maitland Hudson, Alexis P.
Mannion, Rosy N.
Manson, Gara C.M.
Marsh, Aidan C.
Martin, Kevin P.
Meagher, Philip C.
Meagher, Tara P.
Meenan, Alva P.
Molloy, Mary Rose
Moloney, Michael G.
Moroney, Elaine C.
Mulpeter, Margaret M.
Mulroy, James
Murnane, Jane E.
Murphy, Cornelius Noel
Murphy, Daniel A.
Murphy, Paula E.
Murray, James A.
Murray, Jane M.
Murray, Tracey M.
Nagle, Brendan P.
Nicholson, Linda A.
Ní Dhubhghaill,
    Grainne M.M.
Nolan, Tracie M.
Nyland, Mary N.G.
O'Beirne, Barry M.J.
O'Brady, Kevin
O'Brien, James

O'Brien, Jane A.
O'Brien, Joan C.M.
O'Brien, Maria K.
O'Brien, Shane P.
O'Callaghan, Cornelius R.
    (Rory)
O'Connor, Patricia A.
O'Donnell, Anthony B. (Barry)
O'Donnell, Evelyn H.
O'Donnell, John R.G.
O'Donoghue, Shane J.G.
O'Donovan, Donnacha
O'Dowd, Caroline
O'Driscoll, Jeremiah F.
    (Dermot)
O'Dwyer, Niamh E.
O'Gorman, Kevin J.
O'Keeffe, Gail A.
O'Leary, Bridget M.
O'Mahony, Mary M.
O'Mahony, Nora M.
O'Malley, Sharon A.
O'Neill, Ann
Ong, Henry Seng-Lit
O'Reilly, Mary Patricia
O'Reilly, Sarah M.
O'Reilly, Tara H.M.
O'Shea, Carmel H.
O'Sullivan, Charmaine C.
O'Sullivan, John C.
O'Sullivan, John S.
O'Toole, Rachel
Owens, Eileen M.
Owens, Elizabeth Deirdre
Owens, Ursula G.
Phelan, Finbarr A.
Powell, Dermot E.J.
Purcell, Breen J.F.
Queally, E. Marie Louise
Quinn, Kevin J.
Quinn, Niamh C.M.
Quinn, Padraig C.
Quinn, Ronan P.
Rahman, Rebecca M.
Reilly, Bernadette M.
Richardson, Paula R.
Riordan, Margaret Valerie
Riordan, William M. (Liam)
Roche, Fiona M.
Roche, Juliette E.
Roe, Brian A.
Royston, David B.

Ruane, Caroline M.
Rush, Andrew P.
Rushe, Brenda M.
Ryan, Donal G.
Ryan, Catherine M.A.
Ryan, Eamonn M.
Ryan, Timothy J.
Scully, D. Emmet
Shaw, Matthew J.
Sheehan, Eileen
Sheridan, Martina T.
Singleton, Therese M.
Smyth, Donal G.
Spain, Justin F.
Spillane, Patrick J.
Sweeney, Regina M.
Teahan, Nuala M.G.
Tobin, Deirdre M.
Tuohy, Comhnall
Walsh, Catherine M.
    (Catríona)
Walsh, Nicola M.
Ward, Mark J.
Watters, James G.
Weir, Nichola Alicia
Williams, Oran P.
Wise, Peter S.
Woulfe, Katherine E.

1995

Alwell, Anthony J.
Barr, Fionnuala C.
Barry, Aiden G.M.
Barry, Caroline M.E.
Barry, Margaret M. (Marie)
Barry-Murphy, Orla
Beashel, Joseph
Binchy, Daniel O.
Boland, Robert M.
Bradley, Edel P.M.
Brady, Stuart D.B.
Breathnach, Fionan
Bredin, Paula M.
Breen, Kenneth P.
Brennan, Eileen A.
Broderick, Denis
Broderick, Thomas P.
Brooks, Declan O.
Brophy, Imelda L.
Bruce, Alan J.

Buckley, Lucy-Ann
Buckley, Yvonne M.
Bugler, Suzanne M.
Burke, Adrian C.
Burke, Patrick C.
Byrne, Carmel A.
Byrne, Dara M.
Byrne, Margaret M.
Byrne, Michael P.
Byrne, Paul
Cadden, Fabian P.
Cagney, Denis P.
Cagney, Paul W.D.
Cahill, Catherine Mary
Callan, Niamh M.
Callanan, Patrick E.
Candy, Colman J.
Canny, John A.
Carey, Colette B.
Carmody, Katherine M.
 (Caitriona)
Carter, Andrea S.
Caulfield, Anne Marie
Clarke, Garry J.
Coakley, Vincent
Coffey, Philip R.
Colbert, Catherine J. (Kate)
Coles, Richard M.F.
Collins, Brian P.
Comiskey, Eamon P.
Commins, Cormac M.
Conlon, Catherine Nora
Conlon, Dominic R.
Connolly, Mary J.P.
Conroy, Geraldine M.
Corkery, J. Garvan
Costello, Maria
Costello, Sean M.
Craughwell, Amber M.
Crinnion, Leoné M.
Cross, Jacqueline H.
Cuddigan, John J.
Cunniff, Sarah
Curtis, Grace C.
Cusack, Hubert J.
D'Arcy, Brian
Daly, Alan J.
Daly, Bernadette B.
Daly, Maureen
Davoren, Mary M.
de Barra, Cathal L.
Delaney, Patrick E.

Delany, Sandra J.
Devaney, Martina C.
Dockery, Marita
Doherty, Noel M.
Donnelly, Una Anne
Doran, Michael P.
Dorrian, Patricia A.
Dowling, Joan E.
Doyle O'Sullivan, Una
Duchene, Frederique
Duff, Sheila M.
Duggan, Carmel M.
Dunleavy, Nicola M.
Dunne, Trevor M.
Egan, Elizabeth M.
Egan, Kenneth M.
English, Michael G.
Ennis, Jacqueline A.
Falvey, Emer R.
Fanning, P. Colm
Farrell, Rachel S.A.
Fennessy, Ruth Ann
Ferguson, Mel J.
Finlay, Helen O.
Finlay, Martina A.
Finn, James G.
Finnegan, James
Fitzpatrick, John H.
Fitzsimons, Lana S.T.
Foley, Sonja E.
Ford, Diorai
Fox, Patrick M.
Freeman, Robert J.
Fuller, Alan S.
Gallagher, Fergus J.
Gallagher, Maree C.
Gallagher, Norah M.
Gallagher, Sarah J.
Galvin, Turlough J.
Gannon, Patricia M.
Gavin, Joseph M.
Geaney, Ruth N.
Geraghty, James G.
Geraghty, Ursula A.
Gibbons, Sheila M.
Gilhooly, Catherine M.
 (Katie)
Gilhooly, Stuart J.
Gillespie, Francis R.
Gillespie, Michael J.
Gilmartin, Yvonne G.
Given, John O.

Gorry, Marguerite Ann
Greene, John J.
Hall, Geraldine M.
Hanna, Paul R.
Hannigan, Caitriona M.
Harnett, Lucy P.
Harrison, Michael H.
Haughton, Carl J.
Hayes, Siobhan
Hayes, Siobhan M.
Heade, Elizabeth M.
Hearne, Brendan T.
Heffernan, Kenneth P.
Henry, Thomas Anthony
Heslin, Mark J.
Hewitt, Richard A.
Hickey, Barbara A.
Hodgins, Maryann
Holmes, Louise M.
Horan, Patricia A.
Howard, Susan N.M.
Howley, Philippa M.
Hughes, Gillian M.
Hurt, Jacqueline M.
Hussey, Clare T.
Hussey, Rachel
Iu Ting-Kwok
Johnson, Rebecca A.
Jordan, Irene J.
Joyce, Jarlath
Joyce, Orla A.
Judge, Barbara A.
Kane, Hugh E.
Kavanagh, Miriam T.
Keane, Denis J.
Keaney, Claire J.
Kearns, Pauline M.
Kelleher, Anne Marie
Kelleher, Denise E.
 (Elizabeth)
Kelleher, John F.
Kelleher, Margaret M.
Kelleher, Michael W.
Kelleher, Thomas M.
Kelly, John P.
Kelly, Jonathan D.G.
Kelly, Leslie J.
Kelly, Treasa M.A.
Kennedy, Brian D.
Kennedy, Julie S.
Kennedy, Sonja M.
Kennelly, Anne Lucy

Kerins, Selena M.
Kilfeather, Aine
Killilea, Mark P.
Lanigan, Anne M.
Lawless, John
Lawton, Mary (Maura) M.
Lee, Rosario A.M.
Lynch, Bridget C. (Breda)
McArdle, Bernadette G.
McAuliffe, U. Lorna
McCabe, Colman P.G.
McCarthy, John P.
McCarthy, Kieran
MacCarthy, Sheenagh M.
McCheane, Brendan
McCormack, Emer M.
McCormack, Sinead C.
McCullagh, Harry
McEnroe, Patrick G.
McFerran, Cara M.
McGarrity, Joseph A.
McGing, Aileen M.
McGreal, Anthony G.
McGregor, Mary G.
McGuinn, Conleth P.J.
McKendry, Brian W.
McKenna, Eimer M.
McKnight, Catherine M.V.
McLaughlin, Damhnait B.
McMahon, Clodagh M.
McMahon, Sharon M.
McManus, Fidelma
McNamara, Gillian C.
McNamara, Joseph
MacSweeney, Shane P.
McVeigh, Kevin T.
Maguire, Conor J.
Maguire, Gerard T.
Maher, Paul M.
Mahony, Abigail
Manning, Anne V.
Manson, Robert G.
Meehan, Sinead A.
Menton, John F.
Metcalfe, Raymond J.
Moloney, Liam S.
Montgomery, David S.
Mooney, Siona A.
Moran, John A.
Morgan, John G.
Moriarty, Jeanne-Marie
Moriarty, Niamh M.

Morris, Deirdre C.
Morris, Michael G.
Mulcahy, Sylvia M.
Mulherin, Michelle M.B.
Mullarkey, Conor E.
Murphy, Alan D.
Murphy, Brian A.
Murphy, Ciara
Murphy, Dympna M.
Murphy, Nicola Y.M.
Murphy, Nollaig D.
Murray, Fiona M.
Neary, Paul M.
Nestor, Orla M.
Nethercott, Craig R.
Ní Charthaig, Eileanora
Ní Ghríofa, Una M.
Nic Mhurchú, Sorcha
Noone, Darragh B.
Nunan, Michele C.
O'Beirne, Aileen
O'Brien, Ciaran
O'Brien, David H.
O'Brien, Diarmuid S.
O'Brien Raleigh, Maressa
O'Byrne, Sylvester G.
O'Connell, Aoibheann C.K.
O'Connell, John J. (Seán)
O'Connell, Nicola P.
O'Connor, Orla S.
O'Connor, Siona K.
O'Doherty, K. Niamh
O'Donnell, Eric R.
O'Donnell, James F.
O'Donnell, James R.
O'Donnell, Nancy E.
O'Donnell, William
O'Donoghue, Michael (Paul)
O'Donovan, Michael J.G.
O'Flynn, C. Rosaleen
O'Flynn, Deirdre Anne
O'Grady, Juliana
O'Halloran, Susan B.
O'Kane, Judy E.
O'Kennedy, Suzanne M.
O'Leary, Karen A.M.
O'Leary, Marian T.
O'Mahony, Grace O.J.
O'Mahony, Jean M.
O'Meara, Anne M.
O'Neill, Bernard J.
O'Neill, Geraldine T.

O'Neill, Ronan F.
O'Reilly, M. Brigin
O'Reilly, Maurice Killian
O'Shea, John P.
O'Shea, Shaun G.
O'Sullivan, Annette M.
O'Sullivan, Caitriona M.
O'Sullivan, Patrick B.A.
O'Sullivan, Philip A.
Pepper, Deirdre M.
Phelan, Anne M.
Phelan, Chynel
Power, Marcella F.
Quinn, Andrew J.
Quinn, Brendan P.
Quirke, John M.
Rea, Julia M.
Ridgway, Gillian M.
Robinson, Marie-Celine (Feena)
Roche, Nora (Caroline)
Roe, Kieran J.
Rooney, Bernadette A.
Rooney, Niall P.
Rooney, Nicola A.
Rowley, Margaret M.
Ryall, Gearoid T.
Ryan, Catherine M.
Ryan, Marianne L.
Ryan, Michael W.T.
Rynne, John J.
Schuster, Milan
Sheehan, Patrick B.
Sheridan, Anne-Marie
Solan, Dudley F.
Spain, Benedicte M.
Spring, Orlagh M.T.
Synnott, Alan A.
Tait, Andrew A.
Thorne, Mark C.
Tiernan, Cornelius J.
Tiernan, Peter Lorcan
Tierney, Imelda P.
Tunney, James P.
Tynan, Louise A.M.
Waldron, Fidelma M.
Wall, Adrian J.
Wall, Catherine J.
Walsh, Cara
Walsh, Janet C.
Walsh, John F.
Walsh, Michael D.
Walsh, Norman F.

Walshe, Jennifer A.
Walshe, Marie E.
Waters, Micheal J.A.
Welland, Ian P.
White, Darina E.
White, Grainne V.
White, Jonathan W.
White, Nora Mary (Niamh)
Widger, David A.
Wilson, Hazel A.

1996

Acton, Sean P.
Babe, Colin J.
Beer, Andrew M.S.
Bell, Henry J.
Benville, Morya
Bermingham, Caomhan P.
Binchy, Shalom
Bismilla, Naeem P.
Blake, Mary (Anne Marie)
Bohan, Anne-Marie
Boland, Mary G.
Bowen, Lorna M.
Bracken, Taragh M.
Brady, Sinead
Breen, Paul M.
Brennan, Feargal P.
Brennan, Gabriel E.M.
Brennan, Kirsten A.
Brennan, Marian M.
Brennan, Ronan F.
Browne, Catriona
Browne, David F.
Buckley, Claire M.
Buckley, Conor I.
Buckley, Leo J.
Buckley, Marguerite M.
Bulbulia, David S.
Burke, Helen C.
Butler, Caroline A.
Byrne, Joan M.
Byrne, Maria C.
Byrne, Phena M.
Byrne, Sinead P.
Cabry-Kavanagh, Elaine
Cadden, Aoife M.
Cahill, Conor Bill
Cahir, Sharon M.
Callaghan, Francis J.

Canton Airey, Jean
Carey, Edward B.
Carney, Colette M.
Carney, Patrick J.
Carpenter, Jennifer M.
Carrick, Corinna G.
Carroll, Andrea M.
Carroll, John W.
Casey, Denise P.
Casey, Elizabeth A.
Cashman, Jennifer A.
Cassidy, Michelle
Cawley, Susanna J.
Christy, Leslie J.
Clarke, Niamh M.
Cleary, Dominique M.
Cleary, Gerard J.
Cleary, John T.P.
Cleary, Patrick Donough
Codd, Eimear J.
Collins, Maurice A.
Conlan, Elaine T.
Connolly, Rosaleen M.
Coonan, Andrew Robert
Coonan, Robert F.
Corkery, Ellen M.
Cotter, Anne
Cox, Elaine M.
Crawford, Joan C.
Creed, Mary P.
Crowley, Helen M.
Cullen, Karen M.
Cullinane, Mary E.
Curley, Gordon N.P.
Curran, Mary (Brid)
Curran, Richard J.
Cusack, Sandra M.
Daly, Ken D.
Daly, Patrick J.
Davidson, Ashley Hope
Deering, Dermot J.
Delaney, Laura M.
Dempsey, Angela M.
Dempsey, Ethan J.
Dempsey, Feargal P.
Dennis, Patricia D.
Dennison, James
Derrane, Elaine M.
Devine, Fergus M.
Doherty, Maeve E.
Doherty, Muredach P.
Dolan, Aileen R.

Donnelly, Anne-Marie
Donnelly, Brendan P.
Doyle, Fiona B.
Doyle, Gerard W.
Doyle, Michelle T.
Duffy, John J.
Duffy, Patrick
Dunne, Gerard M.
Dunne, J. Evan
Dunne, Riona A.
Edgar, J.P. Hamish
Elly, Richard Charles
Enright, Gail M.
Fagan, David A.
Fagan, Erika L.
Farrell, Graham R.
Farrington, Richard T.
Feeney, Brenda M.
Fennelly, William F.
Fenton, Vanessa M.
Finn, Katherine M.
Finnegan, Michael G.
Finucane, Mark J.
Fitzsimon, Meriel A.
Fitzsimons, Daragh E.M.
Flanagan, Patricia A.
Foley, Aisling B.
Foley, Siobhan T.
Forde, Katharine A.
Fowler, David R.
Fullam, L. Norman
Galvin, Michael J.
Garvey, Rita A.
Gibbon, Ann M.
Gibbons, Patrick J.
Gilvarry, Susan J.
Glynn, Niall B.
Goodman, Beatrice A.
Grace, Michael L.
Griffin, Conor J.
Griffin, Donal F.
Griffith, Thomas A.
Hannon, Iseult
Harte, Anne
Hassett, Grainne M.
Hayes, Maura M.
Heagney, Cora
Healy, Clodiia D.
Healy, Dennis B.
Healy, Janette M.
Healy, Lindsay P.
Healy, T. Barry

Heisterkamp, Frank
Henry, Fiona M.
Herard, Marie Florence
Herron, Niamh M.
Hickey, Fiona B.
Higgins, Cora B.A.
Hodge, Gemma A.
Hogan, Desmond J.
Holden, Niamh E.M.
Holly, Tanya P.
Holohan, Emer M.
Hooper, Sean D.
Hopkins, Clodagh M.
Hough, Mary R.
Hughes, John P.
Hunt, Bernadette M.
Jennings, Elizabeth
Jennings, Martin A.
Jennings, Mary G. (Marian)
Johnston, Matthew
Joyce, Deirdre (Fiona)
Kavanagh, Michael P.
Kavanagh, Niamh M.
Keane, Orla E.
Kearney, Kathryn A.
Kearney, Laurence N.
Keating, Fionnuala M.
Keigher, Donal T.
Kells, Maria T.
Kelly, Alison M.
Kelly, John V.
Kelly, Rosalyn M.
Kennedy, Lorna M.
Kennedy, Valerie F.M.
Keogh, Nicola M.
Kerr, Thomas W.N.
Kerrigan, Anita E.
Kettle, John A.
Kiely, Timothy P.
Kirk, Niamh M.
Lally, Gerard M.
Larsen, Elvi M.
Lavery, Paul J.
Lavin, Emer M.
Leahy, Anne Ita
Leahy, William J.
Lee, Susan E.
Lenehan, James P.
Lennon, Barbara A.
Leonard, Ronan A.
Lloyd, Kim D.
Loftus, Barbara P.

Long, Kimberley M.
Lowe, Eilish P.
Lowey, Caroline M.
Lucey, Stephen A.
Lynam, Michael R.
Lyne, Riobard C.
Lyons, P. Barry
McAllister, Fiona M.
McAuliffe, Catherine M.
McAveety, Mary T.
MacCarthy, Michael P.
McCarthy, Patrick J.
McCarthy, Patrick M.
McDermott, Garrett J.
McDonald, Ethna V.
Mac Donncha, Sean J.
McDonnell, Michael Paul
McFadden, David M.
McGahon, John C.
McGettigan, Ann M.
McGinty, Thomas Anthony
McGovern, Terence M.
McGowan, Donogh V.
McGuire, Gavin J.
McInnes, Peter K.
McKenna, Mini
McKenna, Siobhan M.
McKeone, Cormac
McKnight, Donal (Fergal)
McMahon, Darren P.
MacMahon, Tara P.
McMahon, Ursula M.
McMullin, John B.
McMunn, David J.
McNally, Nora (Saundra)
Mac Niallais, Siobhán
McSweeney, James P.
McSweeney, Patrick J.
McVann, Maura T.
Madden, Jacinta M.
Madigan, Patrick J.
Magennis, Caitriona A.
Maguire, Brendan J.
Maguire, Conor A.
Maher, Jennifer M.
Masterson, Elizabeth M.
Matson, John J.
Molloy, Catherine A.
Monaghan, Garrett R.
Moore, Deborah A.
Moore, Mary B.
Moorhead, Sylvia M.

Moran, Ailish M.
Moroney, Barbara
Moroney, Raymond P.
Mulchrone, Elva M.
Muldoon, Eithne P.
Muldowney, Nicola M.
Mullally, Lisa T.
Mullaney, Mark
Mulligan, Francis M.
Mullins, Avril M.
Mullins, Michael Brendan
Mullins, Patrick J.
Munnelly, Brid A.
Murphy, Antoinette M.
Murphy, Bernard F.
Murphy, Danielle E.
Murphy, Derek W.
Murphy, Mark M.
Murphy, Oisin C.
Murphy, Orla Anne
Murphy, Valerie M.
Naughton, Desmond G.
Neale, Suzanne N.
Nelson, Helen C.
Nelson, M. Michele
Neville, Veronica C.
Ní Mhurchú, Niamh G.B.
Ní Uigín, Renate C.
Nowlan, Ann
O'Brien, Brian E.
O'Brien, John P.
O'Brien, Karen B.
O'Brien, William Kieran
O'Carroll, Cian P.
Ó Cionnaith, Proinsias
O'Connell, Fiona E.
O'Connell, Margaret M.
O'Connell, Mary A.
O'Connell, Matthew G.
O'Connell, Susan M.
O'Connor, Brian
O'Connor, Catherine (Kate) A.
O'Connor, Catherine M.
O'Connor, Grace M.
Ó Cróinín, Séamus
O'Doherty, Eimear
Ó Donnchadha, Orla B.G.
O'Donnell, Elizabeth M.
O'Donnell, Malcolm J.
O'Donovan, Colman P.
O'Dwyer, John M.J.
O'Flaherty, M. Grainne

O'Flynn, Frank M.
O'Gorman, Eoin T.
O'Gorman, J. Finbarr
O'Hanrahan, Kenneth P. Hill
O'Hehir, M. Philomena
O'Loughlin, Orlaith M.
O'Mahony, Carl N.
O'Mahony, Catherine
O'Mahony, David W.
O'Mahony, Robert J.
O'Malley, Breda C.
O'Neill, Alexandra
O'Neill, Jonathan M.
O'Neill, Pamela K.
O'Raghallaigh, Donal S.
O'Reilly, Anthony W.
O'Reilly, Susan E.
O'Riordan, David K.
Orr, Kathryn S.
O'Shea, Brian P.
O'Sullivan, Donal M.
O'Sullivan, Fiona M.
O'Sullivan, Karen A.
O'Sullivan, Patricia A.
Palmer, George Albert
Parte, Bernadette A.
Phelan, Georgina M.
Pigot, Victoria M.C.
Pilkington, Michael J.
Power, Breda
Price, Sonia M.
Pringle, Vanessa
Prior, Patrick M.
Quigley, Garrett T.
Quin, Julie A.
Quinn, Ciaran M.
Redmond, Fiona A.
Reynolds, Mary
Reynolds, Mary T.
Riebesell-Hau, Kerstin
Riley, Margaret A.
Roberts, Irene C.
Rohan, Pauline B.
Russell, Siobhan M.
Ryan, Fiona B.
Ryan, Geraldine M.
Ryan, Oliver R.W.
Ryan, Orlagh M.
Ryan, William A.
Sampson, Eimear M.
Saunders, Mark K.
Sayer, Robert

Shaffrey, Donnough P.
Shannon, Geoffrey E.
Shannon, Lorna I.
Sharkey, Jacqueline A.
Sheehy, Siobhan L.
Sherlock, Dermot P.F.
Sherwin, James
Simms, Daniel Paul
Smartt, Eugene G.
Smith, Bernadette M.
Smith, Sinead M.
Solon, Sean M.
Somerville, James W.R.B.
Spaine, Ann M.
Sreenan, Carmel H.
Stack, Margaret L.
Stronge, Mairin E.
Stuart, George
Tanham, J. Donagh
Thornton, Ellen M.
Tobin, Brenda M.
Tobin, Finbarr P.
Traynor, Mark J.
Tunney, Mary B.
Tyers, Áine M.
Tynan, Anne B.
Van Cauwelaert, Alicia A.
Varian, Mark P.
Walsh, Andrea M.
Walsh, Brendan
Walsh, Francis (Frank) M.
Walsh, Mark J.
Walshe, Elizabeth F.
Ward, Eamonn G.
Ward, Kathryn
Weatherill, Laurence J.
Weldon, Brendan S.
Whelan, Joanne M.
Whelan, John F.
Whelan, Maureen M.
White, Michael L.
Wilkinson, Helen A.
Woodcock, Peter
Wright, Louise M.
Wynne, Paul W.

1997

Agnew, Sheila A.
Allen, Shane M.
Aylmer, Grainne V.

Barr, Michael F.
Barry, Fiona P.
Beattie, Hugh J.P.
Bhogal, Iqbal
Bostridge, Julian O.
Boyle, Kerry Ann
Brady, George E.L.
Brett, E. Sinead
Bryson, Mary C.
Burns, Louise M.
Butler, Gráinne L.
Byrne, Mary Carmel
Byrne, Rosaleen C.
Byrne, Vanessa M.
Cahill, Miriam E.
Candon, James Clarke
Canny, James K.
Cantwell, Barbara E.
Caraher, Alyson M.
Carty, Margaret M.
Casey, Thomas M.
Cassidy, Séamus T.
Cazabon, Elizabeth M.
Chain, Julia S.
Chang, Lavinia Yu Ming
Clancy, Fintan M.
Cole, Adrian E.
Collins, Elaine
Comiskey, Aedamar I.
Connolly, Robert E.
Corrigan, Conall E.
Corry, Micheal G.
Cosgrove, Aileen B.
Costelloe, Margaret A.
Cotter, Valerie A.
Courtney, Aileen C.
Crean, Jeremy D.
Cuffe, Jean M.
Curry, Jennifer M.
Cunningham, Paul A.
Daly, Colin P.
Darby, John C.
Davey, Michael C.
Devane, John D.
Dillon, Brian G.
Dillon, Edmond John
Dillon, Francis David
Dillon, Nicole A.
Donegan, Sally Anne
Doogan, Deirdre P.
Doohan, Siobhan M.
Douglas, Bryan J.

Doyle, Tara M.
Drislane, Declan
Duane, Eilean M.
Dunning, Sharon C.
English, Richard H.
Ennis, Jill M.
Eustace, Joseph K.
Farrell, Anne-Maree
Farrell, Deirdre M.
Farrell, Paul L.
Fay, Leo K.
Finch, Stephen J.
Finegan, Elizabeth (Liza) M.
Finlay, Barry P.
Fitzgibbon, Barra C.M.
Fleming, Aislinn J.
Fogarty, Aengus R.M.
Foley, Sean
Ford, Timothy G.
Gearty, Paula C.
Geraghty, Davitt N.
Gillen, B. Sinead
Glynn, Francis P.
Glynn, James D.
Goggin, Mary Colette
Gordon, Áine A.
Gorman, Margaret M.
Grealy, Winifred
    (Freda) M.C.
Gribbin, Marcelle M.
Gunning, Ciara M.
Hackett, David D.
Halloran-Ryan, Jane A.
Handoll, John T.C.
Hanley, Pamela T.
Harney, Linda M.
Harney, Patrick F.
Harrington-Devine, Joan M.
Harris, Adrian F.
Harrison, Jean B.
Hayes, Conor P.
Heavey, Tara E.J.
Hession, Rachael A.
Hickey, Michael R.
Ho Wei Sim
Hogan, Godfrey P.
Horn, Cornelius
Howells, David J.
Hurley, Noelle M.
Johnson, Sarah J.
Jones, Mary A.
Keane, Siobhan M.

Kearney, Noel
Keating, Gillian M.
Keating, Pauline M.
Keaveny, Michael
Keely, Frances P.
Kehoe, Maureen M.
Kelly, D. Gerard
Kelly, Dermot J.
Kelly, Jeanne M.
Kelly, Jeanne Marie
Kennedy, Robert E.
Keogh, Damien A.
Keogh, James M.
Kiely, Peter C.
King, Eamonn P.
Kings, John C.
Kwan Ka Po
Langford, Kevin J.
Lawlor, Fintan J.
Le Gear Keane, Teresa M.
Lennon, Joyce M.
Lenny, James Andrew
Lynch, Barry A.
Lynch, Maeve
Lynn, Richard M.
Lyons, Aine E.
Lyons, Edward D.
McAdam, Evelyn M.
McArdle, Boguslaw (Bob)
McBride, Kathryn E.
McBride, Richard J.
McCabe, Liam G.
McCloskey, Siobhan V.
McCutcheon, Paul C.
McDermott, Deirdre C.
McDevitt, Stephen C.
McGinley, Margaret M.G.
McGoldrick, Joanne
McGrath, H. Nicola
McHugh, Elisa J.
McInerney, Anne M.
McInnes, Hunter W.
McLoughlin, Ronan F.
McMahon, Marie-Louise
McNamara, Brona M.
McNamara, John C.
McNulty, Suzanne C.
McSharry, Siobhan
McTaggart, Sharon P.
Madigan, Josepha M.A.
Martin, Cliona A.
Matthews, Ciara

Matthews, Paul B.
Meates, James F.
Moloney, Denis G.G.
Molyneaux, John J.
Moran, Clare
Moran, Eileen C.
Morgan, Andrew J.
Mulconry, Eve M.
Muldowney, Hilary P.M.
Mullaney Shipsey, Moira
Mullen, Bernard M.
Murnaghan, Kevin
Murphy, Caroline A.
Murphy, Niall E.
Murphy, Shane P.
Murray, Aisling D.
Murray, Catriona J.
Murray, Paul A.
Naqvi, Riaz Hassan
Neill, Patrick S.
Ní Mhéalóid, Eimear M.
Nolan, Joyce T.
Nolan, Lorraine S.A.
Ó Briain, Conchubhar
O'Brien, Brian P.
O'Brien, David M.
O'Callaghan, Grainne D.
O'Connell, Christopher J.
O'Connell, Kevin F.
O'Connor, Michael A.
O'Doherty, John E.
O'Doherty, M. Francis
O'Donovan, Padraig A.
Ó Muircheartaigh, Donal A.
O'Neill, B. Cecelia
O'Neill, Brian J.
Ó Nualláin, Garbhán B.
O'Regan, Margaret M.
    (Maureen)
O'Reilly, Catherine F.
O'Reilly, Ian P.
O'Roarty, Nessa T.
O Scanaill, Nora
O'Sullivan, Anne R.
O'Sullivan, Aoife
O'Sullivan, Cathal D.
Power, Leonie P.
Power, Susan B.
Price, Gearóid P.
Purcell, Sabina M.J.
Quigley, Neasa A.
Quilligan, Jillian M.

Rankin, Alastair J.
Ransom, Corrine A.
Reel, Stephen H.
Regan, Miriam S.
Reilly, Diane B.
Ring, Vivienne C.
Ross, William Christopher
Rowe, Emily J.
Rush, Jean M.
Ryan, Deirdre A.
Ryan, Deirdre M.
Ryan, Susan P.
Scully, Eimear A.
Shanley, Julie M.
Sheedy, Jeremiah
Sheehan, Patrick A.
Sheehan, Sean R.
Smith, Douglas
Smith, Wendy J.
Spicer, Patrick F.G.
Sullivan, Beulah M.
Swan, Ciara E.
Tayler, Clodagh V.H.
Teevan, Carol Anne
Tierney, Brid M.
Timmins, Hilary M.
Tracey, Siobhan M.
Travers, Thomas J.D.
Tuohy, John J.
Verdon, Craig D.C.
van der Lee, Chris
Wall, Elaine C.
Walsh, Barry J.
Walsh, Deirdre (Dede) A.
Ward, Jane M.
Ward, John Paul
Ward, Nora H.
Wellington, John K.
White, Mark D.
White, Rowan McMurray
Williams, David S.
Wilson, Deirdre M.
Yarr, Julian W.

1998

Ahern, Deirdre
Ahern, Gillian M.
Baily, Brian G.
Barcroft, Peter A.

Barrett, Mary Celine
Barry, Bernadette M.
Baxter, David R.
Beckett, Paul R.
Beecher, Cian T.
Blake, Darina M.
Blaser, Thomas G.
Bolger, Honor P.M.
Boyle, David P.
Brabazon, Thomas J.
Bradley, Aoife E.
Bradley, Fergal M.
Brassil, Mary E.
Breen, John J.
Breslin, Sarah C.
Brien, Una M.
Broderick, Ellen M.
Brophy, Linda M.
Browne, Audrey U.
Buckley, Geraldine C.
Burke, Ailbhe M.
Burke, Edmund J.
Burke, P. Joseph
Butler, Denis J.
Byrne, Rosanne
Cahalan, Aeibhin M.
Cahir, Barry T.
Callan, Emma M.
Callinan, Marie B.
Carroll, Rachel
Carty, Simon O.
Casey, Margaret A.M.
Casserley, Dermot
Cassidy, Isobel St. Clair
Caulfield, Eoin D.
Chapman, Barrett G.
Cleary, Colleen M.
Cleary, Geraldine M.
Cochrane, Gerard V.
Coffey, Maurice A.
Coleman, Daniel J.
Comerford, Ciara G.
Conlon, Eamonn P.
Connery, Niamh M.
Cotter, Michael F.
Coughlan, Sarah M.
Cowley, Richard J.
Craig, Jean T.
Creighton, Niamh F.
Cremen, Rosemary B.
Cunningham, Seána M.
Cunningham-Davis, James N.

Curneen, Sheena M.
Curran, Peter E.
D'Arcy, Shane F.
Deasy, Josephine
Dee, Eoin M.
Dennehy, Aideen
Dennison, Orla A.
Dervan, Gerard P.
Desmond, Paula
d'Estelle Roe, George Declan
de Valera, Eamon H.
Devine, Sharon M.
De Witt, Ian R.
Dockery, Louis J.
Doherty, Frank T.
Doherty, Róisín M.
Dolan, Michelle N.
Donlon, Fidelma
Doorly, Diarmuid F.
Dowling, Fergal M.
Doyle, Brian P.
Doyle, Leonora B.
Doyle, Peter J.
Duggan, Karen A.
Duggan, M. Louise
Dullea, Finian J.
Dunlea, Orla S.
Dunne, Finola M.
Dunne, Siobhan B.
Dunphy, Nicola A.
Enright, Kenneth T.
Fagan, Albert P.
Fay, Joseph G.B.
Feeney, Madeleine S.
Filgate, Vivienne P.
Fitzgerald, John D.
Fitzgerald, Pauline M.
Fitzgibbon, Caroline M.
Fitzpatrick, Arlene S.
Fitzpatrick, Stephen J.
Fitzsimons, Ronan M.D.
Flanagan, Mary E.
Foley, Vivienne M.
Fortune, Margaret M.T.
Fox, Eimear
Fox, Jennifer A.
Foyle, Patrick J.
Frawley, J. David
Fujita, Yuka
Furlong, Peter R.
Gallagher, Martin D.J.
Galligan, James-Paul

Gannon, Aisling C.
Garvey, Aoife
Garvey, Norma
Gibbons, Karen E.
Gillen, Fergus P.
Gilnagh, Claire G.
Gleeson, Patrick P.
Goggin, Kevin G.
Gowdy, Stephen T.
Graham, Peter
Green, Alexander M.S.
Grehan, John
Grennan, Corona M.
Griffith, Moninne M.
Guilfoyle-Carey, Emma M.
Harmon, David P.
Hassett, Daragh J.
Hatton, Kenneth L.
Healy, Fiona C.
Healy, Ivan J.
Hegarty, Daphne J.
Hegarty, Eithne M.
Hickey, Annette
Hickey, Dermot J.
Hickey, Marco W.
Hickey-Dwyer, Clodagh
Hickey-Dwyer, Karen
Holmes, Karen E.
Holmes, Melanie M.
Horan, Damian P.
Howard, Elizabeth B.
Howard, Noreen B.
Hughes, Crona F.
Hurley, Fiona A.
Irwin, David J.
Johnson, Daniel J.
Johnston, David G.
Joyce, Sarah S.
Kavanagh, Paul J.
Kavanagh, Rachel A.
Keane, John W.
Kearney, Mary G.
Keary, Patricia C.
Keating, Liam G.
Keaveny, Conor M.
Keegan, Audrey
Kelly, Miriam S.
Kennedy, Stephanie C.
Kilbane, Dermot J.
Kilroy, Emer F.
King, Donall M.
Kingston, John N. P.

Kirwan, Lorraine M.
Lavelle, Liam H.
Lawlor, Valerie M.
Leahy, Catriona M.G.
Leahy, Imelda
Leonard, James V.
Little, Cormac K.
Little, Mairead
Lohan, Cormac M.
Loughran, Niamh M.
Lupton, Conor P.
Lynch, Ann M.
Lynch, Ann M.
Lynch, Christopher G.
McAlinden, Geraldine M.
McAteer, Theresa N.
McCarthy, Deirdre-Ann
McCarthy, Florence
McConnell, Andreas D.
MacCorkell, Colin V.
MacCorkell, Ian J.
McCormack, Claire E.
McCormick, Karen
McCourt, Conal K.
McElligott, Sharon G.
McEntee, Sonia
McGearty, M. Margaret
McGettigan, Ivor G.
McGinley, Kyran J.
MacGinley, Liz
McGowan, Christina B.
McGrath, Barry J.
McHugh, Mary C.P.
McHugh, Pauline M.
McHugh, Ronan J.
McIlvenna, Leah T.
McMahon, Fiona M.
MacQuillan, Gerard F.B.
Madden, Daphne A.
Mae Wee Linn, Evangelina
Maguire, Maureen M.K.
Maguire, Noreen M.
Maguire, Vanessa A.
Maloney, Stephanie F.
Manning, Fiona
Martin, Emma A.
Martin, Rita
Matthews, Gary C.
Meagher, Emma L.
Mitchell, Jeremy D.
Molloy, Sarah A.
Moloney, Liam

Moloney, Marie E.
Monaghan, Kathryn A.M.
Monks, Sinead E.
Moohan, K. Sharon
Moore, Patricia
Moran, Gemma A.
Moynihan, Damian P.
Mullen, J. Cormac
Mullett, Leonora F.
Mullins, Martina M.
Mulvihill, Sean A.
Murphy, Aoife
Murphy, Elizabeth J.
Murphy, Fionnuala M.
Murphy, Grainne M.R.
Murphy, Jean M.
Murphy, John J.
Murphy, Una
Neiland, Valerie B.
Ní Dhúill, Neasa M.
O'Brien, Aideen M.
O'Brien, Catherine A.
O'Brien, M. Claire
O'Brien, Mary Rose
O'Brien, Regina M.
O'Brien, Sinead A.
O'Callaghan, Mark D.
O Caoimh, Feilim M.
O'Connell, Colm
O'Connell, June P.
O'Dea, Hilary M.
Odlum, Walter
O'Doherty, Hilary M.
O'Donnell, Michael B.
O'Donnell, Michelle T.
O'Donohoe, Aoife M.
O'Gara, Kevin M.
O'Gorman, Ingrid M.
O'Higgins, Sarah Sheena
    Niav
O'Keeffe, Elaine M.
O'Keeffe, Michele E.
Oliver, Patrick J.
O'Mahony, Julie C.
O'Malley, Anthony J.
O'Malley, Mary M.
O'Neill, Catherine E.
O'Neill, Garrett P.
O'Neill, Michael J.
O Riain, Helen L.
O'Riordan, Jennifer G.
Orr, Michael W.M.

Osborne, David R.
O'Shea, Robert G.
O'Sullivan, Richard M.
O'Sullivan, Ronan P.
O'Sullivan, Teresa
O'Toole, Doran W.
Peters, Judith M.
Phelan, David T.
Power, Piaras C.
Quinlisk, Marese A.
Quinn, Patrick Donal
Ringrose, Brendan M.
Ritchie, Joseph O.
Rodgers, Steven J.
Rowley, Thomas M.
Ruane, Kenneth G.
Ruck, Nicholas S.
Ryan, Dorothy M.
Ryan, John J.
Ryan, Marguerite M.L.
Ryan, Sean M.J.
Saunders, Catherine Eavan
Savage, Anne C.
Savage, John G.
Sheehan, Nicola C.
Slattery, Maelbhina G.
Smyth, Brendan P.
Somers, Fiona D.
Stafford, A. Mark
Staunton, Emma M.B.
Staunton, Liam G.
Sutcliffe, John J.O.
Swift, Laura E.
Sycamore, Phillip
Talbot, Eleanor R.
Tangney, Nicholas J.G.
Taylor, Agatha B.
Taylor, Robert A.
Territt, Justine M.
Thomas, Nicholas P.G.
Thynne, Marianne L.
Tuffy, Joanna M.
Tuthill, Suzanne E.
Wales, Matthew P.
Walsh, Aoife B.
Walsh, Padraig L.
Ward, Rachel M.
Ward-Clancy, Martina M.
Waters, Nicholas James
Wheelahan, David J.
White, Joan B.
Widger, Carol A.

Wijnands-Ellis, Louise-Marie
Woods, Karyn A.
Woods, Stephen J.
Wylie, Thomas R.

1999

Addis, Kimberley E.
Ahearn, Margaret
Ahern, Dolores Julia
Aherne, Patrick John
Almond, Catherine
Baker, Catherine T.
Balding, Diane L.
Ball-O'Keeffe, Patricia J.
Ballantyne, Carol M.
Barron, Ciarán P.
Bell, Ian Reeves
Benson, Adrian P.
Black, John J.
Bolster, Fergus
Boylan, Emma M.
Boyle, John
Bracken, Rioghnagh
Breen, Richard J.
Brennan, Michael E.
Brennan, Paul
Broderick, Darryl M.
Broderick, Noreen M.
Brolly, Mary K.
Browne, Fergal G.
Browne, Fiona
Browne, Gillian A.M.
Browne, Mura S.
Buckley, Siobhan R.
Bunbury, Conor P.W.
Bunce, Margaret P.
Burke, Aoife
Burke, Deirdre
Burke, John Ignatius
Burke, Patrick N.
Butler, Andrew Michael
Butler, Jennifer
Butler, Patrick J.
Buyers, John Christian
Byrne, Aisling M.
Byrne, Audrey M.
Byrne, Barbara M.
Byrne, Helene B.
Byrne, Mark D.

Cahill, Carmel Ann
Cahill, John
Campbell, John J.
Canavan, Miceal
Canty, Susan M.
Carbin, Maeve E.
Carley, Eugene G.
Carmody, Anthony T.
Carroll, Wayne
Clarke, Catherine U.
Cody, Justin
Colbert, Aoife M.
Colbert, Tanya C.
Cole, Brian
Collins, Eimear Patricia
Collins, Kevin A.
Collins, Liam J.
Compton, Joyce Annmarie
Conlon, Thomas E.
Connolly, Paul
Connolly, Peter A.
Connor, Bernadette M.T.
Cooper, Glenn J.
Corbet, Robert M.
Corrigan, Joanna L.
Coulter, Diane M.
Crean, William B.
Creedon, Kathleen T.
Crilly, Elizabeth A.
Crombie, Bernadette O.
Cronin, Freda
Crossan, Alan Joseph
Cunnane, Yvonne M.
Cunneen, Claire M.
Cunneen, Eoin K.
Curran, Aisling V.
Dale, Maireadh A.
Daly, Anne Marie
D'Arcy, Patrick Andrew
D'Arcy, Paul W.
Deacon, Ethel M.
Deane, Jane M.
Deane, Simon M.
Dee, Caroline M.
Dempsey, Deirdre M.
Dempsey, Lisa M.
Desmond, Aidan D.
Devaney, Susanne
Dineen, Neil C.
Dixon, Catherine
Doherty, Christopher B.G.
Doherty, Garrett

Doonan, Deirdre, M.
Doran, Joan M.
Dowling, Austin J.
Downey, Kevin Patrick John
Doyle, Mairead A.
Doyle, Peter J.
Duffy, Aileen Therese
Duffy, Conor J.
Dunne, John W.
Durkin, Conor M.
Dyke, Elaine H.
East, Geraldine
Egan, Ronan A.
Enright, Olwyn M.
Fagan, Nora E.
Fahey, Jennifer G.M.
Fahy, Fidelma M.
Farrell, Céline S.
Faughnan, James J.
Fay, Anthony R.
Feeney, Kevin A.
Feeney, Patrick James
Ferns, Margaret
Fetton, Ann B.
Finnegan, Niall P.J.
Finucane, Helen E.J.
Fitzgerald, Cáit P.
Fitzgerald, Mark F.
Fitzpatrick, Anne M.
Flaherty, Ronan S.
Flanagan, Bláthnaid
Flanagan, Dermot A.
Flynn, Aine M.
Foley, Gillian M.
Foley, John P.
Foran, Caroline M.
Fox, Judith M.
Fox, Kate L.
Fuller, Colin S.
Gallagher, Patrick J.
Gaughan, Aoife M.
Gavin, William Barry
Geary, David B.
Geary, Mary P.
Gibbons, Cathal W.
Gifford, Steven W.
Gilmore, Raphael M.
Glazier, Suzanne T.
Gough, Paul Richard
Grace, Fiona M.
Greene, Séamus P.
Griffin, Carol A.

Griffin, Joanne
Guilfoyle, Ita A.
Haigh, Simon Peter
Hallissey, Maurice
Hanly, Maria T.
Hannigan, Hugh-Michael
Hannon, Eleanor M.T.
Hannon, Hugh
Harkin, Patricia A.
Harnett, Helen C.
Harrington, Kelly
Harte, Ada A.
Hayes, Amy M.
Hayes, Louise M.
Heffernan, Ainsley P.
Hegarty, Fidelma J.
Henchion, John J.
Hennessy, Aoife M.
Hennessy, Michael A.
Henry, Michael G.
Herbert, Turlough
Higgins, Brian D.
Higgins, Marianne L.
Hodnett, David J.P.
Hogan, Áine Siobhán
Hogan, Brendan I.
Hogge, Leonie
Howley, Maria J.
Irvine, Catherine
Irwin, William
Jennings, Karen A.
Joy, Aine M.
Kavanagh, Colin D.
Keane, Sarah J.
Kearney, Geraldine R.
Keehan, Geraldine J.
Keeling, Conor
Kelly, Colm J.
Kelly, Deborah A.
Kelly, Maria J.
Kelly, Thomas J.
Kennedy, Frances M.
Kennedy, Patrick Joseph
Kiely, Jennifer S.
Kiernan, Louis M.
Killalea, Karen
Kilroy, Deirdre M.
King, Corann E.
King, Jennifer R.
Lambert, Catherine B.
Lambert, Paul B.
Larkin, Catherine B.

Lavan, John K.E.
Lawless, Gillian C.
Leahy, Aidan J.
Lenny, Claire Patricia
Liken, Maureen C.
Little, Ross D.A.
Long, Brian
Long, Brian P.
Loughran, Oliver M.
Lynch, Blánaid M.
Lynch, John
Lynch, Michelle A.
McAllister, Anarine M.
McCabe, Matthew G.
MacCann, Seán G.
McCarthy, Claire Marie
MacCarthy, David A.
McCarthy, Deirdre B.
McCarthy, Eithne J.
MacCarthy, John F. (Barry)
McCarthy, Shane Finian
McCarthy, Victoria A.
McCormack, Lesley Ann
McCoy, Lorraine M.
McCue, Jason D.
McDwyer, Robert
McEvoy, Linda A.
McGonagle, Caitriona M.
McGuire, Helen P.
McHugh, Niamh M.
McKeon, Niamh M.
McKevitt, Domhnall G.
McKiernan, Eirinn A.M.
McLaughlin, Grainne M.
McLaughlin, John C.
McLister, Sheena M.C.
McLoughlin, Annette M.
McLoughlin, Michelle E.
McManus, Fergal F.
McMullan, Colette P.
McNabola, Louise E.
MacNamara, Niamh Aisling
McNamara, Sinead W.
McNulty, Kevin T.
McPhillimy, John R.
McPhillips, Fiona B.
McWalters, Niall P.
Madden, Aileen
Madden, Kate
Maguire, Louise M.
Maguire, Sarah-Jane
Mannion, Damien A.

Manzor, Sonya A.
May, Catherine A.M.
Meade, Michael G.
Michael, Julian P.
Minogue, Fergus M.
Moher, John W.
Molloy, Donough J.
Monaghan, Rita M.
Monaghan, Seamus E.
Mooney, Gillian F.
Morgan, Sinead
Morrissey, Mary A.
Morrissy-Murphy, Sonya
Mullan, Julie M.
Mulligan, Deirdre M.
Murphy, Conor B.
Murphy, Deirdre A.
Murphy, Eoin B.
Murphy, Gordon P.
Murphy, Jean M.
Murphy, Rhona A.
Murphy, Ruth
Murphy-O'Connor, Julie
Murray, Peter M.
Murray, Roger F.
Murtagh, Aoife A.
Murtagh, Avril C.
Murtagh, Dara E.
Neary, Elizabeth M.
Ní Longáin, Michelle M.
Ní Shé, Ide T.
O'Brien, Maria M.
O'Brien, Orlaith M.
O'Cochlain, Colm P.
O'Connell, Aoife M.
O'Connell, Stephanie
O'Connor, Adrienne
O'Connor, Audrey M.
O'Connor, Jane M.
O'Connor, John C.
O'Connor, Niamh M.
O'Donaill, Maitiú A.
O'Donnell, Dara
O'Donnell, James Desmond
O'Donnell, Susan M.
O'Donoghue, Thomas
O'Donovan, Joan
O'Driscoll, Ann
O'Driscoll, Davnet T.
O'Dwyer, Orlaigh M.
O'Flaherty, Declan G.
O'Gorman, Brian P.

O'Hagan, Cara D.
O'Halloran, Derval
O'Hara, Kelly E.
O'Keeffe, Ciaran J.
O'Keeffe, John G.
O'Leary, Edith S.
O'Malley, C. Sandra
O'Meara, Raymond
Ó Mulláin, Mícheál P.
O'Neill, Grainne
O'Neill, Jennifer E.
O'Neill, Mary D.
O'Neill, Shane M.
O'Reilly, Olga
O'Reilly, Sean J.
O'Reilly, Sean T.
O Riordain, Padraig A.
O'Rourke, Aideen K.
O'Rourke, Cliona S.
O'Rourke, Louise J.
Osborne, Ann Marie
O'Shea, John
O'Sullivan, Audrey M.
O'Sullivan, Cliona K.M.
Pearson, Karen M.
Phelan, Maurice D.
Rabbette, Michelle A.M.
Rasdale, Mark
Regan, Mark E.
Reidy, Martin O.
Reilly, Miriam E.
Rhatigan, Noel
Riordan, Victoria A.
Roberts, Susan B.
Ronan, Elizabeth C.
Ryan, Aine P.
Ryan, Gerard
Ryan, Gregory Eric
Sheedy, Conor
Sheehan, Aoife Mary
Sheehan, Daniel V.
Sheehan, Rosalyn (Lynn) M.
Sherlock, Mikayla
Shiels, Johannah
Singleton, Pauline C.
Slattery, Barbara A.
Smith, Felicity V.
Smith, Philip Antony
Smyth, Gordon Giles
Smyth, Keith
Smyth, Melvin
Stack, Paul J.

Stamp, Thomas J.
Staunton, Myles M.
Stokes, Sheila A.
Stroker, A. Suzanne
Sweeney, Richelle M.
Taaffe, James B.
Taylor, Lucinda A.
Timpson, Richard A.
Townley, Sheena A.M.
Trautt, Gemma E.
Traynor, Gina M.
Tully, Miriam J.
Tunney, Kevin
Tweed, William Paul
Tyson, Nicola
Vint, Philip J.
Walker, Peter D.
Wallace, Charles J.
Walsh, Carole L.T.
Walsh, Rose V.
Ward, Michael O.
Whelan, Seamus
Williams, Eilian S.
Williams, Juliet M.C.
Winters, Gregory J.
Winters, Kevin R.
Woodcock, Mark
Woods, Gavin B.
Woods, Una
Wylie, Norman D.H.
Young, Damien J.

2000

Agnew, Dennis J.
Arkins, Grainne M.
Bainbridge, Vanessa A.
Baker, Robert J.
Ballagh, David R.
Bardon, James S.
Barnett, Richard A.
Barrett, Deirdre M.
Barry, Justin D.
Bate, David K.
Bennett, Ailbhe M.
Bissett, Karen S.
Bleahene, Mary C.
Boland, Neal D.
Bourke, Marguerite M.
Boyle, Aaron K.
Boyle, Emmet

Bradley, S. Sinead
Bradshaw, Julie Ann
Branton, Jonathan R.
Brennan, Alison B.
Brennan, Elsie
Brennan, Gillian A.
Brennan, Mona-Rose
Brennan, Stephen C.
Bright, Philip T.
Broderick, Nigel P.J.
Brophy, Edward J.
Browne, John D.
Browne, Sheila M.
Buckley, Jacqueline M.
Buckley, Valerie J.
Burke, Edward L.
Burke, Elizabeth A.
Byrne, Deirdre P.
Cahir, John J.
Campbell, Kathryn Susan
Cannon, Sarah M.
Carroll, Christine A.
Carroll, Sandra
Carthy, David P.
Carthy, Geraldine M.
Cassidy, Fiona F.
Clarkin, Sarah F.T.
Cleary, Sinead N.A.
Coffey, Francis A.
Colgan, Michelle K.
Colhoun, Mary H.
Coll, Barbara A.
Colleran, Eileen C.
Collins, John M.
Collins, Maeve M.
Collins, Raphoe
Comber, Joy F.
Conneely, Caitriona
Connellan, Michael P.
Conway, Dermot F.
Cooney, Brendan T.
Corbett, Rioghnach T.
Cordwell, Nigel M.
Corrigan, Paula C.
Coughlan, Thomas Oliver
Counihan, Dualta A.
Courtney, Ursula P.
Couser, Siobhan V.
Coveney, Hilary
Coveney, Muireann A.
Cox, Louise A.
Coyne, Niamh B.

Cronin, Gretta
Cronin, Stephanie J.
Crowley, Claire
Cullen, Anne Marie
Cummings, Timothy W.
Cunningham Gilbourne,
    Michelle A.
Cunningham, Michael D.
Curley, Deirdre M.
Curran, Michael F.
Curtis, Sinead B.
Cushen, Louise M.
Daly, Darren N.
D'Costa, Savio R.S.
Deacy, Cathal T.
Deady, Sarah J.
Delahunty, Louise M.
Dennis, Gary T.
de Paor, Moya S.C.
Dermody, Anne-Marie
de Valera, Etain A.M.
Devitt, Lea K.
Dobbyn, Christina J.
Dobson, Rachael B.
Doherty, Gavin P.
Doran, P. Brian
Doyle, Cora T.M.
Doyle, Miriam R.
Duffy, Brian F.
Duffy, Mary B.
Duggan, Graham R.
Dunne, Bryan G.
Dunne, Gemma P.
Dunne, Mary
Elliott, Derek P.
Fahey, Fiona A.
Fahy, Paula B.
Farrell, Adrian J.
Farrell, Ciara M.
Farrell, Mary C.
Farrell, Nichola M.
Ferguson, Garry
Finnegan, Raymond A.M.
Finnerty, Ailish
Finucane, Michael
Fitzgerald, Desmond T.
Fitzgerald, Trudy Fiona
Fitzgerald, John W.
Fitzmaurice, John Karl
Flinter, Paula M.B.
Flynn, Brid M.
Fogarty, Fiona Mary

Forrest, Jeffrey A.
Gaffney, Olga S.
Gallagher, Clodagh M.
Gallagher, Louise M.
Gallen, John P.
Geraghty, John
Gibbons, Deirdre A.
Gibney, Annette
Gleeson, Maria N.
Gorman, Elaine P.
Groarke, Peter S.
Grogan, James C.
Habersbrunner, Eva-Maria P.
Hammond, Leslie C.
Hannon, Leo A.
Hanratty, Lorraine N.
Harper, Sian L.
Harrington, Virginia E.
Harte, Sarah K.
Hayes, Mary M.
Healy, John C.
Hennessy, Olive T.
Herlihy, David P.
Hickey, Patricia M.
Hogan-Chambers, Noëlle G.
Hogan, Anna K.M.
Hogan, Eimear V.
Holmes, Mairéad
Horton, Amanda M.S.
Howard, Rory Gerard
Howlin, Denise M.
Hughes, Mark Q.
Hurley, Fiona M.
Hutton, Marie M.
Hynes, Rosemary
Jennings, Paula
Johnston, Kieran J.J.
Kane, Anthony J.
Kataria, Barinder K.
Kavanagh, Mark N.
Keane, Mary
Keaney, John D.
Kearns, Catherine E.
Keating, Declan A.
Kelleher, Shane P.
Kelly, Catherine F.M.
Kennedy, Ronan P.
Kenny, Peter T. A.
Kenny, Sinead T.
Keogh, Stephen C.
Kirley, Edel M.
Kirrane, Rory

Lacey, Terence C.
Laffan, Robert A.
Lally, Grant M.
Lane, John P.
Lane, Julie M.
Lane, Maureen A.
Larkin, Sinéad
Lillis, Nora H.
Lonergan, Ciara
Lucey, Sinead C.
Lynch, Kay M.
Lynch, Kevin G.
Lyons, Stephen P.
McArdle, Aoife
McArdle, Olivia C.
McArdle, Roisin M.
McCabe, Niall P.
McCann, Ciara M.
McCann, Dorit
McCarthy, Catherine Angela
McCarthy, Colette
McCarthy, Lisa A.
McConville, James W.
McCormack, Barry J.
McCormack, Edel
McCoy, Anne-Marie A.
McDermott, Niamh C.
McDonald, Lisa M.
McDonald, Sinead M.
McElligott, Michael
McEvoy, Yvonne E.
McGahon, Maximilian T.F.
McGarrigle, Anthony J.
McGeady, Daniel D.
McGuigan, Sheila A.
MacGuill, Conor M.
McKeever, Fiona L.
MacKernan, L. Colm P.
McKevitt, Jane A.
McLoughlin, Anna M.
McLynn, T. Anthony
McMahon, Murrough E.
McNally, Karen M.
McNamara, Patricia B.
McNamara, Una C.M.
McPartlin, Eve M.
MacSweeney, Daniel V.
MacSweeney, David F.
Magee, Barry W.
Maguire, Caroline A.
Maguire, Maria T.
Maher, Evelyn M.

Manning, Elizabeth A.
Manning, Siobhan
Mannion, Karina M.
Margey, Killian C.
Martin, Patrick M.
Meade, John B.
Meehan, Jane E.
Merry, Janadia
Michel, Niall
Miller, Eavan M.
Miller, Edward C.G.
Mitchell, John F.
Molloy, Karen M.
Molloy, Nicola
Molloy, Triona M.
Moloney, Shane J.
Monaghan, Louise
Moore, Olive C.M.
Morahan, Dermot B.
Moran, Desmond A.J.
Moran, James P.
Moran, Margaret M.
Morrison, Leo G.
Morrissey, Deirdre N.
Morrissey, John M.A.
Mullany, Martine Lorna
Mullins Treacy, Susan P.
Mulvey, Matthew W.
Murphy, Darragh P.
Murphy, Kathryn P.
Murphy, Rosannagh
Murphy, Sheena M.E.
Murran, Miriam C.
Neilan, Aedin C.
Neville, Colette M.
Ní Fhloinn, Deirdre M.C.
Nolan, Philip J.
O'Boyle, Sinéad
O'Brien, Cathy H.
O'Brien, Emma J.
O'Brien, Rhona A.
O'Callaghan, Clara M.
O'Callaghan, Loraine N.
Ó Catháin, Ruadhairi E.
Ó Ceallaigh, Ruairí
O Cleirigh, Joanelle
O'Connell, Hazel L.
O'Connor, David
O'Connor, Donal K.
O'Connor, Michael M.
O'Connor, Terry M.
O'Donnell, Cait T.

O'Donovan, John M.
O'Driscoll, Denis P.
O'Driscoll, Jean K.
O'Dwyer, Evan T.D.
O'Halloran, Brian P.
O'Halloran, Susan
O'Herlihy, Alva J.
O'Keeffe, Colm E.
O'Keeffe, Judith V.
O'Keeffe, Sheila E.
O'Kennedy, Paraic E.
O'Mahony, Sarah
O'Mullane, Killian F.D.
O'Neill, Conor A.
O'Neill, Niall M.H.
O'Regan, Anita M.
Organ, Adrian M.
O'Riordan, Deirdre A.
O'Riordan, Georgina M.
O'Riordan, Ina
Osborne, David P.
O'Shea, Michael D.
O'Shea, Sarah B.
O'Sullivan, Denis J.
O'Sullivan, Paul V.
Pilkington, Jane M.
Pilkington, Margaret M.
Preston, Gillian P.
Quigley, John G.
Rafferty, Denise
Rafferty, Terence P.
Reilly, Damian M.
Reilly, Gregory J.
Rice, John J.
Roberts, Alan
Ronane, Catherine A.
Rowley, Gerard P.
Ryan, M. Niamh
Ryan, Sarah E.
Ryan, Valerie M.
Saint, Davina S.
Sands, Deborah A.
Shannon, Ultan
Shaw, Valerie A.
Sheehy, Carol A.
Sheil, Karen L.
Sheridan, Patrick J.
Sheridan, William J.
Smith, Tara A.
Smyth, Katrina J.
Storey, Ruth E.C.
Sweeney, Liam P.

Swift, Anthony A.
Tiernan, Mark T.
Treacy, Paul D.
Tuffy, Adeline M.
Tuohy, Tracy A.
Wallace, Shane R.
Walsh, Deirdre A.M.
Walsh, Elaine M.
Walsh, Grahame R.
Walsh, Nicola P.
Walshe, Patrick V.
Ward, Helen M.E.
White, Feargal P.
White, J.A. Berkeley
White, John C.
White, Lizanne
White, Niamh M.E.
White, Seamus B.
Wilkinson, Patrick W.V.
Willis, Richard J.
Wright, John
Wynne, Henry Jonathan

2001

Adams, Alan Paul
Andrews, Patrick J.
Bacik, Milada C.
Bardon, Patrick
Barrett, Anne Marie
Barrett, Maxwell J.
Barry, Lena M.
Barry, Mary T.
Barry, Orla M.
Battye, Susan
Beckett, Sarah P.
Benson, Pamela C.G.
Beresford, Clodagh C.
Bergin, Conall M.
Bourke, Gareth B.
Bourke, Louis M.
Boylan, Peter E.
Bradley, Stephen J.
Bradshaw, Alison M.E.
Brady, Gerard T.
Brady, Mary E.
Brennan, Ann C.
Brennan, Dominic K.
Brennan, Michael M.
Brennan, William J.
Briscoe, Raymond P.

Broderick, Clodagh Olivia
Browne, Catherine M.
Bruen, Noel O.
Bryson, Susan M.
Burke, Adrian T.J.
Burke, Aine A.
Butler, Charles H.E.
Butler, Niamh P.
Byrne, Brendan C.
Byrne, Catriona T.
Byrne, Darragh R.
Byrne, Patricia
Byrne, Thomas B.
Caffrey, Niamh
Cahill, John G.
Campbell, Caroline R.
Campbell, Ciaran
Cannon, Caitriona M.
Carmody, William J.D.
Carney, Andreas M.
Carolan, Thea D.
Carson, Aoife
Carwood, Jennifer L.
Casey, Elaine P.
Casey, Finola M.
Cashin, Clare O.
Cashman, Daniel J.
Champ, Erica M.
Chapman, Linda G.
Cheung, Chimie Victoria
Clancy, Maedhbh
Clancy, Pamela
Clarke, Jennifer M.
Clarke, Valerie P.
Clarke, Victor H.
Clifford, Eleanor M.
Coghlan, Marsha R.
Coleman, Margaret A.
Collins, Gunnel
Collins, Stephen
Conlon, Carthage J.
Conlon, Rebecca L.
Conneely, Maire O.
Connell, Alan
Connolly, Gerard A.
Connolly, Rosemary E.
Conroy, Sarah
Considine, Dearbhla M.
Convery, Paul F.
Coomey, Anthony P.
Corcoran, Sinead M.
Coughlan, Declan K.

Coyle, David B.
Coyle, Shane F.
Coyne, Michele A.
Craig, Anne-Marie
Crossen, Kerri N.
Crossey, William Philip
Crowley, Maire
Crowley, Melanie K.
Cullivan, Breda M.
Cunningham, Diarmaid K.
Curran, Aine B.
Curran, Kieran D.
Currivan, Christian E.
Curry, Aileen M.M.
Dalby, Joseph F.
Daly, Aisling F.
Daly, Eleanor M.
Daly, Gary F.
D'Arcy, Cathriana G.A.
Daveron, Alan J.
Davis, Mark A.
Deane, Susan M.
Deane, Vincent
Deegan, Loughlin A.
Deery, Michael P.J.
Devine, Caitriona A.
Devins, Susan
Devlin, Michael J.
Dobbyn, David P.
Doorly, Fergus P.
Dowling, Nicola C.
Doyle, Aoife M.
Doyle, David
Doyle, Howard T.O.
Doyle, Julie Anne
Doyle, Lisa C.
Doyle, Niamh A.
Duffy, Clara J.
Dullea, Cliodhna J.
Dundon, Catherine A.
Dunne, Colm E.
Dunne, Kerry
Dunne, Kevin P.
Dunphy, Lorcan M.
Ellard, Jennifer M.
Ellis, Thomas
Ellison, Daniel Rhys
Enright, David
Evans, Celeste M.A.
Evans, James P.
Fagan, Michelle M.
Fagan, Sylvia M.E.

Fahy, David J.
Farnan, Keith P.
Farrell, Emilie V.
Farren, Jane
Fay, Andrew T.
Fee, Catherine A.
Feeney, Margaret M.
Fenelon, Laurence R.
Ferris, Brian J.P.J.
Ferriter, Seán M.
Finan, Michèle M.
Fitzgerald, Julie A.
Fitzgerald, Sinead
Fitzgibbon, David M.
Fitzpatrick, Sinead M.
Fitzsimons, Rowena
Fitzsimons, Stephen M.
Flanagan, Garrett P.
Flynn, Sara A.
Fogarty, Shirley M.
Foley, Patrick Desmond
Forbes, Eamonn V.
Forde, Bridget A.
Forde, Domhnall
Fottrell, Conor M.
Fox, Olivia S.M.
Foy, Catherine M.
Furlong, John Kenan
Gabbett, Alec K.
Gallagher, David P.
Gallen, Gerry
Garvey, Aileen T.
Garvey, Kathy
Gately, Olwen M.
Geary, Ronan W.
Gibbons, Alice M.
Gibbons, M. Helen
Gill, Brian G.
Gill, John F.
Gillen, Orla E.
Gilmore, Elizabeth A.
Gilroy, Michael J.
Given, Elaine C.
Gleeson, Alan Eric
Glynn, John G.
Glynn, Yvonne G.
Godfrey, Anne-Marie
Godfrey, Tara D.
Golden, Emma
Gosnell, Frederick V.
Grace, Marie Sinead
Graham, Siobhan

Grant, Bernadette
Guerin, Louise C.
Hall, Eimear M.
Hall, Rachel A.
Hannigan, Brendan J.
Hanrahan, Oliver J.A.
Harrington, Deirdre L.
Harte, Alan S.
Hatch, Niall G.
Haughey, Ronan J.
Hawks, Maria P.
Healy, Shane N.
Heavey, M. Patricia
Heffernan, David F.
Henry, Rhona M.
Heraghty, Pauric C.
Herlihy, Colette M.
Herlihy, David E.G
Herlihy, Emer M.
Hester, Karena M
Hewitt, Victor A.
Higgins, David J.
Hills, Tina A.
Hoban, Joanne C.M.
Hogan, John P.
Holland, Michelle K.
Holohan, Donal F.
Horgan, Kayanne
Horkan, Brian K.
Houlihan, Conor P.
Howard, Carmel J.
Hudson, Rose M.
Hull, Julia M.
Hurley, Catherine D.
Hyland, Mairéad O.
Hynes, Aine T.
Irwin, Gary P.
Irwin, William J.
Joyce, Anthony M.
Juntti, Carina
Kangley, Joanne
Keane, Barbara A.
Keane, Carmel L.
Keane, Peter
Kearins, Valerie R.M.
Kelleher, Linda J.
Kelleher, Veronica T.
Kelly, Aidan
Kelly, Deirdre M.
Kelly, Fergal T.
Kelly, Niamh N.
Kelly, Richard J.

Kennedy, John G.
Kennedy, Stephen
Kenny, Graham P.
Kevane Campbell, Patrice S.
Kiely, Joseph M.
Kieran, Sarah J.
King, Edward
King, Laura M.
Kinsella, Kevin R.
Kirrane, Ailbhe A.
Lacey, Clare M.
Lacy, Johanna E.
Lalor, Eva M.
Lalor, Julia Ann
Lalor, Niamh M.
Lane, Susanna M.
Lanigan, Sonya M.
Lenehan, Darragh W.
Liddy, Kieran G.
Lindsay, Caroline M.
Liston, Rachel N.
Long, Sarah E.M.
Lord, Claire J.
Lucey, Niall B.
Lydon, Shay
Lynch Aidan A.
Lynch, Ruth J.
Lyons, Christine U.
Lyons, Valerie M.
McBennett, Deirdre M.
McCabe, Caitriona M.
McCann, Gary A.
McCarthy, Jacqueline A.
McCarthy, Kevin P.
McCarthy, Patrick M.
McCormack, Roger P.
McCourt, Cian D.
McCracken, Jacqueline A.
McDermott, Mary T.
McDonald, Noelle A.
McDonnell, Kenneth M.
McFadden, Mary A.
McGarr, Robert F.
McGeown, Mary Clare
McGerty, Nessa C.
McGill, Nessa M.L.
McGilloway, Carmel M.
McGowan, Johanna M.
McGrath, Alison K.
McGrath, Niall J.
McGuckian, Christina M.
McHale, Andrew J.

McHugh, Deborah C.
McIlwain, Heather A.
McInerney, Siobhan H.
McIntosh, David A.
McKenna, Eoghan R.
McLaughlin, Claire S.
McLoughlin, Laura M.
McMahon, Laurence J.
McMahon, Maire C.
McManus, Anne R.
McNamara, Elaine M.
McNamara, Fergal A.
MacNicholas, Robert J.
McSweeney, Deirdre E.
MacSweeney, Ronan
Madden, Edward A.
Maguire, Mary K.
Maher, Thomas D.
Mahon, Niamh
Mahon, Sandra M.
Malone, Michael J.
Manley, Patrick J. M.
Martin, Michael D.
Masterson-Power, Sandra T.
Matthews, Gary P.
Maughan, David
Meaney, Caroline M.
Miller, Garrett S.
Miller-Hurley, Jane
Minch, Rachel E.
Minihane, John G.A.
Moloney, Liza M.
Mooney, Alan T.
Moore, Geoffrey
Moore, Ross M.
Moran, Niamh
Morris, Iorwerth J.
Morris, Mary P.
Mossler, Patrick A.
Moyles, Alan P.
Mulcahy, Darren J.
Mullan, Tracy A.
Mulleady, Laura M.
Mulroy, Martin J.
Mulvihill, Timothy David
Murnaghan, Catherine J.M.
Murphy, Darren J.
Murphy, David A.
Murphy, Deborah A.
Murphy, Denis M.C.
Murphy, Donnchadha C.
Murphy, Elizabeth M.

Murphy, John F.
Murphy, Lorraine M.
Murphy, Michael J.
Murphy, Michelle M.
Murray, Ann Marie
Murtagh, Audrey E.
Neary, Elizabeth A.
Neill, John G.
Neville, Ronnie B.
Newton, Enda M.
Ní Cheallaigh, Fiona S.
Ní Mhurchu-Platt, Niamh M.
Nolan, Oisín P.
Noonan, Valerie B.
Ó Baoighill, Donnacha S.
O'Brien, Elizabeth
O'Brien, Niall P.
O'Brien, Tom G.
O'Byrne, Rachel E.
O'Callaghan, Brian J.
O'Callaghan, Ciara E.M.
O'Callaghan, Zelda M.
Ó Ceallaigh, Cormac
O'Connell, Anne
O'Connell, Roisin F.
O'Connor, Catherine A.
O'Connor, Paul J.
O'Connor, Rosanne J.
O'Connor, Stefan P.
O'Dea, Donal Cathal
O'Donnell, Shane P.
O'Donoghue, John P.
O'Donovan, John A.
O'Donovan, Liam P.
O'Flaherty, Gavin J.
O'Gorman, Thomas Keith
O'Hanrahan, Anne-Marie
O'Hare, Ronan M.
O'Hare, Tom
O'Keeffe, Hilda
O'Leary, John A.
O'Leary, Kevin
O'Leary, Peter G.
Oliver, Kieran P.
O'Mahony, Patricia O.
O'Malley, Mary D.
O'Meara, Brian W.
O'Neill, Emma C.
O'Neill, Nóirín M.
O'Neill, Sheila C.
Oram, Bryan
Ó Riain, Katherine N.

O'Riordan, Donal G.
O'Riordan, Michelle C.
O'Shea, Hilda-Clare
O'Shea, Karen A.
O'Shea, Roisin M.
O'Sullivan, Briet M.
O'Sullivan, Cian D.
O'Sullivan, Emer E.
O'Sullivan, Maria B.
O'Sullivan, Mark O.
O'Sullivan, Pauline M.
O'Sullivan, Rhona E.
O'Sullivan, Sheila
Otubu, Celia S.C.
Pedley, David R.
Peters, David M.
Phelan, Orla C.
Pierse, Catherine E.
Plater, David J.
Purcell, Frank
Quigley, Brian P.
Quill-Manley, Stephenie M.
Quinn, Edell M.
Quinn, Elizabeth
Quinn, Maria A.
Raftery, Michael J.
Rees Morgan, Ruth
Reynolds, Mary
Richardson, Lisa P.
Riordan, Louise
Robinson, Paul A.
Roche, Anne T.
Rogers, Ciaran J.
Rosenstock, René M.
Ross, Joanne E.
Rush, Kenneth A.
Rush, Siobhra N.
Ruttledge, Sylvia
Ryan, David M.
Ryan, Eimear M.
Ryan, Jarlath O.
Ryan, Joan
Ryan, Matthew G.
Salvi, Renuka V.
Santoro, Giuseppe R.
Scanlon, James A.
Seymour, James T.
Shanley, Michael J.
Sheehan, Margaret M.
Sheehan, Martha Antone
Shiels, Dessie G.
Simons, Gavin N.A.

Small, Aiden J.
Smith, Gavin P.
Smyth, Pearse M.
Spring, Henry G.
Staunton, Elizabeth J.
Stewart, Joseph Patrick
Sullivan, Josephine
Sutton, Isabelle
Synnott, Adam D.
Tallis, Anita R.
Tedders, Judith M.J.

Thomas, Fiona K.
Torney, Denise H.
Tunney, Peter G.
Tuohy, Alison
Twohig, Paul M.
Twomey, Jill
Twomey, Richelle T.
Wallace, Eoghan P.
Walsh, Eamonn J.
Walsh, Keith G.
Walsh, Lisa S.R.

Walsh, Ruth
Whelan, Dorothy M.
Whisker, Jonathan R.
Whittaker, Alice
Whitty, Carmel E.
Williams, Ivan
Williams, Lorraine E.
Williamson, Fiona M.
Wilson, Eamon
Wyse, Conor M.
Young, Nigel J.P.L.

Select chronology

1607   Reconstitution of the Society of King's Inns (originally founded in 1539).

1733   7 Geo II, c. 5 (Ir.) An act for the amendment of the law in relation to popish solicitors; and for remedying other mischiefs in relation to the practitioners in the several courts of law and equity.

1773   13 & 14 Geo III, c. 23 (Ir.) An act for the better regulation of the admission and practice of attornies.

1774   Formation of the Society of Attornies, first known association of solicitors.

1786   First stone of the new Four Courts building on Inns Quay laid on 3 March 1786.

1791   Law Club of Ireland formed; premises at 13 Dame Street until 1869, then at 25 Nassau Street until 1885, and thereafter at 23 Suffolk Street until 1899 when it was dissolved.

1796   Opening of Four Courts in Michaelmas term 1796.

1802   Four Courts building completed.

1830   Law Society of Ireland formed on 24 June 1830 with premises at Inns Quay. Josias Dunn appointed president.

1839   Dublin Law Institute set up by Tristram Kennedy.

1840   Completion of a building at the rear of the Four Courts erected by the Benchers of King's Inns.

1841   Accommodation in this building made available to solicitors by the Benchers on 29 May 1841.
        The Society of the Attorneys and Solicitors of Ireland formed on 17 June 1841. Josias Dunn elected first president; Edward Iles appointed secretary.

1843   Northern Law Club formed in Belfast, May 1843.

1852 The Society of the Attorneys and Solicitors of Ireland incorporated by royal charter dated 5 April 1852.

1859 Cork Law Society formed.

1863 Solicitors' Benevolent Association established.

1864 Solicitors' Apprentices Debating Society formed.
   Death of secretary, Edward Iles; appointment of John Hawksley Goddard as secretary.

1866 Attorneys and Solicitors Act (Ireland), 1866.

1867 First issue of the *Irish Law Times and Solicitors Journal* published in February 1867 under the sanction of the council of the Law Society.

1876 Northern Law Society formed in Belfast.

1877 Supreme Court of Judicature (Ireland) Act, 1877.

1878 Southern Law Association formed in Cork.

1881 Solicitors Remuneration Act, 1881.

1884 Solicitors Apprentices Debating Society of Ireland (SADSI) reconstituted under new rules.

1886 Annual Law Directory first published by the Society.

1888 Grant of supplemental charter to the Law Society which allowed for representation of the Northern Law Society and the Southern Law Association on the council of the Society by the nomination of five extraordinary members each by both organisations, provided for the nomination of four extraordinary provincial delegate members of the council, one from each province, and changed the name of the Society to the Incorporated Law Society of Ireland.

   Retirement of secretary, John Hawksley Goddard; appointment of William George Wakely as secretary.

1898 Solicitors (Ireland) Act, 1898.

1907 First issue of the Law Society *Gazette* published in May 1907.

1910 Inauguration of the president's medal.

1911 Grant of the Society's coat of arms by the Ulster King of Arms.

1914–18   155 solicitors and 83 apprentices enlisted in the British army in the First World War; a memorial to those who died, 20 solicitors and 18 apprentices, was erected by the Society in the Solicitors' Buildings in the Four Courts in 1921.

1919   Sex Disqualification (Removal) Act, 1919, permitting women to become members of the legal profession.

1920   Government of Ireland Act, 1920.

1921   Provisions of the Government of Ireland Act, 1920 providing for the establishment of the Supreme Court of Judicature in Southern Ireland and the Supreme Court of Judicature in Northern Ireland brought into operation on 1 October 1921. All existing barristers, solicitors and solicitors' apprentices in Ireland on 1 October 1921 had the right of practising in both jurisdictions.

1922   Occupation of the Four Courts, including the Solicitors' Buildings, on 14 April 1922; destruction of the Four Courts, including the Solicitors' Buildings, on 28 June 1922; Law Society moved to temporary premises at 33 Molesworth Street until 1925, and then to 45 Kildare Street, Dublin.
          Northern Law Society incorporated by royal charter on 10 July 1922 becoming the Incorporated Law Society of Northern Ireland.
          Solicitors Act (Northern Ireland), 1922.

1923   Solicitors Act, 1923.
          Admission of first women solicitors; Mary Dorothea Heron admitted to the roll of solicitors on 17 April 1923; Helena Mary Early admitted to the roll on 25 June 1923.

1924   Courts of Justice Act, 1924, establishing new court system.

1929   Legal Practitioners (Qualifications) Act, 1929: an act to make provision for securing that future members of the legal profession shall possess a competent knowledge of the Irish language.

1931   Law Society returned to newly built premises at the Four Courts in September 1931.
          Re–opening of the Four Courts on 12 October 1931.

1937   Adoption of new Constitution, Bunreacht na hÉireann.

1941   The council marked the centenary of the founding of the Society in 1841 by the founding of a centenary Incorporated Law Society of Ireland annuity to be administered by the Solicitors' Benevolent

Association and subscriptions were invited from the members of the Society; the council considered it inappropriate to celebrate the centenary at a time of national emergency.

1942   Death of secretary, William George Wakely; appointment of Eric A. Plunkett as secretary.

1947   Solicitors (Amendment) Act, 1947.

1950   Death of council member, William S. Hayes; admitted a solicitor in 1884, elected to the council in 1892 and re-elected in each successive year to 1950; president of the Society in 1906–07; his portrait by Leo Whelan RHA, commissioned by the profession in 1944, hangs in the Society's council chamber.

1952   Receptions and religious services held in May 1952 to celebrate the centenary of the granting of the Society's charter in 1852.

1954   Solicitors Act, 1954.

1960   Solicitors (Amendment) Act, 1960.
Provision in section 33 of the Act for the Dublin Solicitors' Bar Association to nominate three members of its council to be extra-ordinary members of the council of the Law Society.

1965   Society of Young Solicitors was formed on 29 April 1965; first lecture was given by Thelma King, solicitor, on the subject of hire purchase law in Ireland.

1968   Decision taken by the council of the Law Society to purchase the King's Hospital building, Blackhall Place, Dublin.

1971   Purchase of King's Hospital building completed in January 1971.
Solicitors granted the right of audience in the Superior Courts by section 17 of the Courts Act, 1971.

1972   Eric A. Plunkett retired as secretary; James J. Ivers appointed director general.

1973   The Society became a member of the Council of the Bars and Law Societies of the European Community (CCBE), and an observer member of the European Affairs Committee of the International Union of Latin Notaries (UINL).

1978   Official opening of the Society's new headquarters at Blackhall Place on 14 June 1978 by An Taoiseach, Jack Lynch, TD.

1979   Opening of the Society's new law school and the commencement of
            the first professional course.
                Continuing Legal Education courses commenced.
                European Communities (Freedom to provide services) (lawyers)
            regulations, 1979 S.I. No. 58 of 1979.

1983   Ceremony held jointly by the Law Society and King's Hospital School
            to mark the 200th anniversary of the completion and opening of the
            new King's Hospital School building at Blackhall Place in 1783.

1984   In July 1984 the Solicitors' Apprentices Debating Society of Ireland
            (SADSI) celebrated its centenary.

1990   Retirement of director general, James J. Ivers; Noel C. Ryan appointed
            director general.

1991   European Communities (General system for the recognition of higher
            education diplomas) regulations, 1991 S.I. No. 1 of 1991.
                Qualified lawyers (European Communities) regulations, 1991 S.I.
            No. 85 of 1991.
                Bicentennial ball held to mark the bi-centenary of the founding of
            the Law Club of Ireland.

1994   Solicitors (Amendment) Act, 1994.
                The name of the Society was changed from the 'Incorporated Law
            Society of Ireland' to the 'Law Society of Ireland' by section 4 of the
            Act.
                Resignation of director general, Noel C. Ryan.

1995   Appointment of Ken Murphy as director general.

1996   First appointments of practising solicitors, John F. Buckley, Frank
            O'Donnell and Michael White, as judges of the Circuit Court (as
            provided for by section 30 of the Courts and Court Officers Act, 1995).

1999   Launch of the Law Society's web site.

2000   Official opening of the new education centre and library by President
            Mary McAleese on 2 October 2000.

2002   150th anniversary of the granting of the Society's charter in 1852.
                Solicitors (Amendment) Act, 2002.
                First appointment of a practising solicitor, Michael Peart, as a judge
            of the High Court (as provided for by section 4 of the Courts and
            Court Officers Act, 2002).

APPENDIX 6

Select bibliography of the Law Society and the solicitors' profession

Annual Report of the council of the Law Society of Ireland, 1842–

Brett, C.E.B., *Long shadows cast before* (Edinburgh, 1978)

Committee on Court Practice and Procedure, *Thirteenth interim report: the solicitor's right of audience* (Dublin, 1971)

Cordery on solicitors (14th ed., London, 1995)

Fair Trade Commission, *Report of study into restrictive practices in the legal profession* (Dublin, 1990)

Fanning, R., 'Memoir of Alexis FitzGerald' in P. Lynch & J. Meenan (eds), *Essays in memory of Alexis FitzGerald* (Dublin, 1987) pp 1–17

Gamble, C., *Solicitors in Ireland 1607–1921: the Incorporated Law Society's work* (Dublin, 1921)

Gazette of the Law Society of Ireland, 1907–

Hogan, D., 'Irish lawyers and the Great War', *Law Society Gazette* v. 92 no. 10 (December 1998) pp 20–21

——, 'Reflections on the life and writings of Terence de Vere White', *Law Society Gazette* v. 88 no. 7 (August/September 1994) pp 263–265

——, 'Solicitors and the Four Courts' in C. Costello (ed.,) *The Four Courts: 200 years* (Dublin, 1996) pp 225–233

——, *The legal profession in Ireland 1789–1922* (Dublin, 1986)

——, 'The preparation of the Solicitors Acts, 1954 and 1960', *Irish Jurist* v. 31 (1996) pp 266–279

Irish Law Times and Solicitors Journal, 1867–1980

Keane, E., Phair, P.B., & Sadleir, T.U. (eds), *King's Inns admission papers 1607–1867* (Dublin, 1982)

Kennedy, T.P., 'The shape of things to come: a profile of the number of solicitors of tomorrow', *Law Society Gazette* v. 95 no. 7 (August/September, 2001) pp 30–31

Law Society, *Education policy review group report* (unpublished, 1998)

——, *Guide to the professional conduct of solicitors in Ireland* (Dublin, 1988)

——, *Law directory 1886–* (annual)

——, 'New training course for solicitors' apprentices', *Law Society Gazette* v. 73 (1979) pp 81–82

——, *Record of the centenary of the charter of the Incorporated Law Society of Ireland 1852–1952* (Dublin, 1953)

——, *Solicitors Acts, 1954 to 1960 – a compendium* (Dublin, 1995)

McCague, E., *Arthur Cox 1891–1965* (Dublin, 1994)

McClintock, A.E. & Brady, C., *The law directory for Ireland, and law and equity court guide for the year 1846* (Dublin, 1846)

——, *The law directory for Ireland, and law and equity court guide for the year 1847* (Dublin, 1847)

Morris, J., 'The unattainable heights?: scholarships and prizes awarded to solicitors' apprentices', *Law Society Gazette* v. 75 (1981) pp 33–34

Murray, N.H., 'A short history of the solicitors' profession and of the Incorporated Law Society of Northern Ireland' in *Handbook of the Incorporated Law Society of Northern Ireland* (Belfast, 1959)

National Prices Commission, *Solicitors' remuneration in Ireland* (Occasional paper no. 22, Dublin, 1976)

O'Callaghan, P., *The law on solicitors in Ireland* (Dublin, 2000)

O'Leary, K.F., 'Legal education: the road ahead', *Law Society Gazette* v. 73 (1979) pp 131–136

O'Reilly, S., & Robinson, N., *A new lease of life: the Law Society's building at Blackhall Place* (Dublin, 1990)

Osborough, W.N., 'The Irish legal system 1796–1877' in C. Costello (ed.), *The Four Courts: 200 years* (Dublin, 1996) pp 33–79

——, 'The regulation of the admission of attorneys and solicitors in Ireland 1600–1866' in D. Hogan & W.N. Osborough (eds), *Brehons, serjeants and attorneys* (Dublin, 1990) pp 101–151

——, 'The solicitor's right of audience', *Irish Jurist* v. 8 (1973) pp 84–85

Plunkett, E.A., 'Attornies and solicitors in Ireland' in *Record of the centenary of the charter of the Incorporated Law Society of Ireland 1852–1952* (Dublin, 1953) pp 38–74

Report of the working group on qualifications for appointment as judges of the High and Supreme Courts (Dublin, 1999)

Restrictive Practices Commission, *Report of enquiry into the effects on competition of the restrictions on conveyancing and the restrictions on advertising by solicitors* (Dublin, 1982)

Society of Young Solicitors, 'Report on the education of a solicitor', *Irish Law Times and Solicitors Journal* v. 102 (1968) pp 131–132, 141–142, 151–152, 161–162, 171–172

Walsh, B.M., & Roche, M., *The future of the solicitors' profession in Ireland* (commissioned by the Law Society) (unpublished, 1985)

Index